*Reading with a Passion*

# Reading with a Passion

RHETORIC, AUTOBIOGRAPHY, AND THE AMERICAN WEST
IN THE GOSPEL OF JOHN

JEFFREY L. STALEY

Continuum • New York

*For my wife,*
*Barbara Lynn Wong,*
*whose love reminds me of who I am,*
*and whose faith encourages me*
*beyond what I think I can do.*

1995
The Continuum Publishing Company
370 Lexington Avenue, New York, NY 10017

"Buffalo Bill 's" is reprinted from *Complete Poems: 1904–1962* by E. E. Cummings, edited by George J. Firmage, by permission of Liveright Publishing Corporation. Copyright © 1923, 1951, 1991 by the Trustees for the E. E. Cummings Trust. Copyright © 1976 by George James Firmage.

Printed in the United States of America

*Library of Congress Cataloging-in-Publication Data*

Staley, Jeffrey Lloyd, 1951–
    Reading with a passion : rhetoric, autobiography, and the American
West in the Gospel of John / Jeffrey L. Staley.
        p.    cm.
    Includes bibliographical references and index.
    ISBN 0-8264-0859-1 (hardcover : alk. paper)
    1. Bible. N.T. John—Criticism, interpretation, etc.    2. Reader-
response criticism.    3. Staley, Jeffrey Lloyd, 1951–    .
I. Title.
BS2615.2.S722    1995
226'.506—dc20                                                95-20812
                                                                 CIP

Buffalo Bill 's
defunct
          who used to
          ride a watersmooth-silver
                                   stallion
and break onetwothreefourfive pigeonsjustlikethat
                                                  Jesus
he was a handsome man
                      and what i want to know is
how do you like your blueeyed boy
Mister Death


                              e e cummings
                              (quoted by Breytenbach)

Buffalo Bill 's
defunct
         who used to
         ride a watersmooth-silver
                                  stallion
and break onetwothreefourfive pigeonsjustlikethat
                                                  Jesus
he was a handsome man
                      and what i want to know is
how do you like your blueeyed boy
Mister Death

                         e e cummings
                         (quoted by Breytenbach)

# Contents

# Illustrations

# *Acknowledgments*

There are many people whose love, intellectual interest, and personal encouragement lie hidden in the pages of this book.

Tom Hosinski, C.S.C., introduced me to Tony Hillerman's mystery novels at a serendipitous moment in my life, when I was teaching at the University of Portland, and Jerome Neyrey, S.J., revived my interest in Hillerman a few years later, when I was teaching at Notre Dame. It was also Jerome who encouraged me to "write where my heart was," at a time when I had serious misgivings about the nature and direction of this project.

I am grateful to the many friends and colleagues who took time out from their busy schedules to read all or parts of this manuscript. They have added to its richness with their encouragement and critical insight: Stephen Moore, Alan Culpepper, Mary Gerhart, and Lauren Glen Dunlap, who read the entire manuscript; and Vernon Faillettaz, DeAne Lagerquist, Janice Anderson, Lew Soens, Richard Rohrbaugh, Herman Lombard, and many others who read early drafts of various chapters. Whatever strengths the book has are due in part to these scholars' friendship and observations. Finally, I want to express my appreciation to Frank Oveis, publishing director at Continuum, who believed in this project and saw it through to completion.

Without my family's passionate interest in American history or its curiosity about our family origins, much of this book could not have been written. Grace Johnson's and Bruce Chamberlin's memorabilia have preserved much of my Swedish ancestry. Ruth Sheldrake's amazing address book gave me access to long-lost Canadian, Quaker, and Plymouth Colony roots. Marjorie and Matilda Wong's photographs and stories have given my children a valuable link to their Chinese ancestry. And thanks to my grandfather Lloyd M.

Staley's long life, enthusiasm, and curiosity about his family's origins, I developed an interest in family history twenty years ago. I am grateful to these family members and the many other more distant relatives who have helped me in my journey of self-discovery.

Finally, I want to thank Powell's Bookstore in Portland, Oregon, for stocking their "literary theory" section with works that are always on the cutting edge of the discipline; Joann Patty and Joni Steel, library clerks at the Beaverton Public Library, for their professional help in chasing down my never-ending inter-library loan requests; and Lorena Smith, Phelps County Museum clerk, for her patience in answering my many questions. These women's tireless efforts have added depth to my thinking and richness to the book.

The following articles appear in this book in significantly revised form. An earlier version of chapter 1 appeared as "Stumbling in the Dark, Reaching for the Light: Reading Character in John 5 and 9," in *Semeia* 53; and an earlier version of chapter 3 appeared as "Subversive Narrator/Victimized Reader: A Reader Response Assessment of a Text-Critical Problem, John 18.12–24," in *Journal for the Study of the New Testament* 51.

All translations are from the New Revised Standard Version unless otherwise noted.

# Unbinding the Dead:
# A Decade of Reader Criticism
# in the Fourth Gospel

My aim has been to expose the Fourth Gospel's rhetorical power to analysis by studying the literary elements of its "anatomy."

—R. Alan Culpepper

[R]eader-oriented exegeses can often read disappointingly like the familiar critical renditions of the given biblical passage, lightly reclothed in a reader vocabulary.

—Stephen Moore

In the wider world of literary criticism today, critics and readers are being forced out from behind their masks and asked to own their views as their own. . . .

—Mary Ann Tolbert

Jesus said to them, "Unbind him, and let him go."

—John 11:44

## FORMALIST READER CRITICISM AND THE NEW TESTAMENT

Reader-response criticism has survived as a vaguely defined subfield of literary criticism and literary theory for nearly twenty-five years now. But its impact on biblical criticism has been felt for only about half that long. Instead of being author-centered as so much of earlier literary and biblical criticism had been—instead of answering questions such as What is the historical and biographical context that best explains what this author is trying to do?—reader-response criticism purports to be audience-centered. It has been interested in questions related to the effect of narrative on audiences, theories of how texts effect particular responses, and illustrations of how a narrative can be transformed by the psychology of the individual reader or by particular interpretive communities.

When reader-response criticism burst onto the American literary scene in the 1970s, its popularity grew quickly. In contrast to most earlier approaches, reader criticism was keenly interested in describing and analyzing the persuasive side of literature.[1] The new breed of doctoral candidates in the late 1960s had had their mettle tested in protests against the military-industrial complex, the draft, the Vietnam War, racism, and sexism and had seen how rhetoric could harm and heal. They had lived life with passion and zeal and had developed a distrust and distaste for ordered power structures.[2] Now that they found themselves tenurously seated on the other side of the classroom desk, backs to the chalkboard, audience-oriented criticism was the natural, professional reaction to their mentors' clinical, white-gloved approach to literature. The old "New Critics" who thought they could analyze texts apart from their political, social, ethical, and personal effects were nearly extinct. A new species of reader was crawling out of the oozing slime.[3]

Somewhat similarly to this development in English departments across the United States, in the late 1970s many battle-tested New Testament professors and raw recruits just finishing their degrees were searching for an antidote to the hard-line historical sourcery that had vivisected the biblical text and sucked out its readerly impulse. Having been inaugurated into literary criti-

---

[1] Steven Mailloux is especially helpful at situating this historical shift within the context of institutional rhetoric (*Rhetorical Power*, 19–36). Similarly, Robert Holub discusses this shift in emphasis within the context of an American fixation with the text which was just as easily amenable to French deconstruction and Wolfgang Iser's phenomenological theory of reading as it had been to New Criticism (*Crossing Borders*, 8–13; cf. Mailloux, *Rhetorical Power*, 45).

[2] Linda Hutcheon opines: "In very general terms, the postmodern questioning of this totalizing impulse may well have its roots in some sort of 1960's or late romantic need to privilege free, unconditioned experience" (*The Politics of Postmodernism*, 63; see also Mailloux, *Rhetorical Power*, 30–32; and Greenblatt, *Learning to Curse*, 166–67).

[3] In writing about literary critics' disenchantment with narratology, Christine Brooke-Rose argues that "the chief problem came to be seen as arising not from inherent universal structures but from *reading*, as if analysers had a profound need to experience, not a text or even a story, but *their own mental processes* when faced with a poetic text or story that perhaps did not give them the immediate and unalloyed pleasures that its renown, its place in the canon or histories of literature had led them to expect" ("Whatever Happened to Narratology?" 284; my emphasis). If one were to take out her reference to "*universal* structures," leaving "structures" by itself, her observation would parallel the earlier reaction of reader-response criticism to New Criticism (cf. Suleiman, "Introduction: Varieties of Audience-Oriented Criticism," in Suleiman and Crosman, eds., *The Reader in the Text*, 3–4).

cism by the precision of structuralist thought, these scholars were soon opening up the rhetorically oriented works of Wayne Booth, Wolfgang Iser, and
the important collections of reader-response articles edited by Susan
Suleiman and Inge Crosman, Jane Tompkins, and others.[4] The omens for
change appeared to be good.

Stephen Moore names this new breed of scholars and dissects their work
up through 1988 in his chapter entitled "Stories of Reading: Doing Gospel
Criticism as/with a Reader."[5] And although new names might be added to his
list, the reader-oriented critics' approaches to the Bible have not changed
much in the intervening years.[6]

In contrast to their English Department colleagues across the hall who
believed reader-oriented criticism was a much-needed corrective to New
Criticism's one-sided, constricting emphasis on "the poem itself," New Testament scholars initially saw the more synchronic, formalist, reader-oriented,
narratological approaches as offering a way to hover closely over "the text
itself" and breathe new life into it.[7] Thus, as New Testament scholars began
to search for the "real, super, ideal, encoded, implied" reader in, with, and
under the biblical text, they seemed to have had a threefold hope. First and
foremost, they hoped that the analysis of biblical texts as narratives (complete
with narrator, characters, and plot) could draw back together into one loaf
the fragmentary crumbs of texts left over after historical-critical methodologies had departed. Texts would be interpreted as unified wholes.[8] Texts would

---

[4] Booth, *The Rhetoric of Fiction;* Iser, *The Implied Reader;* idem, *The Act of Reading;*
Suleiman and Crosman, *The Reader in the Text;* Tompkins, *Reader-Response Criticism;* Eco,
*The Role of the Reader;* Fish, *Is There a Text in This Class?;* Mailloux, *Interpretive Conventions;*
Culler, *On Deconstruction;* Holub, *Reception Theory;* and Freund, *The Return of the Reader.*

[5] Moore, *Literary Criticism and the Gospels,* 71–107; and, more recently, "How Jesus' Risen
Body Became a Cadaver," 273–78.

[6] For example, see the more recent assessment of reader-response criticism in The Bible and
Culture Collective, *The Postmodern Bible,* 38–67, 163.

[7] As Stephen Moore puts it so well: "The impression being fostered among biblical students
and scholars . . . is that secular literary criticism, as it pertains to literary narrative, is a discipline
preoccupied with the unity of texts and the autonomy of story-worlds . . ." (*Literary Criticism
and the Gospels,* 11; see also 50–55; cf. Fowler, *"Let the Reader Understand,"* 9–12; Powell,
*What Is Narrative Criticism?* 6–21; Detweiler and Robbins, "From New Criticism to Post-
structuralism: Twentieth Century Hermeneutics," 248–52; and Boers, "Narrative Criticism,
Historical Criticism, and the Gospel of John," 37–38, 43–44).

[8] See, for example, the unitary emphasis in Fowler, *Loaves and Fishes;* Tannehill, *The Narrative Unity of Luke-Acts;* and Culpepper, *Anatomy of the Fourth Gospel.*

be seen as "mirrors" and not only as "windows" to the past.[9] Second, these New Testament scholars hoped that the analysis of the creatively affective and persuasive aspects of story worlds could add a third dimension to their mentors' two-dimensional emphasis on historical events and community concerns. Text pragmatics would replace text semantics.[10] And third, the scholars hoped that this new approach could bridge the growing gap between the academician studying the text as artifact and the layperson reading the text as article of faith.[11] The Bible would be a book motivating laity and scholars alike by its correctly interpreted persuasive power.

Without a doubt, early appropriations of reader-response criticism in the Fourth Gospel have been firmly rooted in formalist literary theory and rhetorical studies.[12] They have typically argued that markers in the text itself guide and manipulate readers' responses. The role of the reader critic, then, has been to uncover and expose the Gospel's rhetorical strategies and to make them obvious to the otherwise unsuspecting reader.[13] My own dissertation, written in 1985 and published in 1988, fell into this category of reader-response criticism but with some subtle twists. In it I explored the purpose of what I interpreted to be a "reader victimization" strategy in the Fourth Gospel: those places where the narrative forced the reader to the wrong conclusions (like false leads in a detective novel), only to correct the reader's mistakes later on.

But like its older sister in the secular realm, biblical reader-response criticism has watched many of its early adherents fly away from formalist, rhetorical constructions of readers to nest with feminist, deconstructive, and other poststructuralist understandings of readers. Along the way, more and more weight is being given to the "real reader"—either the elite, professionally trained, late twentieth century Western (male) reader, or the feminist reader,

---

[9] Petersen, *Literary Criticism for New Testament Critics,* 19. Cf. Moore, "'Mirror, Mirror . . .': Lacanian Reflections on Malbon's Mark," 165–71.

[10] Staley, *The Print's First Kiss;* Fowler, *"Let the Reader Understand";* Wuellner, "Putting Life Back into the Lazarus Story and its Reading: The Narrative Rhetoric of John 11 and the Narration of Faith"; Botha, *Jesus and the Samaritan Woman.*

[11] Meyer, "The Challenges of Text and Reader to the Historical-Critical Method"; White, "Historical and Literary Criticism: A Theological Response."

[12] The Bible and Culture Collective, *The Postmodern Bible,* 38–51.

[13] Porter, "Why Hasn't Reader-Response Criticism Caught on in New Testament Studies?" 278–83; and, more recently, see his "Reader-Response Criticism and New Testament Study: A Response to A. C. Thiselton's New Horizons in Hermeneutics," 94–102. Cf. Culpepper, *Anatomy of the Fourth Gospel,* 5–6; Staley, *The Print's First Kiss,* 27–49; Moloney, *Belief in the Word,* 5–6, 9–13; and Botha, *Jesus and the Samaritan Woman,* 188–200.

or the third-world, postcolonial reader. From this more recent perspective, those earlier appropriations of reader criticism in biblical studies have been criticized for the same reasons that they had been criticized in literary critical circles: for not really being reader-centered at all, but for being just as text-centered as was New Criticism.[14] Even in those places where the early biblical reader-response critics did talk of "readers" and the rhetorical responses that a narrative seeks to elicit from its "readers," what they were really talking about was merely their own idiosyncratic critical moves, lightly masked behind the neologisms and technical language of rhetoric and narratology. It is out of this subjectivist/essentialist scholarly debate in literary theory and biblical studies that the present project was conceived.

### RECENT READER CRITICISM IN THE FOURTH GOSPEL

R. A. Culpepper's *Anatomy of the Fourth Gospel,* published in 1983, established the foundations for subsequent formalist, intrinsic descriptions of readers in the Gospel of John. For over ten years now his book has set the parameters of narratological discussions in the Fourth Gospel. The difficulties Culpepper faced in tackling the issues of implied readers, narratees, and real readers have been reflected in almost all of the critical discussions of Johannine readers since then.[15] And although a growing number of articles and books continue to use his formalist analysis of the Fourth Gospel as the foundation for their own exegetical studies, in the brief summaries below I want to focus only on those subsequent works that try to illuminate the temporal aspect of narrative and attempt to describe the effect of that temporality on the formation of readerly convictions and expectations. The wider range of articles, monographs, and commentaries that selectively utilize elements of formalist literary criticism without giving attention to rhetorical effect,

---

[14] As Mary Louise Pratt notes, although "reader-response criticism often presents itself as a corrective to formalist or intrinsic criticism[, t]his explanation . . . does not seem altogether adequate. On the one hand, formalism and New Criticism are already so discredited in theoretical circles that there seems little need for another round of abuse. On the other hand, much reader-response criticism turns out to be a notational variant of that very formalism so roundly rejected. An antiformalist theoretical stance invoked to uphold a neo- or covertly formalist practice is a contradiction not altogether unfamiliar these days, and one which suggests that in addition to the dead horses being flogged, there must be some live ones running around escaping notice. Gazes must turn outward, beyond the corral" ("Interpretive Strategies/Strategic Interpretations: On Anglo-American Reader-Response Criticism," 26; cf. Spivak, *The Post-Colonial Critic,* 50–52; The Bible and Culture Collective, *The Postmodern Bible,* 51–67).

[15] Culpepper, *Anatomy of the Fourth Gospel,* 206–27; cf. Staley, *The Print's First Kiss,* 11–15.

although numerous and insightful, are beyond the scope of my particular interests and project.

Adele Reinhartz, Mark Stibbe, Lyle Eslinger, Barry Henaut, Willi Braun, and Robert Kysar have each written articles representative of reader-response concerns in the Fourth Gospel.[16] Reinhartz's and Stibbe's studies are the broadest. For example, Reinhartz seeks to show that the pattern of "suggestion, negative response, and positive action" proposed by Charles Giblin is not only exhibited in the microstructure of Johannine signs, as Giblin suggests, but is also reflected in the macrostructure of the book's christological purpose.[17] In a careful analysis of the Johannine dialogues, monologues, and passion narrative, Reinhartz shows how the narrative leads the reader through progressive steps of faith by "articulating or implying Christological expectations . . . then frustrating or negating these expectations . . . [before finally] reinstating and modifying the expectations. . . ."[18]

Stibbe, in his most recent book, applies a number of different literary theories to the interpretation of the Fourth Gospel. He begins with a chapter devoted to a reader-response description of the story's "hero," and like Reinhartz, he focuses on the implications of reader-response criticism for analyzing the Fourth Gospel's Christology. Stibbe's purpose is to show how reader-response criticism helps elucidate the elusive character of Jesus' presence in the story.[19] Using an image from one of his favorite childhood books, *The Scarlet Pimpernel,* Stibbe argues that Jesus acts as a "heavenly pimpernel" who "will not be manipulated or controlled by the political or the ecclesiastical authorities of this world."[20] Like the pimpernel of Baroness Orczy's novel, the Fourth Gospel's "Jesus is a hero who cannot trust those around him."[21]

---

[16] Ingrid Rosa Kitzberger's work also deserves mentioning ("Love and Footwashing: John 13:1–20 and Luke 7:36–50 Read Intertextually"; and "Mary of Bethany and Mary of Magdala—Two Female Characters in the Johannine Passion Narrative. A Feminist, Narrative-Critical Reader-Response"), but I will discuss her work in greater detail in chapter 2.

[17] Reinhartz, "Great Expectations: A Reader-Oriented Approach to Johannine Christology and Eschatology," 63; cf. Giblin, "Suggestion, Negative Response, and Positive Action in St. John's Portrayal of Jesus (John 2.1–11.; 4.46–54.; 7.2–14.; 11.1-44.)."

[18] Reinhartz, "Great Expectations: A Reader-Oriented Approach to Johannine Christology and Eschatology," 66. In her more recent work, *The Word in the World,* Reinhartz devotes an entire chapter to the Johannine implied reader (pp. 29–47). But apart from briefly mentioning the inherent value of sequential readings of the Gospel (pp. 12–13), the explication of narrative temporality has little impact on her analysis of the text.

[19] Stibbe, *John's Gospel,* 5–31.

[20] Ibid., 47; cf. 6, 23, 31.

[21] Ibid., 19.

The elusive character of Jesus thus "acts as a source of hermeneutical seduction, tantalizing and drawing the reader back to the story in order to 'seek' the hero once again."[22] The characters in the story who persevere in their search for Jesus are rewarded with eternal life, and persevering readers will also find their lives grounded in a Jesus who is "*absconditus atque praesans*" (hidden but at the same time present).[23]

In contrast to Reinhartz and Stibbe, the other scholars all focus on smaller segments of the Johannine text. Eslinger analyzes the Samaritan woman pericope, concentrating on the intertextual reading context of ancient Hebrew betrothal scenes at wells.[24] Henaut explores the narrative "disjunctions" in the healing of the royal official's son (4:43–54);[25] Kysar investigates the impact on the implied reader of the four successive "human images" of John 10:1–18;[26] and Braun's attention is directed toward the book's double ending (20:30–31; 21:1–25).[27] In each instance, the impact of reader-response criticism is obvious. For example, although Eslinger is not particularly sensitive to the ways in which breaks in the Samaritan dialogue have an impact on reader expectations,[28] he does conclude his exegesis with the observation that the betrothal type-scene of John 4 is a "strategy designed to mislead the reader so that he may gain an actual experience of the gap between Jesus and his human auditors. . . ."[29]

Barry Henaut, on the other hand, picks out the assumed redactional interstices in John 4:43–54 and argues that, in the way that "so-called traditional scholars" have analyzed the Johannine redactor's use of the signs source, they "have often intuitively made use of 'reader response criticism' without naming it as such."[30] For Henaut, redaction critics' identification of editorial

---

[22] Ibid., 31.

[23] Ibid.

[24] Eslinger, "The Wooing of the Woman at the Well: Jesus, the Reader and Reader-Response Criticism," 168–71.

[25] Henaut, "John 4:43-54 and the Ambivalent Narrator: A Response to Culpepper's *Anatomy of the Fourth Gospel,*" 289–91, 293.

[26] Kysar, "Johannine Metaphor—Meaning and Function: A Literary Case Study of John 10:1-18," 92, 94–96, 101–2.

[27] Braun, "Resisting John: Ambivalent Redactor and Defensive Reader of the Fourth Gospel," 66–71.

[28] Eslinger's "reader" is noticeably missing from three pages of his exegesis ("The Wooing of the Woman at the Well: Jesus, the Reader and Reader-Response Criticism," 177–79).

[29] Ibid., 180.

[30] Henaut, "John 4:43-54 and the Ambivalent Narrator: A Response to Culpepper's *Anatomy of the Fourth Gospel,*" 304.

seams in the signs source help point out to the narrative critic that the Johannine narrator is not only reliable and omniscient, as Culpepper has argued,
but at times can also be ambivalent and indecisive, "if not 'downright
sneaky.'"[31]

In a similar vein, Braun focuses on the classic redaction-critical issue of
Johannine endings. Whereas I criticized Culpepper for failing to hold fast to
his narratological category of narrator when discussing the problem of Johannine endings and for resorting too quickly to a redactional-critical solution,[32]
Braun takes a different approach. Starting with insights drawn from the resistant stance of much of feminist reader criticism, Braun argues that the person
who originally added John 21 was essentially a resistant reader:

> [one who] not only disrupt[ed] the narrative design of the gospel but also dif-
> fuse[d] its affective power. John 21, the continuation of a previously closed
> work, thus constitutes the gospel's permission [I would say instead, a commu-
> nity's permission] for the reader to question the sufficiency of its claims con-
> cerning "the truth" and to expose the dark underside of its justly celebrated and
> eloquent appeal to love.[33]

For Braun, then, the shaky foundations of Johannine redaction criticism are
transformed into the solid ground of a resistant reception history.

Of these six examples of reader-oriented criticism, Kysar's exploration of
Johannine metaphor in John 10:1–18 is the most explicit in its attempt to
account for the successive judgments that the implied reader must make
when confronted with multiple metaphors. Kysar writes of the tension that
"exists between the implied reader's astonishment at the series of metaphors,
on the one hand, and, on the other hand, her or his pleasure in not entirely
sharing the lack of understanding characteristic of the hearers. . . ."[34] His
reader is one who "thinks she or he understands . . . but then . . . is left
behind, struggling to keep up with the temporal flow of the discourse";[35] one

---

[31] Ibid., 300.

[32] Staley, *The Print's First Kiss,* 39–41, 111–12; Henaut, "John 4:43–54 and the Ambivalent Narrator: A Response to Culpepper's *Anatomy of the Fourth Gospel,*" 304; cf. *Anatomy of
the Fourth Gospel,* 43–48.

[33] Braun, "Resisting John: Ambivalent Redactor and Defensive Reader of the Fourth
Gospel," 60, 71; cf. Moore, *Literary Criticism and the Gospels,* 166. Curiously, Braun never
explicitly calls his "ambivalent redactor" a resistant reader. That is my characterization of his
position.

[34] Kysar, "Johannine Metaphor—-Meaning and Function: A Literary Case Study of John
10:1–18," 94.

[35] Ibid.

who can be "put off guard by the images and urged on by them toward clarification."[36] Kysar's exegetical program is thus strongly motivated by a desire to account for both the affective experience of reading and the cognitive, and to relate both experiences to the reader's pilgrimage as she or he attempts to attend faithfully to the narrator's goals.[37]

As with Reinhartz and Stibbe, these four scholars are attentive to the ancient cultural cues, both intertextual and intratextual, which evoke particular readerly expectations and provoke reevaluations of those expectations through surprising twists and turns in the subsequent narrative. Furthermore, all six writers connect these sequences of expectations with the (implied) author's or a later redactor's theological purpose. Finally, all six of these short studies strongly emphasize the unity of the text[38] along with the text's equally strong encoded reader—a reader whom the rhetorically sensitized critic can reconstruct apart from the disconcerting effects of the critic's own social location, personal prejudice, or idiosyncrasies.[39]

Recently two book-length studies of Johannine narrative have been written with sensitivity to a reader-response perspective.[40] In 1993 the Australian Johannine scholar Francis Moloney published the first volume of a commentary on the Fourth Gospel which ostensibly combines reader-response criticism with formalist narrative analysis. At this point Moloney's work covers only John 1–4, but even so, it is already explicit in its positive appraisal of a more formalist, "first-time reader" form of reader criticism. Moloney argues, for instance, that "the implied reader in a narrative is always communicating with the real reader of the narrative, *as the narrative unfolds*" (Moloney's

[36] Ibid., 95.

[37] Ibid.

[38] Braun, I think, would want to describe this narrative unity only in terms of the original Gospel, excluding the disruptive second ending of John 21 ("Resisting John: Ambivalent Redactor and Defensive Reader of the Fourth Gospel," 68, 70).

[39] Schuyler Brown's 1989 essay entitled "John and the Resistant Reader: The Fourth Gospel after Nicea and the Holocaust" is the rare exception to this. It represents one New Testament scholar's attempt to reflect upon the ethical implications of reading the Fourth Gospel in a post-Nicean, post-Holocaust world. However, the exegesis of specific Johannine texts plays a relatively minor role in the essay (ibid., 257–58).

[40] Margaret Davies's work *Rhetoric and Reference in the Fourth Gospel* also deserves mentioning, since she begins by saying that her investigation takes up "the most valuable insights of structuralism and reader-response criticism" (p. 7). However, her concluding chapter, entitled "The Implied Reader or Listener," is primarily an attempt to determine who were the text's "original readers, [as] implied by the strategic rhetoric of the Gospel" (p. 362). For Davies, reader-response criticism is a tool to be used primarily for solving historical-critical questions.

emphasis) and consequently he is interested in the reader "in front of the text."[41] But very quickly Moloney cautions that "[g]ospel criticism must not abandon the pursuits of historical-critical scholarship, which has devoted great attention to the rediscovery of the experience of the Johannine community."[42]

From a reader-response perspective, Moloney is most helpful when summarizing how large narrative segments are arranged to form particular faith responses.[43] Moloney's reader is revealed to be a masterful learner, one who on rare occasions might be tempted, tested, or perturbed by the text,[44] but is never misled by it. His reader thus is always clear-sighted and, strangely, is never caught up by possible ambiguities in the text—even when the commentators quoted by Moloney noticeably have been.[45] Despite his emphasis on the temporal development of the reader's understanding of faith, Moloney offers only limited explication of how Johannine narrative manipulates the implied reader in any word-by-word, phrase-by-phrase sequences. Instead, when Moloney slows down to analyze minute segments of Johannine narrative, the more traditional categories of historical-critical research noticeably obtrude into his commentary. This strategy allows him to ignore the most challenging aspect of formalist reader-response criticism: the attempt to explore, in a freeze-frame manner, the meaning effects of narrative temporality.[46]

In another recent and significant reader-oriented work, the South African scholar J. Eugene Botha has analyzed a smaller portion of the Fourth Gospel. Using speech act theory as his entry into an exhaustive description of Johannine style, Botha's revised 1990 dissertation is more sensitive to the successive interpretive moves that the text elicits from the reader than is Moloney's commentary, and thus Botha's work is more open to the Gospel's wide-ranging rhetorical repertoire. Botha has chosen speech act theory for its ability to enunciate carefully the distinctions between various types of affective inten-

---

[41] Moloney, *Belief in the Word*, 13.

[42] Ibid., cf. xi.

[43] Note especially his "Conclusions" (pp. 51–52, 76, 91–92, 130–31, 175, 191–94).

[44] Ibid., 52, 92, 130–31, 192, 199.

[45] Ibid., 8–9, 13, 82–83, 135–37.

[46] For example, when Moloney discusses the well-known contradiction between John 3:22, 26 and 4:1–2, he fails to address the question of what effect the contradiction might have on the reader's sense of trust and understanding (*Belief in the Word*, 135–37). Even more telling is the fact that Moloney entirely omits from his discussion my analysis of this text. No doubt this is because I described the function of 4:1–3 in terms of a "victimizing strategy," a strategy that Moloney finds "unacceptable" (*Belief in the Word*, 82 n. 21; but see p. 229 for many other references to my work; cf. *The Print's First Kiss*, 96–98; see also Moore, *Literary Criticism and the Gospels*, 98–107).

tions, and this methodology exposes hitherto unseen levels of persuasiveness in Johannine style. For example, Botha's precise and exhaustive classification of linguistic segments in John 4:1–42 according to speech act categories reveals to the critic how Johannine narrative utterances "'involv[e] readers' [and] 'enhanc[e] *attentio*', [thus] 'ensuring reader participation.'"[47] Botha's analysis uncovers a reader who, with regard to the outcome of Jesus' encounter with the Samaritan woman, is kept in suspense through the evocation of the betrothal type-scene; a reader who is "involuntarily involved in the narrative by devices such as irony and misunderstanding."[48] Narrative gaps are exposed and measured for depth and circumference. But beyond these evocative elements of Johannine style, Botha argues that speech act analysis shows how the narrative actually forces its readers "into involuntary association and disassociation with certain characters,"[49] thus trapping the reader. For Botha, all these strategies work together successfully to achieve the communicative goals of the implied author.[50] Without exception, each narrative speech act in John 4:1–42 leaves its christological, sociopolitical, or religious imprint on the implied reader.

### THE CRITIQUE OF NEW TESTAMENT
### READER-RESPONSE CRITICISM

To some scholars, the turn toward synchronic, reader-oriented analyses of New Testament narratives appears to be a radical reaction to problems left in the wake of historical-critical methodology. Yet biblical reader-response criticism has generated a number of challenging responses even from scholars who, like themselves, are disenchanted with historical-critical methods.[51] One of the most pervasive criticisms leveled against biblical reader-response criticism comes from feminist and liberationist interpreters. These interpreters are quick to point out that the critic's social location has generally not been taken into account by the largely white, elite males doing the readerly

---

[47] Botha, *Jesus and the Samaritan Woman,* 190.

[48] Ibid.

[49] Ibid., 191; cf. 115–21.

[50] Ibid., 189.

[51] Rensberger, *Johannine Faith and Liberating Community,* 115; Powell, *What Is Narrative Criticism?* 91–101; Wuellner, "Is There an Encoded Reader Fallacy?" 41; Porter, "Why Hasn't Reader-Response Criticism Caught on in New Testament Studies?" 283–90; Moore, *Literary Criticism and the Gospels,* 98–107.

analysis.[52] In our quest to be part of the biblical critical guild, we reader critics have sacrificed one of the truly original insights of reader-response criticism (that is, what real readers bring to the reading of texts)[53] for "scientific" (read formalist), exegetical objectivity.[54] From this critical perspective, the technical expressions of the reader as "in the text" as an "implied reader," or as an "encoded reader," are merely phrases that, once demythologized, betray the individual interpreter's unfocused ideological and political interests. These "readers" are not objective elements of texts at all. Instead, they are rhetorical devices naïvely used by the interpreter to convince an elite reading audience of the validity of the particular interpretation.[55]

So Temma Berg can write that, in general, biblical reader-response criticism needs

> to keep looking at the words "reader" and "text" and "in" and re-examine what they mean. . . . The reader is in and not in the text. The reader can never be separated from the texts that surround him, partly because "reader" and "text" are interchangeable signs, but also because the reader is an active producer of what she reads. The text exists so that the reader may fill it. The reader exists so that the text may fill her. Neither the reader nor the text has a single, stable center; both the reader and the text may be endlessly changed.[56]

Mary Ann Tolbert's criticism of my work sounds a similar refrain and can be addressed just as easily to the eight studies that I have summarized above.

---

[52] Anderson, "Matthew: Gender and Reading," 3–5, 21–24; Burnett, "Reflections on Keeping the Implied Author an 'It': Why I Love Wolfgang Iser," 14; Wuellner, "Is There an Encoded Reader Fallacy?" 49; Berg, "Reading in/to Mark," 196; Tolbert, "A Response from a Literary Perspective," 208–9; Durber, "The Female Reader of the Parable of the Lost," 59–69; and Segovia, "And They Began to Speak in Other Tongues: Competing Modes of Discourse in Contemporary Biblical Criticism," 18–20, 28–29. In the secular realm, see Schweickart, "Toward a Feminist Theory of Reading," 35–39; and Pratt, "Interpretive Strategies/Strategic Interpretations: On Anglo-American Reader-Response Criticism," 26–30.

[53] Berg, "Reading in/to Mark," 202–3; Segovia, "The Final Farewell of Jesus: A Reading of John 20:30–21:25," 168–69; Beutler, "Response from a European Perspective," 195–96; Tolbert, "A Response from a Literary Perspective," 208–9; The Bible and Culture Collective, *The Postmodern Bible,* 54, 175–76.

[54] Moore, *Literary Criticism and the Gospels,* 106–7, 177–78.

[55] Wuellner, "Is There an Encoded Reader Fallacy?"; Boyarin, "The Politics of Biblical Narratology: Reading the Bible Like/As a Woman"; cf. McKnight, *Post-Modern Use of the Bible,* 14–19, 161–62.

[56] Berg, "Reading in/to Mark," 202; see also Phillips, "'What is Written? How Are You Reading?' Gospel, Intertextuality and Doing Lukewise: A Writerly Reading of Lk 10:25-37 (and 38-42)," 277 n. 30.

"What Staley's generalized reader masks," she writes, ". . . is the critic himself: Staley's reader reads the way Staley does. His analysis . . . is not the reading experience of any reader, but the analysis of the modern biblical critic."[57] Here Tolbert is echoing an argument made by Stephen Moore, an argument that was first put forward by Stanley Fish in a critique of his own early "affective stylistics."[58] Moore's poststructuralist evaluation of reader-response criticism in New Testament studies concluded:

> Reader-response criticism of the Gospels, because it is an enterprise that tends to feel accountable to conventional gospel scholarship, has worked with reader constructs that are sensitively attuned to what may pass as permissible critical reading. That is why reader-oriented exegeses can often read disappointingly like the familiar critical renditions of the given biblical passage, lightly reclothed in a reader vocabulary. The reader of audience-oriented gospel criticism is a repressed reader. Its parents are mainstream gospel exegesis on the biblical side, and reader in the text formalism on the nonbiblical side.[59]

The signs are clear and unambiguous: Warning: Reading in Process. Wash your hands, disinfect your clothing, and check your personal effects at the door.

But on the other side of the critical debate, opposite Tolbert and Moore, stands the social-world perspective of Bruce Malina. Although he can agree with Tolbert that it is salutary to force reader-response critics and readers out from behind their individualistic and anachronistic reading masks, Malina has problems with the "increasingly diverse world of New Testament interpretation," which Tolbert and Moore laud. From Malina's point of view, the high value Tolbert and Moore place on pluralistic and individualistic readings is just another sign of ethnocentric, elitist, middle-class American values being forced upon a radically different, ancient Mediterranean world.[60]

Malina's empirically defined, cultural-anthropological model of reading is one in which contemporary, considerate readers who value "U.S. fairness"[61] will "obviously make the effort to bring to their reading a set of scenarios

---

[57] Tolbert, "A Response from a Literary Perspective," 206.

[58] Moore, *Literary Criticism and the Gospels,* 134–36; Fish, *Is There a Text in This Class?* 21–67, 147–73; cf. Norris, *What's Wrong with Postmodernism,* 79–83; and Porter, "Why Hasn't Reader-Response Criticism Caught on in New Testament Studies?" 285–86.

[59] Moore, *Literary Criticism and the Gospels,* 107.

[60] Malina, "Reading Theory Perspective: Reading Luke-Acts," 18–19, 21.

[61] Ibid., 22. Cf. Moore's evaluation of North American capitalist economy and its influence on biblical exegesis (*Mark and Luke in Poststructuralist Perspectives,* 148–49).

proper to the time, place and culture of the biblical author."[62] From Malina's perspective, reading models that fail to make this effort are sinfully anachronistic, ethnocentric,[63] elitist, and grossly inconsiderate.[64] Strangely, the fairness doctrine to which he appeals seems to get lost in the agonistic rhetoric directed particularly at poststructural and postmodern readings.

In spite of the many important hermeneutical issues that separate social world critics like Malina from reader-response critics like myself, and from poststructuralist critics like Moore, we all nevertheless share a common rhetorical purpose: to radically undercut the churchly ordinariness of the text—that presumed connectedness of the biblical world with our own religious subculture—in order to confront the New Testament as other, as an alien thing.[65] The social world critics, for their part, do this by setting the biblical text in an ancient Mediterranean social context with a nearly unbridgeable chasm between it and our own world.[66] They may provide contemporary readers with a critical drop of water to cool their tongues, but that cultural chasm is one that only their own prophets can cross with ease. Conversely, some reader-response critics—particularly poststructuralist critics—undercut the ordinariness of the biblical text by jarringly juxtaposing it to an ever-widening collection of contemporary literary theorists and intertextual reading frames.[67]

But let me give a different illustration of this rhetorical phenomenon from a related field: that of contemporary historical Jesus research. I find it not at all surprising that the Robert W. Funk-inspired Jesus Seminar has recently, in the final decade before the end of the second millennium, "discovered" that the historical Jesus was a profoundly prophetic, nonapocalyptic figure trying to transform and revitalize Judaism.[68] This peculiarly Lukan-sounding Jesus

---

[62] Malina, "Reading Theory Perspective: Reading Luke-Acts," 16.

[63] Ibid., 23.

[64] Ibid., 17. Compare this with Edgar McKnight's comment: "A reader-oriented approach acknowledges that the contemporary reader's 'intending' of the text is not the same as that of the ancient author and/or the ancient readers. This is not possible, necessary, or desirable" (*Post-Modern Use of the Bible,* 150; see also 151–54; cf. Moore's discussion of intentionality, in *Mark and Luke in Poststructuralist Perspectives,* 61–62, 74–75).

[65] Osiek, "The Social Science and the Second Testament: Problems and Challenges," 94.

[66] Among social world critics there is a widespread emphasis on the ancient Mediterranean "honor/shame culture" with its "dyadic view of person" and "limited good," which diverges widely from Euro-American values (Malina, *The New Testament World,* 28–116).

[67] Fowler, *"Let the Reader Understand,"* 228–66; Moore, *Mark and Luke in Poststructuralist Perspectives,* xv–xix; cf. Culbertson, *The Poetics of Revelation,* 141–85.

[68] For example, see Marcus Borg's *Jesus,* 14, 125–71, and his more recent article, "Portraits of Jesus in Contemporary North American Scholarship."

speaks out against the popular television-evangelist mode of Christianity that is saturated by a gross apocalypticism (e.g., Hal Lindsey, Jim Bakker), a mode of Christianity that is largely uninterested in caring for or protecting the present world and its people (e.g., Jim Jones, David Koresh).

But compare this latter-day reconstruction with Albert Schweitzer's turn-of-the-century work on the historical Jesus. Surrounded by a popular Christian culture that believed the twentieth century would herald the inbreaking of God's kingdom through the cooperative, humanizing agendas of church and state, Schweitzer's historical research uncovered a radically apocalyptic "Markan Jesus"—a different Jesus, whose cataclysmic metaphors opposed the idealistic *Zeitgeist* of Schweitzer's day. Although Schweitzer's research and the Jesus Seminar's research reconstruct the teaching of the historical Jesus along totally different lines (the former accepts Jesus' apocalyptic words as authentic; the latter rejects them as secondary), both share a common but unspoken rhetorical aim: to make Jesus different from their own culture so that "he" can critically speak to it.[69]

I believe that this same phenomenon can be found in the social world Gospels and in the reader-response and poststructuralist Gospels. Although their methodologies differ radically, their goals (conscious or unconscious) are similar: to defamiliarize the Gospel narratives to such an extent that they can speak to contemporary culture in fresh ways.[70] Or perhaps their goals might better be described negatively: all three critical approaches, paralleling historical Jesus research, attempt to defamiliarize the gospel so that it is no longer able to speak in the traditional ways of the past.

Even the great contemporary Jesus scholar John D. Crossan is quick to point out (as was Schweitzer before him) that researchers' reconstructions of the historical Jesus have always had a strangely autobiographical element to them (that is, of course, all reconstructions except his own).[71] In other words, the interests and ideologies of the scholars doing the research are always replicated in their portraits of Jesus. I suspect that the same autobiographical point could also be made of biblical literary critics and their historical-critical

[69] Not surprisingly, McKnight makes the same observation when speaking about scholars' reconstructions of "Paul" (*Post-Modern Use of the Bible,* 148–50).

[70] White, "Historical and Literary Criticism: A Theological Response," 32–34.

[71] Crossan writes: "[H]istorical Jesus research is a very safe place to do theology and call it history, to do autobiography and call it biography" (*The Historical Jesus,* xxviii; cf. xxxiv). However, his methodologies and reconstructions are somehow free from these two viruses that afflict every other portrayal of Jesus (ibid.; see also his "Autobiographical Presuppositions," in *Who Killed Jesus?* 211–15; cf. Davies, *Jesus the Healer,* 8–11).

counterparts. Indeed, it is precisely this autobiographical element that Tolbert's and Moore's criticisms attempt to uncover in us, the reader critics. Thankfully, however, they stop well short of disrobing their fellow scholars or themselves.

In summary, those who challenge reader-response criticism's appropriation by biblical scholars focus on two fundamental issues. The first criticism focuses on reader-response criticism's lack of critical apparatus for analyzing its own interpretive stance. Reader-response criticism often fails or refuses to investigate the social and rhetorical contexts of the interpreter and the implications of those contexts for interpretation. Thus, its interpretations lack a critically reflected subjectivity—in spite of the fact that its interpretations are covertly rooted in the critic's experience as much as liberationist and feminist exegeses are explicitly rooted in the experience of oppression. Although reader-response criticism's failure or refusal to address the social and rhetorical contexts of the biblical interpreter may be due as much to academic or ecclesial politics as to any theoretical oversight, nevertheless more openness in this area is necessary if it is ever going to strengthen its position within the guild. The second criticism focuses on reader-response criticism's interest in appropriating the Bible for the contemporary reader. From this angle, reader-response criticism seems blatantly unconcerned about how canonical texts might have been understood and considered persuasive by first-century audiences.[72]

Thus, biblical reader-response critics fail at both ends of the reader spectrum. For historical and social world critics, reader-response criticism as it is applied to the Bible fails to understand the ancient Mediterranean world or its values—or, worse yet, it has no interest in understanding them. Reader-response criticism is blatantly, pointedly anachronistic. And for feminist and liberationist critics, reader-response criticism fails to account for its own values and advocacy stance. Reader-response criticism is blithely elitist and anarchistic.

HOBBLING OUT OF THE TOMB

Although my particular project addresses the two criticisms mentioned above, it does so within the context of reader-response exegetical studies in the Fourth Gospel. My purpose is therefore not primarily adversarial or theoretical but is instead exegetical, hermeneutical, and self-reflective. I am interested in the application of reader-response criticism to the biblical text, in its appropriateness for and appropriation in contemporary Christian communi-

---

[72] This point is often made in spite of many reader-response critics' expressed interest in orality (see particularly Fowler, *"Let the Reader Understand,"* 48–52; and Moore, *Literary Criticism and the Gospels,* 84–92).

ties, and in my own existential relationship to the approach and the text, more than I am interested in literary theory *qua* theory. Indeed, the three chapters that make up Part One of this book began simply as exegetical studies, with little in the way of explicit theoretical underpinnings. For example, my dissertation's textually defined implied reader is the theoretical starting place for chapter 1 (a dynamic reading of character in John 5 and 9), and, to a lesser extent, for chapters 2 and 3 (an analysis of John 11 from the perspective of a resistant reader, and an analysis of the text-critical problem in John 18:12–24 from the perspective of reception theory). And although in Part One I make a number of references to my earlier, more formalist study of Johannine narrative, this book is intended to be neither a survey of nor an introduction to the varieties of reader criticism—formalist, feminist, receptionist, or postmodern. Many such introductions are already in print and need not be replicated here. Rather, my project begins where most other reader-response critical studies tend to end: with a formalist, reader-response exegetical study of the "encoded reader." Then in Part Two, I explore the implications of my own personal history for my interpretation of Johannine texts.

Borrowing from Stephen Moore's brief definition of formalism as "a methodological attitude in which the meaning of a literary work is located in the details of its structure,"[73] I begin by imagining the reader of John 5 and 9 as a rhetorically defined structure in the text: that is, as an implied or encoded reader. From this formalist model of the reader, I then move on in the next two chapters to explore two more active reading strategies. First, taking a cue from feminist literary theory, I investigate the possibilities of a resistant reading of John 11. Next I use the text-critical problem of John 18:12–24 as empirical evidence of early Christian reading responses and as a window into an agonistic reception history.

As the "real reader" becomes more rhetorically overt in these exegetical chapters, the interpretive value of what actual readers bring to the reading experience begins to take on new significance for me. Consequently, the second half of the book examines the role of the real reader: it addresses the question of the contemporary reader's social location and the implications of that location for reading the Fourth Gospel. In this half of the book I use recent attempts of three Euro-American biblical scholars to situate themselves ideologically and sociologically as real readers, to establish the context for chapter 4,

---

[73] Moore, *Literary Criticism and the Gospels,* 180. See McKnight for an excellent historical survey of the formalist tradition in literary criticism (*The Bible and the Reader,* 15–82).

the book's key theoretical chapter: an analysis of autobiography in contemporary literary theory and its hitherto unexplored implications for reconceiving biblical reader-response criticism.

Whatever overarching thesis this book may have (and I am not convinced that it does have one), I suppose that its origins can be traced to the autobiographical emphasis of Part Two, which is rooted in Mary Ann Tolbert's critical remark quoted earlier: "Staley's generalized reader masks . . . the critic himself: Staley's reader reads the way Staley does."[74] In many respects, this book is my attempt to discover the Staley who is the real reader behind the objectified, implied/encoded reader of my public scholarship. But in this discovering process, I find that I disc over as much fertile soil as I dig up. In my search for a real reader beneath my Johannine implied/encoded reader, I find that I am continually recovering and reseeding in plots no less imaginatively framed than those that I originally built for my Johannine implied/encoded reader. And it is precisely within these newly formed plots that the postmodern and postcolonial perspectives come to play.

Although it is not my purpose to explore all the nuances of postcolonialism and postmodernism any more than it is my purpose to summarize the varieties of reader-response criticism or autobiographics, some concise descriptions of these movements seem in order. Again, Moore's easily accessible definitions prove helpful. Drawing from a wide-ranging collection of literary theorists, he describes postmodernism as

> a discontent within modernity and an incredulity toward its legitimizing "metanarratives" [or its totalizing systems of thought]; . . . a "criticism which would include in its own discourse an implicit (or explicit) reflection upon itself"; . . . "a desire to think in terms sensitive to difference (of others without opposition, of heterogeneity without hierarchy. . . .)."[75]

Similarly, Arif Dirlik defines the goal of postcolonialism as the abolition of "all distinction between center and periphery as well as all other 'binarisms' that are allegedly a legacy of colonial(ist) ways of thinking[, in order to] . . . reveal societies globally in their complex heterogeneity and contingency."[76]

---

[74] Tolbert, "A Response from a Literary Perspective," 206.

[75] Moore, *Literary Criticism and the Gospels,* 181; see also Fowler, "Postmodern Biblical Criticism," 4–6; and Aichele, "On Postmodern Biblical Criticism and Exegesis," 31. Jane Flax helpfully lists eight beliefs "still prevalent in (especially American) culture but derived from the Enlightenment," which "postmodern philosophers seek to throw into radical doubt" ("Postmodernism and Gender Relations in Feminist Theory," 624–25).

[76] Dirlik, "The Postcolonial Aura: Third World Criticism in the Age of Global Capitalism," 329, cf. 332; cf. Appiah, "Is the Post- in Postmodernism the Post- in Postcolonialism?"; and Spivak, *The Post-Colonial Critic,* 50–52.

So to put the underlying issues of Part Two into the language of contemporary literary theory, in the second half of the book I address postmodernism's demolition of the residually Platonic unity of texts and selves (two significant modernist "metanarratives"), and I examine the implications of that demolition for a postcolonial reader-response criticism.[77] Not the least of these implications will be that any conscious turn toward exploring real readers' hermeneutics will be fraught with just as many epistemological difficulties and theoretical dead ends as were the discussions regarding the status of implied or encoded readers. That is to say, the critic's construction of himself or herself—or the construction of a particular reading community—as a heuristic, interpretive device will be no less fictive, no less rhetorically construed, and no less politically neutral than were the earlier and friendlier formalist readers.[78]

On the heels of that last paragraph I have to step back to catch my breath. I feel more than a little uneasy about what I just finished saying, and I am not convinced that I headed off in the right direction. Perhaps I got carried away by my own rhetoric. So let me backtrack. In spite of what I just said in the preceding paragraph, a postmodern dismantling of texts into other texts, and readers into other readers, does not necessarily imply that I am denying the existence of an individual's or a society's historically and culturally mediated consciousness. Instinctively, I feel that I am more than this black ink on white paper; that Jesus is more than a stretch of four Hebrew letters among the thousands of possible consonant clusters posted under Roman directives; that the Holocaust is more than the four words *six million murdered Jews*. And here is where, to my way of thinking, the politics of postcolonialism and feminism jostle uncomfortably with postmodernism's "rejection of a privileged position."[79]

The physical concreteness of the recent past in postcolonial criticism (the memory of casually armed soldiers maintaining "order") and the hierachical, binary ideologies accompanying postcolonialism ("you are subject to us," "it's us against you") are, at the very least, residual traces of "a privileged position"

---

[77] The equally important theological connection between texts and selves is described nicely by Moore, who writes: "[T]he idea of a unified identity, corresponding to the idea of a unified text . . . , is a displaced theological idea descended from the ancient and medieval concept of the soul[; and] the opposite idea of a split or fragmented subject, corresponding to a fragmented text, is an idea no less theological ("'Mirror, Mirror . . .': Lacanian Reflections on Malbon's Mark," 169; cf. van den Heever, "Being and Nothingness," 42–44).

[78] The Bible and Culture Collective, *The Postmodern Bible*, 55–57.

[79] Hutcheon, *The Politics of Postmodernism*, 153.

that still exerts its temporizing power on the borders of postmodernism's "desire to think in terms sensitive to difference (of others without opposition, of heterogeneity without hierarchy. . . .)."[80] Just one example: Knowing that the director of the imaginative fantasy films *Jaws, E.T.,* and *Jurassic Park* also directed *Schindler's List,* a re-creation of the Holocaust in documentary-like black-and-white celluloid, in no way lessens that story's concreteness; nor does it neutralize the hierarchies and binary oppositions of Hitler's Third Reich. Moreover, viewing *Schindler's List* in the context of *Jaws, E.T.,* and *Jurassic Park* cannot merely textualize those living traces who, at the end of the film and in full living color, memorialized their rescuer, Oskar Schindler, by placing stones on his Jerusalem grave in 1993. Postmodernism can bask in the light of heterogeneity without hierarchy, but it is postcolonialism and feminism that refuse to trivialize or remain silent when confronted with the destructive residue of colonialist and modernist hierarchies and their binary oppositions.

So in spite of the tension between postmodernism's politics and the politics of feminism and postcolonialism,[81] all three perspectives play important roles in the latter half of the book. First, these three critical perspectives bring important insights to bear on the theory of autobiography as it is discussed in the field of contemporary literary criticism. Feminism and postcolonialism have been instrumental in challenging and stretching the traditional boundaries of the genre, and postmodernist thought has placed a question mark over the Western understanding of the individual, unified self which had been central to earlier, formalist analyses of the autobiographical canon. Today, interest in autobiography is intense precisely because of the concerns that these three perspectives bring to the genre. So perhaps it is not surprising to find numerous echoes from them in my chapter on autobiography's status in contemporary literary theory.

Second, a postmodern sense of textual and readerly erosion leads me, in chapter 5, to explore an autobiographical reading of myself reading the Fourth Gospel. This erosion provides the basis for a postcolonial reading of myself, which is spatialized naturally in terms of my memories from a childhood spent on the Navajo Reservation in Arizona. The eroding self stretches the boundaries of the autobiographical genre and weaves it intertextually with feminist criticism, myth, geography, genealogy, and popular American culture.

---

[80] Moore, *Literary Criticism and the Gospels,* 181.

[81] For example, see the instructive discussion in The Bible and Culture Collective, *The Postmodern Bible,* 234–67, esp. 262–66.

Third, in chapter 6, the postcolonial reading of myself leads into a postmodern, dramatic reading of the Johannine passion narrative. There, in a dialogue between the three corpses on their crosses (myself as social world critic, as literary critic, and as autobiographer), an eroding sense of self and text wrestle for interpretive control at the site of Jesus' crucifixion.

The book concludes with a brief look at Arnold Krupat's "ethnocriticism," with its commitment to "betweenness" and to dialogue on the epistemological frontier of "transculturalization."[82] I try to imagine the implications of Krupat's vision for a biblical reader-response criticism that tries to account for the critic's social location.

UNBOUND

For the first seven years of my professional teaching career, I required freshmen students to write autobiographical letters describing a crisis event in their lives and then asked them to reflect on how that crisis affected their developing life story. I did not realize at the time that autobiography and autobiographical theory would one day undergird my own move toward postmodern and postcolonial biblical criticism. But now, nine years after initially assigning that exercise in an introductory theology course, I find myself turning to autobiography as I struggle with critical questions of reader-response criticism and biblical hermeneutics.

Speaking providentially as a sometimes-uncomfortable Presbyterian, I discovered when I was nearly finished with this project a just-published collection of essays edited by Diane Freedman, Olivia Frey, and Frances Murphy Zauhar, entitled *The Intimate Critique: Autobiographical Literary Criticism.* Not only did their book give me a name for the criticism I was attempting; it also confirmed my own intuitions. These scholars' attempts to integrate their own personal lives with textual analyses and then to validate them within the professional guild of literary criticism was a breath of fresh air in my musty-smelling, wintry office. Their work gives me hope that spring will come. Perhaps one day all professional interpreters of texts will feel free to examine themselves in their critical enterprises without at the same time fearing that they may have contracted a deadly disease.[83]

---

[82] Krupat, *Ethnocriticism,* 28.

[83] For example, see the recent work of Ched Myers and Wes Howard-Brook, who, as non-professional interpreters of the New Testament, explore their own socially and politically sensitive, self-conscious readings of Mark and John (Myers, *Who Will Roll Away the Stone?;* Howard-Brook, *Becoming Children of God*).

No doubt some will say that all my careful nuancing of postmodern, post-colonial, post-me-up positions is merely another contemporary example of the tail wagging the proverbial dog, a fragrant cloth disguising the stink of Lazarus's decaying flesh; that my final chapters are little more than temporary linguistic flight from the present realities of unemployment, uncertainty, and the malaise of middle age.[84] Yet I cannot help feeling, deep inside (inside the tomb? the womb?), that the tale weighing me down is much larger than the original species of formalist criticism which dogged my original exegetical work in the Gospel of John.

I concluded my first book with this question:

> Can narrative criticism at last arouse Lazarus from the grave [I should have written "from the tome"], and still allow him to be Lazarus? The pressing issue before the biblical critic is whether reader response criticism can unwind those strands of time. Can embracing the medium of print awaken and rouse the text from its death-like slumber, or will the print's kiss sound the death knell? Only the reader can tell.[85]

I think I am still asking those same questions or—perhaps—related questions: Can any form of reader-response criticism arouse Lazarus from that grave tome and still allow him to be Lazarus? Or perhaps I am now more concerned with Mary and Martha, the women; the sisters. After all, they are the ones still alive, the ones left behind who must struggle to make some sense out of the world. So let me try asking the question again: Can packaging the gospel in autobiographical literary criticism and imprinting it with postmodern and postcolonial postmarks send it off to new, unforeseen dustynations?[86] This reader, for one, can't tell for sure. Nevertheless, to adapt for biblical criticism what Patricia Williams once wrote about her own rhetorical aims in the

---

[84] The psychologist Dan P. McAdams argues that at midlife, people like me quite often move toward "postformal modes of thinking" (*The Stories We Live By,* 200). This postformal mode of thinking "rejects the absolute truths of formal operations and focuses instead on situationally specific truths, on solutions and logical inferences that are linked to, and defined by, particular contexts. . . . We . . . struggle to formulate useful statements and viewpoints that are true for the time being and in a particular place. Our thinking about certain issues becomes more radically subjective. We come to accept 'local truths' rather than universal ones; we grow suspicious of general laws about domains of life that are now seen to have multiple and even contradictory meanings" (ibid.; cf. James Fowler's description of "conjunctive faith[, which] involves going beyond the . . . clear boundaries of identity" [*Stages of Faith,* 183, 186–87]). Recently, Paul Anderson has put forward the intriguing thesis that the author of the Fourth Gospel himself evinces a "conjunctive faith" (*The Christology of the Fourth Gospel,* 147–51).

[85] Staley, *The Print's First Kiss,* 122.

[86] Where, perhaps, it could be used to fuel new fires.

legal profession, I have tried to write in such a way that my writing will reveal the intersubjectivity of my exegetical constructions and so lead "the reader both to participate in the construction of meaning and to be conscious of that process."[87] Like hers, my writing is an attempt "to create a genre of [exegetical] writing to fill the gaps of traditional [biblical] scholarship."[88]

Sometimes I wonder if the final chapters of this book haven't raised someone—or something—else, quite different from what I originally intended. Perhaps I should have just let sleeping dogs lie. Were there other bodies in Lazarus's tomb that hot Judean day? It was so dark, I couldn't see inside when I was reading the text. Perhaps there were scores of ossuaries I missed back there, "cases and bins and boxes,"[89] each set in its own niche, each filled with the dust and bones of much different memories; whose traces of stench still lingered imperceptibly in the corners of that hollowed-out hillside.

But then again, perhaps it is the voice that I should be concerned about—not the dead brother, not the still living sisters. The voice that gives a name to the stench and the decay and calls it forth.[90] Gospel.

---

[87] Williams, *The Alchemy of Race and Rights,* 7–8; cf. Berg, "Suppressing the Language of (Wo)man: The Dream as a Common Language," 10–14. But Steven Mailloux points out the "[p]roblems [which] may arise with such rhetorical self-consciousness" (*Rhetorical Power,* 167). For example, he sees three central difficulties, and all three are worth quoting in detail. They express my own fears as I attempt to become rhetorically self-conscious in my biblical criticism.

Mailloux argues: "One danger is that rhetorical candor will be read as narcissistic self-indulgence, that it will be seen not as a necessary theoretical move required by rhetorical theory but as another case of theory's fashionable rereading of itself—self-critique as self-display.

"A still greater danger for a rhetorical hermeneutics is that a demonstration of its rhetoricity will undermine its persuasiveness as theory. This is the rhetorician's nightmare: By arguing that there is no appeal outside rhetorical exchanges, have I undercut the rhetorical force of my own theory? Does rhetorical candor detract from rhetorical effectiveness?

["Finally,] . . . [o]ne other problem must also be faced head on. It is again the question of consequences, the consequences of rhetorical hermeneutics. Certain traditionalists in hermeneutics and conservatives in politics will worry about its purported relativism and anarchic nihilism, claiming that in such a theory anything goes and all is permitted. Some radical revisionists may accuse this same theory of liberal pluralism and political quietism, not because 'anything goes' but because 'everything stays' in such theories; nothing is changed because all is (supposedly) tolerated" (ibid., 167–68; see also Jasper, *Rhetoric, Power and Community,* 69).

[88] Williams, *The Alchemy of Race and Rights,* 7; see also Miller, *Getting Personal,* xi.

[89] Hillerman, *Talking God,* 291.

[90] In the words of Nicole Jouve, "writing criticism as autobiography may be the way to a fuller, more relevant voice" (*White Woman Speaks with Forked Tongue,* 11; cf. Young-Bruehl, "Pride and Prejudice: Feminist Scholars Reclaim the First Person," 15–18).

# PART ONE

# Reading the Text:
# Explorations of the Johannine Reader

In what sense can reading be seen as a form of play, as an act of fantasy or imagining, a model of impersonating, pretending, playing imaginary roles?

—Matei Calinescu

# Stumbling in the Dark, Reaching for the Light: John 5 and 9 and the Encoded Reader

With the exception of music, we have been trained to think of patterns as fixed affairs. "The truth is that the right way to begin to think about the pattern which connects is as a dance of interacting parts, secondarily pegged down by various sorts of physical limits and by habits, and by the naming of states and component entities."

—Daniel Goleman

[Biblical] narrative become[s] an obstacle course, its reading turns into a drama of understanding—conflict between inferences, seesawing, reversal, discovery, and all. The only knowledge perfectly acquired is the knowledge of our limitations.

— Meir Sternberg

Every character is a trap of a certain kind, one which the writer would like his readers to fall into.

—Laszlo Foldenyi

If you were blind, you would not have sin. But now that you say, "We see," your sin remains.

—John 9:41

## READING BETWEEN THE LINES IN BIBLICAL NARRATIVE

One of the shibboleths of reader-response criticism has been the intricate weave of terms its adherents have fabricated for readers. Pick up any discussion of reader criticism in literary theory or biblical criticism, and the emperor's new clothes are soon paraded before the viewing public.[1] But is there really anything there beneath the flowery phrases and bulging postulates of reader criticism? Sometimes it seems hard to say for sure. Yet in spite of the inherent difficulties posed by these varieties of readers,[2] the terms *implied reader* or *encoded reader* best express the rhetorical aspects of texts which I wish to explore in this chapter.[3] What I mean to evoke in the use of these two terms is precisely that: (1) narratives, like arguments, are persuasive in intent and temporal in their mode of expression; (2) by paying close attention to the temporal quality of narratives—that is, by being attentive to the linear sequence of words on the page—the critic will be better able to analyze words' manipulative power;[4] and (3) by being aware of different socio-cultural narrative codes, the critic can better assess the persuasive intent of stories.[5]

Because the miracle stories in John 5 and 9 are constructed in such a way that the encoded reader discovers they were performed on the sabbath only after reading that the miracles occurred, and because the characters' conversations are reminiscent of the dialogues in ancient Hebrew literature, these two stories are excellent places to explore the narratological and theological implications of temporality and ancient cultural codes for Johannine characterization.

In his analysis of characters in the Fourth Gospel, Alan Culpepper quotes Robert Scholes and Robert Kellogg where they describe the difference between Greek and Hebraic forms of characterization (the paragraph is well-worn by biblical scholars):

> The heroes of the Old Testament were in a process of becoming, whereas the heroes of Greek narrative were in a state of being. Process in Greek narrative was confined to the action of a plot. And even so, the action exemplified unchanging, universal laws; while the agents of the action, the characters,

---

[1] Mailloux, *Rhetorical Power,* 31. See also Moore, *Literary Criticism and the Gospels,* 71–72; Fowler, *"Let the Reader Understand,"* 25–40; Porter, "Why Hasn't Reader-Response Criticism Caught on in New Testament Studies?" 278–81; and Machor, "Introduction: Readers/Texts/Contexts," vii–xi.

[2] For example, see Freund, *The Return of the Reader,* 69–89, 136–56; Schweickart, "Reading Ourselves: Toward a Feminist Theory of Reading," 35–39; Mailloux, "Misreading as a Historical Act: Cultural Rhetoric, Bible Politics, and Fuller's 1845 Review of Douglass's *Narrative,"* 4–5; and Wuellner, "Is There an Encoded Reader Fallacy?" 40–54.

[3] Staley, *The Print's First Kiss,* 30–37. The expression "encoded reader" comes from Christine Brooke-Rose (*A Rhetoric of the Unreal,* 105).

[4] What I have in mind here is not a "virginal, first-time reading," but rather a critically informed "second reading" (see, for example, Calinescu's concept of rereading and play in *Rereading,* 112–13, 188–92, 278; cf. Mailloux, *Rhetorical Power,* 34–35).

[5] For example, see Malina, "Reading Theory Perspective: Reading Luke-Acts," 14–23.

became as the plot unfolded only more and more consistent ethical types. Abraham, Jacob, David, and Samson, on the other hand, are men whose personal development is the focus of interest.[6]

Building on these observations, Culpepper notes:

> In John, the character of Jesus is static; it does not change. He only emerges more clearly as what he was from the beginning. Some of the minor characters, the Samaritan woman and the blind man in particular, undergo a significant change. To some extent, therefore, the Gospel of John draws from both Greek and Hebrew models of character development, but most of its characters appear to represent particular ethical types.[7]

A great deal has been written about the nature of ancient Hebrew narrative since Scholes and Kellogg's terse comparisons of twenty-five years ago and since Culpepper's suggestive comments, now more than ten years old.[8] Yet little has been done with Culpepper's observation regarding the "Hebrew model of character" in the Fourth Gospel, beyond taking note of the same point he made. For example, in a more recent study of the characterization of Jesus in the Fourth Gospel, J. A. du Rand does not attempt to delineate any aspects of the "Hebrew model" of characterization in spite of observing: "One can agree with Culpepper that to some extent the Gospel of John draws from both Greek and Hebrew models of character development but that most of the Johannine characters are presented as definite ethical types."[9]

Among the many literary critics working with ancient Hebrew literature, Robert Alter, Adele Berlin, Meir Sternberg, and Shimon Bar-Efrat each have made special efforts to describe the various kinds of characters the biblical writers created and have tried to isolate the narrative modes of their character-

---

[6] Scholes and Kellogg, *The Nature of Narrative,* 169; Culpepper, *Anatomy of the Fourth Gospel,* 103. Erich Auerbach's 1953 essay "Odysseus' Scar," in *Mimesis,* prefigured Scholes and Kellogg's comparisons of Greek and Hebrew literature but is not quoted in Culpepper's chapter on character.

[7] Culpepper, *Anatomy of the Fourth Gospel,* 103.

[8] Cf. Sternberg's critique (*The Poetics of Biblical Narrative,* 232–33, 268). Robert Alter's *The Art of Biblical Narrative,* which appeared in 1981, is mentioned only twice by Culpepper, and Adele Berlin's *Poetics and Interpretation of Biblical Narrative* appeared in 1983, the same year Culpepper's book was published. Subsequently, two other important works on Hebrew narrative have seen print in English. Sternberg's *The Poetics of Biblical Narrative* was published in 1985, and Shimon Bar-Efrat's second edition of *Narrative Art in the Bible* appeared in translation in 1989, five years after its Hebrew publication.

[9] Du Rand, "The Characterization of Jesus as Depicted in the Narrative of the Fourth Gospel," 25, 31–33.

ization. With regard to the types of characters found in ancient Hebrew literature, these scholars—explicitly or implicitly—all take issue with E. M. Forster's often-quoted description that "flat" characters with only one or two ethical traits are a distinguishing feature of Hebrew poetics.[10] Berlin, for example, finds three types of characters in Hebrew narrative (the "full-fledged character," the "type," and the "agent");[11] and, coincidentally, Culpepper describes three types in the Fourth Gospel (the "protagonist," the "ficelles," and the "background characters").[12] There is, however, no one-to-one correspondence between Berlin's three types and Culpepper's three.

But rather than getting into an extended discussion of Johannine character types and attempting to classify either the bedridden man of John 5 or the blind man of John 9 along those lines, I prefer to take my cue from Alter and Sternberg, who eschew any straightforward typology of Hebrew characters. The two of them might well agree with Amelie Rorty, who once developed an insightful, fivefold typology of character and concluded her study saying: "The distinctions that I have drawn are forced; most philosophers and novelists blend the notions that I have distinguished. One would hardly find a pure case. . . ."[13]

If a typology of the Fourth Gospel's characters is not one of my aims, describing the book's modes of characterization and the interweaving of these modes certainly is. For example, in his summary of characterization in ancient Hebrew narrative, Alter discusses its four modes—all of which appear in the Fourth Gospel. These modes are: (1) the narrator's description of a character in terms of actions, appearance, or attitudes and intentions (e.g., John 6:71; 11:2; 12:4; 13:23; 19:39); (2) one character's comments on another (e.g., 1:29, 36; 6:70); (3) the direct speech of the character (e.g., 6:35; 8:12; 11:25); and (4) inward speech (i.e., interior monologue; e.g., 17:1-26).[14] With regard to narration, Alter, Sternberg, and Bar-Efrat argue that the ancient Hebraic narrators are reliable and omniscient and are thus

---

[10] Forster, *Aspects of the Novel,* 68–78. Cf. Scholes and Kellogg, *The Nature of Narrative,* 164–66; Alter, *The Art of Biblical Narrative,* 114; Berlin, *Poetics and Interpretation of Biblical Narrative,* 23, 37–38; Sternberg, *The Poetics of Biblical Narrative,* 191, 525; and Bar-Efrat, *Narrative Art in the Bible,* 90–92.

[11] Berlin, *Poetics and Interpretation of Biblical Narrative,* 23–24, 31–32.

[12] Culpepper, *Anatomy of the Fourth Gospel,* 103–4.

[13] Rorty, "A Literary Postscript: Character, Persons, Selves, Individuals," 319; see also Hochman, *Character in Literature,* 86–89.

[14] Alter, *The Art of Biblical Narrative,* 116–17. Cf. Berlin, *Poetics and Interpretation of Biblical Narrative,* 33–42; Sternberg, *The Poetics of Biblical Narrative,* 322–30, 342–48; and Bar-Efrat, *Narrative Art in the Bible,* 48–86.

accorded descriptive certainty.[15] The same holds true for the narrator of the Fourth Gospel.[16] However, when describing characters, the Hebrew narrators tend to be laconic and highly selective in their use of omniscience.[17] Again, Johannine poetics parallel this peculiarity.[18]

In comparison to such narrators, the characters in Johannine and ancient Hebrew narrative themselves often appear loquacious. But, as Alter states, characters' words ironically "may be more of a drawn shutter than an open window."[19] From this observation Alter goes on to argue that in ancient Hebrew narrative the reader is therefore compelled "to get at character and motive through a process of inference from fragmentary data, often with crucial pieces of narrative exposition strategically withheld, and this leads to multiple or sometimes even wavering perspectives on the characters."[20] Alter thus gives special attention to the dynamic interplay between narration and dialogue and the subtle nuances of repetition.[21] But it is Sternberg who especially concentrates on analyzing the "crucial pieces of narrative exposition strategically withheld,"[22] that is, the manipulation of ambiguity, suspense, curiosity, and surprise that make up a large part of Hebrew characterization.[23] Like Palestinian peasant children guiding their goats through the Judean wilderness, Alter, Berlin, Sternberg, and Bar-Efrat are masters at leading the reader through the sudden twists and sharp turns, the steep ridges and dizzying drop-offs that make up the art of ancient Hebrew characterization.

In view of their observations regarding ancient Hebrew narrative, my analysis of John 5 and 9 will attempt to show that these two miracle stories evince the same combination of rhetorical devices so often found in ancient Hebraic

---

[15] Alter, *The Art of Biblical Narrative,* 117; Sternberg, *The Poetics of Biblical Narrative,* 63–70; and Bar-Efrat, *Narrative Art in the Bible,* 13–45.

[16] Culpepper, *Anatomy of the Fourth Gospel,* 26–34.

[17] Alter, *The Art of Biblical Narrative,* 20, 126; Sternberg, *The Poetics of Biblical Narrative,* 180–85; and Bar-Efrat, *Narrative Art in the Bible,* 48–53.

[18] Staley, *The Print's First Kiss,* 37–41, 95–98.

[19] Alter, *The Art of Biblical Narrative,* 117. See also Alter, *The Pleasure of Reading in an Ideological Age,* 55; Berlin, *Poetics and Interpretation of Biblical Narrative,* 64–65; and Sternberg, *The Poetics of Biblical Narrative,* 346–64.

[20] Alter, *The Art of Biblical Narrative,* 126. See also Berlin, *Poetics and Interpretation of Biblical Narrative,* 67; and Sternberg, *The Poetics of Biblical Narrative,* 230–35.

[21] Alter, *The Art of Biblical Narrative,* 63–116. See also Sternberg, *The Poetics of Biblical Narrative,* 365–75, 436–40.

[22] Alter, *The Art of Biblical Narrative,* 126.

[23] Sternberg, *The Poetics of Biblical Narrative,* 230–320. Cf. Alter, *The Art of Biblical Narrative,* 12.

characterization. And, as in Hebrew narrative, repetition and minute changes in direct speech and narration play major roles in the formation of Johannine characters. As a consequence, Johannine characterization can likewise be complex, and its complexities are multiplied when one tries to account for the effect of narrative temporality on that characterization.[24]

READING WITH THE BEDRIDDEN

The two Johannine healings on the sabbath have often been compared,[25] and Culpepper himself lists eleven parallels in his analysis of the Johannine characters, most of which are easily recognized.[26] The setting in both instances is a pool in Jerusalem, and both unnamed characters are introduced as having long-term disabilities (a thirty-eight year infirmity and blindness from birth).[27] And because both men are healed on the sabbath, the stories share the similar theological themes of work, sin, and the identity of Jesus. The parallels are so remarkable that at least one scholar has been led to see these two stories as complementary units in a giant chiasm that overlays the entire Gospel,[28] and both Brown and Culpepper see them as demarcating a major unit of Johannine narrative.[29] Yet there are also important differences between the two stories, not the least of which is that, whereas John 5 is a miracle story with significant repercussions for the story's larger plot and for Jesus' identity, John 9 begins as a pronouncement story, then turns into a miracle story that is three times as long as the John 5 story, and serves virtually no plot function.

---

[24] John Darr attempts to account for the implications of the reading process for the formation of character in Luke-Acts, but his focus is much broader than mine. He is interested in tracing major characters throughout the entire Lukan corpus (*On Building Character*).

[25] Collins, "The Representative Figures in the Fourth Gospel," 41.

[26] Culpepper, *Anatomy of the Fourth Gospel,* 139.

[27] Sternberg has this to say about unnamed characters in ancient Hebrew narrative: "Anonymity is the lot (and mark) of supernumeraries, type-characters, institutional figures, embodied plot devices. . . . To remain nameless is to remain faceless, with hardly a life of one's own. Accordingly, a character's emergence from anonymity may correlate with a rise in importance" (*The Poetics of Biblical Narrative,* 330). However, quite nearly the opposite is the case in the Fourth Gospel. Here, the nameless mother of Jesus, the Samaritan woman, the blind man, and the beloved disciple are characters with more of "a life of their own" than named characters like Judas, Nathaniel, Caiaphas, or Philip (cf. Beck, "The Narrative Function of Anonymity in Fourth Gospel Characterization," 147–49).

[28] Deeks, "The Structure of the Fourth Gospel," 107–28.

[29] Brown, *The Gospel According to John,* 1:cxliv; Culpepper, "Un exemple de commentaire fondé sur la critique narrative: Jean 5,1–18," 139–40.

While the miracle-story structure of John 5:1–9 is straightforward and simple, it varies significantly from that of the two signs earlier in the Fourth Gospel. John 5:1–9 is the first narrated miracle in Jerusalem (but cf. 2:23–3:2); it is the first miracle Jesus performs for a person of low status; and, consequently, it is the first miracle story in which Jesus initiates the action.[30] Its structure is as follows: Jesus goes up to Jerusalem to participate in a religious festival; while he is there, he sees a sick man lying beside a pool (5:1–6a). After a brief verbal exchange between the miracle worker and the sick man (5:6b–8), the man is healed (5:9a). The only element that fleshes out the skeletal miracle-story form is the conversation between Jesus and the sick man (5:6b–7).

Normally, after the hero has come on the scene and sized up the situation (e.g., "When Jesus saw this man lying there and realized that he had been there a long time . . ." [5:6a]), a miracle is performed. But in this story, rather than Jesus immediately effecting the cure, he asks the man, "Do you want to get well?" (5:6b). For the moment, the question postpones the inevitable cure, whetting the encoded reader's appetite for another impressive sign. At the same time, it forces the encoded reader to concentrate on the developing conversation's peculiarities.[31]

Initially, Jesus' question might seem to reinforce the obvious point in the story—a story that closely follows the pattern of thousands of other miracle stories: of course the man wants to get well![32] Hasn't the narrator just said that

---

[30] Culpepper and Koester both note the differences between this miracle and the first two (Culpepper, "Un exemple de commentaire fondé sur la critique narrative: Jean 5,1–18," 141–43; Koester, "Hearing, Seeing, and Believing in the Gospel of John," 336–37), but neither of them points out the lower social status of this man or the Jerusalem setting of the miracle.

[31] I agree with Haenchen, who says that at this point Jesus' question is "not intended to determine whether the lame man has the desire to become well again (the Johannine Jesus is not trained to practice psychology)" (*John,* 1:255), if Haenchen means by "intended" that the encoded reader would not initially suspect a lack of desire on the part of the sick man. That is to say, Jesus does not ask him, *Mē theleis hygiēs genesthai?* (cf. 3:4; 4:12, 29, 33), which would imply that Jesus expected a negative response from the bedridden man. Thus, Jesus' question naturally expects a positive response.

[32] Haenchen thought that the question by Jesus was "odd," but was one that "permitted the reader to divine that a story of a healing [was] to follow" (*John,* 1:255). I have difficulties with this solution to Jesus' question, since the encoded reader has already read two other miracle stories in this book (2:1–11; 4:46–53) and should have no difficulty in figuring out from the setting (5:1–5) that a miracle is imminent. Jesus' question seems "odd" precisely because the answer initially seems so transparent to the encoded reader, Jesus, and the sick man (cf. 1:42, 47–48; 2:24; 4:17–19).

the man had been ill for thirty-eight years and that Jesus realized he had been there a long time? Yet the sick man does not give a straightforward reply to Jesus' question, such as, "Yes, I want to get well, can you help me?"[33] Rather, he responds with an unusually long sentence, one fraught with innuendo: "Sir, I don't have a person to—whenever the water is stirred up—to put me into the pool. But while I'm coming, someone else gets in before me" (5:7; my translation).[34]

For ancient Mediterranean culture, Jesus' direct, open-ended question and the convoluted, indirect response of the bedridden man reflect the characters' sensitivity to their differing social status. In the Fourth Gospel's first two miracle stories, Jesus' mother and the royal official were in culturally recognized positions of honor from which they could, and did, personally make requests of Jesus. But this sick, incapacitated man is physically impure and thus of lower social status than Jesus.[35] And since "every social interaction [in the ancient Mediterranean world] that [took] place outside one's family or outside one's circle of friends [was] perceived as a challenge to honor,"[36] the sick man is revealing his integrity and respect for social boundaries by not publicly challenging Jesus to respond to his need.[37] So while the illocutionary force of the sick man's response may indeed imply a request for help, it is vague enough to allow a prospective benefactor, if he so desires, to ignore the need without losing face.[38] Thus, taking into account the agonistic nature of ancient Mediterranean honor/shame culture, the sick man's response does

---

[33] John Chrysostom imagines what a more logical response on the part of the Johannine invalid might have been. He writes: "[The sick man] did not rant at his questioner, nor did he say: 'It is to ridicule and make fun of my condition that you ask whether I want to get well'" (*Commentary on Saint John the Apostle and Evangelist,* 360).

[34] Alter argues: "In any given narrative event, and especially at the beginning of any new story the point at which dialogue first emerges will be worthy of special attention, and in most instances, the initial words spoken by a personage will be revelatory, perhaps more in manner than in matter, constituting an important moment in the exposition of character" (*The Art of Biblical Narrative,* 74). Similarly, many Johannine commentators (not trained to write with Alter's poetic precision) have sensed that the bedridden man's opening words are somehow revelatory of his character.

[35] Pilch, "Sickness and Healing in Luke-Acts," 207.

[36] Malina, *The New Testament World,* 37.

[37] Ibid., 39. Note also the similarly veiled request of the socially inferior women, Mary and Martha (John 11:3; see below, p. 64).

[38] Malina, *The New Testament World,* 39–41. By "illocutionary force," I mean what the sentence intends to do, as "distinguished from [its] mere grammatical, or 'locutionary' aspect, and from what [it does] in fact do, [its] effect on the hearer, or 'perlocutionary' aspect" (Chatman, *Story and Discourse,* 161–66; see also Botha, *Jesus and the Samaritan Woman,* 64–66).

not imply a lack of determination on his part to get well,[39] nor is he complaining about his plight.[40] Rather, the social dynamics of the dialogue reveal that Jesus picks up on the sick man's veiled but respectful request and tells the sick man to begin to act on his own behalf. Jesus says to him: "Get up, pick up your mat and keep walking" (5:8, my translation).

Immediately upon being healed—or perhaps as a means to being healed—the man picks up his pallet and walks, and so fulfills Jesus' command.[41] The narrator then adds a temporal notation previously omitted: "Now that day was a sabbath" (5:9b).[42] What began as a relatively simple miracle story with a simple alignment of the encoded reader's sympathies ("Nice work, Jesus!" "Way to go, sick man!") has now turned into something much more complex, with competing allegiances ("Wait a minute! Should Jesus have told the man to carry his mat?"). Healing the man is fine, but did Jesus choose the proper means to effect and illustrate the cure? And what now will happen to the man who so innocently acted on Jesus' sabbath-breaking word?

As noted earlier, in both John 5 and 9 the encoded reader discovers that the healings were done on the sabbath only after the miracle story has been narrated.[43] In this sense they are unique among New Testament sabbath-day mir-

---

[39] Brown, *The Gospel According to John,* 1:209; Culpepper, "Un exemple de commentaire fondé sur la critique narrative: Jean 5,1–18," 148.

[40] Brown, *The Gospel According to John,* 1:209.

[41] Koester thinks that only "*[a]fter* experiencing healing did he take up his pallet and walk" ("Hearing, Seeing, and Believing in the Gospel of John," 338, emphasis mine; see also Culpepper, "Un exemple de commentaire fondé sur la critique narrative: Jean 5,1–18," 142). But the syntax of 5:8–9a is more ambiguous than Koester and Culpepper imply. Is the narrator's phrase "And immediately the man became well" (note that codex Sinaiticus omits the phrase "and immediately") temporally prior to the man's action of picking up his mat and walking, or is it merely logically prior to the man's action? If the narrator were concerned about emphasizing the temporal order of the miracle, he certainly could have used an aorist participle or a temporal adverb with *egeneto.* By way of contrast, in Mark 2:1–12 the actual physical healing of the paralytic (e.g., "Your sins are forgiven," 2:5) is clearly temporally prior to his getting up and walking (2:9–12).

[42] To use Sternberg's term, this is a narrative "gap"; that is, "a lack of information about the world—an event, motive, causal link, character trait, plot structure, law of probability contrived by a temporal displacement" (*The Poetics of Biblical Narrative,* 234–36; cf. Iser, *The Implied Reader,* 33–34; *The Act of Reading,* 168–70). Somewhat facetiously, I might add: That which is now called "gap" was formerly called "aporia" (cf. Haenchen, *John,* 1:257).

[43] Brown and others discuss the "sabbath motif," which is introduced "almost as an afterthought," primarily in terms of source-critical issues (*The Gospel According to John,* 1:210; see also Fortna, *The Fourth Gospel and Its Predecessor,* 113–17). My interest, however, is in the rhetorical effect of the "afterthought," not in its place of origin.

acles. In every other case the miracle stories begin with someone, either the narrator or the characters, noting that the day is a sabbath.[44] But in John 5 and 9, the narrator's belated reference to the sabbath forces the encoded reader to reevaluate the significance of the miracle itself; furthermore, it forces the encoded reader to reevaluate the story's characters. Although in previous stories Jesus challenges certain Jewish religious scruples,[45] he has not actually broken Torah,[46] nor has he told anyone else to do so. However, now with the narrator's added temporal note, the encoded reader must re-view Jesus' heretofore seemingly innocuous words. That Jesus should command the sick man to work on the sabbath, whether in order to be healed or to serve as a witness to his healing, must come as a surprise if not as an outright shock to the reader.[47] And the sick man, whose initial sputtering, convoluted response to Jesus might have appeared sniveling and weak-kneed, in retrospect proves to be a daring, risk-taking individual, a person who unquestioningly acts on a stranger's sabbath-breaking command.

As soon as the encoded reader is clued in to the miracle's temporal setting, the narrator introduces to the story a third party: "the Jews" (5:10).[48] In contrast to Jesus and the sick man, who know that a healing has taken place on the sabbath precisely because the formerly sick man is carrying his mat, and in contrast to the encoded reader, who initially does not know that that day was a sabbath, "the Jews" know only that "it is sabbath; it is not lawful for you to carry your mat" (5:10). There is no evidence that they know anything of

---

[44] Cf. Matt 12:9–14; Mark 1:21–28; 3:1-6; Luke 4:31–37; 6:6–11; 13:10–17; 14:16.

[45] Jesus has challenged purification rituals (2:6–7), attitudes toward the temple (2:13–22), and attitudes toward the Samaritans (4:5–42).

[46] Jer 17:21. Brown, *The Gospel According to John,* 1:208; Yee, *Jewish Feasts and the Gospel of John,* 31–47. Pancaro also adds: "Commanding something unlawful (what precisely is understood by this is not stated clearly, but the sabbath was no doubt included) was punishable with death . . ." (*The Law in the Fourth Gospel,* 15).

[47] Culpepper recognizes the surprise in the belated temporal notation when he says: "By withholding this information [i.e., that it was the sabbath] and supplying it just at this point, the narrator forces the reader to review the healing from a new perspective which catches the reader by surprise" ("Un exemple de commentaire fondé sur la critique narrative: Jean 5,1–18," 149). I just wish to add a note of specificity to his observation by saying that the encoded reader is forced to reevaluate the behavior of *the characters* by the belated temporal notation. Sternberg calls this type of device "character-elevating" (*The Poetics of Biblical Narrative,* 165).

[48] For a full analysis of the expression "the Jews" in this pericope, see Culpepper, "Un exemple de commentaire fondé sur la critique narrative: Jean 5,1–18," 148–50.

the miracle that has just taken place.[49] Thus, the statement "So the Jews said to the man *who had been cured* . . ." (5:10a) is the narrator's point of view—a perspective that Jesus and the encoded reader also share (5:6, 9; cf. 5:13, 14). It cannot be the perspective of "the Jews" (cf. 5:12, 16), for in the remaining dialogue they continue to be concerned with "the one who *said* to you, 'Take it up and walk'" (5:12). "The Jews" are not concerned with anyone "who made [a person] well." The latter characterization of Jesus is that of the healed man (5:11, 15), a characterization of particular interest also to the narrator (5:9, 10, 13).[50]

To the critical observation of "the Jews," "It is not lawful for you to carry your mat" (5:10), the healed man responds, "The man who made me well said to me, 'Take up your mat and walk'" (5:11). "The Jews" neither ask him why he is carrying his mat nor try to find out if someone else told him to carry it. Yet the healed man responds by proclaiming, "The man who made me well said to me. . . ." He does not reveal his benefactor's name, but rather describes his benefactor solely in terms of what he did: "the man who made me well."[51]

Now at this point in the story the encoded reader has no clue that the healed man does not know who his benefactor is. Here, then, is another significant gap in the story, and one that will remain unclarified until 5:13. This gap makes it more difficult for the encoded reader to assess the narrator's evaluation of the healed man, because the man's response to "the Jews'" observation "it is not lawful" could simply be read as juxtaposing the legal authority

---

[49] Contra Haenchen, who says, "It is astonishing that the Jews are unmoved by the miracle, either at this point or in what follows" (*John,* 1:246–47; cf. Brown, *The Gospel According to John,* 1:208).

[50] The narrator, whose descriptions are usually quite limited, uses three different words to denote the formerly sick man. Interestingly, all three are passive verbal constructions with the obvious agent left unidentified. The characters, on the other hand, are limited to the noun *hygiēs.* The narrator's interest is thus in Jesus' act of healing: the "giving of life" as *to poiein,* not in the man's activity of carrying his mat (see Haenchen, *John,* 1:258). This act of Jesus will also be an important point of emphasis in his dramatic monologue (5:21, 24–29, 39–40). The verb *airō* likewise occurs quite often in the miracle story (five times), but the narrator uses it only once, and, not surprisingly, it never occurs in Jesus' subsequent monologue (but cf. 10:18).

[51] Brown says: "The fact that he had let his benefactor slip away without even asking his name is another instance of real dullness" (*The Gospel According to John,* 1:209; see also Beasley-Murray, *John,* 74; but cf. 4:29, 39!). Haenchen, on the other hand, asks: "Should [Jesus] not perhaps have introduced himself to the lame man?" (*John,* 1:247). At this point in the story, however, these commentators' judgments are presumptuous. Such observations can only be made after reading the narrator's aside in 5:13.

of "the Jews" and the authority of a charismatic healer ("*the man who made me well* said . . .").[52] If this particular gap-filling logic were followed, then the healed man's argument essentially would be that the one who has the power to heal also has the power to abrogate sabbath law (cf. 5:17, 19–23).

Conflicts such as this, regarding the authority of Torah and the authority of charismatics, were quite common among Jewish rabbis at the end of the first century C.E. when the Fourth Gospel was being written. For example, after noting that "the one sphere in which supernatural proof was judged totally inadmissable was the definition of lawful conduct (halakhah)," Geza Vermes goes on to relate the following "legendary account of a doctrinal argument . . . between Rabbi Eliezer ben Hyrcanus and his colleagues. Having exhausted his arsenal of reasoning and still not convinced them, he performed a miracle, only to be told that there is no room for miracles in a legal debate."[53]

The question of "the Jews," "Who is the man *who said to you, 'Take it up and walk'*?" (5:12), is thus focused solely on identifying the person who abrogated the Torah proscription of sabbath work. Clearly, "the Jews" are not concerned with the man's testimonial "the man who made me well," for they do not ask him, "Who made you well?" The possibility of a miraculous healing will not affect the infraction that confronts them: a man is carrying his bedding on the sabbath, and, moreover, somebody put him up to it.[54] But before the healed man has a chance to respond to "the Jews'" repeated question, the narrator intrudes and says, "Now the man who had been healed did not know who it was, for Jesus had disappeared in the crowd that was there" (5:13).

What had appeared just moments before to be a spirited theological exchange between the religious elite on one side and, on the other, a weak and

---

[52] Haenchen hints at this when he says: "The man who was healed responds, however, that *the performer of miracles,* who has just healed him, told him to [take up his pallet and walk around]" (*John,* 1:257, my emphasis). John Chrysostom puts it even more strongly. He argues that the healed man's statement, "He who made me well said to me," "was as much as saying: 'You are insane and out of your wits if you bid me, when I have been cured in this way of a long and difficult illness, not to think well of the Healer and not to obey everything He may command.' Yet, if he wished to be ignoble, he could have spoken in quite a different vein; for example: 'I did not do this of my own accord, but because someone else told me to. If this is blameworthy, charge it to the one gave me the order, and I will put down my couch;' and he would have concealed the cure. . . . Actually, however, he did not conceal this, nor did he speak in this way, and he did not plead any excuse, but acknowledged his benefactor and proclaimed him in a loud voice" (*Commentary on Saint John the Apostle and Evangelist,* 363–64).

[53] Vermes, *Jesus the Jew,* 81. See also Pancaro, *The Law in the Fourth Gospel,* 15; contra Bultmann, *The Gospel of John,* 243.

[54] Pancaro, *The Law in the Fourth Gospel,* 15. Cf. John 7:12, 47–48.

timid social outcast recently empowered by Jesus' sabbath command has now been undermined by the narrator's offhand remark. Had the healed man really devised a profound theological argument for replacing Torah with the words of a charismatic healer? Or was the healed man simply revealing the fact that he didn't know his benefactor's name and trying to put the blame for his actions on someone else by saying, "The man who made me well said to me . . . ?"[55] The healed man is not even granted the privilege of speaking the words "I don't know" (cf. 9:12, 25). He will not be permitted to speak for himself again.[56] The reader almost has a sense that the narrator is shielding the healed man from his adversaries by whisking him away from the scene and then intervening to speak on his behalf.[57] But is the narrator guarding the integrity of a character who has fought well and is now on the ropes, or is the narrator protecting the encoded reader from one of the Gospel's least desirable models of faith?[58]

The story continues with Jesus' discovery of the healed man in the temple. It is unclear from the narrator's statement whether this was the place where the man's earlier confrontation with "the Jews" had taken place, but, for whatever reason, the man is there. Jesus, finding him there, says to him, "See, you have been made well! Do not sin any more,[59] so that nothing worse happens to you" (5:14). In response to this injunction the narrator draws the story to a close: "The man went away and told[60] the Jews that it was Jesus who had

---

[55] Brown, *The Gospel According to John,* 1:209; Culpepper, *Anatomy of the Fourth Gospel,* 138.

[56] Even the healed man's final words to "the Jews" are put in indirect discourse. Alter discusses such break-off points in dialogue as strategies that can be a type of "implicit commentary" (*The Art of Biblical Narrative,* 125).

[57] It should be noted that in speaking for the character, the narrator does not blame the character for his failure to know his benefactor's name. Rather, the reason the narrator gives for the healed man's lack of knowledge is *"Jesus had slipped away,"* not "the healed man ran off." Nor does the narrator say after 5:11, "This he said, not because he cared about Jesus, but because he did not know who had healed him." The Johannine narrator is well able to clarify the intent of characters' words when he wishes (see, e.g., 12:5–6).

[58] Culpepper says that "the lame man represents those whom even the signs cannot lead to authentic faith" (*Anatomy of the Fourth Gospel,* 138; see also Collins, "The Representative Figures in the Fourth Gospel," 42–43).

[59] The present imperative *hamartane* is the first occurrence of the verb "to sin" in the Gospel, and the nominal form *hamartia* has been used only once thus far ("Here is the Lamb of God who takes away the sin of the world," 1:29).

[60] The verb *anangellein* has only occurred at John 4:25. But it will reappear in Jesus' farewell discourse (16:13, 14, and 15). There characters will use the word and always with a positive nuance.

made him well.[61] Therefore the Jews started persecuting Jesus, because he was doing such things on the sabbath" (5:15–16).

The account of Jesus' second meeting with the healed man again throws into a quandary the encoded reader's assessments of the story's two major characters. Jesus' observation that the man is well, echoing his initial question to the man (5:6), seems to bring the miracle account to a fitting conclusion. But his injunction "Do not sin anymore" (present imperative)[62] is surprising.[63] The only explicit character trait attributed to the healed man is couched in a prohibition and joined to a warning! But shouldn't the man's healing have been enough evidence of the forgiveness of his sins? And hasn't he just stood up admirably to the legal authorities? So what possible wrong or sin could the man be presently guilty of? Whatever the infraction, it must be significant, for Jesus takes the trouble to find the man and warn him of a worse fate that could befall him.

The suddenness of Jesus' warning and his failure to mention any of the specifics of the man's sin, together with the narrator's lack of interest in illuminating the matter for the encoded reader, have the effect of forcing real

[61] The narrator does not say that the healed man told "the Jews," "Jesus was the one who told him to carry his mat," but rather, "it was Jesus who made him well" (cf. 5:11; also Pancaro, *The Law in the Fourth Gospel*, 15). Alter's insightful discussion of how to read repetitions in direct speech and narrated speech is apropos here: "When there is no divergence between a statement as it occurs in narration and as it recurs in dialogue, or vice versa, the repetition generally has the effect of giving a weight of emphasis to the specific terms which the speaker chooses for his speech" (*The Art of Biblical Narrative*, 77–78).

[62] An aorist imperative would have meant, "Don't start sinning (again), or something worse will happen to you," implying that the act of healing was also an act of forgiving sins and that there was a causal connection between the illness and sin. But the present imperative would seem to imply that the man is still living in sin ("You've been sinning up to this point, now don't do it any more"; see also Koester, "Hearing, Seeing, and Believing in the Gospel of John," 338 n. 25); and thus, perhaps, that the initial healing was not related to the forgiveness of any sins. Compare Luke 8:49; Eph 4:28; and 1 Tim 5:23 (in the textually suspect John 8:11 the phrase "from now on" precedes "do not sin again," giving the latter phrase an aoristic sense).

[63] From the perspective of reader-response criticism, one cannot appeal to Jesus' later statement in 9:3 in order to argue that this earlier statement in 5:14 is surprising (Bultmann, *The Gospel of John*, 243). One can only argue, as Sternberg does, that surprise "catch[es] the reader off-guard due to a false impression given earlier" (*The Poetics of Biblical Narrative*, 259) and that "for the new information to perform its unsettling effect, the old must look settled" (ibid., 309; cf. Schnackenburg, *The Gospel According to St. John*, 1:97; Haenchen, *John*, 1:247). Here the "false impression given earlier" is that the healed man was innocent. The narrator, the healed man, and Jesus have all assumed it up to this point. Only "the Jews" have thought otherwise.

readers to fill the new gap by attempting to explain the healed man's character flaw.[64] Perhaps the healed man has been sinning somehow by flaunting his new-found freedom from Torah in ways that the narrator declines to disclose—perhaps by parading with his mat around the temple courtyard?[65] Jesus had earlier told the healed man to pick up his mat and keep walking, and "the Jews" have just finished telling him that it is unlawful to do what he is doing. Could Jesus be telling the healed man that he is indeed "sinning" by continuing to do what Jesus had previously asked him to do? Has Jesus gone back on his word? (He's beginning to sound just like "the Jews"!) Or, less alarmingly, is Jesus saying, "Enough is enough. You've had your fun parading about the temple precincts. Now put down your mat and get on with living"?

Although the narrative gap raises many questions for readers, especially commentators, most quickly move on to the "meatier" theological issues of the appended monologue.[66] But the effect of the gap should not be set aside in order to hurry on to elaborate the miracle's christological implications. It is true that real readers' gap-filling attempts cannot supply an ultimate answer to why Jesus tells the man, "Do not sin any more." But this is precisely the point of *reading*. Through this gap—and also the previous gaps—the text creates an encoded reader who focuses on earthly questions, a reader who delights in constructing plausible contexts for the characters' words. But later on, in Jesus' monologue, when the encoded reader is finally shown the inade-

---

[64] Compare, for example, the variety of scholarly attempts to explain Jesus' warning either in terms of: (1) Jesus' own understanding of sin (Brown, *The Gospel According to John*, 1:208; Lindars, *The Gospel of John*, 217; Hasitschka, *Befreiung von Sünde nach dem Johannesevangelium*, 285, 337); (2) the author's theology (Bultmann, *The Gospel of John*, 243; Schnackenburg, *The Gospel According to St. John*, 1:97; Beasley-Murray, *John*, 74); or (3) the healed man's life. In the latter instance three possibilities have been proposed. Either the man is being told "don't sin, as you did in the past, when you incurred a debilitating illness" (Collins, "The Representative Figures in the Fourth Gospel," 43; Haenchen, *John*, 1:247); or "don't continue in your sinful ways as you presently are doing" (Countryman, *The Mystical Way in the Fourth Gospel*, 41); or "you're healthy, but you should be concerned about your spiritual condition" (Lindars, *The Gospel of John*, 217; Kysar, *John's Story of Jesus*, 34; Culpepper, "Un exemple de commentaire fondé sur la critique narrative: Jean 5,1–18," 147).

[65] Haenchen hints at something like this when he says, "If one examines verse 8 more closely, it then becomes apparent that Jesus does not give the man who is healed an order like he does in Mark 2:11: the man is not to go home, but is to parade around defiantly with his pallet. That is intended not only to serve as proof that the lame man was healed, but also that he thereby violated the sabbath in accordance with the order given him" (*John*, 1:257). However, this unified reading is one which he later rejects (ibid., 258).

[66] For example, see Schnackenburg, *The Gospel According to St. John*, 1:97; and Countryman, *The Mystical Way in the Fourth Gospel*, 40.

quacies of those earlier gap-filling attempts, the reader will be prepared to accept Jesus' conclusions.

But that is getting ahead of the story. At present, the encoded reader is still stuck in the perplexing narrative gap of 5:14. Perhaps, by the very fact that Jesus has not told the healed man what his sin is, the narrator is giving the encoded reader a clue to the meaning of Jesus' words. The narrator has said that Jesus finds the healed man in the temple (5:14). Maybe the healed man is sinning simply by being in the temple—a religious site about which the encoded reader already knows Jesus has expressed negative sentiments (2:13–22; 4:21–24). But the narrator had also said that the healed man didn't know who Jesus was (5:13). Could Jesus' warning have been precipitated somehow by the healed man's previous response to "the Jews"? Perhaps he was "sinning" in not fully revealing the identity of his benefactor. What does Jesus' "Do not sin anymore" mean in this context? Whatever answer real readers might supply to fill the gap, the phrase seems to raise more questions for readers than it does for the story's character. For that character, having quickly acted on Jesus' command once before, does so again (5:15).

It would appear, then, that the healed man somehow understands Jesus' ambiguous "Do not sin anymore" as relating to his previous conversation with "the Jews," for it is seemingly in response to Jesus' injunction that the man returns immediately to his interrogators with the new information, "Jesus [i.e., not just anybody] was the one who made me well" (5:15). Since the narrator had earlier said that many of the people in Jerusalem had believed in Jesus precisely because of his signs (2:23; 3:1–2; 4:45), the healed man's intentions, ironically, can be understood positively (cf. 11:45–46; 12:9–11, 17–18). Only the encoded reader and Jesus know enough not to trust the level of belief in the Jerusalemites (2:24; 3:10; 4:1–3, 48). As a result of the healed man's proclamation, however, "the Jews" begin to stalk Jesus—because he was doing "these things" on the sabbath.[67]

In view of my interpretation, which seeks to take into account the reading process and the subtle nuances of repetition in narration and conversation, one cannot so easily categorize the character as one who "rats on" or "betrays"

---

[67] Lindars catches the ambiguity of the narrator's conclusion (5:16) when he says, "the vagueness of the expression ["such things"] leaves it doubtful whether Jesus is to blame for causing someone else to break the sabbath, or whether his own act of healing contravened it" (*The Gospel of John*, 217). However, there will be no ambiguity later on, when, in response to the raising of Lazarus from the dead, "some of ["the Jews"] went to the Pharisees and told them what [Jesus] had done" (11:46).

Jesus.[68] Is he really the "super ingrate,"[69] "ready to blame his violation of the sabbath on his benefactor?"[70] Or is he simply a person who shows "persistent naïveté?"[71] Such readings of the character are indeed possible in light of the narrator's and Jesus' earlier, general comments about the people of Jerusalem. But in view of the fact that neither the narrator nor Jesus condemns this man, either explicitly or implicitly (cf. 2:24; 3:10; 4:1–3, 48), a counterreading seems just as legitimate.[72] In his final narrated sentence, the healed man may actually be making a strong argument for the charismatic healer's authority over and above Torah authority—this time supplying the name of the healer in the hope that his interrogators will be impressed (2:23; 3:1–2; 4:45). Perhaps he is not a tattletale, but a character who serves, in his own way and with his own theological argument, as a faithful witness to the performed sign.

In my reading of the character, the healed man is no more a representative of those "whom even the signs cannot lead to authentic faith"[73] than is the Samaritan woman. It should be remembered that her dramatic witness regarding the stranger who "told me everything I have ever done" (4:29a, 39) was a question that expected a negative answer (*mēti houtos estin ho Christos?* 4:29b; cf. 18:35). The characters of John 4:1–42 and 5:1–16 are both imperfect witnesses, and in neither case does the narrator say "she/he believed

[68] Kysar, *John's Story of Jesus,* 34; Smith, *John,* 41; Countryman, *The Mystical Way in the Fourth Gospel,* 41.

[69] Haenchen, *John,* 1:247, cf. 259; Kysar, *John's Story of Jesus,* 34.

[70] Culpepper, *Anatomy of the Fourth Gospel,* 138; Brown, *The Gospel According to John,* 1:209.

[71] Brown, *The Gospel According to John,* 1:209.

[72] Culpepper lists four reasons why the character's final act should be interpreted negatively: "(1) The man's earlier responses have established the trait of seeking to pass responsibility from himself to others; (2) Jesus' warning in v. 14 underlines that he is a sinner; (3) we have seen formal contrasts between this passage and the first two signs, where individuals come to believe in Jesus; and (4) this pericope functions to establish the opposition to Jesus and explain some of the reasons for it" ("Un exemple de commentaire fondé sur la critique narrative: Jean 5,1-18," 148). I have presented important literary-critical and sociological arguments for alternative readings to 1 and 3, and if they are reasonable, then the man's final report to "the Jews" can also be read as rectifying his "sin" (2).

Culpepper's third reason, the formal contrasts in the rendering of the signs, is important, for the contrasts lead to many of the ambiguities in reading this character. It should be noted, however, that the narrator does not particularly value belief based on seeing signs (2:23–24; 4:48; 6:25; 20:29; see particularly my reading of the first two signs in *The Print's First Kiss,* 83–86). Culpepper's fourth reason is dealt with below (p. 44).

[73] Culpepper, *Anatomy of the Fourth Gospel,* 138.

(*episteusen*)."[74] The major difference between the two characters is that the man lives in Jerusalem and announces his good news in a city whose inhabitants have a natural distrust of outside authority figures (1:19–24; 2:18–21), a city unable to trust wholly in Jesus (2:23–25), and whose leaders pose a serious threat to him (4:1–3). The woman, on the other hand, lives far from Jerusalem, in an area that "the Jews" do not control, where "the Jews" cannot take deliberative actions against Jesus.

Finally, I would submit that no character in the Fourth Gospel fully grasps the narrator's perspective that "Jesus is the Messiah, the Son of God" (20:31), except the story's narrator, the Beloved Disciple (21:24–25). Culpepper rightly argues that the individuality of the Johannine characters "is determined by their encounter with Jesus," and that the "characters represent a continuum of responses to Jesus, which exemplify misunderstandings the reader may share and responses one might make to the depiction of Jesus in the gospel."[75] Following Culpepper's lead, one can argue that, in spite of the man's faithful witness, he fails to understand the political implications of announcing Jesus' miraculous, Torah-breaking powers in a city with hostile "Jews" around. But most scholars have been hobbled by the man's misstep— blind to his act of faith and the ambiguities in his characterization. They have condemned the man too quickly, tying him too tightly to the plot (5:15–16; cf. 11:45–46) and to Jesus' subsequent monologue (5:17–47).

## THE BLIND READING THE BLIND

Unlike the bedridden man of John 5, who has rarely been the subject of independent study and is not one of the Gospel's more memorable characters, the blind man of John 9 is both well known and often has been the topic of extended research. Of course, most of the scholarly interest has been generated not so much by the man himself as by the narrator's curious comments about the Pharisees' "synagogue ban" (9:22, 34-35).[76] But no less important have been those studies that direct readers to the story's dramatic elements.[77]

---

[74] Culbertson makes the important observation: "Unbelievers in John's Gospel never admit to needing anything" (*The Poetics of Revelation,* 170). In contrast to unbelievers, both the Samaritan woman and the bedridden man admit their needs, even though they misunderstand how Jesus can fulfill them.

[75] Culpepper, *Anatomy of the Fourth Gospel,* 104.

[76] Martyn, *History and Theology in the Fourth Gospel,* 37–62; Painter, "John 9 and the Interpretation of the Fourth Gospel," 31–61.

[77] Brown, *The Gospel According to John,* 1:376–77.

These studies have noted the sevenfold scenes in the narrative,[78] the rising tempo of the Pharisees' accusations and the increasing insight of the blind man,[79] and the role of the blind man as *eirōn*.[80] Following the leads of the latter studies, my analysis will attempt to show that sensitivity to subtle changes in the blind man's repetitive dialogue and the narrator's descriptions,[81] and sensitivity to the implied author's manipulation of temporal order[82] can give a fuller portrait of the character than scholarship has previously noted.

Although it seems to have gone unnoticed in the history of scholarship, the formal structure of John 9:1–5 is that of a pronouncement story, not that of a miracle story.[83] The scene is set when Jesus, "passing by," sees a man "blind from birth" (9:1). But rather than having the hero effect a cure, as he has done numerous times in the past, Jesus' disciples force their way into the story and interject a theological question (9:2) which leads to a pronouncement by Jesus (9:3–5). From the very outset, however, the narrator teases the encoded reader with the possibility of an ensuing miracle story and with the possibility of double meanings. It is, after all, a *blind man* who is the cause of the disciples' question, not some debatable activity of Jesus or his disciples (cf. Mark 2:13–28). And Jesus' seeing appears to be of two kinds: (1) natural seeing (when a blind man come into his view), and (2) supernatural seeing (realizing that the man has been blind *from birth*).[84] But since the disciples' question shows that they, too, somehow know that the man was blind from birth,[85]

---

[78] Martyn, *History and Theology in the Fourth Gospel,* 24–36.

[79] Resseguie, "John 9: A Literary-Critical Analysis," 299–303; Lieu, "Blindness in the Johannine Tradition," 83–84.

[80] That is, a person who mocks others but is innocent of deceit (Duke, *Irony in the Fourth Gospel,* 119–25; see below, pp. 90–91).

[81] Alter, *The Art of Biblical Narrative,* 63–113.

[82] Sternberg, *The Poetics of Biblical Narrative,* 230–320.

[83] Surprisingly, even Bultmann misses this (*The Gospel of John,* 329–33), and Martyn simply describes the miracle story form (9:1, 6–7), skipping over the intervening verses (9:2–5) as though they didn't exist (*History and Theology in the Fourth Gospel,* 25; cf. Fortna, *The Fourth Gospel and Its Predecessors,* 109–13). Pancaro, however, notes that the story "takes on the form (in its final moments) of a Streitgespräch" (*The Law in the Fourth Gospel,* 17).

[84] Compare, for example, John 5:6, where the narrator used two verbs: "When Jesus saw [*idōn*] him lying there and knew [*gnous*] that he had been there a long time. . . ." At the conclusion of this story Jesus will point out that there are indeed two kinds of sight—one that is open to new spiritual realities, and one that is blind to them (9:40–41).

[85] Bultmann puts the issue this way: "Of course one may not ask how the disciples know that he was born blind" (*The Gospel of John,* 330). In Sternberg's terms, Bultmann is saying

that theological problem along with Jesus' final pronouncement will be the story's ultimate focus rather than the miracle itself.[86]

After Jesus' lengthy pronouncements (9:3–5) a miracle is swiftly narrated (9:6–7). Wordlessly, Jesus spits in the dust, makes mud, and anoints the man's eyes with the mud (the narrator uses the word "mud" twice).[87] In contrast to the bedridden man of John 5, Jesus does not ask the blind man anything and the man says nothing to Jesus. Jesus is wholly the agent; the blind man is wholly the patient.[88] Jesus then gives a terse command—"Go, wash in the pool of Siloam" (9:7a)—and disappears from the story. He will not speak again until he reveals his true identity to the healed man (9:35b–41).[89]

After the narrator's interpretive note regarding the name of the pool, he describes the man's prompt action and its effect: "Then he went and washed, and came back able to see" (9:7b). The blind man will no longer simply be the occasion for the disciples' theological question and Jesus' revelatory remarks, for he now takes on a living presence as one who acts upon the authoritative command of Jesus.

Unlike the bedridden man of John 5, whose plaintive voice caught the encoded reader's ear prior to Jesus' miracle-producing words, this man is voiceless until he encounters those who once knew him as a beggar (9:8–12). And in contrast to the bedridden man who was immediately confronted by the hostile questions of authority figures, this man is given a chance to test his new-found voice on the curious and seemingly harmless questions of his neighbors and acquaintances; people who are close to his social equals.[90] His response to his inquisitive neighbors is almost an exact repetition of the nar-

---

that to ask this question is to be involved in "illegitimate gap-filling" (*The Poetics of Biblical Narrative,* 188).

[86] Duke, *Irony in the Fourth Gospel,* 118.

[87] Pancaro lists the kneading of mud as one of three sabbath infractions in this story. The other two infractions are healing a person whose life is not in danger and using a substance that was not normally used during the week to anoint eyes (*The Law in the Fourth Gospel,* 19–20; see also Brown, *The Gospel According to John,* 1:373; and Bultmann, *The Gospel of John,* 332). But the kneading of mud is the only activity emphasized by the narrator (9:6, 14) and the healed man (9:11). Furthermore, the "how" of the miracle will be the central issue for the Pharisees (9:15, 19, 26).

[88] O'Day, *The Word Disclosed,* 59.

[89] Duke observes that this is Jesus' most prolonged absence in the entire Gospel (*Irony in the Fourth Gospel,* 119).

[90] The questioners begin by talking among themselves about "the beggar" (note the use of the demonstrative pronoun *houtos* in 9:8–9), before finally addressing him directly ("*your* eyes," 9:10).

rator's description of the miracle: "The man called Jesus made mud, spread it on my eyes, and said to me, 'Go to Siloam and wash.' Then I went and washed and received my sight" (9:11). He knows quite well who it was who healed him (cf. 5:13) and the means by which the healing was done, but he is ignorant of his benefactor's present whereabouts (9:12).

The story takes an ominous turn when the narrator says: "They brought to the Pharisees the man who had formerly been blind" (9:13).[91] The encoded reader knows that, in the past, the Pharisees have been suspicious of Jesus (4:1; 7:32, 45–53; 8:13). So when the narrator goes on to add, "Now it was a sabbath day when Jesus made the mud and opened his eyes" (9:14), a reevaluation of the neighbors' apparently guileless questions becomes necessary.[92] In retrospect, perhaps there was an undercurrent of maliciousness lurking beneath those questions.[93]

Furthermore, if the blind man knew that he had been healed on the sabbath, perhaps he should have been more careful in proclaiming the means by which the miracle occurred. Yet, by withholding the temporal notation until after the healed man's conversation with his neighbors, the encoded reader's first assessment of the healed man and the neighbors cannot be construed negatively. Both the encoded reader and the healed man have been innocently caught in a web of words. The healed man has blurted out the name of his benefactor and the means of his cure to his trusted neighbors in a moment of radiant joy, while the encoded reader has had no idea that the day on which this all occurred was a sabbath.

When the Pharisees appear on the scene, there is a peculiar shift in the narrator's description of the healed man. Earlier, in the presence of those who had known him as a beggar, the narrator had described the healed man as "a

---

[91] Lindars accurately assesses the encoded reader's perspective of the neighbors at this point when he says, "it is left to the reader to guess why this was done," that is, why they took him to the Pharisees (*The Gospel of John,* 345).

[92] At this point Pancaro asks the crucial question for reader-response criticism: "Why did Jn wait until v. 14 to mention this fact?" (that is, the fact that it was a sabbath [*The Law in the Fourth Gospel,* 18]). But his answer relates the gap to the miracle's symbolism of baptism—the importance of which lies in the man's (postbaptismal) witness to his neighbors (ibid., 26).

[93] O'Day realizes that "the neighbors are not so guileless" as the healed man (*The Word Disclosed,* 62), and Kysar theorizes that the religious authorities "are brought into this matter because the healing has taken place on the sabbath, and so must determine whether or not the sabbath regulations have been violated" (*John's Story of Jesus,* 49). Neither Lindars nor Beasley-Murray, however, sees any connection between the neighbors bringing the healed man to the Pharisees and the narrator's notation that it was a sabbath (Lindars, *The Gospel of John,* 345; Beasley-Murray, *John,* 156).

beggar" (9:8). Now, in the presence of those who will refuse to recognize the miracle and the miracle-worker, the narrator describes him as "the man who had formerly been blind" (*ton pōte typhlon,* 9:13), or "the blind man" (*tǭ typhlǭ,* 9:17; *hos ēn typhlos,* 9:24). However, in the presence of his parents, who recognize their son, the narrator will call him "the one who received his sight" (*tou anablepsantos,* 9:18). The narrator's epithets betray his ideological perspective[94]—a perspective that surreptitiously leads the encoded reader toward the pronouncement with which Jesus ends the story: Those with eyes to see do not have the ability to peer beneath the surface and find the person with true insight. The Pharisees see nothing more than a blindly ignorant fool (9:41).

The Pharisees' first reaction to being confronted with the healed man is to question the neighbors, and the Pharisees' query gives rise to the story's second gap. Their question is not what the encoded reader might expect: "Why have your neighbors brought you here?" Instead, the Pharisees' question regarding "how he had received his sight" (9:15a; cf. 9:16–17), is directed at the neighbors and presumes that a miracle has occurred.[95] The question implies that the neighbors have already repeated the healed man's story to the Pharisees. The healed man then responds to the Pharisees' question with a remarkably abbreviated account of what had happened to him (9:15b; cf. 9:17c, 25). In response to their question the healed man replies, "*He put* mud on my eyes, then *I washed,* and now *I see*" (9:15b, my emphasis).[96]

---

[94] Sternberg's discussion of the role of the epithet in ancient Hebrew narrative is helpful for the analysis of John 9. He says it is usually "proleptic" (*The Poetics of Biblical Narrative,* 337), for "[i]t shapes the sequence of our expectations (as a foreshadowing device) because it is bound to shape the sequence of events (as a developmental factor). This unusual premise to a coming proposition, then, appears as a cause that signals some effect yet unborn in the world, but already a presence to be reckoned with in the reading" (ibid., 338).

[95] By placing this initial question in indirect discourse and by having the Pharisees discuss the healed man's response among themselves (9:16–17), the implied author puts some distance between the central character and his opponents. Thus, the encoded reader and the character are shielded from the Pharisees' probing, barbed questions. Even after the Pharisees finally ask a question in direct discourse ("What do you say about him? It was your eyes he opened," 9:16), and the man answers, "He is a prophet" (9:17), the narrator immediately intrudes by announcing the calling of the man's parents.

[96] Most commentators have been content to assume that the author somehow gives a summary account of the healing through the voice of the character (that is, a narrative gap occurs in the healed man's shortened account). In this reading, the reader should assume that, in fact, the healed man "told all" to the Pharisees—the author just hasn't told all. Based on a different understanding of narrative (*The Print's First Kiss,* 27–30), I would argue that the neighbors

Although numerous commentators brush off the man's response as merely the author's attempt to shorten what otherwise would be a very redundant account,[97] Alter's and Sternberg's discussions of repetition in ancient Hebrew narrative open up other possible readings.[98] In his opening statement, "He put mud on my eyes," the healed man does not mention his benefactor's name (9:15b)—although he had mentioned it earlier (9:11). Could his omission of Jesus' name at this point be due to the change of his audience? Perhaps he doesn't want to disclose Jesus' identity.[99] This thesis gains further support when the encoded reader comes to the man's next statement. The man does not use the narrator's language of "making mud" (*epoiēsen*) or "anointing" (*epechrisen*) as he had earlier (9:11; cf. 9:6, 14; 9:27); instead, the man switches to the more innocuous phrase "put mud" (*epithēken*, 9:15). The healed man's choice of language thus successfully shields Jesus from two possible sabbath violations.[100] Then, finally, as if to ensure that there will not be the slightest possibility that anyone could accuse his benefactor of sabbath violations, the man omits from his account Jesus' command "Go, wash" (9:7, 11), and instead simply says, "I washed and now I see."[101] In view of the

---

must have repeated the man's story to the Pharisees, and thus that is the place where the narrative gap occurs (see the discussion below of the healed man's words, p. 51).

[97] Haenchen says: "The narrative becomes shorter with each repetition—the reader knows it and should not be bored with the repetition" (*John*, 2:39; see also Schnackenburg, *The Gospel According to St. John*, 2:247–48). Resseguie describes the man in this scene as one who "still lacks color: to the questions of the authorities he responds with short, declarative sentences" ("John 9: A Literary-Critical Analysis," 300). Only O'Day comes close to the real significance of the healed man's brief answer when she says: "Nothing more is offered than the minimum required to answer the Pharisees' question" (*The Word Disclosed*, 63).

[98] Alter, *The Art of Biblical Narrative*, 97–113; Sternberg, *The Poetics of Biblical Narrative*, 365–427.

[99] O'Day astutely observes that "[a]s much as Jesus is talked about in the interrogations of verses 8-34, Jesus' name is never named [by a character] after verse 11. . . . There are many reasons for this reluctance to name Jesus' name. The Pharisees do not name the name of Jesus because to do so would give credence and standing to the one who bears the name. The man born blind does not name the name because the significance of the name will only dawn on him as the narrative advances. The man's parents do not name the name because they are afraid to do so (v. 23)" (*The Word Disclosed*, 56). O'Day's observations are very insightful. However, I would object to the reason she gives for the blind man's deference. He does indeed identify Jesus by name to his neighbors (9:11). Only after he meets the Pharisees does he refuse to name his benefactor.

[100] "Putting mud" on one's body was not necessarily work, but "making mud" and anointing certainly were (Pancaro, *The Law in the Fourth Gospel*, 19–20).

[101] Schnackenburg argues that the choice of the narrator's verb "he opened" (*aneōxen*, 9:14)

extended repetitions of 9:7 and 9:11 and the change of audience, the encoded reader cannot ignore the remarkable brevity and different word choices in the healed man's response to the Pharisees. The man intends to protect his benefactor from his opponents' opening jabs, and he will keep his guard up throughout his interrogation—in spite of the pointed questions peppering him (9:26–27).

If the healed man's account of what had transpired earlier is a cautious feinting, then the Pharisees' pronouncement that "this man is not from God for he does not observe the sabbath" (9:16) comes as a surprise to the encoded reader. The healed man has given them no data for coming to such a conclusion! The Pharisees' observation, then, like their opening question (9:15), cannot be based on anything that the healed man had told them. It, too, must be based on the neighbors' remarks—those remarks which the narrator had left unrecorded.

After the healed man makes his first public declaration regarding Jesus (9:17), the narrator diverts the encoded reader's attention away from the man for the moment and turns to "the Jews'" interrogation of his parents (9:18–23).[102] The dramatic shift is reminiscent of Jesus' dialogue with the Samaritan woman. In that story, immediately after Jesus reveals his identity to the woman (4:25–26), the narrator breaks into the scene to announce the arrival of the disciples (4:27) and so postpones her anticipated response. Similarly in this story, the encoded reader must wait in suspense before hearing the Pharisees' reaction to the healed man's declaration, "He is a prophet" (9:17).

But the narrator's explanation of the parents' fear (9:22–23) opens up yet another narrative gap, a gap that forces the encoded reader to reevaluate the healed man's earlier conversation with the Pharisees. That gap will also sharpen the encoded reader's attentiveness to the healed man's future confes-

---

is "deliberate, since it brings Jesus into prominence as healer and sabbath-breaker" (*The Gospel According to St. John,* 2:247). However, when the man speaks, he uses the plain "I see" (*blepō,* 9:15), which does not necessarily assume that the person who "put mud on his eyes" had any curative powers.

[102] In this scene, as many commentators have noted, the narrator switches from the term "the Pharisees" to the expression "the Jews" to describe those who interrogate the man's parents (9:13, 15–16; cf. 9:40). This phenomenon is not unusual in the Gospel (cf. 1:19, 24; 7:32–35; 8:13, 22), but no perfect answer to the peculiarity has been found. Generally speaking, "the Jews" are found on the scene whenever antagonism toward Jesus reaches a breaking point (e.g., 5:16–17; 6:41, 52; 7:10–15, 35; 8:21–59; 10:19–39; 11:31–54; 18:31–19:22; see Culpepper, *Anatomy of the Fourth Gospel,* 125–32). Here, as elsewhere, the epithet may warn the encoded reader that banners are being unfurled. Battle lines are being drawn tighter, the opposition is closing ranks.

sions. In retrospect, the parents' fear, coupled with "the Jews'" determination to put out of the synagogue anyone who confessed Jesus to be the Christ (9:22), turns a perplexingly unnecessary, rude conversation into a high-stakes courtroom drama.[103] The quotation of the parents' slightly nuanced words, "He is of age, question him" (*eperōtēsate*, 9:23, for *erōtēsate*, 9:21), may also imply that, from the narrator's perspective, this was indeed a legal proceeding.[104] Given that setting, how then will the Pharisees respond to the man's straightforward reply, "He is a prophet"? Will the healed man, like the Samaritan woman, move from perceiving that Jesus is a prophet to recognizing him as the Christ, and thus end up excluded from the synagogue (4:19, 29; cf. 1:19–21; 7:40–41, 45–52)?

After the dramatic interlude in which his parents were called to testify (9:18–23),[105] the Pharisees (now described as "the Jews") again question "the man who had been blind" (9:24–34). The conversation is reminiscent of the earlier dialogue of 8:31–56, where accusers leveled the charges of sin, lying, and dishonorable birth. Ironically, however, the only real liar in this scene is the healed man himself, who responds to the questions "What did he do to you? How did he open your eyes?" with the lie "I have told you already and you would not listen. Why do you want to hear it again?" (9:27).[106] It is precisely because the man did not tell them the whole truth earlier that the Pharisees, becoming more and more exasperated, are still asking him the same questions! Finally, in this exchange, the healed man attains his full stature as a character who opposes the Pharisees, pummeling them with his own ripostes.[107] Even with no direction from the narrator, the irony and biting sarcasm of the healed man's questions are obvious.[108] Amid the debris of the hard-fought battle, his benefactor will meet him once again, and the healed man will show his true colors as he bows down and worships—not the Christ—but the Son of Man (9:35–38). The narrative then closes when Jesus confronts the Pharisees with their own blindness (9:39–41).

---

[103] Martyn, *History and Theology in the Fourth Gospel*, 32.

[104] Bauer, Gingrich, and Danker, *eperōtaō*, in *A Greek-English Lexicon of the New Testament and Other Early Christian Literature*.

[105] See especially O'Day's discussion of this scene (*The Word Disclosed*, 64–65).

[106] Beasley-Murray makes a strong case for understanding the earlier command "Give glory to God" as "a command to the man to confess his sin, i.e., the sin of lying as to his blindness and subsequent healing by Jesus . . ." (*John*, 158).

[107] John 9:30–32. See Resseguie, "John 9: A Literary-Critical Analysis," 299–300.

[108] Bultmann says: "By pretending that he believes [the Pharisees] really to be in earnest, [the healed man] treats the insincerity of the inquiry with the greatest possible irony" (*The Gospel of John*, 336; cf. Duke, *Irony in the Fourth Gospel*, 121–23).

As was the case with the bedridden man of John 5, so also here in John 9 careful attention to repetition, the interplay of narration and direct speech, and the dynamics of reading reveal hidden nuances in the Johannine art of characterization. The healed man's speech (9:15) early in the story alerts the encoded reader to the character's cleverness, and that cleverness is further confirmed by the end of the story.[109] He is indeed, as critics have pointed out, a "quick-witted eirōn"[110] and a man of "dogged loyalty."[111] But I would point out that his quick-wittedness and dogged loyalty show themselves as early as the man's first encounter with the Pharisees (9:13–17), not just during the second interrogation (9:24–34). From the very beginning the man tried to protect Jesus by refusing to tell the Pharisees that Jesus had made mud, anointed his eyes, and told him to wash in the Pool of Siloam. At the same time, the narrator's evasive action gradually unveiled the neighbors' motives for questioning the man and bringing him to the Pharisees. Something more than mere idle curiosity was at stake. Finally, the narrator's choice of epithets in the story was shown to be proleptic. The various descriptions of the healed man led the encoded reader to contemplate the Pharisees' blindness long before Jesus stated it openly (9:39–41).

SABBATH-DAY HEROES

Reading these two miracle stories with close attention to the sequence of sentences and to the gradual accumulation of information and responses reveals a correspondingly more complex portrait of the two men whom Jesus healed on the sabbath. In the first instance, blame for the persecution of Jesus cannot be put at the feet of the bedridden man. It was, after all, Jesus who healed him on the sabbath and told the man to carry his mat. In fact, the bedridden man's argument for the implicit authority of the charismatic healer is one that Jesus himself later picks up and develops, albeit in a different manner (5:17, 19–21; cf. 7:21–23). Yet there are indeed ambiguities in the first man's response. For example, does he respond correctly to Jesus' injunction "Do not sin anymore?" Later, after reading John 9, the encoded reader finds that the first man's ambiguous behavior has become more understandable. The first man had already flagrantly broken the sabbath by the time he encountered

---

[109] Brown, *The Gospel According to John*, 1:377.
[110] Duke, *Irony in the Fourth Gospel*, 125.
[111] Countryman, *The Mystical Way in the Fourth Gospel*, 65.

"the Jews." By way of contrast, the blind man does nothing that could be considered even remotely unlawful.[112] He simply washes his face on the sabbath. Furthermore, he is apparently safe so long as he does not acknowledge Jesus to be the Christ (an acknowledgment that, in fact, the man never makes).

In light of this contrast, there is an element of tragedy surrounding the first character: he is bound to his past. He has publicly broken sabbath law. How can he rewrite history to exonerate his sin? The second character, on the other hand, is comical: he is liberated from his past. Is he the same man who used to sit and beg? Was he really blind? Can he wiggle his way out of the predicament in which his neighbors have put him? These two narratives, filtered through ancient Hebrew models of characterization, together express the double-edged, painful joy of late first century Christian commitment: an experience that stumbles in the dark as it reaches for the light.

## A POSTSCRIPT

In their critiques of the application of reader-response criticism to the Bible, both Temma Berg and Stephen Moore challenge biblical reader-critics to reconceive their nascent "readers." From Berg's perspective, New Testament scholars' readings of biblical texts work—and also fail—precisely because they presume an understanding of reading unlike that of any real reader's reading experience. Their readings are painstakingly slow; there is no room for forgetfulness in them; they trudge on, without ever being interrupted.[113] My readings of the two Johannine miracles fit her criticisms perfectly. But although I will agree that my readings are slow and laborious, I will steady them on the ground that they move light years faster than any other critical readings of the stories. All other readings have been predicated on an immobile text. There the readings lie, begging for aid from their equally paralyzed neighbors, but all the while they lack the courage to move beyond their own shadowy porticos. Those readings prefer the reassurance of the text's encircling grasp to the dangerous excitement of striding wild-eyed into the temple (2:14–19; 5:14; 11:48).

As with Berg's critique of biblical reader-response criticism, Moore's critique recognizes that the biblical text is ideologically motivated and that its

---

[112] Pancaro, *The Law in the Fourth Gospel,* 19.
[113] Berg, "Reading in/to Mark," 188, 195; cf. Mailloux, *Rhetorical Power,* 36–53.

largest reading communities share similar ideological concerns.[114] Nevertheless, he still finds New Testament reader-critics' readings to be overly cerebral and emotionally retarded.[115] Moore's criticism, too, seems to knock the breath out of my readings at the very moment they attempt their first halting steps. I speak of problems that "beg for solutions," of a reader who "reconsiders" the implications of seemingly direct questions, of characters who are "ignorant of things the reader knows."

Whether from mountain or moor, the view is the same: there apparently is a painful stumbling and stuttering in my readings—a blind spot that makes it impossible for me to see the translucent holes beyond the opaque wholes.[116]

Can such blindness lead to insight? Will the bedridden reader ever really walk?

---

[114] Moore, *Literary Criticism and the Gospels,* 125–26, 174–75; cf. Berg, "Reading in/to Mark,"190–92.

[115] Moore, *Literary Criticism and the Gospels,* 95–98, 106–7.

[116] Daniel Goleman describes the physiological basis for the metaphor of the blind spot this way: "At the back of each eyeball is a point where the optic nerve, which runs to the brain, attaches to the retina. This point lacks the cells that line the rest of the retina to register the light that comes through the lens of the eye. As a result, at this one point in vision there is a gap in the information transmitted to the brain. The blind spot registers nothing" (*Vital Lies, Simple Truths,* 15; cf. Moore, "How Jesus' Risen Body Became a Cadaver," 277).

I was made painfully aware of this physiological fact a few years ago when doctors discovered that a prenatal hemorrhage on the left occipital horn of my brain had left me with a shriveled optic nerve to my right eyeball. At that moment I realized that I had never observed the world as a normal person would observe it.

# CHAPTER TWO

# Designing the Seventh Sign:
# John 11 and the Resistant Reader

Supposing truth is a woman—what then? . . . What is certain is that she has not allowed herself to be won . . . .

—Friedrich Nietzsche

What would happen if, for once, one were to reverse the ethos of explication and try to be really precise, to rigorously examine every resistance to meaning?

—Paul de Man

Taking control of the reading experience means reading the text as it was not meant to be read, in fact, reading it against itself.

—Patrocinio Schweickart

. . . they went after her, assuming that she was going to the tomb. . . .

—John 11:31

## STEPPING OUTSIDE THE FORMALIST FRAMEWORK

The two concluding questions in the preceding chapter are ones that have haunted me from the time that I initially wrote them as part of a *Semeia* article four years ago. The first question, which asks whether the blindness revealed in my interpretation of the two sabbath miracles can lead to insight, is, of course, an allusion to Paul de Man's deconstructive reading of Jacques Derrida's reading of Rosseau.[1] And to paraphrase de Man once more, my close reading of

---

[1] De Man, "The Rhetoric of Blindness," in *Blindness and Insight,* 102–41; esp. 116–17, 139–41.

the stories in John 5 and 9 sought to outdo the closeness of reading that had been held up to the texts in the past and to show, by reading the texts and the commentaries more closely, that they were not nearly close enough.[2] But except for the conclusion of the chapter, where I hint that there may be more "I" in the readings than first meets the eye, the reader I uncovered there was one who seemed to lie passively under the power of text, one who could perhaps be aroused by the text's rhetorical ploys or perhaps moved in response to them, but could never flirtatiously initiate the seductive dance of interpretation.[3]

It is not unusual that of all reader-response critics, we in the biblical realm should find microscopically close readings to be the most amenable to our discipline. When compared with other literary canons, the biblical canon is small. Yet the number of tools that have been developed to analyze that relatively miniscule canon abound. Concordances and lexica, statistical analyses of grammar and syntax, historical and cultural studies, and histories of interpretation are multitudinous, relatively inexpensive, and much more easily available to the scholar than they are in other disciplines. Furthermore, relatively stable interpretive communities have treasured and transmitted for centuries the male, hierachically defined biblical commentaries, texts, and interpretive strategies of the pre-print era. So when these chirographic resources and strategies are added to print-era tools, and then electronically digitalized for speed and breadth of research, the possibilities for closer and more carefully nuanced readings are magnified a hundredfold.

At another level, however, I cannot help but think that my own personal history makes close readings doubly advantageous. I am naturally nearsighted, and I grew up in a family of readers and in a tradition where the peculiarly close readings of the dispensational *Scofield Reference Bible* were considered nearly as inspired as the sacred text itself. So perhaps I was born

---

[2] Paul de Man described contemporary criticism this way, as seeking "to outdo the closeness of reading that had been held up to them and to show, by reading the close readings more closely, that they were not nearly close enough" (quoted in Holub, *Crossing Borders,* 11; see also Moore, *Literary Criticism and the Gospels,* 160). Robert Holub astutely recognizes why deconstruction seemed more amenable to the American literary scene in the 1970s than German "reception theory," in that deconstruction's focus on the text cohered nicely with New Criticism's interest in "the text." At the same time, however, deconstruction appeared to contain the more radical critique of New Critical presuppositions (*Crossing Borders,* 11–13, 19–20, 22–36; see pp. 2 n. 1, 5 n. 14 above).

[3] See Stephen Moore's description of biblical critics as having "Victorian scruples [that] regulate [their] reading habits" (*Mark and Luke in Poststructuralist Perspectives,* 150; cf. 157).

and raised with a natural disposition for the painstakingly slow, microscopic readings that Temma Berg derides.[4]

But despite my continued attention to slow, close readings of Johannine texts, the attentive reader will discover a subtle change in the ends to which the readings are put in the present chapter. In this chapter, my close readings of texts—and their ever-present intertexts[5]—become consciously chosen boundaries and strategies.[6] In the formalist reader criticism of the last chapter, however, my readings were more positivist or essentialist "uncoverings" of texts. They centered on the implicit, print-generated, sociorhetorical strategies that real readers must ingest if they are to remain true to the narrative world of the encoded reader.

Although at one time I might have made the claim that my readerly interpretation of John 5 and 9 accurately described how the encoded reader ought to respond to the printed text, today my less than formalist-oriented self would not want to voice such an absolutist claim for my reading of those texts or for the reading of John 11 that follows below. Nevertheless, I am purposefully committed to whatever liberating aims a reader might find in any of my interpretations—regardless of how far short they fall from their intended exegetical goals, and in spite of their tentativeness. Using Elisabeth Schüssler Fiorenza's liberating hermeneutic, I believe that biblical scholars need "to

[4] Berg, "Reading In/to Mark," 188–89; see p. 53 above.

[5] For a helpful definition of intertextuality, with its "dangerous 'feminine' or 'effeminate' overtones," see Michael Worton and Judith Still's "Introduction," in *Intertextuality*, 30. They write that intertextuality recognizes that "a text cannot exist as a hermetic or self-sufficient whole, . . . [since] the writer is a reader of texts before s/he is a creator of texts, and therefore the work of art is inevitably shot through with references, quotations and influences of every kind." Moreover, "a text is available only through some process of reading; what is produced at the moment of reading is due to the cross-fertilisation of the packaged textual material . . . by all the texts which the reader brings to it" (ibid., 1–2). Or, as Gary Phillips puts it: "reading . . . intertextually is a different way not only of speaking about the history of [a] . . . text as a history of its readings; it is a way of speaking about our present locus as readers as well" ("'What is Written? How Are You Reading?' Gospel, Intertextuality and Doing Lukewise: A Writerly Reading of Lk 10:25–37 (and 38–42)," 290. See also Kitzberger, "Love and Footwashing: John 13:1–20 and Luke 7:36–50 Read Intertextually," 191–93, 205.

[6] In commenting on Iser's sense of narrative "gaps" (*The Implied Reader*, 34–40), elements that played a major role in my interpretation of John 5 and 9, Patrocinio Schweickart notes, "one can argue that the 'gaps' that structure reader's response are not built into the text, but appear (or not) as a result of the particular interpretive strategy employed by the reader ("Reading Ourselves: Toward a Feminist Theory of Reading," 530; cf. 541; cf. Freund's and Holub's analyses of the Fish/Iser debate in *The Return of the Reader*, 148–51; and *Crossing Borders*, 25–28, respectively).

engage in a disciplined reflection on the public dimensions and ethical implications of our scholarly citizenship," in order to become "significant participant[s] in the global discourse seeking justice and well-being for all."[7] At the
same time, however, to the extent that my interpretations bend toward post-
structuralism or postmodernism and fail to engage in such issues of critical
praxis—to the extent that my interpretations remain mesmerized by the simulacrum of undecidability—they can easily become simply elitist posturings
before equally elitist audiences.[8] Thus, the readings I offer can be as paralyzing to the real reader as were the formalist readings they supplant. While the
paralyzing effect of formalist reader criticism arises from the totalizing power
it grants to texts, making no allowances for readings that resist its own apparent coherence, the paralyzing effect of poststructuralist and postmodern
moves can be traced to texts' bewildering interpretive possibilities. For the
uninitiated reader, critical praxis often seems to be precluded in the presence
of polyvalency.

It is precisely at this impasse that feminist criticism proffers its proposal.
Drawing on the language of "resistance" that was central to Judith Fetterley's

---

[7] Schüssler Fiorenza, "The Ethics of Biblical Interpretation," 17. Linda Hutcheon's warning, however, is worth heeding. She notes that "there is also a very real sense in which the postmodernist notions of difference and positively valorized marginality often reveal the same
familiar totalizing strategies of domination [evident in imperialist and patriarchal discourses],
though usually masked by the liberating rhetoric of First World critics who appropriate Third
World cultures to their own ends" (*The Politics of Postmodernism,* 38).

[8] See, for example, Holub's concluding chapter, where he discusses poststructuralists'
defense of de Man's and Heidegger's early associations with German National Socialism ("The
Uncomfortable Heritage," in *Crossing Borders,* 148–201; see also Bauman, *Modernity and the
Holocaust,* 126–28; and DuBois, *Torture and Truth,* 137–40) and Hutcheon's astute observation that "postmodernism, caught as it is in a certain negativity that may be inherent in any critique of cultural dominants . . . has no theory of positive action on a social level. . . ." (*The
Politics of Postmodernism,* 22; cf. 167–68).

Of course, we modernist and postmodernist New Testament scholars are not without our
own "uncomfortable heritage." For example, lurking behind the implied author of an anti-
Jewish sounding *Religionsgeschichte* with its fascination with Heideggerian thought is a real
author—Rudolf Bultmann—who cannot be divorced completely from the sociopolitical
world of Hitler's National Socialism. Although Bultmann did, at times, voice opposition to
Nazi policies, his diminutive criticisms never seriously jeopardized his professorial chair at
Marburg during Hitler's reign of madness (Rubenstein and Roth, *Approaches to Auschwitz,*
205–6; Jaspert, *Karl Barth/Rudolf Bultmann Letters 1922-1966,* 78–79, 135–39; Johnson,
"Power Politics and New Testament Scholarship in the National Socialist Period," 19). I, for
one, have not yet fully comprehended the apparent Bultmannian distinction, existentially
speaking, between *Historie* and *Geschichte* in the death of one particular Jew under Pax
Romana and *Historie* and *Geschichte* in the death of six million Jews under the Third Reich.

groundbreaking feminist reader-response criticism, Patrocinio Schweickart describes her own readerly activity as opposed to strategies of partition and control (i.e., formalism), and opposed to impossibility (i.e., deconstruction), and instead "grounded in the interest of producing a community of feminist readers and writers, and in the hope that ultimately this community will expand to include everyone."[9] Without using the word resistance, Schüssler Fiorenza has described her own feminist hermeneutical task in the New Testament with a quaternion of like-minded terms ("suspicion," "proclamation," "remembrance," and "creative actualization") that also reflect similar concerns for the formation of community.[10] Still more recently Willi Braun has picked up the language of resistance in his analysis of John 21, footnoting both Fetterley's and Schüssler Fiorenza's work.[11] However, the implications of his resistant reading for liberation and community formation are not central to his exegetical interests. For all Braun's rhetoric of resistance, his reader is ultimately relegated to a relatively passive role, being invited by the aporia of John 21 to approach the narrative with "critical ambivalence."[12]

Braun's advocacy of critical ambivalence for the Johannine reader may seem as though it is a positive step beyond the totalizing, tranquilizing effect of formalist theory in Culpepper's *Anatomy of the Fourth Gospel* and in my own appropriation of reader criticism.[13] But without the final step of what

---

[9] Schweickart, "Reading Ourselves: Toward a Feminist Theory of Reading," 55. Cf. Freedman, Frey, and Zauhar, "Introduction," in *The Intimate Critique,* 1–3; Fetterley, *The Resisting Reader,* vii–x. Susan Durber also utilizes Schweickart's language in her analysis of Lukan parables ("The Female Reader of the Parables of the Lost").

[10] Schüssler Fiorenza, *Bread not Stone,* 15–22; cf. Schneiders, *The Revelatory Text,* 180–86. However, in contrast to Schüssler Fiorenza's and Schneiders's approaches (see respectively *In Memory of Her,* 333; *The Revelatory Text,* 186–88; cf. Brown, *The Community of the Beloved Disciple,* 183–98), I do not wish to argue that my interpretations necessarily imply anything about the early Johannine community. With Turid Karlsen Seim, my literary approach will "not presuppose that the roles of women as described in the text correspond to or mirror without reservation a practical function in a specific historical situation" ("Roles of Women in the Gospel of John," 57).

For a helpful summary of feminist biblical criticism, both literary and historical, see Janice Capel Anderson, "Mapping Feminist Biblical Criticism: The American Scene, 1983–1990."

[11] Braun, "Resisting John: Ambivalent Redactor and Defensive Reader of the Fourth Gospel."

[12] Ibid., 71. Cf. Robert Fowler's description of Mark as an "ambivalent narrative" (*"Let the Reader Understand,"* 261–66).

[13] Although Braun does not mention my application of reader-response criticism to the Fourth Gospel (*The Print's First Kiss*), his criticism of Culpepper would probably also apply to my early work.

Schüssler Fiorenza calls "creative actualization," the reader's reflective ambivalence can all too quickly lose its critical edge. That kind of ambivalence, no matter how critical or self-conscious, elides its weakened prefix and leaves nothing but an empty vale behind.

And so on to my final troubling question from the last chapter: Will the bedridden reader ever really walk? Clearly, I was not contemplating the possibility of a dancing reader when I wrote that.[14] Just to be able to resuscitate a paralyzed, anesthetized, and dissected reader—to be able to resist the inexorable downward pull of gravity—would have been, for me, a minor miracle in itself. Thus it is with a degree of irony (and nagging fear lest I fail in my endeavor) that I now attempt to arouse a more active, lively reader from the foul-smelling crypt of Lazarus.

Enough of this hermeneutical shuffle on the borders of Judean Bethany. While I have been busily writing, the position of Lazarus has not changed. The corpse remains undisturbed, Mary and Martha still weep at Jesus' feet, and the male disciples continue to wander about aimlessly. It is time, I think, to try and wake the zombie-reader from his formalist tomb.[15]

## CRACKS IN THE NARRATIVE FOUNDATION

Of all the assured results of twentieth-century Johannine scholarship, perhaps the greatest consensus is in regard to the Fourth Gospel's literary structure. The book begins with a clearly defined, concentrically constructed prologue (1:1–18) that is then followed by "The Book of Signs" or "Jesus' Public Ministry" (1:19–12:50). The next major section, comprising 13:1–20:31, is variously designated "The Book of the Passion" or "Jesus' Private Ministry."[16]

---

[14] For example, Alan Culpepper writes: "Readers dance with the author whether they want to or not, and in the process they adopt his perspective on the story" (*Anatomy of the Fourth Gospel,* 233). Picking up this metaphor, Willi Braun argues that Culpepper's reader, "whether the scripted, implied reader or the real reader, either ancient or modern [is] . . . a co-operative, assenting. reader. Culpepper's interpretation does not recognize any wall flowers in the Johannine dance" ("Resisting John: Ambivalent Redactor and Defensive Reader of the Fourth Gospel," 61–62; cf. Kolodny's use of the dance metaphor in "Dancing through the Minefield: Some Observations on the Theory, Practice, and Politics of a Feminist Criticism," 5, 7, 17, 22).

[15] Leigh Gilmore writes: "The zombie is an extension of another's will; it rises only to do another's bidding" (*Autobiographics,* 72).

[16] Dodd, *The Interpretation of the Fourth Gospel,* 289. Rudolf Bultmann more idiomatically calls these "The Revelation of the *doxa* to the World," and "The Revelation of the *doxa* Before

The work concludes with an "appendix" or "epilogue" (21:1–25) that seems to have been added later. Alan Culpepper's narrative analysis, to date still the most comprehensive literary approach to the book, does not deviate from this norm.[17]

The twofold delineation of Johannine narrative structure as a Book of Signs and a Book of the Passion focuses on a shift in the book's christological emphasis. The second description, however, which is probably unconsciously based on the same christological observation, ostensibly concentrates on plot movement.[18] But what is the book's plot? Again, the general consensus has been that, whatever its theological and historical origins might be, the prologue accurately summarizes the narrative's basic plot: the one who existed at the beginning of the world enters the world, comes to his own people to reveal something about God, is rejected by them, and returns to God. The revelation of Jesus as the one "sent from the Father" and the crisis of responses ignited by that revelation are what dominates Jesus' public ministry. In this regard, John 11 is viewed by most scholars as the climax of Jesus' public life, but not as the plot's major transition.[19]

However, a small number of scholars working independently of one another have recently argued for a different ordering of the narrative's structure and plot. These studies by Mathias Rissi, myself, Gunnar Østenstad, and, to a certain extent, by George Mlakuzhyil, each view John 11 both as the structural center of the book and the major turning point of its plot.[20]

---

the Community" (*The Gospel of John,* 111, 457; see also Thyen, "Die Erzählung von den Bethanischen Geschwestern (Joh 11,1–12,19) als 'Palimpsest' über Synoptischen Texten," 2025–26; and Lombard and Oliver, "A Working Supper: John 13:1–38 Introduces Jesus' Farewell Discourses," 359–61).

[17] Culpepper, *Anatomy of the Fourth Gospel,* 88–89, 94.

[18] See Marchadour's excellent summary of the logic behind this division (*Lazare,* 94–110).

[19] Ibid., 99–101. However, F. R. M. Hitchcock, writing in 1923, took exception to this general assessment of the Johannine plot. He argued that the raising of Lazarus had to be the "moral centre" and the "plot centre" of the book, since "[i]t is the true centre, . . . at once [the] highest point and [the] turning point, *apex* and *vertex*" ("Is the Fourth Gospel a Drama?" 16, cf. 20; emphasis his).

[20] Rissi's "Der Aufbau des Vierten Evangeliums" was published in 1984. My article "The Structure of John's Prologue: Its Implications for the Gospel's Narrative Structure," was published in 1986 and made reference to Rissi's work, although the basic insights were formed independently of his article. The results of Østenstad's research, formulated in "The Structure of the Fourth Gospel: Can it be Defined Objectively?" were published in 1991 but make no reference to either Rissi's or my work. Finally, Mlakuzhyil's dissertation, entitled *The Christocentric Literary Structure of the Fourth Gospel,* was published in 1987. Although he mentions Rissi's and my work, Mlakuzhyil also developed his thesis independently of Rissi and me.

It is tempting to argue that our perspectives were each influenced by the formalist narrative critical turn in New Testament studies of the early 1980s, which favored plot and narrative cohesiveness over theology and aporiae. But the works of Rissi, Mlakuzhyil, and Østenstad show no evidence of a literary or theoretical interest. For example, Rissi's work focuses entirely on the symbolic plot structure of Jesus' journeys, finding a narrative pattern that moves from darkness to light, and from territories outside Judea to Jerusalem.[21] His footnotes reflect a knowledge only of standard Johannine scholarship. Somewhat similarly, Mlakuzhyil, Østenstad, and I each worked with a slightly different understanding of repetitive concentric structures in the Fourth Gospel and tried to relate these to the book's plot or its theology, or both.[22] But again, except for a few passing references to formalist literary theory in my work, these three studies show no awareness of recent trends in New Testament narrative studies. Nevertheless, I cannot help but think that the "spirit of the age" has provided some of the impetus to all four of our approaches.

Current trends in New Testament narrative studies are most obvious in Fernando Segovia's recent analysis of the Gospel's plot. His argument, as outlined in "The Journey(s) of the Word of God: A Reading of the Plot of the Fourth Gospel," works with a historical sense of genre, is well informed by contemporary literary theory regarding plot, and similarly challenges the received tradition. Segovia sees John 11 as significant to the narrative's plot in that John 11 represents "the fourth and final journey of Jesus to the city of Jerusalem, . . . a visit which contains within itself the concluding narrative of death and lasting significance."[23] But for Segovia, chapter 18 represents the more natural narrative dividing point, since it seems to fit most closely with the tripartite structure of the ancient biographical genre.[24] While I am not totally convinced by his argument that the threefold division of the ancient

---

Somewhat similarly to Bultmann, Mlakuzhyil argues that John 11–12 is a compromising "bridge section" hinging the "Book of Jesus' Signs" and "the Book of Jesus' Hour" (ibid., 238–41; cf. Bultmann, *The Gospel of John,* 392; Byrne, *Lazarus,* 25–26; and Marchadour, *Lazare,* 94–99, 104–10).

[21] Rissi, "Der Aufbau des Vierten Evangeliums," 52.

[22] More recently Hartwig Thyen, making reference to both Mlakuzhyil's and Østenstad's work, has also argued for placing the major narrative division of the Fourth Gospel at 10:42 ("Die Erzählung von den Bethanischen Geschwestern (Joh 11,1-12,19) als 'Palimpsest' über Synoptischen Texten," 2026–28; cf. Schneiders, "Death in the Community of Eternal Life: History, Theology, and Spirituality in John 11," 45).

[23] Segovia, "The Journey(s) of the Word of God: A Reading of the Plot of the Fourth Gospel," 44.

[24] Ibid., 45; cf. 32–33.

biographical genre is more crucial to the explication of Johannine plot than is the fourfold journey motif, nevertheless Segovia's attempt to combine these two elements is likewise a literary challenge to the traditional twofold theological division of the book.

All these recent readers of Johannine narrative structure, with inner ears attuned to repetitive phrasing and feet tapping to the rhythm of the plot, unconsciously simulate the totalizing proclivities of formalist literary theory.[25] But when those proclivities are viewed within the interpretive tradition of Johannine studies as conscious attempts to read the Gospel text in a different way, against the grain of established exegetical norms, they bear the seeds of a resistant reading of the Lazarus story. And every such seed, regardless of origin, is important in Mary's and Martha's garden plot on the outskirts of Jerusalem.

Although I have no irrefutable evidence to back up my intuitions, the Enlightenment's rejection of the miraculous, coupled with a Lutheran and Reformed emphasis on the preaching of the gospel, was probably just as much responsible for popularizing the division of Johannine narrative between chapters 12 and 13 as were source-critical theories or references to Johannine theology. Bultmann himself recognized that the raising of Lazarus has "decisive consequences for [Jesus'] destiny," since it is this particular story where "his last act leads to the decision of the authorities to kill him, and his last words lead to the final division between faith and unbelief."[26] Furthermore, Bultmann wrote that "the whole [Lazarus narrative] forms the transition to the Passion Narrative, and to the scene of Jesus' departure from his own that precedes it."[27] From the perspective of Johannine narrative structure, one could hardly find a clearer summary of reasons for arguing that the raising of Lazarus is the plot's climax and turning point. The structure of Bultmann's commentary and the subsequent history of Johannine scholarship, however, have left different imprints.

But beyond the formalist machinations of plot and the totalizing effects of Johannine narrative symmetry, there is another significant way in which John 11 marks a major dividing point in the book. With this final sign the implied author introduces a new, personal element to the story, one that is evident in the unusual characteristic of naming the miracle's participants (Mary, Martha, and Lazarus), in the surprising appeal to Jesus' affections

---

[25] See, for example, Petersen, *Literary Criticism for New Testament Critics,* 49–80; Powell, *What Is Narrative Criticism?* 32–50.

[26] Bultmann, *The Gospel of John,* 392, 393.

[27] Ibid., 392.

("Lord, he whom you love is ill," 11:3; "See how he loved him," 11:37),[28] and in Jesus' untypical display of distress and grief (11:33, 35, 38).[29]

One can debate whether the references to Jesus' love are simply intended to reflect Jesus' personal affection for the Bethany family or whether they should be understood in more concrete rhetorical terms as a covert request by female clients to their prospective patron, Jesus.[30] Nevertheless, it is the first time in the book that any appeal is made on the basis of love—regardless of its intentions. And Jesus' public display of grief at Lazarus's tomb would seem to suggest Jesus' close personal relationship with the family. These responses, therefore, signal a change in tone and emphasis—a change that will continue to evolve throughout the last half of the book. Moreover, the story's repetition of *agapan* and *philein* ([love], 11:3, 5, 11, 36), and the consequent formation of a community in response to the loss of a beloved friend and brother (celebrated by Mary washing Jesus' feet, 12:3), are part of a metaphorical matrix that, a few days later, Jesus himself will draw from when trying to describe his own changing relationship to his disciples (13:2–38; 15:14–15; 20:17).[31]

---

[28] For another description of this change, see my article "The Structure of John's Prologue: Its Implications for the Gospel's Narrative Structure," 258–62; cf. Marchadour, *Lazare,* 100–101.

[29] In spite of Beasley-Murray's arguments to the contrary (*John,* 192–94), Lindars is no doubt correct in arguing that the specific context of John 11:33–39 demands that *enbrimēsato tō pneumati* (11:33) be translated as "deeply moved" ("Rebuking the Spirit: A New Analysis of the Lazarus Story in John 11," 102–4).

[30] Schnackenburg rightly notes: "Implicit in . . . [the message the sisters sent to Jesus] was the plea for a cure" (*The Gospel According to John,* 2:322; cf. Culpepper, *Anatomy of the Fourth Gospel,* 110–11; Wuellner, "Putting Life Back into the Lazarus Story and its Reading: The Narrative Rhetoric of John 11 as the Narration of Faith," 116; and Koester, "Hearing, Seeing, and Believing in the Gospel of John," 342). By contrast, in John 4:46–53 the royal official's gender and social position provided him with the cultural status to sense that he could explicitly request Jesus to "come down before my little boy dies" (4:49).

For a broader discussion of the ancient Mediterranean patronage system and the language of friendship, see Moxnes, "Patron-Client Relations and the New Community in Luke-Acts," 242–50, esp. 244–47; cf. Karris, *Jesus and the Marginalized in John's Gospel,* 86.

[31] Turid Seim hints at this when she writes: "When Jesus washes and wipes the feet of the disciples, he is acting towards them as Mary did towards him. This also implies that she in advance has fulfilled his request to the disciples in 12:14ff" ("Roles of Women in the Gospel of John," 73; cf. Kitzberger, "Love and Footwashing: John 13:1–20 and Luke 7:36–50 Read Intertextually," 204, contra Bultmann, who argues that "[l]ike th[e] enemy [Caiaphas], the woman disciple did more than she realised" [*The Gospel of John,* 416]). Likewise when Jesus says, "Whoever serves me must follow me. . . . Whoever serves me the Father will honor," he is describing behavior typified first by Martha (12:26, cf. 12:2; Michaels, "John 12:1–11," 289; and Schüssler Fiorenza, *In Memory of Her,* 330).

Nevertheless, the arguments that a more personal tone emerges in John 11 and that the miracle story represents the major turning point of the book's structure and plot must not be separated from the foregrounding of the sisters, Martha and Mary, the two central characters in the miracle. Until their peculiar role in the story is situated within the broader context of the book's plot, the contemporary reader cannot begin to see the actual ideological implications of a reading resistant to standard androcentric interpretations.

In contrast to the Synoptic passion narratives, what is unique about the machinations of the Johannine passion plot is precisely this: Lazarus's sisters' desperate cry is the only narrative context for bringing a purposeful Jesus back to Judea and to a saving, community-transforming death (11:8–10; cf. 10:7–18, 26–30). Or more simply: what propels Jesus to his crucifixion in the Fourth Gospel is the calculated risk he takes in expressing his love for two women (11:7–10), and the calculated risk the women take by telling Jesus of their brother's illness.[32] In the Synoptic Gospels, however, it is not Jesus' relationships with people that draw him to Jerusalem. Prior to his entrance into the city those texts offer no clue that Jesus even knows anyone there. Instead, Jerusalem seems to act almost as an impersonal, cosmic magnet that pulls Jesus, like a moth circling a flame, ever closer to its deadly clutches. Thus, the Synoptics give their readers little context for understanding Jerusalem's hold on Jesus—apart from the obvious fact that the chief priests and scribes, those who have the power to condemn him to death, reside there (Mark 10:33; cf.

Robert Karris argues that Martha's designation of Jesus as "teacher" (11:28) should also be understood as a positive theological designation and part of the metaphorical language that Jesus adapts for his own purposes, since Jesus will use it later to describe himself (13:13–14; *Jesus and the Marginalized in John's Gospel,* 89). But Martha is not the first person in the Fourth Gospel to call Jesus *didaskalos* (cf. 1:38; 3:2), and twice Jesus connects *didaskalos* with *kyrios* in the footwashing scene (13:14–15). Karris's argument would thus have been stronger if he had noted that Martha, like the male disciples (11:8, 12), calls Jesus *both* teacher and Lord (as well as Son, Christ, and the Coming One, 11:27–28). Martha's doubled designation and Mary's subsequent anointing of Jesus function, therefore, to confirm these women as disciples—and the only disciples whose actions and words are the matrix for Jesus' own soon-to-be-completed mission.

[32] Mary's later act of anointing Jesus' feet (12:1–7) would seem to imply that she has had, like Thomas (11:16), some premonition of what Jesus' return to Judea could cost him. "Unless his body is anointed now, it never will be," says John Crossan (*Jesus,* 192). Crossan is speaking of the unnamed woman in Mark 11:3–9, but the remark fits equally well with Mary's action in John 12 (contra Brown, who thinks that the anointing is an "unconscious prophetic act" on Mary's part [*The Gospel According to John,* 1:449, 454]). Since Lazarus's sisters must be well aware of the hostile Judean attitude toward Jesus, one can say that the sisters take a "calculated risk" in making their need known to him.

Matt 2:1, 13; 15:21; Luke 13:31–35). But the Fourth Gospel plays the divinely dealt hand differently. In John's story, Jesus has already been to Jerusalem for festivals on a number of occasions (2:13–3:21; 5:1–47; 7:10–10:39); he has met numerous people in Jerusalem; and his words and actions there have sparked much controversy. So although I believe that there are important structural reasons for dividing the Fourth Gospel at chapter 11 rather than at chapter 13, I want to argue here for a deeper narrative logic: a resistant ideology that has gone unnoticed in past androcentric exegesis. For only in this Gospel does human need in any way impinge on Jesus' decision to return to Judea and Jerusalem.[33] In this Gospel Mary and Martha's premeditated action functions as the key to unlock Jesus' passion.

## STACKING THE CORPSES

Recent work in the New Testament from the perspective of cultural anthropology has emphasized the social significance of kinship and the pivotal values of honor and shame in the ancient Mediterranean world.[34] In that world, the proper sphere of women—woman as the embodiment of positive shame —was symbolized by the household and those tasks related to its care and upkeep. Under normal circumstances women's status in the wider (male) community was directly proportional to their ability to bear male heirs. Moreover, a woman's access to this wider, public sphere, the sphere of men, depended on her relationship to a man. If a woman was married, that access was mediated by her husband. If she was unmarried or widowed, access to the male sphere (that is, to justice, security, and property) was vouchsafed through her father, her brothers, or her sons.[35] Taking this cultural scenario

---

[33] The emphasis in this sentence should be on the phrase "in any way." Surely Charles Giblin is right in arguing that in the Fourth Gospel, Jesus disassociates himself "from the predominantly human concerns of those who, by merely human standards, would also seem to be rather close to him. . . . He never fails to attend to the situation presented to him, but in doing so he acts radically on his own terms" ("Suggestion, Negative Response, and Positive Action in St John's Portrayal of Jesus [John 2.1–11.; 4.46–54.; 7.2–14.; 11.1–44.]," 210). I just want to make it clear that the Fourth Gospel is the only Gospel where Jesus' decision to go into Judea and the environs of Jerusalem is linked to another human concern—irrespective of how, when, or for what ultimate reason the Johannine Jesus responds to that concern (cf. Schneiders, "Death in the Community of Eternal Life: History, Theology, and Spirituality in John 11," 48).

[34] Malina and Neyrey, "Honor and Shame in Luke-Acts: Pivotal Values of the Mediterranean World," 25–65.

[35] Ibid., 44–46. See also Malina, *The New Testament World,* 48–50.

into account, then, what is immediately apparent in the "family novella"[36] of John 11 is that the two sisters,[37] rather than Lazarus's wife, his sons, or Mary's or Martha's husbands or sons, are the characters who fill the story's center position and take the public role of finding the benefactor, Jesus.

Given the social dynamics of the ancient Mediterranean world, however, the sisters' role in the unfolding of the Johannine sign is understandable. As Bruce Malina points out, in the ancient Mediterranean family "the tightest unit of diffuse loyalty [was] the descent group of brothers and sisters. . . . The affection we expect as a mark of the husband and wife relationship [was] normally a mark of the brother-sister and mother-son relationships."[38] So rather than undermining the highly emotional context of the miracle scene, the sisters' presence actually symbolizes the deepest level of family affection and loyalty. The narrator's description of Mary and Martha as Lazarus's sisters further supports my argument that John 11 demarcates a narrative shift away from the less personal tone of the first half of the book (cf. 19:26–27).

But the sisters' central position in the funeral scene raises a more pressing set of issues for the story's culturally sensitive reader. For example, it is unusual that, as the narrator says, the Jerusalem mourners come to visit Martha and Mary "at home" rather than visiting Lazarus's immediate family members at their home (11:19, 20, 31, 45). Since Jewish funeral customs dictated that condolences be expressed at the family home,[39] the culturally attuned, encoded reader can assume either that Lazarus had never been married or that he was a widower and childless.[40] If he had a spouse and children, the mourners would be found with them, and Mary and Martha probably

---

[36] This is Hans Windisch's term ("John's Narrative Style," 37).

[37] Byrne is correct in noting that there is "no evidence initially [in 11:1] that Lazarus is related to Mary and Martha" (*Lazarus,* 37).

[38] Malina, *The New Testament World,* 121–22; see also 128–29.

[39] Byron McCane writes: "The first stage of mourning was a week of intense grieving, . . . during which the relatives of the deceased 'stayed away from work, sitting at home upon low couches, heads covered, receiving the condolences of relatives and friends.' For the first three days, family members would leave home only to visit the tomb, either to grieve there or to ensure that their loved one was truly dead" ("'Where No One Had Yet Been Laid': The Shame of Jesus' Burial," 475).

[40] Since Lazarus's cameo appearance in the Fourth Gospel has so many parallels to the life of Jesus (e.g., women play an important role in both of their lives; the chief priests want to kill both men; both men die, are wrapped in linen, and entombed; and both men come back to life again), the culturally encoded reader could easily assume that Lazarus, like Jesus, was not married. Moreover, using Jesus as a model, it is likely that the encoded reader would presume that Lazarus had never been married.

would be at their house. But here, in lieu of a wife and children, Martha and Mary represent Lazarus's closest living relatives, the only ones to whom condolences are expressed. Furthermore, since both Martha and Mary function as hostesses at the later party in Lazarus's honor (serving food, anointing the guests' feet, 12:1–3; cf. Luke 7:44), the encoded reader can assume that they either live with him or he with them.[41] This is also unusual. Why would two adult women be living with their brother? The most natural cultural scenario is one in which the two women have lost spouses.[42] This scenario would explain why Lazarus's sisters take the initiative in making their need known to Jesus and why the guests in mourning come to them: (1) Lazarus has no father or mother, sons, or wife who can make an appeal on his behalf; (2) Mary and Martha have no other brother, and no husbands or sons who can make a public appeal on their behalf; and (3) the naturally close bond of loyalty between sister and brother demands that they take some action. Thus, the sociological scenario that this story suggests is one in which Mary and Martha are widows who have been living with their unmarried brother, Lazarus. As Mary and Martha's next of kin, Lazarus would have been responsible for his sisters' welfare. However, with his death, the sisters lose not only their dearest family member but also their only voice in the public sphere of justice.[43]

In this scenario—an intertextual reading that foregrounds a concern for ancient Mediterranean social systems and is sensitive to the unwritten cul-

[41] Bultmann states, "Jesus is a guest with the sisters, as in Lk. 10.38–42" (*The Gospel of John*, 414 n. 7; see also Kitzberger, "Mary of Bethany and Mary of Magdala—Two Female Characters in the Johannine Passion Narrative: A Feminist, Narrative-Critical Reader-Response," 15; Nortjé, "The Role of Women in the Fourth Gospel," 26). But Schnackenburg takes the more traditional exegetical position based upon the Markan parallel (14:3–11): "the meal is somewhere in the village, but not in the house of the family with which Jesus is friendly" (*The Gospel According to John*, 2:366; see also Haenchen, *John*, 2:86).

[42] Kitzberger, in the original version of her essay presented at the Society of New Testament Studies meeting in Chicago, 1993, called these sisters "single women, not defined by a man, either husband or son. And they are autonomous and independent women. . . ." But she did not explain why she thought they were single women ("Mary of Bethany and Mary of Magdala—Two Female Characters in the Johannine Passion Narrative: A Feminist, Narrative-Critical Reader-Response," 27).

[43] My between-the-lines reading of the family relationships in John 11 may appear to some as a gross overreading of the minimally narrated scene. But it is important to remember Malina's description of the Mediterranean world as a "high context" society which "produce[s] sketchy and impressionistic texts, leaving much to the reader's or hearer's imagination. . . . This is because people have been socialized into shared ways of perceiving and acting. Hence, much can be assumed" ("Reading Theory Perspective," 20).

tural elements in the story—the modern reader discovers not only the socio-economic implications of Lazarus's death for the two sisters but also the unnamed deaths of at least two other people. For Mary and Martha, death is an ever-present reality, a reality slowly sucking their lives and livelihood from them. But it will only be by celebrating the death of a life-giving man (12:1–9) that the sisters will find the courage to live without a man (cf. 20:1–18).[44] In this, the last of the Johannine signs, it is the men who die or are at the edge of death: Lazarus (twice, 11:14; 12:10), Mary and Martha's unmentioned husbands, Jesus (11:8, 51–53), Thomas and his compatriots (11:16), and the entire priestly, patriarchal hierarchy of Judaism (11:47–50).[45] Only the women break out of these manacles of death and, in that process, present Jesus with the familial model he will appropriate to sustain his disciples beyond his departure (13:34–35; 14:18, 21; 15:9–17).

But let me step back for a moment from this reading scenario and add an important qualification to what I have just described. By adopting an ancient Mediterrranean cultural intertext I do not intend to exclude other ancient or modern intertextual relationships from the conversation with John 11. Nor am I attempting to establish a hierarchical reading strategy that implies that all readings of the Johannine text must begin at this same intertextual level—namely, ancient Mediterranean culture. So although I am sympathetic to Bruce Malina's concept of "reading scenarios" that "consider the text as setting forth a succession of explicit and implicit mental representations of scenes or schemes [and which,] in turn, evoke corresponding scenes or schemes in the mind of the reader,"[46] my broader, less absolutizing sense of intertextuality—coupled with a profound sense of the ideological constraints on interpretation—leads me to reject a simple, historical prioritization of one intertextual reading scenario over another. I give historically and culturally sensitive readings of texts no precedence, a priori, over other kinds of readings, especially when those "historically and culturally sensitive readings" fail to reflect critically upon the ideological interests of the text or the interpreter.

Following Judith Still and Michael Worton, I am more comfortable with arguing that

---

[44] Kitzberger rightly argues that the reader is encouraged to place the story of Mary Magdalene's encounter with Jesus within the context of Mary and Martha's previous encounter with him ("Mary of Bethany and Mary of Magdala—Two Female Characters in the Johannine Passion Narrative: A Feminist, Narrative-Critical Reader-Response," 17–20).

[45] Marchadour observes that in the Fourth Gospel, Judea as a whole functions symbolically as the place of death (*Lazare,* 137–38).

[46] Malina, "Reading Theory Perspective: Reading Luke-Acts," 14–15.

[b]oth axes of intertextuality, texts entering via authors [which is Malina's historical-cultural concern] . . . and texts entering via readers [which is more specifically my interest], . . . are . . . emotionally and politically charged; the objects of an act of influence, whether by a powerful figure (say, a father) or by a social structure (say, the church), does not receive or perceive that pressure as neutral.[47]

However, those "passionate and power-relations aspects have . . . been neutralized by certain theoreticians who present the acts of writing or reading as formal structures, without attending to the love-hate which motivates the transfer of texts."[48] It is the "emotionally and politically charged" aspects of intertextuality that Malina seeks to defuse with his elaboration of cultural "reading scenarios" and with his appeal to "considerate readers."[49] But it is precisely the real world, "love-hate," liberating potentialities of writing and reading that motivate my conscious selection of ancient and modern intertexts.[50]

SHATTERING TIME

If a reading scenario posited by the intertextual weave of ancient Mediterranean texts and modern anthropological monographs lays a stack of corpses at the doorstep of Mary and Martha by defining their story's unwritten cultural elements, a much different set of intertextual connections helps delineate the text's temporal signification. Here, formalist reader-response critics' attention to the distinction between "story time" and "discourse time"[51] and

---

[47] Still and Worton, "Introduction," in *Intertextuality,* 2; cf. Phillips, "'What is Written? How Are You Reading?' Gospel, Intertextuality and Doing Lukewise: A Writerly Reading of Lk 10:25-37 (and 38-42)," 286–91.

[48] Still and Worton, "Introduction," in *Intertextuality,* 2.

[49] Malina, "Reading Theory Perspective: Reading Luke-Acts," 16–17, 21.

[50] See pp. 82–84 below. Cf. Kitzberger, "Mary of Bethany and Mary of Magdala—Two Female Characters in the Johannine Passion Narrative: A Feminist, Narrative-Critical Reader-Response," 6–7; Kitzberger, "Love and Footwashing: John 13:1–20 and Luke 7:36–50 Read Intertextually," 191–93; and Schüssler Fiorenza, *Bread not Stone,* 15–22.

[51] The distinction between story and discourse is commonly used by biblical critics who have adapted formalist models of literary theory in their exegetical method (see Chatman, *Story and Discourse,* 62–84; Genette, *Narrative Discourse,* 27–29, 33–34, 86–87; cf. Powell, *What Is Narrative Criticism?* 23; Culpepper, *Anatomy of the Fourth Gospel,* 53–70). Because of its Platonist-sounding language (does an ideal "story" exist above and beyond all its possible discursive representations?), this distinction has been severely criticized by other narrative the-

the constantly changing judgments made by readers in the process of reading through a text join with biblical form-critical analysis of the miracle story structure.

In the previous chapter I looked at the two sabbath-day miracles in the Fourth Gospel and noted their deviations from the formal structure of most miracle stories. That formal structure, as many have noted, has four basic elements: (1) the statement of the problem; (2) the entrance of the hero or savior figure; (3) the savior figure or hero's solution; and (4) the evidence of the solution.[52] Both healings in John 5 and 9 were narrated quickly and both similarly characterized "the Jews'" responses, but the stories differed significantly in the way they formed their central characters. Moreover, the implied author masterfully manipulated the encoded reader's expectations at step 4, especially in the second sabbath miracle, by narrating in comic and dramatic fashion a variety of responses to the man's changed status and problematic identity. Now in the raising of Lazarus, the final miracle of Jesus' public ministry, the implied author once again exploits the encoded reader's expectations. But here the titillation comes between steps 2 and 3 in the miracle story structure: between the entrance of the hero and the hero's solution.[53]

Typically in miracle stories the reader must read only a few sentences to move from the entrance of the hero to the occurrence of the miracle. In other words, the miracles themselves take up very little discourse time. For example, with Jesus' first miracle in the Fourth Gospel, the discourse time is marked by the seventy-two Greek words between the moment when Jesus' mother tells

---

orists (cf. Moore, *Literary Criticism and the Gospels,* 64–68). However, quite apart from any latent metaphysical connotations, I find the distinction between story and discourse rhetorically useful. It reminds me that the arrangement of narrative episodes and their duration are inventions and thus infinitely malleable (see also Kitzberger, "Mary of Bethany and Mary of Magdala—Two Female Characters in the Johannine Passion Narrative: A Feminist, Narrative-Critical Reader-Response," 5 n. 22).

[52] Bultmann and Dibelius, of course, did much of the initial categorizing of miracle stories. But Bultmann's analysis isolated only three elements (*History of the Synoptic Tradition,* 209–44; cf. Wire, "The Structure of the Gospel Miracle Stories and Their Tellers," 83–84, 108–10).

[53] This structural peculiarity of the narrative has led John Painter to categorize it as a "quest story" ("Quest and Rejection Stories in John," 30) rather than a miracle story. But Painter's typology seems to miss the obvious fact that the author of the Fourth Gospel knows the miracle-story form very well and is able to manipulate it for his own rhetorical purposes, and in a variety of creative ways. In words that apply as much to the miracle-story form as to the Deuteronomic author's manipulation of the cyclical plot of the book of Judges, Sternberg says: "The variations prove no less integral to structure and effect than the uniformities" (*The Poetics of Biblical Narrative,* 271).

him "They have no wine" (2:3) and the narrator's acknowledgment that a miracle has occurred (2:9).[54] In Jesus' second miracle, it is marked by the sixty-two words between the narrator's observation that a royal official's son was ill (4:46) and the servants' report that the official's child was alive (4:51). In Jesus' first sabbath miracle, discourse time is marked by the fifty-three words between the entrance of the hero and the occurrence of the miracle (5:6–9); in the feeding of the five thousand, by the ninety-eight words between these two moments (6:5–11); and in the second sabbath healing, by the 101 words between them (9:1–7).

The raising of Lazarus, however, is the only Johannine miracle in which story time is explicitly marked in the narration. Here, nearly a week transpires between the time when Mary and Martha send their desperate message to Jesus and the time when Lazarus is raised from the dead.[55] Moreover, in terms of discourse time, there are thirty-nine verses, or 641 words between the time that Jesus gets the message of Lazarus's illness and the miraculous event when Jesus raises Lazarus from the dead (11:4–43). So not only is there a dramatic delay in story time, since Jesus remains in Bethany beyond the Jordan two days after hearing of Lazarus's sickness, but there is also a dramatic delay in discourse time. Ironically, the encoded reader is led to expect a miraculous healing by being introduced to the healer in 11:3; but, like Mary and Martha, the encoded reader is forced to wait a significant amount of time for the event to occur (11:44).[56]

There is also an additional irony in the structuring of this final sign. Since the encoded reader already knows that healings can occur from a significant distance (4:47–53), neither Jesus' delay in Bethany beyond the Jordan nor his return to Judea bears any necessary connection to the anticipated miracle. In fact, the sisters' statement, "Lord, he whom you love is ill" (11:3), and Jesus' statement, "This illness does not lead to death; rather it is for God's glory . . ." (11:4), seem to be explicit allusions to the healing of the royal official's son, who was, by contrast, at the point of death when the father approached Jesus

---

[54] I am counting every definite article, particle, and conjunction. Talk about painstakingly slow reading!

[55] This estimate of the number of days is based on the combination of three factors: the fact that Lazarus was still alive when the sisters sent their message to Jesus, the fact that Jesus stayed two more days in Bethany (beyond the Jordan) before heading for Judea, and the fact that Lazarus's corpse had been in the tomb four days when Jesus finally arrived in Bethany.

[56] Suspense in the miracle story is created through the rhetorical ploy of narrative retardation (see Auerbach, *Mimesis,* 4–5; Hägg, *Narrative Techniques in Ancient Greek Romances,* 326–27; and Sternberg, *The Poetics of Biblical Narrative,* 271–72).

(4:47, 49).[57] In view of that earlier miracle and the omission of the corresponding imperative "Come down" (4:49), the encoded reader now anticipates another cure from a distance (cf. 4:50; 11:11–12). Moreover, as I have argued elsewhere, even Jesus' command "Let us go to Judea again" (11:7) initially cannot be understood as a turn toward Mary, Martha, and Lazarus. Instead, it must be understood as a continuation of Jesus' own unarticulated purpose.[58]

To my knowledge, in no other miracle story from the ancient Mediterranean world is the hero's initial reaction seemingly so unrelated to the eventual miracle, and in no other miracle story is there so much (I hesitate to say the words) patently unnecessary discourse time between the plot elements of the miracle-story form.[59] Thus, the reactions of Jesus and the extended discourse time both raise the encoded reader's expectations for a miracle, and both reinforce what that reader has learned from the narrative's previous signs: this miracle-worker needs neither additional time nor the proximity of space to effect cures.

Formalist reader-response criticism does have a vested interest in narrative manipulations of readers' expectations through dramatic delays such as the one in John 11; however, its interest does not end with the mere observation of the phenomenon.[60] The content of the material that prolongs the pause is also crucial to narrative argumentation. For example, in the only Markan miracle story similar to the raising of Lazarus, a woman with a chronic menstrual flow intrudes into the story of Jairus and his daughter and is healed when she touches Jesus' garments (Mark 5:22–43).[61] As with the raising of Lazarus, the Markan Jesus' decision to interrupt his journey to Jairus's house

---

[57] These are the only Johannine miracles that are initiated by immediate family members and performed on behalf of another male family member.

[58] This is because the only Bethany that has been mentioned up to this point in the narrative has been "Bethany beyond Jordan" (1:28; 10:40; cf. 11:18; *The Print's First Kiss,* 106).

[59] Wire, "The Structure of the Gospel Miracle Stories and Their Tellers," 101–3.

[60] Wilhelm Wuellner's rhetorically oriented narrative criticism has much in common with reader-response criticism. His analysis of John 11 is sensitive to the persuasive force of the story, and he argues correctly that the "subversive effect of [the narrative's] rhetorical coherence . . . gets recognized both *while* reading John 11, as well as *before* reading John 11 . . ." ("Putting Life Back into the Lazarus Story and its Reading: The Narrative Rhetoric of John 11 as the Narration of Faith," 125, his emphasis). But, strangely, he fails to develop that subversive element as it is expressed in the implied author's manipulation of the miracle story form (ibid., 116–17).

[61] Schnackenburg's comparison is particularly useful, although he does not mention the lengthy delay (*The Gospel According to St. John,* 2:341).

by publicly affirming the woman's trust shows that the Markan Jesus too has his own priorities and timetable. And as in John 11, Jesus' delay will make the anticipated miracle more impressive.

But while the Markan intercalation adds a certain element of dramatic tension to the story of Jairus's daughter (Will Jesus get to her before she dies?), insofar as the story merely narrates another miraculous event, it continues to reinforce precisely those qualities of Jesus' authority that will heighten readers' trust in him.[62] In John 11, however, there is no trust-enhancing, intervening miracle that causes Jesus to postpone attending to Mary and Martha's need. In fact, the situation is just the opposite. Here, the initial absence of the miraculous, coupled with Jesus' opaque reasoning for his delay, and the bewildering cacophany of reactions to Lazarus's sickness and death, boldly expand the narrative's discourse time, challenging and undermining the basic intention of this and all miracle stories. Although the raising of Lazarus is essential for the book's plot (11:47–53), the miracle itself occurs almost as an afterthought in the formal structure of the miracle story.[63] Thus, the manipulated miracle-story form poses these questions for the encoded reader: In view of the author's ideology, what is the point of the story? Is it Jesus' power (11:37, 40, 44), Martha's prevenient trust (11:21–27), or Mary's postresurrection perception (12:1–8)?

As I mentioned above, the miracle-story form in John 11 is prolonged by the addition of characters whose various reactions to Lazarus's illness and subsequent death expand the space between the hero's appearance and the actual miracle. For example, the narrative incorporates into its structure thirteen different responses of Jesus to Lazarus's death. Jesus begins with the reflection that Lazarus's "illness is not going to lead to death" (11:4) and then tells the disciples an opaque, tenuously related proverb about walking in the daylight (11:9–10). Next, Jesus reveals to his disciples the fact that Lazarus is finally resting (11:11); Jesus then has to correct their misunderstanding by telling them that Lazarus is actually dead (11:14–15). When Jesus arrives in Judean Bethany, he talks to Martha about Lazarus's resurrection and his own power over death (11:23, 25–26), responds to Martha's surprise with a rhetorical question (11:40), and prays at the tomb (11:41–42). Moreover, the narrator

---

[62] "*Pistis,*" Bultmann writes, ". . . is a trust in the miracle worker which is his proper due" (*History of the Synoptic Tradition,* 219).

[63] Brendan Byrne describes the tension by speaking of two points of climax in the story: a theological climax, which comes with Jesus' "I am" revelation, and a dramatic climax, which arrives when Jesus shouts "Lazarus, come out" (*Lazarus,* 32).

reports the fact that Jesus remained beyond the Jordan after hearing of Lazarus's illness (11:5–6), Jesus' journey back to Judea and his arrival at the outskirts of Bethany (11:17–20), his distress and tears (11:35–38a), and his arrival at the tomb (11:38b).

The miracle story also includes ten responses of Mary and Martha to their brother's illness and death, most of which are recorded as direct speech. First, the sisters tell Jesus of Lazarus's illness (11:3). Martha then has two conversations with Jesus which reflect five different reactions to Lazarus's death and which, in a variety of ways, affirm Jesus' power (11:21–27, 39). Mary, on the other hand, has only four responses to Lazarus's death. She falls at Jesus' feet, weeps, and sadly wishes Jesus had come earlier (11:32–33). Her final response occurs a week later when she anoints those very feet that have brought the story's tragic hero back to her, to Martha, to Lazarus, and to the hero's own anticipated death in Jerusalem (11:2; 12:1–8).

"The Jews" have seven different responses to Lazarus's death. The narrator describes them as consoling Martha and Mary (11:19, 31) and weeping (11:33). They point out Lazarus's grave to Jesus (11:34). They seem impressed and surprised at Jesus' reaction to the death (11:36–37). Finally, after Jesus raises Lazarus from the dead, the narrator notes "the Jews'" twofold reaction to the miraculous event (11:45–46).

The disciples have the fewest responses to Lazarus's death. All three responses occur near the beginning of the story, just after Jesus has decided to go back to Judea and to Lazarus. First, the disciples address an incredulous question to Jesus (11:8). Then they misunderstand Jesus' metaphoric allusion to Lazarus's death by responding, "Lord, if he has fallen asleep, he will be all right" (*sōthēsetai,* 11:12). In spite of this misconstrual, their prognosis is ironically correct. Lazarus will indeed "be rescued" (*sōthēsetai*) from the deep sleep of death. The disciples' final response (11:16) echoes their initial question and marks an *inclusio* around Jesus' decision to return to Judea. Voiced by Thomas, its edge of resignation will grow and cast a shadow of death over the last half of the book.

In view of these multiple responses to Lazarus's sickness and death and the role of Mary and Martha in the story, it seems strange that the narrator concludes the miracle without offering the encoded reader any immediate insight into the sisters' reaction to receiving back their brother (cf. Mark 5:42). Jesus does not publicly restore Lazarus to them (cf. Luke 7:15–16), nor does the narrator make a note of the disciples' reaction (cf. John 2:11). Only "the Jews" are given narrative space to respond to the miracle (11:45–46). As David Beck puts it:

What distinguishes [the named characters in John 11] is their lack of recorded faith response. Martha verbally expresses her belief but is challenged to no *act* of faith. A faith response is not asked of Mary, and Lazarus's response to Jesus' command is not the faith response of a human being but the reanimation of one who has lost his capacity to believe or respond.[64]

Although the story offers only two responses to the raising of Lazarus, the implied author amazingly has incorporated thirty-two different responses into the miracle story structure *prior* to the occurrence of the miracle. Furthermore, the narrator names five different characters, along with the two stereotypical character groups (the disciples and "the Jews"), and four different geographical locations. Thus, those real readers who would be culturally attuned to the simple miracle-story form are faced with an enormously complicated structure in John 11. Can they wend their way through the labyrinth to a satisfying resolution? Perhaps. In the end, however, it is only the miracle story's function in the overall plot that makes any resolution possible. Real readers can read through the cacophony of disruptions to find the melody, the single tone: Lazarus's resuscitation sets in motion the plot to get rid of Jesus (11:47–51). But can readers hear the dissonant countermelody that attempts to train their ears to a different pitch, a higher tone?

## DIVIDING THE SISTERS

The amount of space that recent commentaries and articles have devoted to analyzing Martha's conversation with Jesus and Mary's actions in this final Johannine sign proves that many readers have indeed found in the miracle story a stirring crescendo. Feminist critics, especially, have heard in Martha's carefully nuanced confession (11:27) a tone that shatters both the stereotypi-

---

[64] Beck, "The Narrative Function of Anonymity in Fourth Gospel Characterization," 153, my emphasis. Mark Stibbe, on the other hand, thinks that "the greatest 'gap' in the story is the narrator's omission of any response from Lazarus." For Stibbe, "[t]he silence of Lazarus is more deafening than the cry of Jesus" ("A Tomb with a View: John 11.1-44 in Narrative-Critical Perspective," 54; see also Stibbe, *John's Gospel,* 106). And Hans Windisch describes the omissions this way. "The dramatic shape of the conclusion leaves something to be desired from our point of view: there is no description of the immediate impression the resurrection makes, especially the greeting between brother and sisters, a corresponding gesture, or a word from Jesus along the lines of Lk 7.15's 'he gave him back to his mother,' the touching conclusion to the family novella. The scene is broken off prematurely; the creative touch goes lame, or rather the joy of narrating is extinguished after the fact of the miracle has been demonstrated" ("John's Narrative Style," 37).

cal patriarchal reconstructions of the Johannine community and the ideology that underlies those patriarchal reconstructions.[65] But my purpose is not simply to hum along with those feminist voices by concentrating only on Martha's bold affirmation of Jesus' power. Instead, I want to listen to the subtle rhetorical shifts in the sisters' direct speech statements and show how the deaths of the story's male characters empower these women, freeing them to ever bolder speech and action.

In the miracle story, the first sentence attributed to the sisters is the one Jesus receives through an unnamed intermediary: "Lord, please [*ide*], he whom you love is ill" (11:3, my translation). It is the only time in the entire account that the women are portrayed as speaking or acting in unison, and the sisters' use of the second person singular verb *phileis* must strike the encoded reader with surprise. This is because, as noted earlier,[66] the encoded reader has previously been given no intimation of Jesus' love for particular characters in the story. And yet now, without actually naming their brother (something that, in fact, the sisters never do), Jesus knows exactly to whom they are referring (11:11).

The sisters do not explicitly request Jesus to come to them, nor do they repeat the royal official's condescending command, "Come down" (4:49). And because of the earlier miracle performed from a distance (4:46–54), the encoded reader could easily understand the sisters' initial reticence ("Lord, he whom you love is ill") as evidence of their strong faith.[67] But why are the sisters unable to speak with their own voices and say to Jesus, "Lord, *help us!* Lazarus *our brother,* the one whom *we* love, is ill?" Perhaps this first sentence also expresses the sisters' feeling of powerlessness. Perhaps it is a verbal act of

[65] See, for example, Raymond Brown's *The Community of the Beloved Disciple,* Culpepper's *The Johannine School,* Cullmann's *The Johannine Circle,* and Hengel's *The Johannine Question* (80–135). None of these historical reconstructions of the origins and development of the Johannine community gives much place to the role of women in the community. Brown's study went the furthest, but he relegated his discussion to an appendix (*The Community of the Beloved Disciple,* 183–98). He never asks how women might have reworked the Jesus tradition that they inherited and transmitted. But compare these studies to the historical investigations of Elisabeth Schüssler Fiorenza (*In Memory of Her,* 329–30), Sandra Schneiders ("Death in the Community of Eternal Life," 52–55), and Ingrid Kitzberger ("Mary of Bethany and Mary of Magdala—Two Female Characters in the Johannine Passion Narrative: A Feminist, Narrative-Critical Reader-Response," 11–12). All these scholars find important historical, theological, and ecclesiological implications in the Fourth Gospel's portrayal of women.

[66] See pp. 63–64.

[67] Gail O'Day puts it this way: "[T]he reader senses that even though the women ask nothing of Jesus, they address him because they expect him to know what to do" (*The Word Disclosed,* 81).

deference, expressing their fear of putting any explicit, public challenge to Jesus (cf. Mark 5:27–28, 32).

Later on, however, when Jesus finally arrives at Judean Bethany, each sister in turn publicly reproaches Jesus to his face with the identical words, "Lord, if *you* had been here, *my* brother would not have died" (11:21, 32; my emphasis).[68] At that time they do not allude to Jesus' friendship with Lazarus. They do not simply say, "Your friend has died" (cf. 11:3). Thus, it appears that the death of their brother brings with it the sisters' discovery of their own personal voices. Correspondingly, what the encoded reader at first might have assumed to be an expression of the sisters' strong faith (the absence of the royal official's "Come down"), could now in retrospect appear to have been merely the reader's idealization of the characters. Contrary to the implied author's perspective (14:1–31), and much like the perspective of the earlier royal official (4:46–54), the women have all along presumed that physical presence bears with it the promise of salvation ("Lord, if you had been here . . . ," 11:21, 32).

Although initially the sisters had spoken in unison and mouthed what they hoped would be Jesus' concern (11:3), they now speak for themselves, individually, out of their own personal sense of need. Furthermore, the repetition of the sisters' words ("Lord, if you had been here . . .") reemphasizes the mystery of Jesus' decision not to come immediately to their aid, reemphasizes the awful fact of their brother's death, and reemphasizes their own misunderstanding of the meaning of Jesus' presence. But just as importantly, their private meetings with Jesus and their slightly different responses to his arrival have the dramatic effect of separating the sisters from each other.[69] From a narrative standpoint, the death of Lazarus literally puts space between the two female characters.

If, as I argued earlier, the sisters were indeed knowingly taking a calculated risk in covertly asking Jesus to return to Judea and heal their brother, then Jesus' arrival, after Lazarus's death, is doubly poignant for them. The sisters

---

[68] Note, too, that Jesus responds to Martha—not by naming the name Lazarus or by describing a mutual relationship to the deceased ("the one whom we love") but by saying, "*Your brother* will rise again" (11:23).

[69] Giblin astutely notes that "their statements differ only by the more emotional tone in which Mary expresses her personal loss (the emphatic position of *mou*)," ("Suggestion, Negative Response, and Positive Action in St. John's Portrayal of Jesus [John 2.1–11.; 4.46–54.; 7.2–14.; 11.1–44.]," 209; cf. van Tilborg, *Imaginative Love in John,* 193–94). For other examples of the use of emphatic pronouns in the Fourth Gospel, cf. 13:6–9 (*mou*); 18:17, 25–26; 21:15, 17 (*sy*); and 18:35 (*egō*).

have already lost their brother. And now, without solving their problem, their presumed benefactor has put his own life under the threat of death by belatedly answering their request. Thus, in view of the disciples' question (11:8) and Thomas's statement (11:16), the encoded reader might reasonably hear in the sisters' doubled cry "Lord, if you had been here . . . ," the additional anxious, unvoiced question: "And now that you are here, what will happen to you?" In other words, "What a heroic act for you to come to us! But how foolish, now that our brother is dead! In coming back to Judea 'you have lost your own life and you have not saved his.'"[70]

Indeed, Martha's indecorous act of leaving the house of mourning and going to meet Jesus (11:20), and her private remark to Mary (11:28), may be read as protective acts (cf. 11:54). Since the encoded reader knows that "the Jews" were "just now trying to stone [Jesus]" (11:8) and that "many of the Jews had come to Martha and Mary to console them" (11:19), Martha's encounter with Jesus outside the village and her words to Mary may appear as attempts to keep Jesus from a volatile confrontation with his opponents.[71]

As most scholars have noted, Martha's response to Jesus' question (11:23) is the theological climax of the miracle story. Bultmann and many feminist interpreters after him have argued that "[t]he answer of Martha (v. 27) shows the genuine attitude of faith."[72] But for Elisabeth Schüssler Fiorenza, Martha's statement implies much more. It means that "Martha represents the full apostolic faith of the Johannine community, just as Peter did for the Matthean community. More importantly, her faith confession is repeated at the end of the Gospel in 20:31, where the evangelist expresses the goal of her/his writing of the Gospel. . . ."[73] However, Schnackenburg and others argue that Martha's "'yes' to Jesus' question does not mean that she has understood the meaning of her words. . . . For the evangelist, who holds Jesus' meeting with Martha up to his readers as a mirror of their own faith, Martha's attitude is an example of faith which proves its worth in a critical situation."[74]

---

[70] Lewis, *The Lion, the Witch and the Wardrobe,* 141.

[71] Bultmann also finds an attitude of expectancy—or perhaps a need for consolation—in Mary's quick movements toward Jesus (11:29; *The Gospel of John,* 405–6).

[72] Ibid., 404.

[73] Schüssler Fiorenza, *In Memory of Her,* 329; cf. Schneiders, "Death in the Community of Eternal Life: History, Theology, and Spirituality in John 11," 52–53. Sjef van Tilborg calls Martha "the perfect reader model" (*Imaginative Love in John,* 192).

[74] Schnackenburg, *The Gospel According to St. John,* 332. Brendan Byrne puts it slightly differently: "If Martha's faith is perfect at this point, the actual sign (the raising) becomes, at least for her, superfluous. If she still has some way to go in her journey of faith, then the sign is not an anticlimax" (*Lazarus,* 54). In a similar fashion, Kitzberger initially characterizes Martha as

Not surprisingly, those scholars who argue that Martha represents the Johannine ideal of Christian commitment concentrate their attention on the dialogue in 11:21–27. Those scholars who argue, on the other hand, that Martha is a less than ideal example of faith focus on the conversation in 11:39–40. But recognition of the temporal nature of narrative and the rhetorical significance of narrative sequence actually allows for both interpretations of Martha's response. The encoded reader initially is given no textual clues from which to conclude that Martha's faith statement might be inadequate. But later on, at the tomb, the tone of Jesus' conversation with Martha leads the reader to reconsider that earlier, positive evaluation.[75]

A major reason why the encoded reader can first respond positively to Martha is simply because her conversation with Jesus ends so abruptly (11:28).[76] Since the encoded reader finds neither Jesus nor the narrator responding negatively to Martha's bold words (11:27; cf. 1:49–51; 3:3–4; 6:67–70), the reader assumes that the implied author must agree wholeheartedly with Martha's confession. But tagging along behind the sudden break in their dialogue is the first of the story's two potential narrative gaps.[77] For curiously, in the place of any confirming statement from Jesus or the narrator (cf. 9:38b–39), the encoded reader finds only Martha's mundane words to Mary: "The Teacher is here and is calling for you" (11:28).

Since the encoded reader has not heard Jesus say anything like "Go, call Mary," the abrupt end of Martha's theologically charged conversation dramatically accentuates the narrative gap it creates. Clearly, the implied author has withheld part of Jesus and Martha's dialogue from the reader. Later on, when Jesus asks Martha, "Did I not tell you that if you believed, you would see the glory of God?" (11:40), the encoded reader will discover the second narrative gap in Jesus and Martha's earlier dialogue. For there is no narrative

---

"active and reacting spontaneously" ("Mary of Bethany and Mary of Magdala—Two Female Characters in the Johannine Passion Narrative: A Feminist, Narrative-Critical Reader-Response," 10–11; cf. O'Day, *The Word Disclosed,* 88–90).

[75] In response to Martha's exclamation in John 11:39, van Tilborg writes, "Martha's faith must have been defective" (*Imaginative Love in John,* 195; cf. 192). Although the encoded reader's reevaluation of Martha's faith statement is not nearly as dramatic as that elicited by Peter's confession and confusion in Mark 8:29, 32–33 and Matt 16:16–23, it is, nevertheless, similar in effect. Furthermore, as I noted earlier, Schüssler Fiorenza correctly observes that in terms of faith statements, Martha is the Johannine equivalent of Matthew's Peter (*In Memory of Her,* 329).

[76] Schnackenburg, *The Gospel According to St. John,* 333. Similar sudden breaks in dialogue occur between John 4:26 and 27; 8:58 and 59; and 9:17 and 18.

[77] Van Tilborg, *Imaginative Love in John,* 194–95.

account of Jesus having made this statement to Martha. In point of fact, however, Jesus' question reads like the missing conclusion of their earlier conversation (cf. 1:50–51; 3:10; 5:14; 9:39).[78]

These two examples of reported speech involve previous conversations between Jesus and Martha, and both examples give the encoded reader the feeling that not everything that could have been told has been told, that perhaps only the most crucial elements of their dialogue have been divulged. But what is most perplexing for the encoded reader is the belated discovery that Jesus' earlier confirmation—or correction—of Martha's confession has somehow been misplaced. The encoded reader, who might at first have assumed that Martha's confession was laudatory,[79] was not given any immediate evidence of Jesus' "Yes!" It is not until after Martha exclaims repulsively "Lord, it stinks" (11:39, my translation), that the encoded reader discovers Martha's earlier words might have said more than she intended.[80]

Of course, regardless of how real readers initially settle the issue of Martha's confession (Is it full and comprehending, or is it incomplete and unreflective?)—in the end it comes closest to the narrator's image of "having the right stuff" (20:31).

## CRITICAL RESISTANCE

I have tried to make clear in this chapter that any attempt to explicate the design of the Johannine seventh sign must reckon with its own de-signing of

[78] Margaret Davies takes a different perspective, arguing that "Jesus' rebuke, 'Did I not tell you that if you would believe you would see God's honor' (11:40), is not quite fair, . . . because Jesus had said no such thing to Martha. His remarks had been directed to the disciples before he set out for Bethany (11:4)" (*Rhetoric and Reference in the Fourth Gospel,* 372). But this is not quite right. Jesus did indeed say something to the disciples about the "glory of God," but it was not tied in with belief (11:4; cf. 11:15). Thus, I think it is still more reasonable to read Jesus' question as the rhetorically significant "misplaced" conclusion to Jesus and Martha's earlier conversation.

[79] Schüssler Fiorenza, *In Memory of Her,* 329; Schneiders, "Death in the Community of Eternal Life: History, Theology, and Spirituality in John 11," 52–53.

[80] Sandra Schneiders correctly notes that Martha's "shock at Jesus' order to remove the stone shows that she did not in any way anticipate a resuscitation of Lazarus" ("Death in the Community of Eternal Life: History, Theology, and Spirituality in John 11," 54). But for Schneiders, "[t]his is not . . . due to lack of faith. She who knows that Lazarus, even though he has died yet lives, has no reason to think the final resurrection will be anticipated in his case" (ibid). However, Schneiders's exegesis fails to wrestle seriously with the subsequent and qualifying question that Jesus puts to Martha: *Ouk eipon soi hoti ean pisteusēs . . .* (11:40; Schneiders, "Death in the Community of Eternal Life: History, Theology, and Spirituality in John 11," 55).

itself; its radical reconfiguration of *Dasein*.[81] For, as I have argued, this sign, above all other signs in the Fourth Gospel, is the death sign of patriarchy and a resigning of Jesus' absence. Unlike Ruth, who, according to Jewish tradition, hatched a desperate plot to continue her lifeline by first anointing herself and then uncovering the feet of Boaz (Ruth 3:3–4), in the Johannine story Mary celebrates the death of her redeemer—her *gōʾēl*—by anointing his feet with perfume (John 12:3–4). Its pungent odor erases the final traces of Lazarus's decaying flesh at the very moment when those outside the house are beginning to plot Jesus' death and her brother's second death (12:9–11).

As a male, I want to be an assenting reader of this story. I want to identify with the feminist readings of Martha's bold confession and Mary's brazen anointing. And, of course, I want to say yes to the resistant reading I have just completed. Yet I find myself resisting any identification with the stinking corpse of Lazarus, the one bound up in linen cloths. For it is only while the male character lies entombed and alone, lost to family and community, that the sisters finally are free to explore their own voices. As long as Lazarus is alive, the sisters must rely on him. He is the source of their unified voice. He is the origin of their need. But when Lazarus dies, the sisters become separated from each other. Now, in their separate meetings with Jesus, they each speak independently. And even when they use the exact same words to reproach him for his lack of presence in their time of desperate need, the structure of their individually formed sentences changes ever so slightly. Martha's incredulous outburst at the tomb, coupled with Mary's invisible silence, underscore the sisters' separateness and individuality even more dramatically than Martha's earlier confession.[82]

By the time the sisters are reunited with Jesus and their brother (12:1–12), their sisterly bond has moved beyond a unanimity of words and a unanimity

---

[81] For example, see Page DuBois's discussion of the Heideggerian concept of *Dasein* (*Torture and Truth*, 134–35, 145–46; and Herman Waetjen's analysis of the concept in relation to reader-response criticism ("Social Location and the Hermeneutical Mode of Integration," 75–76, 81, 92).

[82] The narrator's choice of the descriptive epithet "Martha, the sister of the dead man" (11:39) rather than simply "Martha," or "Martha, the sister of Mary," or "Martha, the sister of Lazarus" emphasizes Martha's perspective that the dead will not rise in this age (11:24), just before she expresses the perspective again with her own voice. But the epithet also betrays the narrator's ideological point of view. As I argued earlier (p. 48), epithets such as these are proleptic. So by associating Martha with death instead of life, the narrator may be momentarily distancing himself from her and her sharp response which follows (11:40; O'Day, *The Word Disclosed*, 94). On the other hand, one might read the epithet as legitimating Martha's new-found voice. That is, there is no brother (he is "*dead*") or sister (Martha is "*sister of the dead*," not, "sister of the living [Mary]") who can speak for her.

of need. And unlike the parallel scene in Luke 10:39–40, neither of the Johannine women needs to appeal to Jesus as an authority figure. As Elisabeth Schüssler Fiorenza points out, "[i]n John, Mary and Martha are not seen in competition with each other, as is the case in Luke [10:38–42]."[83] Although only Mary recognizes the temporary nature of the family reunion and celebrates it by anointing Jesus' feet, Martha is her equal in ministry.[84] Encircled by dying men, the sisters' purposeful, independent actions reflect a sense of community whose unity is based on noncompetitive diversity.

In spite of the ideal community that Mary and Martha represent, there is an important sense in which I as a male reader am still a resistant reader. For although I have been reading the miracle story looking for its natural points of resistance to traditional notions of meaning and looking for resistances within the history of interpretation, I now find myself suddenly resisting certain parts of the critically resistant reading that I have just read in the text. What I find doubly disturbing is this: that as a male reader I read through this sign, with its multiple disruptions and designing strategies, as if I were the one become dead, the one without a voice, pretending to experience precisely that which I find impossible to experience—the silence of the zombie-like Lazarus.[85] In this miracle (and what a miracle it is!) the men are the ones who die: Lazarus (twice), Jesus, Thomas and his compatriots, and the Jewish leaders. Only the women live—two women with their pulsating doubts and their fragmentedly formed, tensive trust.

Feminist reader-response criticism has given me a strategy that stirs my blood, but paradoxically the stir is the premonition of my own death, the silencing of my androcentric voice. So now I begin to resist Mary and Martha's community, a community that seems to have no room for sisters who say "our brother" or "my brother" while any brother is still alive. To be alive in this text as a male is to be a participant in the destructive power of patriarchy and androcentrism. To be alive in this text as a male is to live the death of Lazarus, whose death is the means whereby the sisters' verbs are transposed into active voice. To be alive in this text as a male is to have one's

---

[83] Schüssler Fiorenza, *In Memory of Her,* 330.

[84] Ibid.

[85] As Rosa Braidotti has suggested: "Lacking the historical experience of oppression on the basis of sex [white, male, middle-class intellectuals] paradoxically lack a minus. Lacking the lack, they cannot participate in the great ferment that is shaking up Western culture; it must be very painful indeed to have no option other than being the empirical referent of the historical oppressor of women and being asked to account for his atrocities" ("Envy; or, With My Brains and Your Looks," 235, as quoted in Newton, "Historicisms New and Old: 'Charles Dickens' Meets Marxism, Feminism, and West Coast Foucault," 463).

death celebrated prematurely, to discover that only the hero's absence can make the women's hearts and minds grow strong.

I scratch again at the surface of Bultmann's classic commentary and fumble with his footnotes (the scholar's attempt to keep his bottom clean), hoping to bring a Teutonic (two-gin-and-tonic) scent of order back to my reading of John 11. I am afraid that my male attempt at a resistant reading may be only a parody; that my reading cannot and should not be taken seriously by contemporary feminist interpreters of the New Testament.[86] But in Bultmann's commentary I uncover one lightly perfumed note that gives me a whiff of hope. "Even more fantastic," he writes, "is Grill's exposition . . . [that] Mary and Martha are originally the dawn and dusk of Indian mythology, Lazarus is the moon, and Jesus is Sabazios-Dionysus."[87] Now I feel better. If Bultmann can privilege Grill's fancy with such a note of seriousness, perhaps my reading may be granted similar favor. To be read, noted, and toasted—then resisted and roasted—is at least to have had a voice. I am suddenly grateful for Martha's quick, impassioned rejoinder to Jesus, "Lord, it stinks!"

So bring on the next Johannine death scene. I have barely bloodied my nose in this act of resistant reading. Find me another poker-faced zombie to challenge and raise from this overwrought tome. But this time I want familiar ground to fight on, and I want some formal rules that I can recognize, a foe that I can understand and see. So lead me back again to my reliable Johannine narrator and to his victimized encoded reader.[88] Then let me and the two of them duke it out in the confines of Caiaphas's courtyard, while Peter and his buddies tally up the score. Perhaps this time a healthy dose of textual variants mixed with a shot or two of reception theory and Kentucky whiskey will convince me once again, as I was convinced in the past, that the revenant—I mean the referent—that I am fighting against is really rooted in a text.

---

[86] Adrienne Rich writes: "The personae we adopt, the degree to which we use lives already ripped off and violated by our own culture, the problem of racist stereotyping in every white head, the issue of the writer's power, right, obligation to speak for others denied a voice, or the writer's duty to shut up at times or at least to make room for those who can speak with more immediate authority—these are crucial questions for our time" (*Blood, Bread, and Poetry,* 131). To continue with her words: I guess what this solitary white male needs is "a history that does not simply 'include' peoples of color and white women, but that *shows the process* by which the arrogance of hierarchy and celebration of violence have reached a point of destructiveness almost out of control" (ibid., 144; my emphasis).

[87] Bultmann, *The Gospel of John,* 395 n. 1. Julius Grill's two-volume work, entitled *Untersuchungen über die Entstehung des vierten Evangeliums,* was published in 1902 and 1923 respectively.

[88] Staley, *The Print's First Kiss,* 95–118.

# CHAPTER THREE

# Fighting for Assistance:
## John 18:1–24 and the Agonistic Reader

[L]iterary criticism was and largely remains a kind of secular theodicy. Every decision made by a great artist could be shown to be a brillant one; works that had seemed flawed and uneven to an earlier generation of critics . . . were now revealed to be organic masterpieces.

—Stephen J. Greenblatt

It is almost as though he had decided to let whatever . . . disunity there is . . . unravel itself and gamble on being able to posit an authorial intention that would pull it all back together again.

—Stephen Moore

For is it only the desire for a masterful author that makes one into a slavish reader.

—Dennis Foster

Then Annas sent him bound to Caiaphas the high priest.

—John 18:24

### SUBVERSIVE NARRATORS, VICTIMIZED READERS

I'm back in an arena I know well—the stuff out of which dissertations are made. A brief introduction to a critical issue in literary theory, some historical examples to buttress an otherwise weak-sounding argument, a highly technical exegetical discussion about a rather minor problem in Johannine textual transmission, and I'll be on my way. My goal in all this will be to show conclusively, on the basis of early scribal evidence, that the Fourth Gospel had the effect of undercutting ancient readers' assumptions about the story that was being narrated. And by undercutting readers' expectations regarding the story, I believe that readers' ideological presuppositions were also being challenged.

If I do my work well, you will be convinced at the end that contemporary readers do not need to devise extratextual, rhetorical strategies for resisting the Fourth Gospel's message. The Fourth Gospel and its early copyists initiated that resistant work for us centuries ago. To put my thesis another way: If I do my work well you will see that the type of consciously constructed, resistant reader with which I concluded the last chapter was an unnecessary rhetorical conceit. For my argument in this chapter rests on the assumption that early Christian scribal activity proves that the Fourth Gospel contains within itself all the fractures required for fostering its own spectrum of resistant readings. In order to discover all the Fourth Gospel's natural lines of resistances we must not only peer into the text more closely than we have in the past; we must also pay more careful attention to the history of its textual transmission.

Having marked out the lines of my argument, let me begin by briefly introducing the critical issue of narration in biblical literary theory. For in the Fourth Gospel, the narrator is the source of the book's most subversive rhetorical strategies.

With the introduction of contemporary literary theory into the arena of New Testament studies in the late 1970s, attempts to describe Gospel narrators in contrast to redactors or authors were at the forefront of the developing agenda.[1] Issues such as the narrator's omniscience and omnipresence, reliability, and ideological point of view were discussed at length and in contrast to authorial intention and historical reference.[2] The dialogue was fruitful, and scholars gained important insights from the exchange. Without raising much controversy, scholars categorized Gospel narrators as undramatized, reliable, omniscient, and omnipresent.[3]

---

[1] For example, see Rhoads and Michie, *Mark as Story*, 23; Fowler, *Loaves and Fishes*, 166–67; Culpepper, *Anatomy of the Fourth Gospel*, 15–49; Pamment, "Focus in the Fourth Gospel," 71–75; Sternberg, *The Poetics of Biblical Narrative*, 50–128; Tannehill, *The Narrative Unity of Luke-Acts*, 6–9; Kingsbury, *Matthew as Story*, 31–37; Powell, *What Is Narrative Criticism?* 23–32; Fowler, *"Let the Reader Understand,"* 61–126; and Davies, *Rhetoric and Reference in the Fourth Gospel*, 31–43.

[2] The starting point for most of these discussions was Wayne Booth's *The Rhetoric of Fiction* (pp. 149–65), and Seymour Chatman's *Story and Discourse* (pp. 197–212).

[3] For example, see Culpepper, *Anatomy of the Fourth Gospel*, 16–34; cf. Sternberg, *The Poetics of Biblical Narrative*, 82–83; Gunn, "New Directions in the Study of the Biblical Hebrew

But by the mid-1980s other voices were beginning to raise questions about these all-encompassing definitions of biblical narrators and narration which were being generated by the new "narrative critics." Two such questioning voices can be heard: in James Dawsey's 1986 work, *The Lukan Voice: Confusion and Irony in the Gospel of Luke,* and in my own *The Print's First Kiss: A Rhetorical Investigation of the Implied Reader in the Fourth Gospel,* published in 1988.[4] Similar studies followed soon thereafter.[5] Stephen Moore documents the beginnings of the debate regarding the nature of Gospel narrators in his excellent study of the application of contemporary literary theory to biblical texts. There he uses Robert Tannehill and James Dawsey as dialogue partners over the narrative of the third Gospel.[6]

As Moore notes, the narrator whom Dawsey discovers in his meticulous articulation of the various voices in Luke's narrative is one whose view is "in some ways contradictory" to that of Jesus—the latter being a perspective with which the author sides over against that of the narrator.[7] The purpose of this "confusion" lies in the author's rhetoric of irony,[8] and Dawsey describes that strategy in the following manner: "One can imagine that the purpose of the irony at play in the views of the narrator and of Jesus would . . . be to chafe the audience into a change in perspective."[9] Later, he expands on this notion by saying:

> the narrator's misunderstanding of Jesus was the bridge that allowed for full participation in the story and led to decision. The meeting of Jesus and his community would have become possible when the community became so

---

Narrative," 65–71, esp. 69–71; and Gunn, "Reading Right: Reliable and Omniscient Narrator, Omniscient God, and Foolproof Composition in the Hebrew Bible," 53–64.

[4] Dawsey's book was a revision of his 1983 Emory Ph.D. dissertation entitled "The Literary Function of Point of View in Controlling Confusion and Irony in the Gospel of Luke"; mine was a Ph.D. dissertation done at the Graduate Theological Union in 1985.

[5] Henaut, "John 4:43–54 and the Ambivalent Narrator: A Response to Culpepper's *Anatomy of the Fourth Gospel*"; Braun, "Resisting John: Ambivalent Redactor and Defensive Reader of the Fourth Gospel"; Botha, "Reader 'Entrapment' as Literary Device in John 4:1–42"; Hedrick, "Authorial Presence and Narrator in John"; Kysar, "Johannine Metaphor — Meaning and Function: A Literary Case Study of John 10:1–8"; and Fowler, *"Let the Reader Understand,"* esp. 195–227.

[6] Moore, *Literary Criticism and the Gospels,* 29–40.

[7] Dawsey, *The Lukan Voice,* 104, 110, 143–56; cf. Moore, *Literary Criticism and the Gospels,* 32; and Darr, "Narrator As Character: Mapping A Reader-Oriented Approach to Narration in Luke-Acts," 43–60.

[8] Dawsey, *The Lukan Voice,* 154; see also 123–42.

[9] Ibid., 155.

immersed in the character of the narrator that it could be confronted by the incongruity between its words and Jesus' words.[10]

As Moore rightly points out, literary critics have invented a term for what Dawsey claims to have unearthed in Luke's Gospel, some two thousand years prior to its resurrection in the novels of Mark Twain and Henry James.[11] It is the "unreliable narrator," who, as Wayne Booth defines, does not speak for or act in accordance with the norms of the work, "which is to say, the implied author's norms."[12] Moore's challenges to Dawsey's reconstructed Lukan narrator are substantive and compelling: the possibility of a first-century author creating a consistently unreliable narrator such as Dawsey's "Lukan voice" seems indeed remote.[13] But in spite of these criticisms of Dawsey's work and some recent challenges to my own analysis of Johannine narrative strategies,[14] I still believe that my descriptions of the Johannine narrator are accurate.

My work, independent of that of Dawsey, followed a similar furrow but plowed a different field. I chose to focus my attention on the narrator of the Fourth Gospel, digging out the curious corrections and delayed descriptive statements that lie partially exposed in the topsoil of Johannine narrative style. But somewhat differently from Dawsey, I found the Johannine narrator at times contradicting *himself* along with his contradictions of minor characters' statements (John 3:22, 26; 4:2) and Jesus' words (7:1, 3–4, 8–9, 10).[15] At other times the narrator withheld information that later would prove essential to the meaning of the text, or the narrator simply prolonged the story beyond its seemingly logical conclusion.[16] Like Dawsey, I described all

---

[10] Ibid.

[11] Moore, *Literary Criticism and the Gospels*, 33.

[12] Booth, *Rhetoric of Fiction*, 158; Chatman, *Story and Discourse*, 223–37.

[13] Scholes and Kellogg, *The Nature of Narrative*, 264–65; Moore, *Literary Criticism and the Gospels*, 33. Sternberg, commenting on narrators in ancient Hebrew literature, writes: "[J]ust as the narrator is not the victim of irony on the author's part, so does he not indiscriminately traffic in irony at the reader's expense: his ironies, many and diverse, are situational rather than verbal" (*The Poetics of Biblical Narrative*, 51).

[14] For example, Culpepper has expressed his reservations in "Preface to the Paperback Edition" of *Anatomy of the Fourth Gospel* (p. x), as has Moloney in his book review of my dissertation and, more recently, in his *Belief in the Word* (p. 13 n. 51; p. 82 n. 21).

[15] From a redactional perspective, these texts have been traditionally understood as editorial glosses (e.g., Bultmann, *The Gospel of John*, 175–76; Brown, *The Gospel According to John*, 2:164–65; Schnackenburg, *The Gospel According to St. John*, 1:422 n. 6; Culpepper, *Anatomy of the Fourth Gospel*, 116). Some of these texts, like the one that is the focus of the present study, have also undergone textual emendation (e.g., 7:8, 10).

[16] See my analysis of John 2:1–12; 5:9; 6:59; 9:14; 10:40; 11:18; 13:1–30; and 20:30–21:25, in *The Print's First Kiss*, 95–105, 107 n. 57.

these embedded, narrative-busting elements as heavily ironized rhetorical ploys.[17] However, in spite of the narrative's contradictions and withheld information, I emphasized that the Fourth Gospel's narrator should be characterized as reliable, since he always corrected his "mistakes" or "oversights," thus reestablishing a trustworthy relationship between himself and his narratees/implied reader.[18]

I believed at the time, and still believe, that characterizing the Johannine narrator as reliable, and yet as one who was willing to use a "victimizing" or "entrapping" strategy to educate his implied reader, is a better solution to the Fourth Gospel's narratological problems than is arguing for the narrator's pervasive unreliability or confusion.[19] As Wayne Booth has noted, "most of the great reliable narrators indulge in large amounts of incidental irony, and they are thus 'unreliable' in the sense of being potentially deceptive. But difficult irony is not sufficient to make a narrator unreliable."[20] More recently, other studies in Johannine narrative have seemed to confirm my original conclusions.[21] For example, Stephen Moore says that the reading he enacted of John 4:1–15, 7:37–39, and 19:28–34 implied "that the recipients of the Fourth Gospel are the ultimate victims of its irony,"[22] and both Eugene Botha and

[17] Ibid., 83–90, 105–18.

[18] Ibid., 116–17. Regarding the relationship between the implied or encoded reader and the narratee in the Fourth Gospel, I have argued that its narratee is "only tenuously distinguished from the implied reader" (ibid., 46). Similarly, Robert Fowler observes that in Mark, "the roles of the narrator and narratee are covert and effaced and therefore virtually identical with the roles of the implied author and implied reader, respectively; the distance involved in these relationships is absolutely minimal" (*"Let the Reader Understand,"* 33; see also Howell, *Matthew's Inclusive Story*, 205–11, 243–45; and Reinhartz, *The Word in the World*, 7).

[19] Staley, *The Print's First Kiss*, 98. I borrowed the language of victimization from John McKee (*Literary Irony and the Literary Audience*, 82–87; see also Richter, "The Reader as Ironic Victim," 135–51), while the language of entrapment came from John O'Neill ("The Experience of Error: Ironic Entrapment in Augustan Narrative Satire," 278–90; see also Fish, *Is There a Text in This Class?* 21–67; Foster, *Confession and Complicity in Narrative*, 1–19; and Mailloux, *Rhetorical Power*, 43–44).

[20] Booth, *The Rhetoric of Fiction*, 159; see also his *A Rhetoric of Irony*, 233–77.

[21] For example, see Eslinger, "The Wooing of the Woman at the Well: The Reader and Reader-Response Criticism," 169–70, 173 n. 16, 175; Reinhartz, "Great Expectations: A Reader-Oriented Approach to Johannine Christology and Eschatology," 72; Henaut, "John 4:43–54 and the Ambivalent Narrator: A Response to Culpepper's *Anatomy of the Fourth Gospel*," 300; Braun, "Resisting John: Ambivalent Redactor and Defensive Reader of the Fourth Gospel," 61–62, 70–71; Grayston, "Who Misunderstands Johannine Misunderstandings?" 9, 14; and Hedrick, "Authorial Presence and Narrator in John," 84–93.

[22] Moore, *Literary Criticism of the Gospels*, 168. More recently he has argued that "Jesus . . . is the main ironic casuality" (*Poststructuralism and the New Testament*, 62 n. 68).

Robert Kysar have found numerous instances of "reader entrapment" or "reader victimization" strategies in John 4 and 10.[23]

But granting the point that such a phenomenon could exist in Johannine narrative poetics, what would be its function within the author's overall purpose? Here I argued that in a story designed for insiders (20:30–31), the narrator's contradictions and withheld information—like the strategy of a Socratic *eirōn*—force the implied or encoded reader into the role of an outsider: the implied reader is necessarily an error-prone reader who can never feel as though his grasp of Jesus or the life of faith is absolute.[24] Nevertheless, the implied or encoded reader must also be one who learns from his mistakes and hasty judgments, since the group of characters with whom he shares his errors and confusions shifts from being the Pharisees and Jesus' unbelieving brothers, to being the disciples and, finally, Peter.[25]

To my surprise, I later discovered that my description of the Johannine implied reader closely resembled Robert Fowler's characterization of the Markan reader, who, Fowler says, probably operates at a level of faith development "where persons are able to deal comfortably with ambiguity, irony, and paradox."[26]

### SOCRATES' IRONY, CLITOPHON'S TRICKERY

In *Socrates, Ironist and Moral Philosopher,* Gregory Vlastos begins his careful study of Socratic irony by noting that, from Aristophanes to Theophrastus,

---

[23] Botha, "Reader 'Entrapment' as Literary Device in John 4:1–42," 41–45; and Kysar, "Johannine Metaphor—Meaning and Function: A Literary Case Study of John 10:1–8," 94–95.

[24] Staley, *The Print's First Kiss,* 98, 107. My use of masculine pronouns to denote the implied or encoded reader is purposeful. The shared reading conventions of the ancient Mediterranean world would presume that when the gender of narrators and narratees was unmarked in public texts, these entities (and thus their corresponding implied authors and encoded readers) would be masculine (ibid., 28, 43; cf. Burnett, "Reflections on Keeping the Implied Reader an 'It': Why I Love Wolfgang Iser"; Malina and Neyrey, "First-Century Personality: Dyadic, Not Individual," 72–83).

[25] Staley, *The Print's First Kiss,* 98, 102–3, esp. n. 40, 116.

[26] Fowler, *"Let the Reader Understand,"* 226; cf. Anderson, *The Christology of the Fourth Gospel,* 147–51. See also Fowler's later chapter, entitled "An Ambivalent Narrative?" 261–66 (cf. Liebert, "That You May Believe: The Fourth Gospel and Structural Development Theory," 67–73; and Durber, "The Female Reader of the Parables of the Lost," 59–78). Descriptions of ideal, first-century readers tend to read like the psycho-biographies of the late twentieth-century biblical scholars doing the literary analysis. The connection should not be overlooked. However, that connection lies at the root of another story, one that will be elaborated in chapters 4 and 5 (below).

the root *eirōn* in Greek literature consistently denotes "sly, intentionally deceptive speech or conduct."[27] Vlastos's argument, however, is that, in the case of Socrates, the word takes on a derivative but crucially different meaning. When describing the central character of Plato's *Dialogues,* the word *eirōn* implies "speech used to express a meaning that runs contrary to what is said—the perfect medium for mockery innocent of deceit."[28]

Thus, part of the enjoyment of reading Plato's *Dialogues* comes from the reader's knowledge that Socrates is constantly mocking his interlocutors' false wisdom—without their knowing that they are being duped. This gentle mockery or Socratic irony is meant, of course, to lead Socrates' students to knowledge of the truth. Even in the difficult case of the young, virile Alcibiades, who is led to believe that Socrates is sexually attracted to him and so climbs in bed with him (only to find a cold shoulder in his face), Vlastos argues that Alcibiades deceives himself. Socrates simply refuses to do anything to dispel Alcibiades' misconstrual of his doubled language.[29]

It is one thing to argue that, in the Fourth Gospel, Jesus is like Socrates, doubling words and phrases at his interlocutors' expense—or even to point out that Nicodemus and the Samaritan woman function as Jesus' Alcibiades. But it is quite another thing to imply that the *narrator* of the Fourth Gospel likewise acts with Socrates' argumentative agenda. Even granting the rather minor point I have just argued for—that the narrator of the Fourth Gospel is reliable rather than unreliable—one is left to ask whether there exists any evidence from the ancient world that authors invented narrators who, although reliable, nevertheless occasionally feign ignorance and suppress their own knowledge for the sake of educating or entertaining their audiences.

In his article entitled "Authorial Presence and Narrator in John," Charles Hedrick seems to be searching for exactly this evidence. He observes how, in the Fourth Gospel, "intrusive comments that do not derive from the 'principal narrator' of the showing of the story . . . improve the showing of the story by clarifying what is apparently conceived as obscurity in the story's showing . . . [and, among other things,] correct errors made by the principal narrator."[30] Although Hedrick's discussion exhibits some confusion regarding the narratological distinction between implied authors and narrators, his work is

---

[27] Vlastos, *Socrates, Ironist and Moral Philosopher,* 25. See also Michael Stokes's discussion of "Platonic questions" (*Plato's Socratic Conversations,* 7–35; cf. Teloh, *Socratic Education in Plato's Dialogues,* 24–40; and Swearington, *Rhetoric and Irony,* 55–94).

[28] Vlastos, *Socrates, Ironist and Moral Philosopher,* 28.

[29] Ibid., 43–44.

[30] Hedrick, "Authorial Presence and Narrator in John," 92.

useful, particularly for its attempt to find in other ancient texts Johannine-like "extraneous voices . . . that compete with the principle [*sic*] narrator of the story."[31]

Hedrick's search for correcting and clarifying narrators in nonbiblical literature takes him to the ancient Greek romance *Leucippe and Clitophon*. In this third-century C.E. work attributed to Achilles Tatius, Hedrick finds a voice, other than that of the principal narrator, intruding at various points in the story, giving "learned digressions (diatribes) on various subjects for the moral edification of the (implied) readers."[32] Hedrick's argument is that this secondary interpretive voice, or "hermeneut" as he calls it, is the same phenomenon that biblical scholars have named "redaction" in Johannine literature.[33]

Although Hedrick has pointed out some important narratological congruencies between the Fourth Gospel and *Leucippe and Clitophon,* he fails to mention an additional point of similarity: the romance contains perhaps the most extravagant examples in ancient literature of a reliable narrator who victimizes his readers. This happens quite graphically on three occasions; and in a fourth and final variation on the strategy, the narrator tellingly lets the reader in on the joke prior to its revelation to the unsuspecting character.[34] *Leucippe and Clitophon* opens with a detailed description of a votive painting which the unnamed first-person narrator sees during a tour of Sidon. But when another character interrupts the narrator's intense preoccupation with the picture by exclaiming, "How well I know it—for all the indignities Love has made *me* suffer,"[35] the narrator quickly relinquishes his role to Clitophon, the one who "has suffered Love's indignities." The original first-person narrator then becomes the narrative's narratee.

The implied author has made it evident from the opening scene of the romance that a painting can represent prolepsis and prefiguration in a central

---

[31] Ibid.

[32] Ibid., 91.

[33] Ibid., 93.

[34] *Leucippe and Clitophon,* 3:7–15; 5:7–8; 5:17–19; 7:1–6, 15–16. See also Hägg, *Narrative Technique in Ancient Greek Romances,* 133–35.

[35] *Leucippe and Clitophon,* 1:2. It is important to note that Clitophon is introduced singly, and as a man who has suffered much because of love. Thus, the opening scene of the romance overdetermines the narrative's hermeneutic code in order to reinforce the victimization strategy found much later, when Clitophon's lover, Leucippe, appears to die (Hägg, *Narrative Technique in Ancient Greek Romances,* 124–26, 239–40; for a definition of narrative "overdetermination" and "codes," see p. 95 n. 49 below).

character's life.[36] So later on, when Clitophon and his lover Leucippe are entranced by a painting of Andromeda and Prometheus as prisoners, chained to rocks, the reader knows that this does not bode well for the lovers.[37] Thus the reader is not surprised when, in the next series of events, Leucippe is ritually slaughtered by pirates and cannibalized.[38] Clitophon, the retrospective narrator, reinforces the scene's authenticity with his eyewitness depiction of Leucippe being led to the sacrificial altar.[39] A few paragraphs later, however, the reader discovers that Leucippe's apparent death had been a carefully planned ruse to free her from the pirates. In this text, then, the character Clitophon, the pirates, and the reader have all been unsuspecting victims of Clitophon the narrator's storytelling trickery.

In the next instance of reader victimization, the narrator once again introduces upcoming events with a painting. This time, however, the character Clitophon realizes that the painting he is viewing is an ominous sign, and so he delays sailing to Pharos.[40] But in spite of Clitophon's attempts to ward off disaster, Leucippe again is kidnapped by pirates. This second group of pirates decapitates the unfortunate woman. The narrative episode concludes with the grief-stricken Clitophon burying his lover's headless body on the beach.[41] Neither the reader nor Clitophon discovers that Leucippe is still alive until Clitophon receives a letter from her, six months after her apparent death.[42]

The final instance of reader victimization takes place in the sixth month after Leucippe's "second death," when Clitophon sails to Ephesos and takes a tour of the estate of his new wife, Melite. There, in the orchards, a slave woman throws herself at Melite and Clitophon's feet and begs for her freedom. Although the woman gives her name as Lakaina and says that she is from Thessaly, Clitophon thinks she looks much like his erstwhile beloved Leucippe, recently beheaded and buried. But it will be another page and a half before Clitophon and the reader know for sure that Lakaina is indeed Leucippe.[43]

---

[36] Of course, dreams also represent prolepsis. For example, Leucippe's mother has a dream that her daughter is butchered by bandits (*Leucippe and Clitophon*, 2:23; Hägg, *Narrative Technique in Ancient Greek Romances,* 237–42).

[37] *Leucippe and Clitophon*, 3:7–8.

[38] Ibid., 3:15.

[39] Ibid.

[40] Ibid., 5:3–5.

[41] Ibid., 5:7–8.

[42] Ibid., 5:18.

[43] Ibid., 5:17–19.

The victimizing ploys in *Leucippe and Clitophon* are unusually bold, and they differ in two important ways from the Fourth Gospel narrator's entrapment strategy. In the romance, reader victimizations occur in major plot developments and for no apparent educative purpose. The victimizations seem to function only as entertainment devices, to hold the reader's attention and deepen the narrative's suspense. By way of contrast, the encoded reader's knowledge of Christian tradition made it less likely that the Fourth Gospel's narrator could have freely manipulated that story's major plot.[44] Thus, the Fourth Gospel's victimization strategy is found only within minor plot developments. Furthermore, like Socratic irony, the Fourth Gospel's victimization strategy is used more to educate the reader than to entertain the reader. Despite these differences, the third-century romance *Leucippe and Clitophon* proves that an ancient writer could on occasion create a narrative with a reliable narrator who nevertheless could mislead his readers. And Plato's portrayal of an ironical Socrates provides the rhetorical context for using the strategy in more open ideological narratives such as the Fourth Gospel.

In the discussion below I intend to continue to explore the implications of the Fourth Gospel's subversive narrator along with its strategy of victimizing, or entrapping, the encoded reader. But there is an added twist to my argument in this final foray along the borders of formalism. In order to wrest from John 18:12–24 some objective evidence of the Johannine encoded reader, I will use as hermeneutical double agents ancient textual variants and modern attempts to reconstruct the sources behind the text. First, the double agents will function as spies, exposing the rhetorical strategy of the Johannine narrator. Then they will become my war trophies; my prisoners captured in the exegetical battles of reader criticism—proof that other flesh-and-blood readers have attempted to fight off the covert entrapment strategy of the Johannine narrator.

---

[44] Once again, my understanding of the reader as an "encoded reader" has it roots in my dissertation. There I defined the implied reader as an "intratextual" property of texts that "interconnected with a myriad of other worlds," as being "denoted in the temporal quality of narrative," yet sensitive to the "text's [overarching] strategies" (*The Print's First Kiss*, 33–36; see also p. 28 above; cf. Fowler, *"Let the Reader Understand,"* 9–58; Reinhartz, *The Word in the World,* 7–14).

I noted earlier that this rhetorical, formalist reader has not been lacking for critics (Wuellner, "Is there an Encoded Reader Fallacy?"; Berg, "Reading in/to Mark"; Tolbert, "A Response from a Literary Perspective"; see also pp. 11–13 above). But as I argued in the preceding chapter, I am now more comfortable with saying that my previously textually defined "implied" or "encoded reader" is better conceived as a consciously chosen reading strategy rather than as an inherent property of the Johannine text (p. 57 above; see further Moore, *Literary Criticism and the Gospels,* 71–73; Calinescu, *Rereading,* 44–56; Brooke-Rose, *A Rhetoric of the Unreal,* 105).

THE MENACE OF JOHANNINE PASSION PLOTTING

Like ancient Greek romances, the plot structure of the Johannine passion narrative is straightforward, sequential, and "syntagmatic" rather then episodic, thematic, or "paradigmatic."[45] It opens with a betrayal in a garden (18:1–3) and is followed by Jesus' arrest (18:4–18) and his two questionings (18:19–19:16). The arrest and questionings lead to Jesus' crucifixion and death (19:17–37) and his subsequent burial by a secret disciple (19:38–42). There is, then, a sequence of events which is causally and temporally connected and can be easily followed by the reader.[46]

But beyond the simple analysis of plot or "proairetic code,"[47] the passion narrative also exhibits a chiastic structure,[48] which emphasizes or "overdetermines" the author's ideological and argumentative concerns.[49] These concerns comprise the text's "hermeneutic code."[50] As many scholars have noted, the opening and closing scenes (*a* and *a´*) both take place in gardens (18:1–3 and 19:38–42), and both evoke negative images of discipleship.[51] In *a*, the negative image is captured by the epithet "Judas, who betrayed him" (18:2), while in *a´*, the portrayals of Joseph of Arimathea and Nicodemus are more positive, but still less than ideal.[52]

---

[45] For a discussion of "syntagmatic" and "paradigmatic" plot arrangement, see Funk, *The Poetics of Biblical Narrative,* 17–18, 46. For a broader view of my analysis of Johannine plot structure, see "The Structure of John's Prologue: Its Implications for the Gospel's Narrative Structure," 241–64.

[46] Cf. Smith, *John,* 99–100; Culpepper, *Anatomy of the Fourth Gospel,* 89–98; Giblin, "Confrontations in John 18,1–27," 210–15, 230–31.

[47] Brooke-Rose (*A Rhetoric of the Unreal,* 38–42; cf. Calinescu, *Rereading,* 211–12) uses the language of "codes," following Roland Barthes. For Brooke-Rose, the "proairetic code" is the "code of actions," which includes plot and sequence (*A Rhetoric of the Unreal,* 38).

[48] This type of narrative structuring is probably derived from oral rhetoric (Fowler, *"Let the Reader Understand,"* 151–52). Clearly, chiasms are not something contemporary readers hear. We are dependent on our eyes for noting this phenomenon.

[49] Christine Brooke-Rose defines "overdetermination" as instances when a narrative code's "information (narrative, ironic, hermeneutic, symbolic, etc.) is too clear, overencoded, recurring beyond pure informational need" (*A Rhetoric of the Unreal,* 106).

Unless otherwise denoted, when I use the term "author" I mean an "implied author," which is "that pragmatic category of narrative which distances reader from author and forces the role of interpretant upon the reader . . . , that singular consciousness which the reader constructs from the words of a text" (*The Print's First Kiss,* 29).

[50] Brooke-Rose, *A Rhetoric of the Unreal,* 39.

[51] For example, see Peter Ellis, *The Genius of John,* 254–55.

[52] Sylva, "Nicodemus and his Spices," 148–51; Bassler, "Mixed Signals: Nicodemus in the Fourth Gospel," 635–46; Senior, *The Passion of Jesus in the Gospel of John,* 130–33; and Countryman, *The Mystical Way in the Fourth Gospel,* 122.

In the next set of frames, *b* and *b'* (18:4–32 and 19:23–37), eight prophecies are fulfilled. In *b,* the four prophetic references are intratextual, as Jesus' and Caiaphas's statements from earlier in the narrative are fulfilled (18:9, cf. 10:28; 17:12; 18:14, cf. 11:50–52; 18:17–18, 25–27, cf. 13:38, 16:32 [here Peter's false testimony is interrupted by Jesus' faithful testimony, vv. 19–24]; 18:31–32, cf. 12:31–33). But in *b'* the four prophetic references are intertextual, since events surrounding Jesus' crucifixion are related to four unnamed texts from ancient Jewish writings (19:23–24, cf. Ps 22:18; 19:28–30, cf. Ps 22:15; 19:31, cf. Exod 12:46 [also Num 9:12; Ps 34:20]; 19:33–34, cf. Zech 12:10). Additionally, in *b',* the true witness of "him who saw" the lance thrust into Jesus' side (19:35) stands in contrast to Peter's wild-slashing sword and his threefold denials (*b*).

Finally, the center of the passion narrative's chiastic structure focuses on the ideological issue of Jesus' sonship ([*d*] 19:7–11) and is framed by the political implications of Jesus' alleged kingship ([*c* and *c'*] 18:33–19:6 and 19:12–22).[53] Within this central framing section there is also an oblique balancing of private and public scenes, with Pilate questioning Jesus inside (18:33–38a; 19:1–3, 9–11), followed by either Pilate's legal judgments or the Jewish leaders' accusations made outside (18:38b–40; 19:4–8, 12–22).[54]

Thus, the plot structure and ideologically contrived, chiastic symmetry can be set out as follows:

| *Plot Structure* | *Chiastic Symmetry* |
| --- | --- |
| (1)  Betrayal, 18:1–3 | (a)  In a garden, 18:1–3 |
| (2)  Arrest, 18:4–18 | (b)  Four prophecies fulfilled, 18:4–32 |
| (3)  Official questionings, 18:19–19:16 | (c)  Questions about kingship, 8:33–19:6 |

---

[53] For example, Raymond Brown (*The Gospel According to John,* 2:857–59), Peter Ellis (*The Genius of John,* 264), and Ernst Haenchen (*John,* 2:186) all note the author's careful balancing of kingship claims but fail to see that the center of the chiasm focuses on the ideological issue of Jesus' sonship and takes its dramatic turn when Pilate "grows more fearful" (19:7–8; cf. Brown, *The Gospel According to John,* 2:891). See also Giblin for a slightly different structuring ("John's Narration of the Hearing before Pilate [John 18,28-19, 16a]," 221–39, esp. 222–24).

[54] Brown, *The Gospel According to John,* 2:859; Ellis, *The Genius of John,* 258, 260; Schnackenburg, *The Gospel According to St. John,* 2:242; and Haenchen, *John,* 2:186. Donald Senior's observation is more to the point: "The power of the trial scene is found not in the symmetry of its structure but in the dynamism of the narrative" (*The Passion of Jesus,* 69; cf. 90–91; Schnackenburg, *The Gospel According to St. John,* 259–60).

|  |  | (d) | Questions about divine sonship, 19:7–11 |
| --- | --- | --- | --- |
| (4) | Crucifixion and death, 19:17–37 | (c′) | Questions about kingship, 19:12–22 |
|  |  | (b′) | Four prophecies fulfilled, 19:23–37 |
| (5) | Burial, 19:38–42 | (a′) | In a garden, 19:38–42[55] |

From an authorial perspective—that is, from a static, comprehensive, and wide-angle view of the text—the passion narrative's symmetry reinforces a particular reading and ideological stance over and above its simple plot line: a reading and stance where, in spite of the cacophony of characters and mixed motives that propel Jesus to his death, God's (and thus Jesus') purpose is being accomplished.[56] As early as his discourse on the shepherd and sheep (10:1–30), Jesus had clearly and forcefully laid down the body of his mission before his opponents. There he had spoken of himself as the "good shepherd [who] lays down his life for the sheep" (10:11; cf. 19:28–31); there he had said that no one could take his life from him, for he had "power to lay it down, and . . . take it up again" (10:18; cf. 19:10–11).[57]

Now, once again, that most explicit revelation of Jesus' purpose is echoed in the unusual clustering of words found in the opening scenes of the passion narrative (18:1–40). For a second time the nouns "gatekeeper," "gate," "courtyard" (*aulē*), and "bandit" from the shepherd discourse are used. In this latter context, however, it is to the "other disciple" and Peter that the gate-keeper opens the gate (18:17; cf. 10:3, 18:37).[58] But characters like Judas,

[55] For two other recent assessments of chiastic structures in the Johannine passion narrative, see Ellis (*The Genius of John,* 247–49, 278–79) and Mlakuzhyil (*The Christocentric Literary Structure of the Fourth Gospel,* 228–35, 335–39).

[56] Ignace de la Potterie put it this way: "The careful reader will be struck by two details [in the Johannine passion narrative]: the complete self-awareness of Jesus, several times indicated, and also the majesty with which he goes forward to his Passion" (*The Hour of Jesus,* 16; cf. Schnackenburg, *The Gospel According to St. John,* 3:218–20; Senior, *The Passion of Jesus,* 31–39, et al.). By way of comparison, note how Jesus' own words in 18:11 and 19:11 confirm the author's ideological stance.

[57] See especially Sabbe, *John 10 and its Relationship to the Synoptic Gospels,* 75–93; cf. Howard-Brook, *Becoming Children of God,* 384.

[58] Brown, *The Gospel According to John,* 2:859. By having the gatekeeper open the gate to the "other (beloved?) disciple," the encoded reader is being led to shift his allegiance from the community of Jesus, where Jesus was shepherd (10:2–3), to a later community of Jesus, where a disciple will be "shepherd" (cf. Neyrey, "The Footwashing in John 13:6–11—Transformation Ritual or Ceremony?" 210–12; and Stibbe, *John as Storyteller,* 100–104).

who do not enter through the gate (10:1, cf. 18:16) into the courtyard (10:1, cf. 18:15), are thieves and bandits (10:1, cf. 12:6; 18:30). Not coincidentally, Jesus' earlier confrontation with "the Jews" had also taken place during the winter (10:22; cf. 18:1); and the temple (10:22–30) was the place where, as Jesus now says, he had "spoken openly to the world" (18:20).[59]

Thus, the strongly overdetermined proairetic code (plot), hermeneutic code (symmetry), and symbolic code (allusions and echoes) all work together to constrict and limit real readers' penchant for aberrant interpretive moves.[60] Yet, paradoxically, it is precisely in the context of the author's attempt to control tightly the encoded reader's sense-making activities that real readers' forward flow of thought has been disturbingly arrested, reading after reading. For there in the high priest's courtyard (18:12–28) a cohort of variant readings rise up and bear witness to the confusion of many real readers: Who is the high priest (*ho archiereus,* 18:19) to whom Jesus has been taken? Is it Annas or Caiaphas? Into whose courtyard have the other disciple, Peter, and readers been admitted?

## TEXT CRITICISM AS RECEPTION HISTORY

In the pre-print era, real readers of the Fourth Gospel were just as often the producers and transmitters of the text as they were its consumers. But as copyists, they could become writers of new texts in ways that contemporary critics cannot, easily fitting George Steiner's description of the contemporary reader-critic who "is judge and master of the text."[61]

Like modern-day commentators, many of those copyists were either well-versed in the Synoptic trial tradition or knew the Fourth Gospel well enough to realize that only Caiaphas had previously been called "high priest" by the narrator. So for either or both of these reasons, many of these pre-print-era reader-critics simply "corrected" the text to fit what they knew to be "right."

---

In a few moments, when Jesus is about to die, the encoded reader will see this shift of allegiance more explicitly. There the author will have Jesus transfer his role of "son" to the "Beloved Disciple" (19:26–27).

[59] Schnackenburg and Fortna both note a number of allusions to John 10 in John 18—in the form of christological statements—but neither of them mentions the "gate" metaphor itself (*The Gospel According to St. John,* 2:225–26; *The Fourth Gospel and its Predecessor,* 159).

[60] Following Roger Poole and Harold Bloom, Willi Braun would call this the "menace of the gospel text" ("Resisting John: Ambivalent Redactor and Defensive Reader of the Fourth Gospel," 63).

[61] As quoted in Fowler, *"Let the Reader Understand,"* 27, 31.

And while certainly not all ancient readers would have been disturbed by the minor discordant refrain of John 18:24,[62] the textual variants are nevertheless vivid testimonials to real readers' readings. They are the silent witnesses to the fact that the narrator's statement and placement of John 18:24 has, for nearly two thousand years, forced readers to reassess their constructions of the interrogation scene.

My purpose here, however, is not to review the numerous text-critical problems of John 18:13–24, nor to summarize the variety of source-critical solutions that have been proposed for this pericope over the past hundred years.[63] Rather, my intention is simply to point out that the history of the text's transmission and of scholars' reconstructed sources speaks eloquently to the variety of ways in which some real readers have sought to make sense out of a disruptive text.

So instead of using the various manuscript traditions, erasures, and source-critical theories to ascertain the original, or "copy text,"[64] my approach will be to use this data as an empirically verifiable "reception history."[65] From this evidence of real readers' readings I can then move on to show how reader-response criticism's theoretical concern for the reading process might make rhetorical sense out of the narrator's statement and placement of 18:24. From the evidence of real readers' readings I can also make rhetorical sense out of the history of the text's reception, without taking recourse to rewriting John 18:24 or hypothesizing earlier sources.

To paraphrase for the Fourth Gospel what Robert Fowler says of Mark, I will be arguing that modern scholars and ancient readers have unconsciously been impressed by the rhetorical or pragmatic function of the language of the Fourth Gospel, that is, by the ways it is designed to affect the reader. In other

---

[62] For example, see Malina's description of "low context" and "high context" societies ("Reading Theory Perspective: Reading Luke-Acts," 19–21).

[63] For example, see the text-critical studies of Bernard (*A Critical and Exegetical Commentary on the Gospel according to St. John,* 1:xxvi–xxviii), Mahoney ("A New Look at an Old Problem [John 18, 12–14, 19–24]," 137–44); the theological and literary-critical studies of Chevallier ("La comparution de Jésus devant Hanne et devant Caïphe [Jean 18/12–14 et 19–24]," 178–85), Giblin ("Confrontations in John 18,1–27," 222–26), and Charbonneau ("L'interrogatoire de Jésus, d'après la facture interne de Jn 18,12–27," 191–210); and the source-critical studies of Fortna (*The Fourth Gospel and Its Predecessors,* 155–63) and Matera ("Jesus Before Annas: John 18.13, 14, 19–24," 38–55).

[64] McGann, *A Critique of Modern Textual Criticism,* 24–26.

[65] For a description of reception theory, see especially Holub, *Reception Theory,* xi–xiv, and Jauss, *Toward an Aesthetic of Reception,* 32–45. For a practical demonstration of its methodology, see Mailloux, *Interpretive Conventions,* 159–91, and his more recent *Rhetorical Power,* 36–53.

words, the pragmatics of the narrative have asserted themselves throughout the centuries, and in spite of modern critical and ancient scribal approaches designed to bypass pragmatics in favor of semantics.[66]

The plethora of variant readings and reconstructed sources for John 18:13–24 share one common concern: to move 18:24 ("Then Annas sent him bound to Caiaphas the high priest") to a position earlier in the text, placing it just after 18:13a or 18:13. Thus, the "original text" would have read something like this: "First they led him [Jesus] to Annas, who was the father-in-law of Caiaphas, the high priest that year. Then Annas sent him bound to Caiaphas the high priest. Caiaphas was the one who had advised the Jews . . . ."[67] In this way the disquieting question, Who is the high priest before whom Jesus appeared? is easily and quickly answered—or rather it is no longer a question that would even arise for a reader, since the one and only named high priest in the story is Caiaphas.[68] The reading sequence is thereby "smoothed out," and

---

[66] See Fowler, *"Let the Reader Understand,"* 53.

[67] Bruce Metzger's and Edwyn Hoskyns's arguments regarding the textual variants are based on intertextual evidence. Hoskyns simply argues that the variants were "attempts to harmonize the Fourth Gospel with the synoptic tradition" (*The Fourth Gospel,* 512), while Metzger believes that the order of the Sinaitic Syriac text (18:13, 24, 14–15, 19–23, 16–18, 25–27) is probably governed more directly by Tatian's second-century *Diatessaron* (*A Textual Commentary on the Greek New Testament,* 251–52). Although it has long since disappeared, Fowler describes the *Diatessaron* as still a "powerful reading grid" in the contemporary Christian world (*"Let the Reader Understand,"* 264–66).

The Synoptic/*Diatessaron* texts provide possible solutions as to why John 18:24 was rearranged, but they are not the reason why Caiaphas is mentioned in the first place; nor do they create the problem of the narrator's *delayed* reference, a reference that could have been placed earlier, after 18:13. The problem of the delayed reference is strictly an intratextual problem (cf. Senior, *The Passion of Jesus,* 57–63). For some of the narrator's less disruptive delayed references, see John 1:28; 6:59; and 11:18.

[68] The noun *archiereus* is normally plural in the Fourth Gospel (7:32, 45; 11:47, 57; 12:10; 18:3, 26, 35; 19:6, 15, 21) and is usually translated "chief priests." This perplexing plural has led most commentators to propose a historical solution to the Fourth Gospel's problematical picture of the Jewish high priesthood.

For some commentators, the ambiguity over the high priesthoods of Annas and Caiaphas simply reveals the author's ignorance of Second Temple Judaism: the narrator's phrase *hos ēn archiereus tou eniautou ekeinou* (11:49, 51; 18:13), must imply that the author thought Judaism had a rotating high priesthood—perhaps like those found in pagan temples of Asia Minor (Bultmann, *The Gospel of John,* 410 n. 10; Brown, *The Gospel According to John,* 1:439; Haenchen, *John,* 2:75, 167; et al.). Or perhaps Annas is given the title by honor (Brown, *The Gospel According to John,* 2:820–21). But regardless of these solutions, the fact remains that Caiaphas has been the only person explicitly called high priest (singular noun) in the Fourth Gospel (*eis de tis ex autōn,* 11:49). Because of the earlier reference, John 18:15–24 was confusing enough to elicit rewriting the scene.

readers are not forced to go back and re-read the scene in order to see where and how they missed a nonexistent reference to "Annas who was also called high priest."

But apart from the textual or source reconstructions which seek to rectify a later problem (18:24), there is no ambiguity at the beginning of the scene (18:12–14) and no reason for the reader to question the narrator's veracity. As a matter of fact, when Annas is first introduced, the narrator takes pains to situate him in the story world since Annas is a man hitherto unknown to the encoded reader, and is a curiosity-arousing addition to the narrative.[69] Annas is thus "the father-in-law of Caiaphas the high priest," a character who had been introduced earlier in the text. Furthermore, as the scene shifts to the attempts of Peter and "another disciple" to get close to the proceedings (18:15–18), the subsequent parenthetical references to the high priest do nothing to disrupt the reader's reconstruction of the events: another disciple, who was known to the high priest (Caiaphas) brings Peter into the courtyard of the high priest's house. Logically, at this point, the reader can only make the gap-filling deduction that Annas must be at Caiaphas's house, for Peter and "another disciple" have followed Jesus (18:15), and the narrator has just finished saying that Jesus had been brought to Annas (18:12).[70] Yet even this somewhat surprising development creates no disturbances in the reading sequence—only in the reader's reconstruction of a sparsely painted scene.

Curiously, once Peter gets inside the high priest's courtyard the narrator's scenic description begins to get more detailed (18:16–18). Now the narrator mentions a number of kinds of people (a woman who is the gatekeeper, slaves, and the temple police), the weather (it was cold), and the seemingly inconsequential fact that some people were standing around a charcoal fire, warming themselves. This scenic description works to heighten the drama of the story, since it momentarily postpones the inevitable confrontation between Jesus, Annas, and the high priest (18:19–24) which the encoded reader has been led to expect (11:45–52; 18:12–14). But, more importantly,

---

[69] Annas is obviously unknown to the encoded reader, for he is introduced by the qualifying phrase "the father-in-law of Caiaphas" (18:13; cf. Culpepper, *Anatomy of the Fourth Gospel,* 213–16; Staley, *The Print's First Kiss,* 44–45).

[70] Augustine's conjecture—"Annas and Caiaphas lived in different wings of the same palace," which were "bound together by a common courtyard" (Brown, *The Gospel According to John,* 2:823; Schnackenburg, *The Gospel According to St. John,* 3:239–40)—is another way that real readers might at this point fill in the limited scenic frame. However, Augustine's attempt to fill the apparent scenic gap is merely one of many possible readerly reconstructions of the Johannine story world, and should not be treated as though it were a real-world reference.

through this most visual scene of Peter's denial, the encoded reader is led to reflect on the meaning of true discipleship.

Earlier in the story the encoded reader had fully identified with the character Peter. It was he of whom Jesus had said, "You are to be called Cephas" (1:42), and it was he who confessed, "Lord, to whom can we go? You have the words of eternal life. We have come to believe and know that you are the Holy One of God" (6:67–69). Yet the encoded reader has subsequently learned to disassociate himself from Peter because of his inability to understand what Jesus was about to undergo (13:6–9, 36–38; 18:10–11).[71] In the high priest's courtyard, as in the dramatically visual footwashing and meal scene (13:6–11, 21–30), Peter is not in control of the situation. Here in the courtyard Peter acts like an outsider, both by denying that he had been one of Jesus' disciples (18:17),[72] and by choosing to stand beside the charcoal fire with the high priest's slaves and the temple police (*hoi douloi kai hoi hypēretai*, 18:18). Although Peter had depended on another, unknown disciple in order to get inside the courtyard and mingle at the insiders' fire, Peter now seems to have been abandoned. The "other disciple," after performing his narrative function of getting Peter into the courtyard, has mysteriously disappeared. That other disciple will not emerge again until Jesus is near death, at a time when, significantly, Peter is nowhere in sight (19:25–27).[73]

While the character Peter was originally introduced in the Gospel as a positive model of discipleship, the temple police (*hypēretai*) are agents—far from fully developed characters—who are never described positively (cf. 7:32, 45–46; 19:6). They, along with Judas and the cohort, appeared abruptly on the scene as the narrative tension began to rise (18:3). Only once does any of them speak, and that is when one slaps Jesus and asks him, "Is that how you answer the high priest?" (18:21–22). So while the author gives the reader no reason to identify with them, it is precisely with these *hypēretai* that Peter has positioned himself. Furthermore, the narrator intensifies the encoded reader's inclination to associate Peter with them by repeating the verbs for standing

---

[71] Just as Peter denies Jesus three times (18:15–18, 25–27) and then is asked three times if he loves Jesus (21:15–19), so also he misunderstands Jesus three times prior to the denials. He misunderstands Jesus' footwashing (13:6–11), Jesus' remarks about leaving (13:36–38), and Jesus' refusal to defend himself (18:10–11).

[72] This is a significant difference from the Synoptic Gospels, where Peter denies *having ever known* Jesus (Mark 14:66–72; Matt 26:69–75; Luke 22:54–62).

[73] I follow Brown, Haenchen, and many others who believe that "the other disciple" and "the disciple who Jesus loved" are one and the same (Brown, *The Gospel According to John*, 2:822–23; Haenchen, *John*, 2:167).

and warming (*heistēkeisan/hestōs; ethermainonto/thermainomenos*) in reference to both (18:18, 25), just as he had earlier done with Judas (18:5).[74]

Thus, the Fourth Gospel's encoded reader, who all the while has been discovering what it means to follow Jesus, now places Peter alongside Judas and Jesus' antagonists and completely disassociates himself from these epitomes of failure. Ironically, it is precisely Peter's first denial that dramatically affirms the encoded reader's faith in Jesus, for Jesus is the one who earlier had predicted that this very thing would happen (13:38). Peter's denial strengthens the reader's conviction that Jesus is knowingly drinking "the cup that the Father has given him" (18:11). Without giving the encoded reader any reason to doubt his portrayal of the story, the narrator has separated the reader completely from Peter as a model of discipleship and at the same time has closely aligned that reader with Jesus. But as we shall see momentarily, the text's subversive narrator will force the encoded reader into his own misconceptions and denials of the story he thought he knew well.

The narrator opens the next scene (18:19–24) with a surprise: Annas, the one to whom Jesus had first been taken, has totally disappeared from the story.[75] But this gap is easily filled. Since the new scene opens with the high priest interrogating Jesus (and since Caiaphas is the only high priest known to the encoded reader, 18:9), the reader must conclude that Annas had met with Jesus and talked to him while the eyewitness narrator was outside watching Peter deny that he was a disciple.[76]

---

[74] This behavioral correspondence is similar to that found in John 5:19–20. There the narrator positively observed that Jesus made himself "equal to God" because he did the same things that God did. Here, however, is the negative side of that equation (cf. 8:39–47): Peter is equal with the sinister *hypēretai* because he does what they do (cf. the use of *histēmi* in 3:29; 18:3, 5).

[75] Brown wants to argue that Annas has not disappeared at this point, saying: "John calls Annas 'the high priest'" (18:15, 16, 19, 22; *The Gospel According to John*, 2:820). But this observation can only be made retrospectively, after the reader has come to v. 24. Based on a sequential analysis of the reading experience as evidenced by the textual variants, there is no reason for any reader to presuppose Brown's hypothesis. For only Caiaphas has been called *archiereus* (11:49, singular noun).

[76] From an intratextual reading perspective, the encoded reader has been nicely primed to fill in just this sort of gap, since the narrator had earlier described two co-temporal events. For example, in John 4:27–39, the Samaritan woman's witness to the villagers and Jesus' response to the disciples' unasked questions both take place at the same time (note especially the resumptive function of *oun* in 4:28, 40; cf. 11:17, 20, 21; and 18.19). Furthermore, if the encoded reader's intertextual repertoire includes the knowledge of a Mark-like passion narrative, then the encoded reader is well aware of similar scenes described co-temporally (Mark 14:53–72; see Bultmann, *The Gospel of John*, 641–42, 647).

The scene continues with Jesus' sarcastic response to the high priest
(18:20–21), the brutal reaction of one of the temple police (18:22), and Jesus'
closing question (18:23). But never in the course of the narrative has the
reader been led to suspect what the narrator ostensibly knows: that Jesus is all
the while talking with Annas, not Caiaphas. Furthermore, the encoded
reader's straightforward construction of the scene is additionally confirmed
by one of the temple police standing by who asks, "Is that how you answer the
high priest" (18:22)?[77]

But of course, as the history of the text and its interpretation make clear,
many real readers' sequential sense-making and gap-filling activities are radically undermined by the narrator's final remark: "Then Annas sent him
bound to Caiaphas the high priest" (18:24).[78] It is at this point (and at this
point only) that the reading process has so often been arrested, with real readers having to turn around and recheck all the knots they had just finished
tying.[79]

### READING, WRITING, AND FIGHTING

By believing that the narrator's original construction of the scene was accurate
(Jesus is with the high priest, Caiaphas), and consequently believing the temple
police as well (who are part of the conspiracy to get rid of Jesus), many real readers have suddenly found themselves caught in the wayward strands of an unrav-
eling narrative. For if the narrator's final context-revealing remark (18:24) is to
be believed, then either the narrator had betrayed the readers at 18:19, forcing

---

[77] As I have noted elsewhere, a similar rhetorical ploy is found in John 3:22, where the narrator says that Jesus was baptizing. This is then confirmed by characters in the story (3:26),
only to be negated later by the narrator (4:1–3) as a rumor the Pharisees had heard (Staley, *The
Print's First Kiss,* 96–98). A similar rhetorical situation is found in 7:1–10. There the narrator
says: "Jesus went about in Galilee. He did not wish to go about in Judea" (7:1–9). This is then
confirmed by Jesus when he says, "I am not going to this festival" (7:8; note the textual variants
here also!). However, the narrator negates these statements by turning around and saying that
Jesus did in fact go up to the festival (7:10; *The Print's First Kiss,* 103–5). Again, if the author
had wanted to make explicit that Annas was intended in 18:22, he could have made the temple
police retort, "Is that any way to answer a [no article] high priest?" or "Is that any way to
answer *one of the chief priests?*" (cf. 11:49).

[78] Schnackenburg describes the effect in the following manner: "The thoughtful reader
comes up against the following stumbling block. . . . Who is this, Annas or the officiating high
priest Caiaphas?" (*The Gospel According to St. John,* 3:228).

[79] Compare, for example, the phenomenon of the two Bethanys in the Fourth Gospel
(1:28; 11:1, 18; Staley, *The Print's First Kiss,* 105–7).

them to trust the brutalizing temple police who likewise had misnamed Jesus' interrogator "the high priest" (18:22), or the text has undergone some corruption or poor editing. Not realizing that the narrator could have a rhetorical purpose for occasionally misleading the encoded reader, many real readers have reverted to righting the text.

Whether real readers tie up the unraveled narrative by rewriting the text or by positing a narrator who occasionally misleads, the textual variants and source reconstructions are empirical evidence that the narrative's discourse has, in the past, disturbed real readers' reading habits and that it still, in the present, disturbs real readers reading. From the perspective of a rhetorically inclined reader-response criticism, then, the belated remark in 18:24 has created a reader who can only make sense out of the preceding scene (18:19–23) by denying and fighting against the construal which the narrator and the temple police originally led him to make (18:13–14, 22).[80]

Only the reader had the unique privilege of being brought inside the high priest's chamber, of seeing one of the temple police slap Jesus, of hearing him ask Jesus, "Is that how you answer the high priest?" (18:22). And that privileged reader had no recourse but to take each statement at face value. The disciple Peter, like the reader, had also been privileged by being brought inside. Peter had slipped inside the high priest's courtyard with the help of the "other disciple" only to become an outsider by denying Jesus and associating with the temple police (*hypēretai*).

Ironically, by first believing the narrator's (mis)construal of the scene and by then rejecting it, the encoded reader is put in the same company with Peter, the temple police, and Judas, characters from whom the narrator had earlier distanced that reader. The narrator's context-revealing remark in 18:24 forces the reader to acknowledge that he too has become an outsider through his construal of the preceding scene. Like Peter, the reader has had his failure exposed. The reader must feel that he has been victimized and betrayed by his misunderstanding.[81] Moreover, the agonistic, rhetorical power of the narrative's discourse has been evoked through the assistance of a momentarily misleading narrator and the brutalizing action of the high priest's assistants (*hypēretai*).

---

[80] The rhetorically oriented reader-response criticism I am following here is closely aligned with Fowler's (*"Let the Reader Understand,"* 9–58; cf. Staley, *The Print's First Kiss,* 6–49).

[81] Again, the choice of masculine pronouns is deliberate (see above, p. 90 n. 24). I have argued elsewhere that this rhetorical ploy of entrapment serves a distinct purpose for the implied author, one that seeks to evoke a particular kind of faith response (Staley, *The Print's First Kiss,* 116–18; cf. Liebert, "That You May Believe," 69, 71–72).

In these opening scenes of the Johannine passion narrative, the encoded reader has himself been trapped by the narrator's offhand remark and made to feel the stinging slap of the temple police.[82] Thinking he has been following Jesus into Caiaphas's rooms, he has been forced to recognize his own inability to reconstruct the events of the story—not insignificantly, at the same time Peter is failing in his loyalty to Jesus. Here, in the high priest's house, the confrontational, discourse-denying readings of a few ancient manuscripts, an odd assortment of scholars' source-critical reconstructions, and numerous commentators' notes testify to the narrative's rhetorical power at the very moment that the encoded reader is falling victim to that power. In real readers' anxious attempts to find assistance for their readings, to rewrite the text and fight through to some kind of unperturbed closure, these readers have inadvertently lopped off the ear of the assistant standing by to help them.[83]

Later, in Pilate's halls, a badgered Jesus will speak out publicly about his followers. But he will not call them by the more familiar and more positive terms *mathētai* ("disciples," 8:31–32; 15:8), *douloi* ("servants"), or *philoi* ("friends," 15:12–15). Ironically and tellingly he will call them *hypēretai,* or "followers [who] would be fighting to keep me from being handed over. . . ." (18:36). Not coincidentally, both Peter and many real readers have been just that in John 18:1–24: Peter has cut off the ear of the high priest's slave and denied being a disciple; many real readers have been discourse-denying, Annas-bound *hypēretai.* The history of the text's reception reveals the latent desires of a readership whose wild swipes at the text have tried to clean it up and rectify its loose-ended scenes.[84]

For one brief moment, however, the Fourth Gospel's narrator wrestles his Judas-dipped plot from the reader's grasp and in so doing opens another *thyra* (gate) into the high priest's *aulē* (courtyard). Here in the high priest's cramped courtyard, the narrator's belated reference to Caiaphas defies the comfortable framework of the previously described scene. Like Clitophon's entrapping narration in *Clitophon and Leucippe,* the Fourth Gospel's narrator stands

---

[82] To use Steven Mailloux's words: "Trial thus becomes entrapment" (*Rhetorical Power,* 49).

[83] John 18:10, 22, 36. Cf. Fowler, *"Let the Reader Understand,"* 195–227.

[84] In words that fit the Fourth Gospel as well as the Hebrew Bible, Sternberg argues, "the more active and cunning the reader, the greater is his vulnerability to the traps set by the narrative all along. But then so is his enjoyment of the game of art, and so is the insight he carries away with him. Underreaders may get things right, but at the lowest level and for the wrong reasons. In contrast, so far as the implied reader falls victim to the text's misdirections, he gains in understanding even or especially where he went astray: he does right to go wrong and will be rewarded accordingly" (*The Poetics of Biblical Narrative,* 272).

alongside the disruptive *hypēretai* and fights against a simplistic closure to the story by subverting his own straightforward account of the arrest, trial, and death of Jesus. This subversion notwithstanding, the allegiance of the Fourth Gospel's encoded reader is quickly won back and the ironic narrator's reliability is reaffirmed with the recounting of Peter's third denial (18:25–27). Whereas the encoded reader has been made aware of his error (18:24), Peter is still denying Jesus, standing with the *hypēretai,* and warming himself by their fire.

So despite the threat of overdetermined hermeneutic, proairetic, and symbolic codes, the reception history of John 18:12–24 reveals that it is still able to incite a riot from its readers. It is a text whose disorderly conduct challenges readers to draw their interpretive weapons, to reach down and pick up the bloodied ear lost in the panic of the midnight commotion. In this Gospel, only a readerly response like Peter's, which struggles through the smoldering embers of violent misunderstanding and denial, and the humbling effect of the narrator's misconstrued scenes, can stand one day on the shore of Lake Galilee and feel the weight of the simple words, "Follow me" (21:4, 9, 19).

"Contradiction forces the reader into an interpretive dilemma," writes Dennis Foster. And although Foster is writing about a "confessional turn" in modern literature, his words apply just as well to the Fourth Gospel. He goes on:

> the desire to resolve the confusion is aroused while the means to resolve it are undermined. By taking their readers through this dilemma, these books offer the possibility of refusing understanding (the mastery of meaning) as a purpose of narrative. The writers pose as masters of their texts, but only to disclose finally the illusory nature of the category, for both writers and readers. For is it only the desire for a masterful author that makes one into a slavish reader.[85]

Something is obviously not quite right in that last sentence. Either there should be a question mark at the end of the sentence, or else the "is it" ought to be transposed. Was this a proofreading oversight or Foster's consciously planned "mistake" to trapographically expose his readers' desires for a masterful author? Frankly, I didn't even catch the error the first time I read the paragraph. But now that I see it, I want to correct it. I have a desperate need to make things right.

Is John 18:12–24 the work of a masterful author—a Socratic *eirōn,* a crafty theologian? Or does my reading merely prove that I have been trained to be a

---

[85] Dennis Foster, *Confession and Complicity in Narrative,* 19. See also Liebert, "That You May Believe," 71–73.

good, slavish reader? Or—perhaps more importantly—are there other metaphors for describing readers beyond those of master and slave, resistance and submission?[86] Regrettably, the metaphors of master/slave and resistance/submission have tended to dominate the first three chapters of this book. But in today's postcolonial world I think we must find a way of doing reader-response criticism without having to submit or resist, without having to fight against ourselves and our foundational texts.

Biblical reader-response criticism needs new, noncombative, nonhierarchical metaphors for reading. Or perhaps we biblical reader-response critics should be adding metonymies to our metaphors. And when those metaphors and metonymies are found, I suspect we will discover that a postmodernist, postcolonialist feminist ethic of reading has led us to them. For if postmodernist, postcolonialist, and feminist critics have done anything for contemporary literary theory, they have at least made other theorists aware of the powerful roles that metaphors play in our private and public discourses. Moreover, postmodernist, postcolonialist, and feminist scholars have already added their own critically reflected, wide-ranging metaphors and metonymies to the conversations of literary theory. I'd like to try some of them on for size. I want to play dress-up.

In the remaining chapters of this book I revert to childhood and learn to read all over again. I'll pretend to be Merlin,[87] spinning swords with words and making mud spurt blood. I want to try alchemy[88] and splice genes and genres to generate electricity. Maybe I'll build a cyborg.[89]

"One should not mix genres," publishers tells me. "It just doesn't work. It won't sell." But I'm stubborn, and I want to do it anyway. After all, alchemy is

---

[86] As Donna Haraway points out, "encoded" metaphors like those that I have been using in the last three chapters are particularly problematic today. For example, she argues that "communications sciences and modern biologies are constructed by a common move—*the translation of the world into a problem of coding* [her emphasis], a search for a common language in which all resistance to instrumental control disappears and can be submitted to disassembly, investment, and exchange" ("A Manifesto for Cyborgs: Science, Technology, and Socialist Feminism in the 1980s," 83; see also 69, 82).

[87] Berg, "Suppressing the Language of (Wo)man: The Dream as a Common Language," 12.

[88] The metaphor comes from Patricia Williams (*The Alchemy of Race and Rights,* 256–57. Patricia Hampl writes: "The golden light of metaphor, which is the intelligence of poetry, was implicit in alchemical study. To change, magically, one substance into another, more valuable one is the ancient function of metaphor, as it was of alchemy" (as quoted in Freedman, *An Alchemy of Genres,* 54; see also 18, 20, 77; cf. Miller, *Getting Personal,* xii).

[89] This metaphor comes from Donna Haraway ("A Manifesto for Cyborgs: Science, Technology, and Socialist Feminism in the 1980s," 65–72). On the relationship between gender and genre, see Gerhart, *Genre Choices, Gender Questions,* 98–101.

a form of gambling.[90] It's easy to convince yourself that the solution you're presently working with—or surely the next one—will be the one that works; the one that smokes out the demons. And cyborgs—well, they don't die so easily either. So I'm going to go ahead and try to break down the confusing compounds of differences and distances that have defined biblical criticism and its readers. I want to discover why the Johannine text matters so much to me. I want to find out why I dissolve so quickly when I read it. I want to renovate—no, reinvent—no, relevate out of the reverential toolbox of readers in texts and texts in readers that we biblical reader-response critics have climbed into. And somewhere beyond that entombing toolbox, I think, is where hope lies.

[90] Or to put it another way: "Thinking is not the management of thought, as alas it is too often taken to mean these days. Thinking means putting everything on the line, taking risks, writerly risks, finding out what the actual odds are, not sheltering behind a pretend and in any case fallacious and transparent objectivity" (Jouve, *White Woman Speaks with Forked Tongue,* 5).

# PART TWO

# Reading the Reader:
## The Autobiographical Turn
## in Reader Criticism

Would'st thou be in a Dream, and yet not sleep?
Or would'st thou in a moment laugh and weep?
Wouldest thou lose thyself, and catch no harm,
And find thyself again without a charm?
Would'st read thyself, and read thou know'st not what,
And yet know whether thou art blest or not,
By reading the same lines? O then come hither,
And lay my Book, thy Head and Heart together.

—John Bunyan

# CHAPTER FOUR

# The Father of Lies:
# Autobiographical Acts in Recent Biblical
# Criticism and Contemporary Literary Theory

There is no theory that is not a fragment, carefully prepared, of some autobiography.

—Paul Valéry, as quoted in Lionnet, Miller, Olney, et al.

All autobiographers are unreliable narrators, all humans are liars. . . .

—Timothy Adams

[L]istening carefully to lies is sometimes very revealing of the truth.

—Tony Hillerman

When he lies, he speaks according to his own nature, for he is a liar and the father of lies.

—John 8:44

## MAKING WHOPPERS

The arguments raised against formalist reader-response criticism have finally worked their way under my thick skin, and no matter how hard I have scratched, I haven't been able to get rid of them. At first I thought the itching was caused by a mosquito bite or a tick—something that would irritate me for a few days and then disappear. But here I am, four chapters into this book, and the itching still won't go away. I've been scratching so long, I've broken through the skin and the raw places have gotten infected. Now I have a raging fever.

Sometimes I get delirious. I imagine that a giant eyeball is rolling down on top of me, suffocating me. I can't find a place to run or hide from the two-ton eye. And the textually encoded, rhetorically defined readers of my earlier chapters won't protect me either. I try to pull myself under the covers of this book—this page—this "I"—to shield myself and find a place to breathe freely. But it's impossible. I can't get away from the omnipresent eye.[1]

Finally I awake from the nightmare and take off the gauze mask[2] that has been precariously perched on the edge of my nose. It's spring in the Pacific Northwest, and I remember that my allergies are particularly bothersome at this time of year. I get up, take an antihistamine and walk around a bit. I sneeze a few times and then begin to ask a few simple questions to clear my head—like, Who is the "who" who has been doing the writing of those chapters on the Johannine encoded reader? And what power does that "who" have over the reading experience and the reading *of* experience? My head is beginning to clear. The itch is starting to go away.

Although these two questions may seem to have obvious answers, don't expect a quick response on my part or any sudden disclosures. When you've been hiding behind implied and encoded readers as long as I have, it's not easy to slip into something more comfortable, curl up in a chair, and tell a stranger who you are.[3] It's going to take me some time to unwind, and I'll probably talk about a lot of other people before I finally actually talk about myself. But that's not necessarily bad. After all, this is supposed to be a theoretical chapter, sort of a bridge between "me" the formalist reader and "me" the some-other-kind-of-reader. So if it looks as if I'm tensing up into some contorted form of academese, please bear with me. Eventually I'll find my voice and scream. Right now I'm still in transition—not quite ready to give birth. No, that can't be right. I'm male and over forty years old. The transition must be a symptom of male menopause. Real men don't give birth—they just kidnap metaphors.[4]

---

[1] The text is an eye, then. More precisely, the text is an eyeball (*bulbus oculi*), snug in its bony cavity (orbit) . . . (Moore, "How Jesus' Risen Body Became a Cadaver," 276; cf. Synnott, *The Body Social,* 206–27; esp. 222–27).

[2] "The propogated mask of the imagined literary critic, the language club of hyperauthenticity, the myth of a purely objective perspective, the godlike image of generalized, legitimating others—-these are too often reified . . . as 'impersonal' rules and 'neutral' principles, presumed to be inanimate, unemotional, unbiased, unmanipulated, and higher than ourselves" (Williams, *The Alchemy of Race and Rights,* 11).

[3] "Part of me would like to go back to doing the kind of criticism I used to do. I feel awkward and exposed, and it would be easier, in one way, to hide again behind the implied author I know so well how to invent: magisterial, elegant, controlled and controlling" (Carlton, "Reading Middlemarch, Rereading Myself," 241).

[4] "Is autobiography somehow always in the process of symbolically killing the mother off by telling her the lie that we have given birth to ourselves?" (Johnson, "My Monster/My Self," 4).

I make a pot of coffee and sneeze a few more times, and another jumble of germ-filled questions comes spewing out.

So what if those readers that I and others have been discovering in the biblical text and writing about for the past ten years were, as some critics have been saying, just our own selves disguised by the critical language of academic discourse?[5] Could we then turn around and do an exegesis of souls that parallels our exegesis of texts? Or would there be an explosion when we began consciously to investigate the intertwining and fusing of our lives to canonical literature? What would be the fallout if we unearthed elements in our personal experience—outside of our professional training—that might have influenced our views of the Bible's rhetorical strategies as much as, or perhaps more than, our reading in critical theory? The caffeine rush from the first cup of coffee is beginning to have its effect.

Suppose someone could show me, for example, that the theory of Johannine reader victimization that I espoused in the preceding chapter was rooted in my own childhood experience of being a victim of ethnic and racial discrimination as much as it was rooted in my professional reading of literary criticism.[6] Then wouldn't the critics of biblical reader-response criticism be proved right? For in this scenario, what I thought I had been reading as "something really there" in the Fourth Gospel would have been nothing more than reading my own unconscious desires into the text.[7] The critics would then tell me that my very real but unnamed desires had simply led me to the discovery of the literary-critical language of irony and reader victimization, that critical language merely provided the professional legitimization for what was, in fact, a purely subjective reading of myself in the text.[8]

So perhaps the biblical reader-response critic's objectivist pajamas have finally fallen down. (This, of course, is not a problem for me, since I am

---

For the significant role of birthing metaphors in literature, see Friedman, "Creativity and the Childbirth Metaphor: Gender Difference in Literary Discourse," esp. 371–80; and Cochrane, "The Grave, the Song and a *Gestalt* Theology as Pregnant with Context: Contextual Impregnation as the Substance of Theology (Local Theologies and the Integrity of Faith)," 123.

[5] "The more criticism I read, the more I think that it is a scrambled form of autobiography, which seeks to conceal the self in the writing" (Jouve, *White Woman Speaks with Forked Tongue*, 37).

[6] This, in fact, will be one of my major arguments in the next chapter, "Not Yet Fifty: Postcolonial Confessions from an Outpost in the San Juan Basin."

[7] "In the hermeneutics of desire the reader finds in the text what she wants it to say" (Ostriker, *Feminist Revision and the Bible*, 122).

[8] But "subjectivity may be as severe and demanding a discipline as objectivity," writes Alicia Ostriker (*Feminist Revision and the Bible*, 110).

already walking around the kitchen half naked.) For the interpretive manner
in which we reader-response critics get dressed always seems to begin and end
in the same way: with an unreflected self viewing a text. In between we move
out to try with the help of literary and historical tools and scientific-sounding
language, to dress up the readerly responses engendered by the text. But the
end always looks the same. Someone tells us, at the conclusion of our exegetical dress-up, after we have amassed all our objective data, that our rhetorical
analysis and imagined readerly responses simply originated within ourselves
and not with the text. We look surprised and, curious and distracted, examine
our behinds. We decide our critics are probably right, climb back into bed,
and shut our eyes.

But should reader-response criticism be excluded from the exegetical
breakfast just because its pajamas got twisted between its legs on the way to
the table? James Olney, for one, would say no. He would argue that the
reader-critic's clothes are no different from anyone else's. He writes:

> With his yearning for order—a yearning greater, I should think, than his desire
> for knowledge—man explores the universe continually for laws and forms not
> of his own making, but what, in the end, he always finds is his own face: a sort
> of ubiquitous, inescapable man-in-the-moon which, if he will, he can recognize
> as his own mirror image. Man creates, in fact, by the very act of seeking, that
> order that he would have.[9]

At this point I want to collect my change of clothing and squeeze back into
my recently vacated space at the breakfast table. With or without the exegetical clothes, I think we reader-response critics have an important role to share
at that meal. (Please pass the butter and jam.) For surely, if all our readings of
texts are in some important sense readings of ourselves, each shaped by our
peculiar situation of living in the world, there ought to be some way for us to
go about the critical investigation of ourselves as readers—an investigation
that would have hermeneutical significance not only for the individual but
for biblical reader-response criticism and biblical criticism at large. And if any
one should be doing this kind of self-critical investigation, it ought to be we
reader-response critics.

Within this context of concerns, it seems to me that recent work in the literary theory of autobiography might offer the biblical critic shiny new utensils
and a bold-colored tablecloth for imagining readers and their relationships to
texts. What better place could one find to begin an exegesis of the soul than
with autobiographical theory, which investigates the ways people inscribe

---

[9] Olney, *Metaphors of the Self,* 4; cf. 8–9.

themselves? Moreover, autobiographical theory is particularly attuned to the problematics of self and distance in narrative, or those rhetorical tricks whereby writers define the narrating self and then separate that self from the narrated experience.[10] The problematics of self and distance reflected in the autobiographer's "I" is intimately related to the hermeneutical quest for an impermeable, distance-enhancing membrane that would protect the reader from invading any given text and would protect the text from invading the reader.[11]

Not insignificantly, recent movements toward more active and proactive readers in biblical reader criticism have already led to the development of a new, autobiographical topos in biblical scholars' professional papers and published articles. And although these vignettes have yet to be found under the covers of our most prestigious journals, they are symptomatic of what many biblical scholars must feel is an insidious disease invading our discipline, threatening its solidly modernist, dispassionate, professional bodies. However, the autobiographical intrusions that some might find destructive to scholarship are still at the early stages of development as an academic epidemic.[12] Thus white, middle-class, heterosexual, male biblical critics have

---

[10] For example, see Sidonie Smith, *A Poetics of Women's Autobiography*, 46–47; Sprinker, "Fictions of the Self: The End of Autobiography," 322–25, 342; and Benstock, "Authorizing the Autobiographical," 11–16.

[11] This sentence is essentially a quote from Sandra Schneiders, who writes: "If naïveté is the nearness of the subject matter through a transparent text, criticism is the process of distancing the text. There are two purposes to this distancing: *to protect the reader from the text* and *to protect the text from the reader*" (*The Revelatory Text*, 169 [her emphasis]; cf. 142–44, 171–72).

Schneiders's language of protection seems to draw on the image of the body's immune system, which, in popular imagery, fights off foreign invaders. But "[i]n the early 1970s, the Nobel Prize winning immunologist, Niels Jerne, proposed a [radically different] theory of immune system self-regulation, called the network theory." In Jerne's theory, "there could be no *exterior* antigenic structure, no 'invader', that the immune system had not already 'seen' and mirrored internally. 'Self' and 'other' lose their rationalistic [and nationalistic] oppositional quality and become subtle plays of partially mirrored readings and responses" (Haraway, *Simians, Cyborgs, and Women*, 218 [her emphasis]). Using this theory of the immune system, Haraway can then argue for a postmodern turn whereby "[t]he internal, structured activity of the system is the crucial issue, not formal representations of the 'outer' world within the 'inner' world of the communications system that is the organism" (ibid., 219, cf. 224; cf. Fisher, "Self in Text, Text in Self," 139; and van den Heever, "Being and Nothingness," 42–43).

[12] Susan Sontag notes that, historically, certain incurable diseases have been associated with unbridled, indiscriminate human passion (*AIDS and Its Metaphors*, 23, 25). This has certainly been true of the AIDS epidemic in the late twentieth century, and I suspect that the more recent appearance of AIDS in biblical criticism (Autobiographical Intrusions Destroying Scholarship) is viewed in like manner by objective, scientific exegetes. For if, as Haraway

little to fear from the virus. Our autobiographical moments—when they are found—seem to function most often as rhetorical imperfections on the epidermis of our antiseptic papers. And since they barely scratch the surface of our critical thinking, the lesions have not yet begun to bleed or infect exegetical argumentation as a whole. Bury the autobiographical skeleton in a tentative footnote, and most readers will easily overlook it.

Even when our autobiographical vignettes do appear in boldface print, they often read as bland-name combinations of the ubiquitous McDonalds and Burger Kings, which grow like ragweed alongside U.S. interstate highways. "I am Male and Caucasian," their oversized, blinking billboards blare; a "Wealthy, Heterosexual Oppressor who happens to be Protestant; and a Professionally-trained, Euro-American Reader of the Bible." In a word, "I am a McWhopper." With a few cosmetic changes the creed works just as well for Caucasian women or Roman Catholics of European origin.[13] Like McDonalds's and Burger King's

---

argues, "the immune system is a map drawn to guide recognition and misrecognition of self and other in the dialectics of Western biopolitics" (*Simians, Cyborgs, and Women*, 204; cf. 214, 223), then what makes AIDS so frightening is that the body's immune system loses its ability to discriminate between self and other. Similarly, with literary AIDS, autobiographical intrusions in scholarship begin to destroy the rhetorical boundary between objective critic and subjective person, making it difficult to determine the status of either one. For many white, well-established male professors, the problem is compounded by the brooding fear that these Autobiographical Intrusions Destroying Scholarship may have come from a place only recently legitimated by the professional body of Western scholars. As it has been argued for Acquired Immune Deficiency Syndrome, that place of origin is the Two-thirds World—particularly among women (Sontag, *AIDS and Its Metaphors*, 24, 26, 51–52, 62–63, 71–72, 83–84; cf. Freedman, Frey, and Zauhar, *The Intimate Critique*, 1–2, 10).

[13] The necessity of accounting for social location among white biblical interpreters has been voiced numerous times by Elisabeth Schüssler Fiorenza ("The Ethics of Biblical Interpretation: Decentering Biblical Scholarship," 3–9; and "Biblical Interpretation and Critical Commitment," 5–6). More recently her call has been echoed by Wilhelm Wuellner ("Is There an Encoded Reader Fallacy?" 46, 49), Mary Ann Tolbert ("A Response from a Literary Perspective," 210; and "The Politics and Poetics of Location," 311–14), and Norman Gottwald ("Social Class as an Analytic and Hermeneutical Category in Biblical Studies," 21–22). It is therefore not surprising that a number of white New Testament scholars are beginning to speak autobiographically in the academic arena, and occasionally they even reflect upon their social location. See, for example, Borg, *Meeting Jesus Again for the First Time*, 3–19; Fowler, "Postmodern Biblical Criticism," 9–12; Schneiders, *The Revelatory Text*, 1–5; Anderson and Moore, *Mark and Method*, 20 (see also Moore's *Literary Criticism and the Gospels*, 176–77; his *Mark and Luke in Poststructuralist Perspectives*, 154–55; and his *Poststructuralism and the New Testament*, 95, 114, 124–25); Parsons, "Anatomy of a Reader"; and Patte and Phillips, "A Fundamental Condition for Ethical Accountability in the Teaching of the Bible by White Male Exegetes," 17–23.

fast foods, most of these professional autobiographical acts hide shrunken burghers and oversized white buns wrapped tightly in thin waxy paper. They are flat, tasteless, barely distinguishable bits of fat-fueled calories which other scholars wolf down in a flurry before they rush out to the meatier concerns of the big bad exegetical world.[14] As biblical exegetes, we have barely begun to explore the problematics of our little white lies or the interpretive implications of our autobiographical acts.[15]

Having picked up a few scraps of wisdom from literary critics and the Proceedings of the Modern Language Association, we biblical critics typically "offer up in the spirit of 'honesty' autobiographical information about [our]selves usually at the beginning of [our] discourse[s] as a kind of disclaimer. This is meant to acknowledge [our] own understanding that [we] are speaking from a specified, embodied location without pretense to a trancendental truth. But," as Linda Alcoff goes on to note,

> such an act serves no good end when it is used as a disclaimer against [our] own ignorance or errors and is made without critical interrogation of the bearing of such . . . autobiograph[ies] on what is about to be said. It leaves for the listeners all the real work that needs to be done. For example, if a middle-class white man were to begin a speech by sharing with us this autobiographical information and then using it as a kind of apologetics for any limitations of his speech, this would leave those of us in the audience who do not share his social location to do the work by ourselves of translating his terms into our own, appraising

---

For the problematics of white, (upper) middle-class scholars speaking from a liberationist perspective, see Abel, "Black Writing, White Reading: Race and the Politics of Feminist Interpretation," 470–98, esp. 488–90; Myers, *Who Will Roll Away the Stone?* 5–7, 132–39; Howard-Brook, *Becoming Children of God*, 5–8, 399; and Patte, "Acknowledging the Contextual Character of Male, European-American Critical Exegesis." As a member of the bicultural Hispanic American community, Fernando Segovia is attempting to bring his own social location into dialogue with his approach to Johannine exegesis ("Towards a New Direction in Johannine Scholarship: The Fourth Gospel from a Literary Perspective," 16–17, 21; *The Farewell of the Word*, vii–ix, 328–29; and "Toward a Hermeneutics of the Diaspora"; see also Maldonado, "'¿La Conquista?' Latin American (*Mestizaje*) Reflections on the Biblical Conquest").

[14] I must confess that I worked at McDonalds for nine months when I was seventeen. Back then you could buy a Big Mac, an order of fries, and a milk shake for ninety-nine cents. At one time I believed that I could distinguish the taste of McDonalds's french fries from Burger King's. I am not as sure about this possibility as I once was.

[15] "Perhaps every white person should affix an authorial health warning to their texts," writes Nicole Jouve. "It's not because you are aware of a danger, nor because you mean well, that your words or actions do not harm. . . . Writing is never innocent. White writing is less innocent than any other" (*White Woman Speaks with Forked Tongue*, viii).

the applicability of his analysis to our diverse situation, and determining the substantive relevance of his location on his claims.[16]

Not surprisingly, Alcoff's hypothetical illustration is the norm for most autobiographical acts in biblical criticism today. The gap between autobiographical topoi and interpretive acts is rarely bridged—except in the works of oppressed and colonialized peoples. And even there, where the sociopolitical context of the interpreter is self-consciously central to the hermeneutical task, specific autobiographical material is often lacking.[17] On the other hand, when a connection between autobiography and biblical interpretation is explicitly made by a McWhopper, the primary emphasis in the tentative, blushing unveiling is on that person's intellectual journey. Our stories are about disembodied minds.[18] And after lengthy struggles with life-threatening questions, these minds are finally able to find release—*moksha*, salvation—in mature, objective, reevaluations of the biblical tradition.

Of course, none of us set out in our careers to be autobiographers, even though most of us, in private, are intensely self-reflective people. First and foremost, we are biblical scholars. The modernist model of objective, distanced scientific writing that we were taught in graduate school leaves no room for first-person narration or public self-revelatory acts. So it may seem unfair for me to focus attention on those places where the frayed hems of biblical scholars' slips are showing. I know full well the courage it takes sometimes just to get out of bed in the morning—let alone to get out on the ballroom floor and dance with a stranger. Nevertheless, I want to explore briefly three atypical autobiographical vignettes by white Euro-American biblical scholars—scholars who explicitly write about their lives and then attempt to relate those inscribed lives to their scholarship. My hope is that by

[16] Alcoff, "The Problem of Speaking for Others," 25. Cf. Krupat, *Ethnocriticism*, 33; Miller, *Getting Personal*, xiii; and Patte and Phillips, "A Fundamental Condition for Ethical Accountability in the Teaching of the Bible by White Male Exegetes," 17–19.

[17] Itumeleng Mosala's *Biblical Hermeneutics and Black Theology in South Africa* typifies this approach. From the title of the book to its concluding sentences Mosala makes clear that his work is grounded in his own personal life—in "the historical and cultural struggles of the black people" (ibid., 67; esp. 67–99). However, perhaps in an effort to be heard by "First World" theologians and biblical scholars, Mosala and others like him rarely write in an openly autobiographical voice.

[18] This is made explicit at the annual meeting of the Society of Biblical Literature, where, each year, a senior biblical scholar is invited to give an autobiographical talk on the topic "How My Mind Has Changed (or Remained the Same)." Typically, when these minds have changed, it is because of the reading of some new book. Change is rarely caused by any human experience other than reading texts.

uncovering the rhetorical shape of their textual reflections and virginal unveilings, I might find new ways of addressing those hidden seams that tie texts to readers.

At the conclusion of the preceding chapter I chose three unusual metaphors which feminist scholars have used to illustrate the peculiar mixing of genres found in some women's writings. These three images were the hybrid of machine and organism symbolized by the cyborg, the wacky word-wizardry symbolized by Merlin's magic, and the complex, imaginative experiments of alchemy. I particularly like these three metaphors because they attempt to express the effects of combining personal experience and autobiographical reflections with academic, scholarly discourses.

Although none of the biblical scholars' works which I will investigate can live up to the powerful pictures that cyborgs, Merlins, and alchemy evoke for the mixing of genres, nevertheless these scholars' writings do stand out from those of their Caucasian peers. This is not simply because these scholars write about the need for connecting lives and scholarship. There are, in fact, many biblical scholars writing about the need for that. But from these three scholars' work a reader clearly senses that they are critically engaged in the task of making explicit connections between their personal lives and their scholarship. And I believe that this sense comes from each scholar's conscious choice to place side by side in his or her text two kinds of writing: autobiographical and scientific.

I have chosen three recent works by Marcus Borg, Sandra M. Schneiders, and Mikeal Parsons because I am particularly interested in these Euro-American scholars' views of the self and the rhetorically explicit bridges that they build between their autobiographical selves and their scholarship.[19] But, more importantly, I also hope to uncover those areas in their writing where their subjective, personal autobiographies inadvertently cross the boundaries into their objective, public scholarship. I want to be a subversive alchemist, a mad-eyed Merlin, mixing up the stuff of autobiography and exegesis which these three scholars still think they can keep separate and uncontaminated. My purpose, therefore, is not to go outside their texts to interview the real living people behind the writing in some kind of tabloid exposé.[20] Rather, my

---

[19] Or, in Albert Stone's words, I see my task as "identify[ing] and connect[ing] the mythic and ideological components of an individual's story, noting the distinctive ways each author manipulates ideas to make bridges between public life and private experience, past and present, between writer and reader" (*Autobiographical Occasions and Original Acts,* 16).

[20] As James Olney points out, this was an early interest of autobiographical criticism and one that still creates problems for the critic (*Autobiography,* 20, 24; see also Sidonie Smith, *A Poetics of Women's Autobiography,* 4–5).

goal is to focus specifically on those revelatory fragments of the self that these authors offer to their readers through their own words, and to explore how those fragments are related to the wider body of these scholars' work.[21]

Now the exposure of the scholarly body to autobiographical antigens can be quite dangerous. It could lead to a breakdown of those natural resistances that our discipline has built up over decades, leaving our professional, scientific writing open to an uncontrollable proliferation of autobiographical infections. My intention, I maintain, will be to describe the symptoms of that disease so that others will be aware of the impending danger. I just hope I can keep my antiseptic mask, my sterilized implements, and my resistance-enhancing pills close at hand so that I won't be contaminated by the writings I'm about to unvestigate.

## A CYBORG MEETS JESUS

In his recent book *Meeting Jesus Again for the First Time,* Jesus Seminar spokesperson Marcus Borg sets a peculiar task before himself. His earlier book *Jesus: A New Vision* had been an attempted revision of the historical Jesus, an attempt to flesh out the socioreligious context of Jesus' public life and to hear again his prophetic voice in the political machinations of Second Temple Judaism. But Borg's newest work is almost a midrash on that earlier study. In contrast to *Jesus: A New Vision,* his latest book attempts to put flesh on himself as a scholar and as a person of faith, thereby showing readers how to connect with the reconfigured Jesus of contemporary American biblical scholarship.

Borg's intent is laudable, and the goals he sets for himself are challenging. For as anyone familiar with past quests for Jesus knows, a scholar must be able to hide behind the rhetorical mask of objective, dispassionate discourse in order to legitimize his or her historical research. Borg, however, begins his book by boldly baring private parts of his life to his reading public. Instead of disguising his personal interests and his spiritual and theological questions, he lays them out in a sixteen-page autobiographical narrative. But Borg's autobiography should be read as carefully as the rest of the book. As literary

---

[21] Although there is some similarity between my critical interests and Norman Holland's theory of "identity themes" ("Unity Identity Text Self," 124), it corresponds more closely with what Sidonie Smith argues is constitutive of "a new concern [in autobiographical studies] for the *graphia,* 'the careful teasing out of warring forces of signification within the text itself,'" where the reader plays a central role (*A Poetics of Women's Autobiography,* 6).

critics are quick to note, the rhetorical power of autobiography (no less than the rhetorical power of historical Jesus research) lies precisely in its apparent openness and candor. And the openness and candor often efface a more covert purpose.[22]

In his first chapter, entitled "Meeting Jesus Again: My Own Story," Borg describes his spiritual and intellectual journey from midwest American, Scandinavian Lutheran pietism to Oxford-trained New Testament scholar. The seven-part narrative begins in chronological fashion with a childhood spent in a small North Dakota town near the Canadian border. He writes that his earliest images of Jesus are rooted there, wound around Bible verses memorized in Sunday School and inspirational hymns sung in worship. Not insignificantly, the most memorable scene from Borg's autobiographical sketch is of a country church gathering, where, in an unfamiliar place and surrounded by strange people, he sang hymns and listened to missionaries tell about their experiences in China. The warmly familiar Christian songs overlaid with an unfamiliar but nonthreatening country church function as a key metaphor for his own spiritual pilgrimage.[23]

Even more importantly, the images of the friendly Canadian border near his hometown and the strange yet comfortable country church mirror Borg's sketch of the historical Jesus. For the image of Jesus as a boundary crosser is central to Borg's analysis of Jesus' relationship to Jewish purity systems. He writes: "[T]here is something boundary shattering about the *imitatio dei* that stood at the center of Jesus' message and activity."[24] And although Borg's Jesus breaks through the borders of purity systems, he does not seem to incur the physical pain and sociopolitical stigma that often accompany such trespassing. Like the strange but friendly border scenes from Borg's autobiography, Borg's Jesus challenges stereotypical American religiosity from the outside and simultaneously soothes white middle-class American fears about the cost of radical sociopolitical engagement and subversive boundary crossing.[25]

---

[22] Cf. Adams, *Telling Lies in Modern American Autobiography,* 61, 72, 88.

[23] Borg immediately follows this description with the perceptive sentence: "It is tempting to see the course of my life ever since as a living out of the messages of those hymns" (*Meeting Jesus Again for the First Time,* 6). However, Borg does not pursue that dangerous temptation by consciously blurring the boundaries of his autobiographical and scholarly writing.

[24] Ibid., 58; see also 50–61.

[25] There are many other borders that are not so safe. For example, Diane Freedman notes: "Danger has long lurked in the borderlands [of the American Southwest]. It's risky to succeed in border crossing, in the making of a new life, in assimilating. Inside, one is perhaps even more the outsider, the migrant, the marginal" (*An Alchemy of Genres,* 48; cf. Anzaldúa, *Borderlands/La Frontera,* "Preface").

If the metaphor of boundaries surreptitiously breaks out of Borg's autobiography to infiltrate his more objective, scholarly view of Jesus, the image of life as a spiritual and intellectual journey is a consciously chosen metaphor intended to bind the autobiographical reflections to his scholarly work. For Borg, the "understanding of the Christian life as a journey of transformation is grounded in [an] alternative image of Jesus."[26] Yet Albert Stone notes that the journey or pilgrimage motif is also rooted "in the mainstream of American personal narratives,"[27] and that it is "most frequently chosen to dramatize the inward search for God."[28] Moreover, transformation, which is central to Borg's autobiographical summary, has been important to many Western autobiographical acts and to American autobiography in particular. Again, Stone argues that "[m]ost autobiographers . . . achieve self-consciousness through a kind of *metanoia*. They write as if, and after, some transforming event or inner crisis has occurred."[29]

Borg does not mention the significant role that the journey metaphor has played in the Euro-American myth of identity, or how that Euro-American story might have affected his own self-understanding. Instead, near the end of the book he points out how Israel's stories of its relationship to God are dominated by the journey motif: from slavery in Egypt to freedom in the Promised Land; from exile in Babylon to return to Jerusalem.[30] Even more importantly for Borg, Jesus' teaching emphasizes "the religious life as a journey. Jesus teaches a 'way,' and the gospels are about 'the way.'"[31]

When he turns to Jesus' wayward teaching, Borg focuses on the meaning of the word "disciple" as a "follower," since "[d]iscipleship in the New Testament is . . . a following after Jesus, a journeying with Jesus."[32] For Borg, this journey with Jesus involves listening to his teaching, eating at his table and experiencing his banquet, and becoming part of an alternative community. As important as the journey metaphor is for Borg's understanding of Jesus' purpose, the liturgical and Markan emphasis on the destination of Jerusalem and the cross are curiously unrelated to following Jesus. Discussions of Jesus' death are buried in footnotes.[33] Precisely at this point, however, the borders of autobiography once again inadvertently overlap his scholarship. Just as his

---

[26] Borg, *Meeting Jesus Again for the First Time,* 3.
[27] Stone, *Autobiographical Occasions and Original Acts,* 33.
[28] Ibid., 59.
[29] Ibid., 92 (his emphasis).
[30] Borg, *Meeting Jesus Again for the First Time,* 133.
[31] Ibid., 134.
[32] Ibid., 135.
[33] Ibid., 31; 88 n. 3; 140 nn. 24 and 25.

own spiritual and intellectual journey is textually uncontaminated by the troubling questions raised by rejection and death, so also Borg's Jesus is an open-ended sentence, unmarked by a period. Jesus' quest for a relationship with God is neither disrupted nor scandalized by a politically charged death.

Moreover, in spite of Borg's insistence that "discipleship is not an individual path,"[34] his spiritual quest seems to be nurtured primarily by private, mystical experiences. Out of the seven segments into which Borg divides his life, human relationships play a significant role in only the first three.[35] In the lengthiest segment ("Seminary and Beyond"), the course of his spiritual and intellectual journey is shaped by experiences of nature mysticism which cause him to respond with "radical amazement."[36] These highly personal events—which Borg never describes in detail—serve as another bridge between his autobiographical quest for a relationship with God and his scholarly quest for the historical Jesus.[37] For Jesus' experience of God—as a man of spirit who practiced the politics of compassion—undergirds Borg's own self-understanding.[38] Both Borg and Borg's Jesus are men guided by a passionate desire to give themselves wholly to God.

But whether Jesus had a core group of followers, or whether Jesus intended to form a community of like-minded spirit-people who would act out his politics of compassion, is an irrelevant historical question for Borg. Although he can argue that Jesus was a "movement founder"[39] with an "inclusive vision" that negated "the boundaries of the [Jewish] purity system,"[40] the terms "movement" and "founder" remain undefined. Corresponding to his silence on these historical questions is the striking absence of the church in Borg's autobiographical sketch of his adult life. After childhood, the only community that appears to sustain him is the intellectual one dominated by New Testament scholars. So although Borg's intent is to build bridges between the secular Jesus scholar and the wider Christian community, his autobiographical sketch veers off in a different direction. Using his autobiography as a mea-

[34] Ibid., 135–36.

[35] These seven segments are: "Childhood," "Adolescence," "College," "Seminary and Beyond," "How I See Jesus Now," "The Pre-Easter and the Post-Easter Jesus," and "Beyond Belief to Relationship" (*Meeting Jesus Again for the First Time*, 3–17).

[36] Ibid., 14.

[37] One can speculate that Borg's spiritual life is nurtured by the same experiences he associates with Jesus: fasting and prayer, contemplation, and perhaps visions (*Meeting Jesus Again for the First Time*, 35).

[38] Ibid., 14; cf. 31–38, 58–61, 88, 109–10.

[39] Ibid., 30.

[40] Ibid., 56.

sure, an individual's commitment to a spiritual community would seem to serve little purpose. Consequently, the journey motif that runs through both Borg's autobiography and his sketch of the historical Jesus guides the spiritual quester down a different path: a path that leads into a borderland where seekers have "nowhere to lay [their] head."[41]

It should come as no surprise, then, to find that the self Borg inscribes fits easily within the stereotyped, male-defined model of the autobiographical genre. This model, as some have argued, tends to "assume a certain ideology of selfhood [which is] grounded in the metaphysical notion of the essential self, one that privileges individuality and separateness over connectedness."[42] So while Borg's view of God and Jesus changes radically through the course of his autobiographical sketch, and while his scholarly emphasis on Jesus' politics of compassion highlights the significance of human relationships and connectedness to the world, Borg's autobiographical self remains remarkably stable, ethereal, unified, and unaffected by the intricacies of interpersonal commitments.[43]

My purpose in this autobiographical critique is not to argue that Marcus Borg should have written his autobiographical sketch differently, nor is it intended to be a theological critique of Marcus Borg's particular reconstruction of the historical Jesus. Borg has, in fact, done an excellent job of communicating the best of two worlds—both the scholarly and the experiential—to the curious bystander. But since I am beginning to believe that all readings, like all scholarly reconstructions of Jesus, are circular and autobiographical, my intention instead has been to point out some of the inadvertent connections between Borg's autobiographical reflections and his critical assessment of Jesus. That is, I have been particularly interested in finding those places, both explicit and implicit, where the carefully constructed border between Borg's scholarship and personal life breaks down and is unintentionally crossed.

Even more importantly, my goal has been to ask the theoretical question: Would a more conscious awareness of the modes of autobiographical writing have caused Marcus Borg to inscribe himself or his Jesus differently? In choosing to write about his spiritual and intellectual experience, and then set-

---

[41] Ibid., 135.

[42] Smith, *A Poetics of Women's Autobiography,* 12; cf. 13–15. Cf. also Costello, "Taking the 'Woman' out of Women's Autobiography: The Perils and Potentials of Theorizing Female Subjectivities," 131.

[43] In other words, it is a docetic view of self. It is a "[s]elf-conception . . . formed without the body" (Gilmore, *Autobiographics,* 84; see esp. 82–86).

ting that autobiographical sketch apart from the scholarly sketch of Jesus, his readers are invited to view both lives objectively, as separate entities unaffected and uninfected by one another. But what if a reader were to meet Borg again, and discover a Borg who, for the first time, had accepted the cyborg's challenge to mix completely self and science?[44] Would the rhetorical gains offset the imagined losses of borders?

## NOTHING IN THE TEXT ABOUT MERLIN

Like Marcus Borg, Sandra M. Schneiders has an abiding passion for finding ways to connect contemporary biblical scholarship with what is largely a biblically illiterate Christian community. So it is not surprising to find her recommendation on the dust jacket of Borg's *Meeting Jesus Again for the First Time.* But Borg's focus is on the historical Jesus and depends almost exclusively on the shovels and picks of historical criticism to dig through layers of ecclesiastical tradition and uncover that Jesus. On the other hand, Schneiders's work, *The Revelatory Text: Interpreting the New Testament as Sacred Scripture,* exposes the reader to a much wider range of exegetical methodologies, concentrating primarily on the final shape of the biblical narrative.

In her autobiographical vignette, Sandra M. Schneiders reveals to the reader how her own intellectual quest led her to write this book. She writes that her academic career largely has been a search to find legitimate ways of introducing into her study of the New Testament the lived experience of Christian faith and a belief in the Bible as divine revelation. This legitimizing desire has grown out of her professional education and study, since "the type of objectivity that was the ideal of historical critical exegesis and that controlled its agenda and methodology seemed to forbid, if not any interest in such matters, at least any explicit intrusion of such concerns into the scholarly study of the text."[45] Thus, Schneiders's goal is to develop a theologically reflective, hermeneutically sophisticated, and exegetically sensitive context for reading Scripture as the enlivening, challenging, transformative word of God which Christians claim it is. In order to legitimize her endeavor, she will be careful to keep her own autobiographical reflections from intruding into her hermeneutical praxis.

Unlike Marcus Borg's lengthier, more general autobiographical sketch,

---

[44] This is Donna Haraway's "manifesto" in her essay "A Manifesto for Cyborgs: Science, Technology, and Socialist Feminism in the 1980s" (see esp. 66–67).

[45] Schneiders, *The Revelatory Text,* 2.

Sandra M. Schneiders's personal reflections cover only five pages of her two-hundred-page book. Her autobiography focuses only on a small segment of her adult life, or the "final shaping" of her intellectual journey. Schneiders, who describes herself as a white, middle-class woman, and a European-trained, Roman Catholic New Testament scholar, concentrates all her autobiographical reflections on a few significant moments in her professional life. Yet even those selected moments bleed over into her scholarly discourse. For example, where Marcus Borg began his autobiography with his auditory memories of singing hymns in church and then moved to the oral tradition behind the Gospels, Sandra M. Schneiders's autobiography, like her scholarly investigations, is centered on visual experiences with written texts. Tellingly, her autobiography is subtitled "*Genesis* of the Project" (my emphasis).

Like a modern-day disciple of Merlin, the inspirational and revelatory moment of Schneiders's autobiographical vignette is marked by a strange incantation muttered over the sacred text. Paradoxically, the patriarchal intonation of "*rien de tout,*" uttered by a famous, unnamed Parisian Old Testament scholar[46] becomes the very stuff that energizes her scholarly career. It is the puff of professorial smoke that tickles her nostrils, exciting her to connect spirituality and scholarship.[47] The professor's "nothing at all" is a direct response to Schneiders's question regarding the implications of inspiration for interpreting the biblical text. And since that male-defined absence is the mark of her autobiographical presence,[48] it is not surprising to find Sandra M. Schneiders beginning her hermeneutical discussion of metaphorical thinking and the meaning of the expression "Word of God" by evoking the lingering absence and negativity in Paul Ricoeur's understanding of language.

Sandra M. Schneiders's second and third chapters, "The New Testament as the Word of God" and "The New Testament as the Church's Book," lay out the central theological tenets of her arguments for constructing a theology of the revelatory text. She argues from Paul Ricoeur and Sallie McFague that the Word of God is a root metaphor in Christian theology; that is, it is "an

[46] Ibid., 2.

[47] Summarizing two central ideas from Luce Irigaray and Jacques Lacan, Ann Rosalind Jones writes, "women, because they have been caught in a world structured by man-centered concepts, have had no way of knowing or representing themselves" ("Writing the Body: Toward an Understanding of *l'écriture féminine,*" 359), for "the father [has been] the bearer of language and culture" (ibid., 362).

[48] "A feminist practice," writes Julia Kristeva, "can only be . . . at odds with what already exists so that we may say 'that's not it' and 'that's still not it.' By 'woman' I mean that which cannot be represented, what is not said. . . ." (as quoted in Jones, "Writing the Body: Toward an Understanding of *l'écriture féminine,*" 359).

extraordinarily enduring and powerful image" which "nourishes ever new growth and meaning."[49] In contrast to how it is understood in fundamentalist and evangelical theology, this understanding does not allow the expression "Word of God" to be translated into a literal meaning. For it is an unstable linguistic entity that exists "in and even as linguistic tension involving a simultaneous affirmation and negation of the likeness between the two terms of the metaphor. The metaphor contains an 'is' and 'is not,' held in irresolvable tension."[50]

The way in which Sandra M. Schneiders appropriates Ricoeur's description of metaphor as an "is/is not" linguistic phenomenon is particularly helpful for developing a critically sensitive understanding of how the metaphor "Word of God" functions in the Christian tradition. And at first glance this description of metaphor seems to mark a break in Schneiders's defenses, a place where her autobiographical reflections inadvertently intrude into and infect the body of her scholarly work. But it is precisely at the point of the whispered "is not" that the knotty strings of her Parisian Old Testament professor's remark begin to untie and critique her legitimizing address. For example, when Schneiders talks about the referent of the metaphor "Word of God," she speaks of it as "divine revelation," which, through the medium of language, is "our encounter with the real."[51] And near the conclusion of her book, when talking about the biblical text as written discourse, she can speak of the "truth claims of the text, what [it] says about reality."[52]

At these points I want to stop Sandra M. Schneiders and ask her if I can bring back the revelatory naughtiness of her autobiographical vignette and, with her Parisian professor, whisper a reverential "is not" after the words "divine revelation," "real," and "reality." For aren't these terms also metaphors and signs of deferment? Yet again it is at these places that her autobiography and the professor's diseased "*rien de tout*" are excluded from her scientific, theological discourse. For instead of finding a feminist "that's not it, that's still not it"[53] marking her language of "divine revelation" and "the real," one discovers the politically charged language of power beginning to dominate her arguments. Listen for a moment to her description of Ricoeur's concept of distanciation: "Distanciation does indeed raise serious *challenges* for the exegete who

---

[49] Schneiders, *The Revelatory Text,* 32.
[50] Ibid., 29.
[51] Ibid., 34.
[52] Ibid., 141.
[53] Kristeva, as quoted in Jones, "Writing the Body: Toward an Understanding of *l'écriture féminine,*" 359.

*must overcome* the distance in order *to establish* as nearly as possible the original meaning of the text, but it also offers immense possibilities to the interpreter who *will exploit* the distance to derive augmented meaning from great texts that no longer belong exclusively to one time, place, or people."[54]

Or again, with regard to the indices of valid interpretation, Schneiders writes in a commanding voice:

> First, a valid interpretation *should account* for the text as it stands or establish, independently of the proposed interpretation, why and how it *should be emended.* . . . Second, a valid interpretation *has to be consistent* with itself, that is free from internal contradictions. . . . Third, a valid interpretation *should be equally as or more successful* than its competitors at explaining anomalies in the text. . . . Fourth, a valid interpretation *ought to be compatible* with what is known from other sources. . . .[55]

I have not chosen these particular texts with the intent of undermining Sandra M. Schneiders's theological method, her exegetical priorities, or her pastoral purpose. Rather, my goal is to approach her book autobiographically, in order to show how the revelatory moment of her life story inadvertently bleeds over into her scholarly task and also offers a critique of it. For there seems to be a clear line of development from her professor's *"rien de tout,"* to her own appropriation of Paul Ricoeur's understanding of metaphor (the not-ness of the Word of God) and to its ultimate circumscription and displacement by a need for "a norm against which interpretations can be judged,"[56] or for "criteria of validity" in interpretation.[57] In Sandra M. Schneiders's thinking, the legitimization of interpretation seems to imply a hermeneutical system that will somehow limit the supplementarity of the linguistic signifier, or the "is/is not" quality of ultimate metaphors.

No doubt Sandra M. Schneiders would be among the first to agree with Diane Freedman that among her many mentors "continental critics (especially male critics) do not make a point of theorizing out of a personal history made accessible to the reader. . . . [T]heir goals are generally not self-disclosure, comfort, warmth, and intimacy with the reader, but instead disruption and 'distanciation.'"[58] So it is not surprising to find that Schneiders makes a concerted effort to keep the self-disclosures of her autobiographical introduction from

---

[54] Schneiders, *The Revelatory Text,* 144 (my emphasis).

[55] Ibid., 165–66 (my emphasis).

[56] Ibid., 145.

[57] Ibid., 164.

[58] Freedman, *An Alchemy of Genres,* 99; cf. Schüssler Fiorenza, "Biblical Interpretation and Critical Commitment," 7.

intruding into the body of her scholarship. For identification, as Diane Freedman goes on to note, "is the opposite of distanciation, an almost onomatopoetic term."[59]

Nevertheless, at the conclusion to her work, Sandra M. Schneiders turns to a more personal and feminist emphasis as she begins to analyze the Johannine story of the woman at the well. In the story's dialogue the Samaritan woman recognizes Jesus as the one who reveals "all things" and, like Schneiders's description of the revelatory experience itself, there is a complementarity to their ensuing conversation.[60] The woman, Schneiders writes, "is a genuine theological dialogue partner gradually experiencing Jesus' self-revelation even as she reveals herself to him."[61] At this point I feel as though I am reading Sandra M. Schneiders through the Johannine character, and I wish I could see more of the appropriated magic.[62]

In Schneiders's exegesis, Jesus, the one who needs nothing at all, seeks something from the woman and is satisfied. In contrast to the Parisian professor's "*rien de tout*" and Paul Ricoeur's "is/is not" which open Schneiders's book, the Samaritan woman's negative statement, "Surely this couldn't be the Messiah, could it?" is carefully elided from the Johannine text. She never vocalizes the *Mēti* ("Surely not") of John 4:29.[63] The feminist whispering "that's not it, that's still not it" is barely audible as Schneiders elaborates the woman's christological witness to the Samaritan villagers who come out to meet her.

What I find powerfully compelling about Schneiders's work is her desire to bridge the gaps between the church's theological reflection, the believer's spiritual experience, and the scholar's exegetical practice. She does an excellent job of finding a dialogical and theoretical language to bridge those gaps, but I wish Schneiders had spent less effort trying rhetorically to separate *her own personal life* from the search for definitive "norm[s] against which interpretations can be judged."[64]

---

[59] Ibid.

[60] Schneiders, *The Revelatory Text,* 191; cf. 177. "Conversation" and "dialogue" are also crucial metaphors in Schneiders's interpretive theory of appropriating the biblical text (ibid., 140–42).

[61] Ibid.

[62] See her discussion of "meaning as appropriation" (*The Revelatory Text,* 172–78).

[63] Ibid., 191, 193. When used in an interrogative sentence, the negative adverb *mē* anticipates a negative response, and *ti* functions as an intensifier (Blass and Debrunner, *A Greek Grammar of the New Testament and Other Early Christian Literature,* 220–21, 226). For other examples of *mēti* in the Fourth Gospel, see John 8:22; 18:35.

[64] Schneiders, *The Revelatory Text,* 145. For example, see Nancy Miller's practice of "personal criticism" in *Getting Personal,* 1–29.

In light of Sandra M. Schneiders's truncated autobiography, it may seem presumptuous of me to ask any questions regarding the nature of the self revealed in her autobiographical vignette. Nevertheless, an answer to my questions—regardless of how tentative it might be—will help the reader better understand my summary of autobiographical criticism below.[65] Like the Samaritan woman of her final chapter, Sandra M. Schneiders's consciously constructed self is a bodiless person, one who is strongly unified by a determined will and a focused intellectual quest. In these respects it shares much of the same ideology of the unified self with Marcus Borg's literarily constructed portrait, but with a more conscious concern for making connections—past and present—to a particular Christian community.[66]

I have no idea what the *M* of Sandra M. Schneiders stands for, and I'm afraid to call her to find out the truth behind the scarlet letter on her book's cover. Personally, I like to think that the *M* stands for Marilyn—although *Sandra Marie* has a much nicer sound to it than *Sandra Marilyn*. Nevertheless, I've chosen the name Marilyn because it sounds like Merlin and conjures up images of wizardry. And Merlin's wizardry is Temma Berg's metaphor for feminist mixings of autobiographics and scholarship.[67]

Like Merlin, Sandra M. Schneiders whispers hermeneutical incantations and waves plastic metaphorical wands over the canonical text as she lifts new insights from the Christian affirmation of the Bible's divine inspiration. Yet I can't help but think, when all is said and done, that the ghost of the old Parisian biblical scholar still hovers over her desk and pen. So what I want to ask Sandra M. Schneiders is this: What groups of people grant authority to the interpretive norms you delineate, and in whose interests are those norms determined? What power structures and ideologies are served by the desire for "valid criteria" in biblical interpretation?

I think I know the answers that she would give at the beginning and at the conclusion of her book. In those two places sparks seem ready to fly as she "challeng[es] the androcentric, patriarchal, sexist, and misogynist misinterpretations that pervade the history of New Testament scholarship and that have deeply affected the Christian imagination through the scholarly and homiletic tradition."[68] But in the middle portion of the book, where Schneiders seeks to

---

[65] See the following subsections, "A Myth of Origins" and "Losing the Formula," pp. 136–44.

[66] I'm thinking here particularly of her three pages of personal acknowledgments (pp. xi–xiii) and her "Hermeneutical Appropriation" of the Samaritan woman story (pp. 195–97), both of which reflect her strong commitments to the Roman Catholic Church.

[67] Berg, "Suppressing the Language of (Wo)man: The Dream as a Common Language," 12.

[68] Schneiders, *The Revelatory Text,* 186.

legitimize the appropriation of Scripture with a theory of carefully established interpretive norms, this Merlin seems to be conjuring for the very audience she is trying to undermine. Perhaps Jane Tompkins is right in saying "that theory itself, *at least as it is usually practiced,* may be one of the patriarchal gestures women *and* men ought to avoid."[69]

## A Reader's Alchemy

Unlike Marcus Borg's and Sandra M. Schneiders's autobiographical vignettes, Mikeal Parsons's self-reflections were originally written for a very small audience. They were prepared specifically for a ten-year review of a Society of Biblical Literature seminar group.[70] Nevertheless, his analysis of his own reading context is important precisely for its difference from the other two I have just finished reviewing. Taking up the challenge of Fernando Segovia, who has argued that New Testament "readers [need] to read readers" with the same energy that they read texts,[71] Parsons exegetes his own "middle-class, middle-aged, Southern, white American" male identity, as one presently "living in the Southwest [whose] confessional commitment is Christian, profoundly shaped by Baptist traditions."[72]

Parsons's social description of himself starts off in a much more critically developed fashion than does either Borg's or Schneiders's, but, unlike them, he does not attempt to present a chronologically arranged personal narrative alongside historical or textual analysis. His autobiographical portrait is more emotionally transparent than theirs, and it is more consciously "American" in its troubled search for rootedness. His approach, which he calls "cultural-literary criticism,"[73] is in fact an elaborate expansion of the McWhopper topos that I described at the beginning of this chapter.

Since Mikeal Parsons describes cultural-literary criticism as taking "seri-

---

[69] Tompkins, "Me and My Shadow," 24, as quoted in Miller, *Getting Personal,* 21 (Miller's emphasis).

[70] It first appeared in the 1992 *SBL Seminar Papers* as "What is 'Literary' About Literary Aspects of the Gospels and Acts?" and will soon be published in *Biblical Interpretation* under the title "Anatomy of a Reader." Throughout my analysis I will be using his latest and more accessible title, but I will continue to use the page numbers from the *Seminar Papers,* since this is the only published version currently available to me.

[71] Segovia, "Towards a New Direction in Johannine Scholarship: The Fourth Gospel from a Literary Perspective," 22 (as paraphrased by Parsons, "Anatomy of a Reader," 20).

[72] Parsons, "Anatomy of a Reader," 21.

[73] Ibid., 20.

ously the assumptions that texts, readers, and methods are all historically and culturally conditioned and the fact that texts, readers, and methods have particular ideological perspectives,"[74] he begins his self-description in broad terms of his participation in Western society. But eschewing a simple autobiographical narrative that might illustrate the significance of this context, Parsons prefers instead to read himself intertextually through the lenses of other New Testament exegetes.

For example, Parsons uses Krister Stendahl's essay "The Apostle Paul and the Introspective Conscience of the West" as a way to help him understand his membership in Western society. He then turns to Clarence Jordan's *Cotton Patch Bible* and the form of Baptist-like public confession to critique his own growing consciousness of his racial and ethnic identity. Of all the elements in his elaboration of the McWhopper topos, Parsons's discussion of his troubled masculine identity reads the most like an autobiography. Here he views himself through the screen of the Davidic succession narrative as it is interpreted by Philip Culbertson in his *New Adam*. And when Parsons describes age as a social factor in his identity, he uses the ABS video "The Gerasene Demoniac" and Hanna Barbera's animated video version of Bible stories for children as ways of illustrating important differences. Finally, he analyzes the ideological constraints behind the eighteenth-century invention of "Paul's three missionary journeys" in Acts as a way of showing how "control beliefs" have molded his social location. However, as Parsons himself is quick to point out, perhaps the most glaring omission from his analysis of social locaters is that of socioeconomic class.[75]

Unlike Marcus Borg's and Sandra M. Schneiders's autobiographical selves, which project the classic Western image of the individualized, unified self with its introspective turning points, Mikeal Parsons's autobiographical self leans more toward a postmodern perspective, as if the self were something entirely socially constructed or merely a linguistic, rhetorical trope.[76] For although certain hints of individuality persist in his analysis, Parsons seems to imply that these markers are primarily constructed intertextually and are socially embedded in Western culture and American mythology. Thus, like his own lost Scotch-Irish roots, his personal story is nearly obliterated behind the pages of social description.

Parsons concludes his description of himself by arguing that cultural-literary criticism "demands that the scholar get in touch with the driving

[74] Ibid.
[75] Ibid., 29 n. 10.
[76] For a discussion of the postmodern view of the self, see pp. 138, 141 below.

myths about gender, race, age, and ideologies in popular western culture."[77] For him that means "learning more about Western culture, especially the South," where he comes from, and the Southwest, where he now resides.[78] Parsons knows that biblical scholars cannot begin every exegetical essay with a thoroughgoing analysis of social location like his own. Nevertheless, he does "envision the interpreter deciding in each moment of interpretation which of these social locaters is most important, recognizing of course, that these choices are themselves conditioned to some extent by the social location of the reader."[79]

Since the focus of Mikeal Parsons's essay is the assaying of the reader rather than the exegesis of a specific biblical text, I cannot offer the same type of autobiographical critique of his work as I did with Borg's or Schneiders's books. For in Parsons's analysis, the history of exegesis functions as a preliminary step toward understanding the self, rather than as a preface to interpreting the biblical text. In point of fact, the wide assortment of secondary sources Parsons uses tends to blend in with his own self-description. The sources become tainted blood transfusions infiltrating Parsons's semipermeable borders. In contrast, Parsons, the scientific-like narrator in this readerly experiment, remains relatively stationary and passive. He is read by other readers of the New Testament but does not himself become an active reader of any biblical text.

The letters of the word *alchemy* produce the anagram *Mychael*—a rather unusual spelling for the common proper name. Or, working in the opposite direction, beginning from the nearly phonetic spelling of Mikeal Parsons's first name, one gets the nearly phonetic spelling *alkemi*. I think that without too much trouble Mikeal Parsons could become a practitioner of literary alchemy in the genre-mixing modes of Diane Freedman and Patricia Williams.[80] For instance, Mikeal's essay begins and ends with quotations from novels, and throughout his scholarly discourse on social location he blends personal asides with snatches of literary and cultural theory and professional-looking footnotes. But since he spends no time actually exegeting a biblical text in the essay, his readers will have to wait until a later date to see whether my suspicions are confirmed regarding how "cultural-literary criticism" works its way out in his New Testament research. What I would like to see in Mikeal's work is a volatile chemical reaction: something that would combine the cyborg's

---

[77] Parsons, "Anatomy of a Reader," 29.
[78] Ibid.
[79] Ibid.
[80] Freedman, *An Alchemy of Genres;* Williams, *The Alchemy of Race and Rights.*

sense of autobiography, Merlin's textual magic, and his own alchemic analysis of the reader. That formula, however, has yet to be written.

I feel good about myself. In the process of critiquing these three autobiographical vignettes by biblical scholars, I've been careful to keep my distance from them. I've kept my critical mask up over my nose and mouth, and I think I've made it through without getting infected by any toxic autobiographical antigens exuding from their pores. I actually feel stronger than I did when I began the chapter, as though I've built up, in the process of writing the last few pages, a certain physical resistance to autobiographical intrusions. So now I'm going to finish my breakfast, get dressed, and then exercise my muscles a bit on the machinery of autobiographical theory.

## A Myth of Origins

As I noted earlier, despite the obvious structural inadequacies and largely uncritical nature of most biblical scholars' autobiographical acts, autobiography is by no means an insignificant area of research in contemporary literary theory.[81] Rejuvenated largely by feminist critics interested in uncovering the little-known works of so-called "nonliterary," "noncanonical" women authors and a poststructuralist fascination with the textualized, disappearing self, interest in autobiography has recently spilled over into the seminars of the American Academy of Religion.[82]

Although it has been common to begin the study of autobiography with St. Augustine's *Confessions,* the word *autobiography* has its origins in the English language of the late eighteenth century.[83] For example, Robert

---

[81] As late as 1972 James Olney could write: "Surprisingly little has been written about autobiography at all, and virtually nothing about its philosophical and psychological implications" (*Metaphors of the Self,* ix). Within a few short years, however, scholarly interest in autobiography would rise significantly (see, for example, Weintraub, *The Value of the Individual;* Olney, *Autobiography;* Gunn, *Autobiography;* Eakin, *Fictions in Autobiography;* Lejeune, *On Autobiography*). More recently, a shift has been made toward the rhetorical implications of national and ethnic autobiography (e.g., Lionnet, *Autobiographical Voices;* Folkenflik, *The Culture of Autobiography;* Fischer, "Ethnicity and the Post-Modern Arts of Memory," and Pease, "National Identities, Postmodern Artifacts, and Postnational Narratives").

[82] For example, see Sidonie Smith, *A Poetics of Women's Autobiography;* Gilmore, *Autobiographics;* and Costello, "Taking the 'Woman' out of Women's Autobiography: The Perils and Potentialities of Theorizing Female Subjectivity." In religious studies, see Henking, "The Personal is the Theological: Autobiographical Acts in Contemporary Feminist Theology."

[83] Folkenflik, *The Culture of Autobiography,* 1–5; cf. Shea, "The Prehistory of American

Folkenflik points out that the earliest reference to the word is "in the preface to the 1786 edition of Ann Yearsley's *Poems*. . . . Hence, the first use of any form of the term appeared in the apologia of a lower-class woman poet generally condescended to in literary histories under the name Lactilla, the Milkmaid Poet."[84] Folkenflik thus makes a strong argument that autobiography, as a stable literary form, was born on the outskirts of public intercourse and out of wordlock.[85] Its conception was not immaculate, let alone virginal, nor was it without siblings. As Folkenflik goes on to note: "By the middle of the 1820's, there was an institutional recognition of the term and a budding [bulging?] canon."[86]

The original elements of the thrice-spliced, word-grafted term *auto-bio-graphy* present a helpful and, in a general sense, an accurate history of the troubled genre's critical investigation. For example, Sidonie Smith argues that during the first half of the twentieth century the emphasis in autobiographical literary criticism was on the *bio* of the author.[87] Speaking of this period of criticism, James Olney describes

> a rather naive threefold assumption about the writing of autobiography: first that the *bios* of autobiography could only signify 'the course of a lifetime' . . . ; second that the autobiographer could narrate his life in a manner at least approaching the objective historical account . . . ; and third, that there was nothing problematical about the *autos,* no agonizing questions of identity, self-definition, or self-deception—at least none the reader need attend to. . . .[88]

But a second generation of critics, still confident "in the referentiality of language and a corollary confidence in the authenticity of the self," "attuned itself to the 'agonizing questions' inherent in self-representation."[89] Thus interest shifts from the *bio* element of autobiography to the *auto* and its fictive constructions. Smith writes that, for this group of scholars working in the 1960s, "truthfulness becomes a much more complex and problematic phe-

Autobiography," 25; Olney, "Autobiography and the Cultural Moment: A Thematic, Historical, and Bibliographic Introduction," 6–7; and Sprinker, "Fictions of the Self: The End of Autobiography," 325.

[84] Folkenflik, *The Culture of Autobiography,* 1–2.

[85] Ibid., 5.

[86] Ibid., 6; cf. 8–9.

[87] Sidonie Smith, *A Poetics of Women's Autobiography,* 4.

[88] Olney, "Autobiography and the Cultural Moment: A Thematic, Historical, and Bibliographic Introduction," 20.

[89] Sidonie Smith, *A Poetics of Women's Autobiography,* 5.

nomenon."[90] The psychological dimensions of truth have taken precendence over those of fact or morality.

Finally, Olney and Smith want to argue that a third phase of autobiographical theory can be discerned in the contemporary scene where *graphy*, or the concentration upon inscripted selves and readers, has taken over center stage. Here, an emphasis on the death of the unified self has led to a concern for the rhetorical, linguistic function of "selves" and "readers," with a "careful teasing out of warring forces of signification within the text itself."[91] Not surprisingly, writing epitaphs for the self-polluting *auto* have been the norm in autobiographical studies of the 1970s and 1980s. Nicole Jouve's internal monologue describing the demise of the self is not untypical of the topos:

> Contemporary theory has problematized the subject in manifold ways that preclude the search for the self that you propose. Psychoanalysis would demonstrate to you, through Lacan in particular, that 'I' is always another, first grasped as an imago. And what about the unconscious, the divided self and all that? Self-knowledge is a mirage, a hangover oasis from the Greeks. And you speak about the autobiographical voice as if there was such a thing, as if the prodigious wealth of recent studies on autobiography, first male then female, hadn't endlessly questioned its existence as a genre.[92]

Nevertheless, as scholarly interest in cross-cultural and bicultural autobiography has expanded, there is a growing need to readdress the confessional, "naïve" mode of representation exhibited by much of marginalized self-writing. From the perspective of ideological criticism, Leigh Gilmore asks the crucial questions:

> Has the claim of representativeness, which characterized autobiography as practiced by an elite group, become passé and naïve because the poststructuralist critique of such a grounding has been overwhelmingly persuasive? Or has representativeness been marginalized with the effect of forcing those who now claim it to the 'margin' of representation? Why does the coincidence of poststructuralist skepticism and 'truth telling' produce a judgment of naïveté when representative identity is self-claimed by a non-'representative' person (in terms of the dominant culture)?[93]

---

[90] Ibid.

[91] Barbara Johnson, *The Critical Difference*, 5, as quoted in Sidonie Smith, *A Poetics of Women's Autobiography*, 6. Cf. Olney, "Autobiography and the Cultural Moment: A Thematic, Historical, and Bibliographic Introduction," 22.

[92] Jouve, *White Woman Speaks with Forked Tongue*, 9–10.

[93] Gilmore, *Autobiographics*, 228; cf. 82; see also Gerhart, *Genre Choices, Gender Questions*, 110; and Tolbert, "The Politics and Poetics of Location," 310–11.

But I'm getting ahead of myself. I'm ready to walk out the front door, and I still haven't brushed my teeth or put on my shoes and socks. I need to sit back for a moment and plan a more pleasing presentation for the origins of autobiographical criticism before I leave the house. So let me try putting on this myth in another way.

Many recent studies in autobiography look to Roy Paschal's 1960 book *Design and Truth in Autobiography,* as the turning point in modern study of the genre.[94] This is because Paschal's theoretical approach is a formalist bridge linking the strictly historical delineation of canonical autobiography of the 1920s–1940s with the antiformalist theories of the 1970s and beyond. Not surprisingly, Paschal begins his study with an attempt to clarify autobiography as a genre, comparing it with diaries, memoirs, autobiographical writings, and philosophical reflections on the self. For Paschal, autobiography is "historical in its method, and at the same time, . . . represent[s] . . . the self in and through its relations with the outer world."[95] "It involves the reconstruction of the movement of a life, or part of a life, in the actual circumstances in which it was lived,"[96] and "is . . . an interplay, a collusion between past and present; its significance is indeed more a revelation of the present situation than the uncovering of the past."[97]

Paschal's study has three essential foci: (1) the history of autobiography as a literary genre, (2) the structure of autobiography and its various subtypes, and (3) the issue of truth in autobiography. For Paschal, and most other male critics, Augustine's *Confessions* represented the genesis of the genre which, he argues, has also been "essentially European."[98] For Paschal, autobiography is the "distinctive product of Western, post-Roman civilisation, and only in modern times has it spread to other civilisations."[99] This argument is convincing, of course, only insofar as he and others define autobiography specifically in terms of "a preoccupation with the self [which] . . . holds the balance

---

[94] For example, see Adams, *Telling Lies in Modern American Autobiography,* 1; and Olney, "Autobiography and the Cultural Moment: A Thematic, Historical, and Bibliographic Introduction," 11. Another important scholar working in the area of autobiography in the early 1960s was William Spengemann (see especially his later work, *The Forms of Autobiography*).

[95] Paschal, *Design and Truth in Autobiography,* 8. Philippe Lejeune's definition is very similar: "[W]e shall define autobiography as the retrospective prose narrative that someone writes concerning his own existence, where the focus is his individual life, in particular the story of his personality" (*On Autobiography,* viii, 149–50).

[96] Paschal, *Design and Truth in Autobiography,* 9.

[97] Ibid., 10.

[98] Ibid., 22.

[99] Ibid., 180.

between the self and the world, the subjective and the objective, [and] . . . is inspired by a reverence for the self . . . in its delicate uniqueness."[100] Most women and Third World autobiographers are automatically excluded from this definition, for they blur that "balanced" distinction between the self and the world.

For Paschal, the literary critic must wait until the sixteenth-century Renaissance to find the "extraordinary psychological insight" that marks truly great autobiography.[101] And the classsical age of autobiography is represented only by the late eighteenth- and early nineteenth-century works of Rousseau, Goethe, and Wordsworth, who "were inwardly turned, deeply concerned with their sensibility and imagination."[102]

In terms of the structure of autobiography and its various subtypes, Paschal is careful to distinguish four categories: "autobiography as the story of a man's theoretical understanding of the world," the "essayist autobiography," the "autobiography which restricts itself to childhood," and "innovations of method."[103] Finally, Paschal describes autobiographical truth in terms of an internal narrative consistency where "that unique truth of life . . . is seen from inside."[104] For him, "truth lies in the building up of a personality through the images it makes of itself, that embody its mode of absorbing and reacting to the outer world, and that are profoundly related to one another at each moment and in the succession from past to present."[105]

Over the past thirty years, the three foci of Pascal's work—the history of the genre, the structure of autobiography, and the issue of truth—have remained important to theoretical discussions of autobiography. But each focal point has been scrutinized and strongly criticized. Not surprisingly, feminist and postcolonial critics have challenged the classical definition of the genre and its history for its male, European bias, and the narrow structure of autobiography for its Western emphasis on the ideology of the individual and internal change. What this has meant for feminist and postcolonial critics is that, today, autobiography is shaped by a "nonessentialist aesthetics [which is] tied to the emergence of occluded oral cultures, to the articulation of a reality that emphasizes relational patterns over autonomous ones, interconnected-

---

[100] Ibid., 180–81.
[101] Ibid., 30.
[102] Ibid., 36.
[103] Ibid., 56.
[104] Ibid., 195.
[105] Ibid., 188.

ness over independence, isomorphic analogies over unifying totalities, and opacity over transparency."[106]

Similarly, poststructuralist critics have completely rejected Paschal's understanding of truth in autobiography and his concept of the unified self. "It has become a commonplace of contemporary literary and critical theory," writes Martin Gloege, "to think of the 'self' as a 'construction,' as counterfeit and artificial as opposed to authentic and natural, as a product of society, as a narrative or rhetorical device, trope, or strategy of and within language."[107]

Finally, I'm on my way out the front door.[108] My shoes and socks are on, and I'm ready to face the world. I've eaten a bowl of cereal, had a methamphetamine with my third cup of coffee (that will take care of my allergies for another four hours), and now I'm ready to metamorphose into a bit of my own autobiographical metacriticism. Meta-autobiographical criticism. That's what I'm going to call my new outfit. It is a metaphase—or, better, a metastasizing of autobiographical criticism and human skin. A new metaphrastic metaphor.

## LOSING THE FORMULA

I put off writing this chapter until the rest of the book was nearly completed, thinking that I would need the extra time to read everything I could on the current status of autobiography in literary criticism. Using the dissertation formula, I figured that if

> I did not begin this [chapter] with the requisite prefatory litany of past adventures in criticism, buying into the sort of paranoia ("If I don't cite earlier critics, my readers won't find my case credible") that the Academy seems to foster by equating scholarship and objectivity with an ability to run a CD-ROM search

---

[106] Lionnet, *Autobiographical Voices,* 245.

[107] Gloege, "The American Origins of the Postmodern Self," 59; see also van den Heever, "Being and Nothingness," 42–45.

[108] "[A]utobiography," Robert Sayre writes, "is, or can be that second house into which we are reborn, carried by our own creative power. We make it ourselves, then remake it—make it new.

"The comparison to architecture (rather than to clothes, the more traditional metaphor for autobiography) is also apt because of the effect the lives and works of Americans have had on the American landscape. The 'building' of civilization in the United States has been like the construction of a vast enclosure over the continent. . . ." ("Autobiography and the Making of America," 148–49; see also 156, 168).

of the MLA Bibliography, I [would] risk being accused of lacking professionalism and/or rigor.[109]

And God knows, I didn't want that curse hanging around my neck. But the more I read in autobiographical theory, especially on the feminist side of the issues, the less convinced I was of the value of writing in the same dry, formulaic manner as I had previously.

My original and primary intention was to do a survey of the theoretical literature, writing a short summary of the critical problems and general movements in order to make biblical scholars aware of the significance of autobiography for a reader-oriented hermeneutics. But I also found in my reading that autobiographics is a cross-disciplinary exercise, involving anthropology, psychology, literature, and philosophy. How was I ever going to pull together so many fields of research into a coherent summary for biblical scholars? My original goals seemed far too broad and unwieldy. And even though I have actually just completed a short variation of the survey-of-literature topos, I'm not sure now that my summary of autobiographical literary criticism has been particularly useful to my reader.

As I explored the secondary literature, what really began to interest me was the role American myths have played in Euro-American autobiography,[110] and the construction of the person in autobiographical material from non-Western peoples.[111] Since I am a Euro-American reader who was strongly influenced in childhood by a Native American subculture, I began to think that I should give particular attention to the distinctive qualities of Euro-American and Native American autobiography and how those ways of imagining the self might have influenced the way I read myself.

For if there is any truth in Paul de Man's argument that autobiography "is

---

[109] Torsney, "'Everyday Use': My Sojourn at Parchman Farm," 73. Or in Dorothy Dinnerstein's words: I make "no effort to survey the relevant literature. Not only would that task be (for me) unmanageably huge. It would also be against my principles. I believe in reading unsystematically and taking notes erratically. Any effort to form a rational policy about what to take in, out of the inhuman flood of printed human utterance that pours over us daily, feels to me like a self-deluded exercise in pseudomastery" (*The Mermaid and the Minotaur*, ix).

[110] For example, see Stone, *Autobiographical Occasions and Original Acts;* Eakin, *American Autobiography;* Payne, *Multicultural Autobiography;* Adams, *Telling Lies in Modern American Autobiography;* Gloege, "The American Origins of the Postmodern Self"; Sayre, "Autobiography and the Making of America"; and Wilson, "Producing American Selves: The Form of American Biography."

[111] For example, see Brumble, *American Indian Autobiography;* Krupat, *For Those Who Come After,* and "Native American Autobiography and the Synecdochic Self"; and Wong, *Sending My Heart Back Across the Years.*

not a genre or a mode, but a figure of reading or of understanding that occurs, to some degree, in all texts,"[112] and if autobiography does not reveal reliable self-knowledge but rather "demonstrates in a striking way the impossibility of closure and of totalization,"[113] then the questions that de Man's analysis raised for me were these: What are the figures of reading that have guided my understanding? And do those figures reveal reliable knowledge of myself and the Fourth Gospel or, instead, do they demonstrate the "impossibility of closure and totalization"?

For example, Daniel Shea charts the sources of American autobiography showing how, "[b]y reputation, if not chronology, John Smith stands first in the line of American self-writers who found that they could not write themselves into the New World text without writing the native identity to some extent as their own."[114] Paradoxically, however, Arnold Krupat notes that "from the first days of settlement until the end of the nineteenth century, the American self tended to locate its peculiar national distinctiveness in relation to a perceived opposition between the European, the 'man of culture,' and the Indian, the 'child of nature.'"[115] Strangely, the conflict of ideologies represented in the two perspectives of wanting to write the Native American identity as one's own and of seeing oneself as a European transplant, opposed to the Indian, seemed to reflect my own autobiographical ambivalence. Moreover, I found Krupat's description of the Native American self as an "I-am-We experience . . . where such a phrase indicates that I understand myself as a self only in relation to the coherent and bounded whole of which I am a part,"[116] reflected my own self-awareness as well as the ancient Mediterranean view of person[117] and certain elements in what some have called feminine self-consciousness.[118]

---

[112] De Man, "Autobiography as De-facement," 921.

[113] Ibid., 922.

[114] Shea, "The Prehistory of American Autobiography," 29.

[115] Krupat, *For Those Who Come After,* 41.

[116] Krupat, "Native American Autobiography and the Synecdochic Self," 174.

[117] Brumble, *American Indian Autobiography,* 37, 118.

[118] Hertha Wong argues: "There are a few similarities between how feminists characterize female personal narrative and . . . pre-contact Native American self-narration. According to feminist autobiographical theory, women's autobiographical narrative, unlike men's, tends to be circular (cyclical) rather than linear, and their autobiographical focus communal rather than individual. Although these women are Westerners, like Native Americans they share a sense of identity that is based on belonging to and participating in a larger pattern—-the cultural patterns of family and social relations . . ." (*Sending My Heart Back Across the Years,* 23; but cf. Vizenor's important critique, in "Ruins of Representation: Shadow Survivance and the Literature of Dominance," 24–26).

As Jeane Costello argues, the point is not

> that men see themselves as autonomous individuals and women [or Native
> Americans] see themselves as connected to others . . . , but [rather] that any
> conception of individuality is an ideological construct. For postmodern theo-
> ries have shown us the ways in which all subjects, not just female [and non-
> Western], are situated and relational. . . . There is no absolute autonomy for
> anyone.[119]

The more I research I did, the more I felt myself beginning to fracture and
follow the fissure lines of my feverish late-night reading. What was I really
doing when I tried to describe myself as a reader of the Fourth Gospel, when I
tried to come out from behind my well-wrought mask of implied and
encoded readers? Would the reader I discovered myself to be, be any less a fiction than the implied or encoded reader I had previously disked over in the
Fourth Gospel? Was I discovering myself? Or inventing myself? Suddenly I
began to understand William Maxwell's dictum: "[I]n talking about the past,
we lie with every breath we draw."[120]

## WHERE THE FUTURE LIES

So who or what will I be when I go back inside and reread the Fourth Gospel
without the help of my masked, encoded reader? That question troubles me,
and I don't quite know how to answer it. Will I be a cyborg, meeting myself
again for the first time? Or a Merlin, looking at the revelatory me in a pur-
loined text? Perhaps I'll become a blurry-eyed alchemist and combine fairy
dust and esoteric roots in order to conjure up some new sylph.

Whatever I become, I know that my reading in autobiographical criticism
has taught me I can never escape from turning to behold the man, the autobiographical *I*. "It's in the *I* of the beholder," they say. It's in the *I* of the storm;
in the voIce of the "AmerIcan be anything undivIdualist." It's in the dIseased
*I* of AIDS.

Like the Johannine *I Am* sayings of Jesus, my *I* marks the dropping of only
one of many masks—that antiseptic shield protecting me from allergies,
infection, and death. But with that mask gone, this McWhopper is finally

---

[119] Costello, "Taking the 'Woman' out of Women's Autobiography: The Perils and Potentials of Theorizing Women's Subjectivities," 131 (see also Wong, *Sending My Heart Back
Across the Years*, 16–17).

[120] As quoted in Adams, *Telling Lies in Modern American Autobiography*, 15; cf. 169–70.

ready to move beyond the purity and monoculturalism of Burger King and McDonalds to the All-Nite Truck Stop on the other side of the tracks. I'll go inside, sit with greasy eighteen-wheelers, and swap tall tales all night long in the classic American tradition of Washington Irving and Mark Twain.[121] I'll be transformed into a McWhopper—a McWhopper telling whoppers.

And I know I can lie with the best of them. In fact, one of my earliest childhood memories is of lying.[122] I must have been about five years old at the time, trying to remain a part of my older brothers' group of worldly-wise buddies. They all had girlfriends, or so they claimed, and they were bragging about how many times they had kissed them. So I lied and said that I had smacked one on Debbie Becker a few weeks earlier, behind the old outhouse next to Elm Springs Gospel Chapel.[123] But to my chagrin, the lie didn't do the trick. Instead of becoming my ticket into an elite community of first- and second-grade boys, my lie became a source of scorn and grounds for exclusion.

Little did I know that a conspiracy of lies was floating about that day. The boys' shocked silence was testimony that none of them had ever kissed a girl or had a girlfriend. And in the instant I blurted out my story I knew that I had crossed an invisible line into a new land from which I could not return. I had tainted my soul and would never be admitted into that secret brotherhood of jokes, pokes, and sly winks. None of my tearful pleadings or swear-on-the-Bible, cross-my-heart-and-hope-to-die confessions could restore me to their fellowship.

I keep reading that AIDS is spreading, even contaminating elite white male heterosexuals like myself. And now I'm beginning to think that those Autobiographical Intrusions Destroying Scholarship have infected me too. I feel weak-kneed and queasy. I'm itching all over and breaking out in hives. I'm no

[121] According to Timothy Adams, "the characteristic blend of truth and lie common to the [American western] tall tale is suggestive of the . . . perennial paradox of the autobiographer, whose writing always lies on the frontier" (*Telling Lies in Modern American Autobiography,* 38).

[122] Michel Tournier observes: "Childhood is given to us as ardent confusion, and the rest of life is not time enough to make sense of it or explain to ourselves what happened" (as quoted in Vizenor, *Interior Landscapes,* frontispiece).

[123] For Robert Folkenflik, "[o]ne very special form of the self as other is dependent on the lie. The telling of a lie as a special way of presenting the self to others as different from what one consciously knows oneself to be differentiates one from others and at the same time makes of one's self a private thing (one's 'own' self) that cannot be known by another. The lie seems particularly important in autobiographies devoted in whole or in part to childhood" ("The Self as Other," 225).

Folkenflik's primary example of how lies function in autobiographies of childhood comes from Edmund Gosse's *Father and Son* (pp. 33–35). Like Gosse, I grew up as a "member of an obscure fundamentalist sect [called] the Plymouth Brethren" ("The Self as Other," 225).

longer able to resist the onslaught of disease. I don't think I can make it across the tracks to that truck stop after all.

Perhaps I'll feel better if I lie down here for awhile. Lying, my mother used to say, is great therapy for most common, generic illnesses. "Just lie for a spell," she would say. "It's good for the body *and* the soul."[124]

---

[124] "Lies mean," writes Nicole Jouve, "not lies but creating the elaborate conditions within which 'truth' might be glimpsed" (*White Woman Speaks with Forked Tongue*, 28; see also Johnson, "My Monster/My Self," 4; cf. Silko, *Ceremony*, 191).

# CHAPTER FIVE

# Not Yet Fifty:
## Postcolonial Confessions from an Outpost in the San Juan Basin

The deepest side of being an American is the sense of being like nothing before us in history. . . .

—Alfred Kazin

I am I because my little dog knows me.

—Gertrude Stein

Very truly, I tell you, before Abraham was, I am.

—John 8:58

If representation of the self—indeed, the very concept of self—is problematic in contemporary autobiographical theory and postmodern literature, it is no less an issue in the Fourth Gospel. In that book, too, Jesus' hidden, mistaken, intertextual, transhistorical identity is crucial to the plot. Although the reader is told from the very beginning who Jesus is (John 1:1–18), his antagonists never seem to get it right (7:40–42; 8:25–28; 11:41–42; 19:33). Even his own disciples are unable to figure him out until just hours before his death (16:29–30). Working with cultural-anthropological models in biblical criticism, Bruce Malina has noted that in the Mediterranean honor/shame culture of Jesus' day, to ask who you were was to inquire where you were from and who your family was.[1] This is certainly true for the Fourth Gospel. Every question about Jesus' identity is ultimately an issue of who his parents are and

---

[1] See his discussion of the "dyadic personality" in *The New Testament World,* 63–73, esp. 69. Karl Weintraub puts it this way: In classical antiquity "[i]ndividuals were embedded in the social mass of given blood relations" (*The Value of the Individual,* 2).

where he is from (6:42; 8:14, 19; 16:28; 19:9). In the southwestern United States where I grew up, personhood was constructed along similar lines.[2]

Like many others in our academic discipline of New Testament studies, I have come to the guild of biblical scholarship through the roots of American Protestant fundamentalism. But the anti-intellectualism that I was raised with, in the fierce primitivism and sectarianism of the lay-led Plymouth Brethren, was tempered by a childhood spent exploring the eroded cliffs and canyons of the Navajo Indian Reservation in northeastern Arizona. There, as the son of a missionary school teacher and a school cook, I encountered a culture radically different from that of my own family.

## METAPHOR[3]

I was seven years old and already enamored with Indians when we moved to Immanuel Mission from the plains of central Kansas in the spring of 1959. When my two older brothers and I played cowboys and Indians with the

---

[2] David Brumble goes so far as to compare explicitly the ancient Mediterranean world's view of the person with that of Native Americans (*American Indian Autobiography,* 3–5, 46, 115–16, 122, 136–37; cf. also Cheyfitz, *The Poetics of Imperialism,* xii–xiii).

Those distinctive qualities of the Indian persona are dramatically illustrated by Tony Hillerman in his novel *People of Darkness.* There the Navajo tribal policeman, Jim Chee, meets a white woman who asks him about himself. After a lengthy answer to her question, the woman is baffled by his response and says, "You're not playing the game. . . . I told you about me. You're just telling me about your family."

The statement surprises Chee, since he "defined himself by his family. How else? And then it occurred to him that white people didn't. They identified themselves by what they did as individuals" (p. 105; see Bakerman, "Cutting Both Ways: Race, Prejudice, and Motive in Tony Hillerman's Detective Fiction," 22; Erisman, "Hillerman's Uses of the Southwest," 13; and Pierson, "Mystery Literature and Ethnography: Fictional Detectives as Anthropologists," 24–29).

In a strange way, I have discovered much about myself from reading Hillerman's books. For, as Ward Churchill notes, "through [Hillerman's] efforts, an appreciable portion of the American reading public . . . have for the first time found themselves identifying directly with native characters, thereby understanding at least some aspects of the modern Indian circumstance in ways which have never before been possible for them" (*Fantasies of the Master Race,* 267).

[3] Jacques Derrida writes: "Thought stumbles upon metaphor, or metaphor falls to thought at the moment when meaning attempts to emerge from itself in order to be stated, enunciated, brought to the light of language" ("White Mythology," in *Margins of Philosophy,* 233). And Eric Cheyfitz adds: "Metaphor marks the frontier between the domestic and the foreign precisely by blurring that boundary" (*The Poetics of Imperialism,* 94; cf. 106–9).

neighborhood boys in Ramona,[4] Kansas, we were the only ones who willingly chose to be the underdogs.[5] Usually after the proper number of cowboys had been selected, the rejects would become our camp stragglers, complaining all afternoon about their horrific fate. But not us. We were wild-eyed warriors, raiding the westward headed wagon trains with their U.S. Cavalry escorts. I have a photograph of my brothers and myself at the ages of six, seven, and eight, standing stiffly in front of our house with store-bought bows, tomahawks, and feather war bonnets, and the fiercest looks we could muster for our camera-crazy aunt (see illustration 1).[6]

I can still remember the worst whipping I ever got as a child. It was for a secret war dance my brothers and I once held after sundown. The predetermined spot for the celebration had been carefully scouted earlier in the day, and if no enemies were lurking about, we would assemble after supper at the smoldering backyard trash can, next to our neighbor's tinder dry, stubble-strewn field. Two miles south of that field ran the original Santa Fe Trail (see illustration 2),[7] and local farmers would tell of occasionally plowing up Indian arrowheads or iron scraps from freight wagons abandoned along the trailside. We imagined ourselves to be Pawnees on the warpath that evening, plotting to raid a few of those slow-moving, overloaded wagons. With a hot, dry Kansas wind blowing from the east, showers of sparks flew from our fiery brands like a Fourth of July fireworks display. We hopped, whooped, and hollered, waving our glowing wands in intricate airborne patterns. But suddenly a stranger stepped out from the shadow of the dilapidated garage. From the strong, purposeful gait we knew it was our father, returning late from school. In an instant the sacred spell was shattered. Like some primitive pictograph, our bruised

---

[4] The farming community of Ramona, whose name probably derived from the *mestiza* heroine of Helen Hunt Jackson's vastly popular 1884 novel of the same name, had a population of about one hundred in the mid-1950s (see further May, *The Annotated Ramona,* i–xvi; Scheick, *The Half-Blood,* 44–45, 82–85; for a postcolonial definition of *mestiza/o,* see Lionnet, *Autobiographical Voices,* 14, 18).

[5] Rayna Green discusses the origin of the children's game "cowboys and Indians" in "Poor Lo and Dusky Ramona: Scenes from an Album of Indian America," 88–89, esp. n. 17.

[6] "The photograph acts toward the self like a harshly lit mirror," writes Michael Ignatieff, "like the pitiless historian confronted with the wish fulfillments of nationalistic fable or political lie" (*The Russian Album,* 7; cf. Sontag, *On Photography,* 37–38, 41).

[7] Although I did not realize it at the time, the "Holy Faith" Trail had already played an important role in my family's history. My father's great grandmother's uncles traveled it in 1848; in 1880 my father's great uncle helped lay track for the railroad that was following it; and my father's father was a postal clerk on the Santa Fe railway line in the 1940s and 1950s.

1. *Pretending to be Indians.* Ramona, Kansas, 1958. I am in the center.

2. *Ramona, Kansas, and the Santa Fe Trail.* Ramona is southeast of Dickinson, and the road below Ramona, with the bulge between Tampa and Lost Springs, is the Santa Fe Trail. (Map courtesy of the Kansas Department of Transportation)

and battered buttocks would bear the bitter memory of that evening for days.[8]

But now it was May 1959 and the Kansas prairie with its imaginary Indians was fading quickly into the distance. Pawnee Rock, Fort Larned, and Dodge City were far behind us, and we were simply a tired family of seven making a hot, dusty, eight hundred mile trip to live with real Indians in Arizona. On that endless four-day journey to the other side of the world, one of my two older brothers, Robert or Gregory, usually got to ride in the cab of Orville Robson's old farm truck which carried our household belongings. That left six of us uncomfortably glued to each other and to the sweat-soaked seats of our Ford sedan—my two younger sisters, Brenda and Beth; two of us boys; my father; and my mother, who was seven months pregnant with David, her sixth and last child in a ten-year span (see illustration 3).

At about noon on the third day of our journey we crossed the Continental Divide at Wolf Creek Pass, in southern Colorado. We stopped and had lunch at a roadside picnic area near the headwaters of the San Juan River, a short distance beyond the divide. I would spend the next ten years immersed in the sun-parched basin that river drained.[9] It would set the boundaries of my childhood world (see illustration 4).

We lived our first fourteen months at Immanuel Mission (see illustration 5)[10] in a two-room adobe and stone cellar, sharing the single bathroom with Yellowhair, an ancient Navajo who knew no English and was a survivor of the "Long Walk."[11] Yellowhair was more than a hundred years old when we first met him, and when he smiled, his face would wrinkle and crease, making him look like the loose skin that covered the joint of my thumb. For twenty years he had been the only baptized Navajo in Morning Meeting.[12]

Yellowhair's room adjoined the basement bathroom. And occasionally, on

---

[8] We were playing with fire in spite of our parents' numerous warnings, and knowing full well that they lived by the biblical adage, "Spare the rod, spoil the child" (see Prov 20:30; 22:15; 23:13–14; cf. Gosse, *Father and Son*, 43).

[9] Symbolically, my two older brothers and I were buried beneath the cold waters of baptism our first Sunday on the reservation.

[10] The name *Immanuel* means "God [is] with us" and comes from Isaiah's prophetic oracle of salvation (Isa 7:14; cf. Matt 1:23). For the mission staff the *us* part (-*ānû*) was a crucial, exclusivistic term. God could only be found with us, on that ten acres of fenced desert, and nowhere else within a fifty-mile radius.

[11] This is what the Navajo people called their 1864 journey into exile at Bosque Redondo in central New Mexico (Hillerman, *Listening Woman*, 126–27).

[12] We used the phrase "Morning Meeting," a term betraying its antisacramental, Quaker origins, to refer to our weekly "Breaking of Bread" or communion service (Gosse, *Father and Son*, 101–2, 142).

3. *On the road to Immanuel Mission in late May, 1959.* My sister Beth is in the foreground. "Shiprock," a one-thousand-foot-high volcanic plug, is in the background.

4. *Exploring a New World.* My oldest brother, Robert, and I investigate the Yazzie family's abandoned *chaha'oh,* or "pole arbor" as Tony Hillerman would call it (June, 1959).

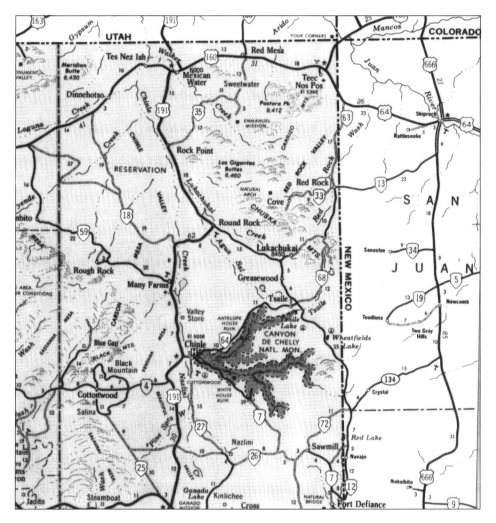

5. *Immanuel Mission.* Immanuel Mission has always been spelled with a capital *E* on U.S. road maps, although we never spelled it that way. The mission is about twenty miles southwest of the Four Corners monument (the name given to the place where Utah, Colorado, New Mexico, and Arizona meet), and in 1959 it was forty-five miles from the nearest highway, which stopped at the New Mexico state line.

Under the vision and guidance of Harry Ironside and Carl Armerding, the Holcomb family established the mission in 1922 on the site of an old abandoned trading post. When we moved there the mission consisted of eight buildings on about ten fenced acres. There was a two-room school, a garage, a shop and storage building, one private residence, a building that housed the diesel generator that supplied our electricity, the "big house" (a three-story dormitory, dining room, and staff residence), a hogan used for overnight Navajo guests, and a new, partially completed dormitory. (Map courtesy of *Arizona Highways* magazine)

his way to empty his slop-bucket in the morning, he would stand and silently watch my mother getting dressed. With a sudden feeling of strange eyes upon her, she would turn and glimpse his shuffling shadow or hear his door scraping shut on the hard-packed dirt floor of his windowless room. Lately I have found myself yearning to find a place where I could meet Yellowhair once again, speak his language, and explore the shriveled memories of his youth.

In the windstorms of early summer the front room of our apartment would fill with fine-grained sand that seeped through the ground-level windows, and during late summer thunderstorms, chocolate colored water would flood the room. On those days we were allowed to stay in bed a little longer as my father shoveled and swept the room clean. Sometimes a snake or two would find our cool, den-like cellar of adobe and rock, and the shrill shriek of its discoverer—usually one of my sisters—would bring the entire family running.

Within two years we had built our own four-bedroom, cinder-block house with all the conveniences of the modern world. It never flooded and it kept out unwelcome visitors better than the two-room cellar ever did. We had electricity, gas heat, running water, two indoor toilets, and a bright yellow, van-like "carry-all" (bought for fifty dollars at Army Surplus in Phoenix). But outside the mission compound no one had these comforts, and no one seemed to miss them. Most of the *Diné*[13] I saw rode horseback or in horse-drawn wagons. They lived in hogans—one-room mud huts with crude, oil-drum, wood-burning stoves in the center. They traveled for miles to fill their barrels with drinking water, and their toilets were any bushes tall enough or ravines deep enough to hide them from the curious eyes of a roving white boy.

Inside our house we read the Bible daily around the dining room table and in Sunday School I memorized verses that spoke of a Holy Spirit poured out on Jews thousands of years ago. But outside our front door I was getting to know people who encountered spirits, witches, and holiness (*hózhǫ́*, harmony)[14]—all within a quarter-mile walk of Immanuel Mission's fenced compound.

Inside our house we kept a dog as a pet, and it usually slept at night curled

---

[13] This is what the Navajo people call themselves. It can best be translated as "the people" (Hillerman, *Dance Hall of the Dead*, 20).

[14] Hillerman, *The Dark Wind*, 55–58. Although there is no "*r*" sound in the Navajo language, Hillerman spells the word "*hozro*," on a number of occasions. In a recent interview, however, he acknowledges his earlier misspellings of the word (Breen, "Interview with Tony Hillerman," 51).

up on our front doorstep.[15] But beyond our front door the name for dog was *łéchąą'í* (shit-eater), and I saw starving, cowering dogs kicked at every opportunity.[16] Occasionally laughing Navajo children would throw live puppies into the mission's garbage dump fires. It was not unusual to find their small blackened bodies the next morning, mixed in among the empty cans and broken bottles.

My most vivid childhood memories are of dogs.[17] They haunt my dreams.

---

[15] As David White notes, in many Indo-European traditions "[t]he dog either remains stationary, on the threshold between night and day or between indoors and outdoors; or it constitutes a moving periphery, enclosing the herd that it guards from savage predators (often its cousins, wolves) or human rustlers, or providing a moving horizon between nature and culture as it pursues wild game, running ahead of its master, the hunter, who follows its bark.

"Ultimately, the dog, with its ambiguous roles and cultural values, its constant presence in human experience coupled with its nearness to the feral world, is the alter ego of man himself, a reflection of both human culture and human savagery" (*Myths of the Dog-Man,* 14–15; cf. Gottlieb, "Dog: Ally or Traitor?" 486–88). The coyote and skinwalker share this "alter ego" role in Navajo culture and mythology. For example, Hillerman writes: "He reminded Chee how Coyote always sat in the doorway of the hogan when the Holy People met in Council, neither quite part of these representatives of cosmic power, nor totally allied with the wilderness of evil outside" (*Coyote Waits,* 70, cf. 234–36; *Listening Woman,* 48–50, 81–82, 101–2; *Dance Hall of the Dead,* 163). In classical Greek culture, the cynic philosphers played this ambiguous role. Leif Vaage describes the cynics, whose name was derived from *kyōn,* the Greek word for dog, as "stray dogs on the margins of their world, barking and doing whatever at the edge of town" ("Like Dogs Barking: Cynic parresia and Shameless Asceticism," 36).

[16] This translation of *łéchąą'í* comes from somewhere in one of Tony Hillerman's novels—the specific book and page I cannot recall. Although the Navajo word for dog was one of the first words I learned on the reservation, it never dawned on me to connect it with *chąą'* (excrement)—another word I learned very quickly—until I read it in the Hillerman novel (cf. Scobie, "Slums, Sanitation and Mortality in the Roman World," 418–20). Strangely, it was this particular translation, now lost to me, that rekindled my interest in my childhood years on the Navajo reservation.

In Homer's *Iliad,* "scorned women are 'dog flies,' or 'bitches,' or bitch-eyed,'" (Friedrich, "Sanity and the Myth of Honor," 289), and in ancient Greek culture, women were quite literally the shit-eaters. Von Staden writes: "When confronted with the female body, and especially the female reproductive parts, the Hippocratic healing hand did not hesitate to draw on the excrement of animals [for potions and poultices] . . . , ingredients shunned in Hippocratic treatment of males" ("Women and Dirt," 12; for the role of excrement in cynic behavior, cf. Sloterdijk, *Critique of Cynical Reason,* 151; cf. Greenblatt, "Filthy Rites," in *Learning to Curse,* 59–79, esp. 64–65; for the use of human excrement in dehumanization and torture, see Des Pres, "Excremental Assault," 203–20).

[17] "Recollection, I have found, is usually about half invention," writes Wallace Stegner (*Crossing to Safety,* 64). Or, in Timothy Adams' words, "memory is the self's autobiography, an unwritten narrative with an unreliable narrator" (*Telling Lies in Modern American Autobiography,* 169). This is because, as Daniel Goleman explains, "[t]he self has in its power all the

Their silvery shadows flit across the moonlit edges of my unconscious. I remember two dogs that we owned in Kansas, although the first, Chloe, lives in my memory only as a name. The second was named Bimbo, and from time to time my brother Greg and I would pretend that we were she. We would crawl around on all fours, bark ferociously, and eat her dry dog food from the bowl on our back porch.

In our first few years on the reservation, our family selected dogs for pets from among the many Navajo strays that made their home in the mission dump. Our first transformed stray was named Blackie. In our home she grew to be sleek, healthy, and alert.[18] But to the Navajos, a well fed, grinning dog meant only one thing: a cunning killer. She could only have gotten fat by killing and eating sheep. One day I found Blackie under the mission's old Studebaker, lying in a puddle of blood, turned inside out by a bullet through her side.[19] My eight-year-old eyes watched her life slowly pour out on the

---

tools—and temptations—of a totalitarian state. The self acts as a censor, selecting and deleting the flow of imagination" (*Vital Lies, Simple Truths*, 95). In spite of this difficult state of affairs, Andrée Collard is quick to point out that "without memories there [is] no present" (*Rape of the Wild*, 92).

[18] Collard writes: "Properly reared pets have a great deal in common with the well-adjusted women and people of colour whom the white man has conquered/colonised/enslaved. The dog is considered 'properly reared' when it whimpers and allows itself to be petted. Women are well bred, well adjusted when they efface themselves behind joyless smiles, limp voices and demure mannerisms that make them tractable. Slaves and colonised people are well adjusted when they assimilate white values and behaviour patterns and allow themselves to be petted, i.e. show deference to whites" (*Rape of the Wild*, 87; see also Churchill, *Fantasies of the Master Race*, 257–60, 264–69, 276–79; but cf. Davis, "The Moral Status of Dogs, Forests, and Other Persons," 50–59).

The association of dogs with women goes back millennia. White argues: "Perhaps the most striking of all [ethnographic details] is the juxtaposition, in Europe, India, and China, of races of Dog-men with Amazons, or with a Kingdom of Women. . . . In fact, when we look closely at many of the world's traditions of the ancestral union of a male dog with a human woman, we find certain recurrent motifs that point . . . to mythic themes. . . ." (*Myths of the Dog-Man*, 187–88; cf. 47–70; see also Estés, *Women Who Run with the Wolves*, 115–29, esp. 123–24). Similar stories also circulated among the conquistadores in the New World (Varner and Varner, *Dogs of the Conquest*, 125; cf. Greenblatt, *Learning to Curse*, 21–24).

[19] In connecting wombs, wells, and altars together in the biblical tradition, Elaine Scarry argues that "what had been the interior lining [of the womb and well] now becomes the exterior, table-like surface [of the altar]. . . . That the altar's surface is the reversed lining of the body is made more imagistically immediate in all those places where blood is poured across the altar. . . ." And just as the altar is a turning of the body inside out, so too "belief in the scriptures is literally the act of turning one's own body inside out—[since] imagining, creating, the capacity for symbolic and religious thought begin with the capacity to endow interior physical events with an external, nonphysical referent" (*The Body in Pain*, 190; cf. John 19:32–37).

hard-packed adobe. She had crawled home to her favorite hiding place, to nurse her four newborn pups one last time.

The second stray our family took in appeared to be part German shepherd. He was larger than Blackie and light-colored,[20] and after a few weeks in our home he had changed from a cowering creature into a spirited and loyal friend. But one day his rightful owners came to our door accusing us of theft, and the dog, of killing sheep. They demanded the dog back. Then they took the dog and tied an old piece of briar-like barbed wire around his neck. With the husband pulling him, the wife kicked the dog the entire mile to their house. We children watched in horror as they made their way across the desert sand. The dog never got off his haunches. He cried like a newborn pup but never opened his mouth to bite them.[21]

Two days later the dog returned to us. His tail was wagging and the wire was still wound tightly around his neck. We were overjoyed to see him, but our joy turned to anguish when our parents made us take him back to his original owners. He wouldn't leave us, so we threw stones at him to chase him away. I don't remember what happened to that dog. I can't recall its name.

Inside my childhood missionary home I was a boy who had lived until age seven in rural Kansas. But that was not how the Navajo children outside my front door viewed me. Most of them had been weaned on nightmarish tales of nineteenth-century *bilagáana*[22] savagery. Consequently, they believed that I was a direct descendant of Kit[23] Carson, the white man who had burned

---

[20] White points out that the "Indo-European dogs of the dead generally moved around in pairs. . . . Most often, one of these dogs was black and the other white, symbols of a path that led not only from a past life to a present death, but also from death to a future life" (*Myths of the Dog-Man,* 39).

[21] Isa 53:7. "Melzack and Scott have shown through animal torture what torturers throughout history have known all along: it is possible to traumatize the sense out of living creatures and bring them to the point at which they submit to any atrocity without a whimper while becoming hopelessly dependent upon their torturers," writes Collard (*Rape of the Wild,* 63). Primo Levi concurs: "To destroy a man is difficult, almost as difficult as to create one: it has not been easy, nor quick, but you Germans have succeeded. Here we are, docile under your gaze; from our side you have nothing more to fear, no acts of violence, no words of defiance, not even a look of judgment" (*Survival in Auschwitz,* 135–36).

[22] This is the Navajo word for white person (Hillerman, *Skinwalkers,* 11; *Talking God,* 14). It is probably a corruption of the Spanish *Americano.*

[23] Christopher Carson's nickname "Kit" is fortuitous for American mythology. General James H. Carleton, the staunch Calvinist under whom Carson served, planned the removal of all Navajos from their native land in part to "teach them the truths of Christianity" (Trafzer, *The Kit Carson Campaign,* 184; cf. 230–31, 237–39; see also Sheehan, *Seeds of Extinction,* 243–75). But with the diminutive nickname Kit, Christopher Carson loses all symbolic con-

their family orchards and cornfields, starved their old women and young children, and forced those who survived into exile in a foreign land.[24]

It should not have come as a surprise, I suppose, to discover that my Navajo playmates' accusation of my complicity in Kit Carson's scorched-earth warfare was actually much closer to the truth than I once thought.[25]

---

nection with his superior's missionary zeal and that of the other famous "Christ-bearer" in the New World: Christopher Columbus.

St. Christopher has often been portrayed in Christian iconography with the head of a dog; a giant who ate human flesh before his conversion (White, *Myths of the Dog-Man,* 31, 34–36, 47; see illustration 6). Not surprisingly, his namesake Christopher Columbus is credited with inventing the word cannibal (White, *Myths of the Dog-Man,* 63; cf. Cheyfitz, *The Poetics of Imperialism,* 43, 61–62; and Arens, *The Man-Eating Myth,* 44–48, 53–54) and with introducing human-eating dogs into the New World on his second voyage in 1493 (Varner and Varner, *Dogs of the Conquest,* 4). Spanish greyhounds were first used in battle on May 5, 1494, in the landing on Jamaica. After their formal use in pitched battle on the Vega Real a year later, they became a standard element in the Spanish subjugation of Native Americans (ibid., 5, 8, 11). Within twenty years, hungry Spanish war dogs were being fed live Indian babies, torn from their mothers' arms (ibid., 13, 82–83; see illustration 7). They were first used in tracking escaped African slaves by Christopher Columbus's son, Diego, in January 1522 (ibid., 22, 57–58; a strategy subsequently employed by North American slave owners) and later as instruments of God's ultimate judgment upon Indians' homosexual activity, zoophilia, and lapses into heresy (ibid., 41, 193, see also xvi; and illustration 8; cf. Williams, "The Abominable Sin: The Spanish Campaign against Sodomy and its Results in Modern Latin America," in *The Spirit and the Flesh,* 131–51, esp. 134–40). To this day in many parts of Mexico, the common nickname for boys named *Jesús* is *chucho,* which in some Spanish dialects can mean a mutt or a mangy stray dog.

Unlike the Christus Victor myth associated with Christopher Columbus, American legend and art transformed "Kit" Carson into a wily young fox who outsmarted numerically superior foes, or into an innocent little kitten, who was forced to fight for his life when cornered by wild, vicious "critters and varmits" (Carter, *'Dear Old Kit',* 3–36; cf. Steckmesser, *The Western Hero in History and Legend,* 24–53). Thus, Thelma Guild can write that Carson's "adventures have an epic quality like those of Homeric heroes of the ancient Greeks. . . . Americans do well to remember Kit Carson as one of their heroes, for Fortune has seldom smiled upon a more deserving character" (*Kit Carson,* 294–95).

[24] Hillerman, *Dance Hall of the Dead,* 75–76.

[25] But I find solace in Walter Benn Michaels's perspective; he argues that "[v]irtually all the events and actions that we study did not happen to us and were not done by us. In this sense, the history we study is never our own; it is always the history of people who were in some respects like us and in other respects different. When, however, we claim it as ours, we commit ourselves to the ontology of the 'Negro' [or the 'Indian,' or the 'Euro-American'], to the identity of 'we' and 'they' and the primacy of race" ("Race into Culture: A Critical Genealogy of Cultural Identity," 682; see also Knapp, "Collective Memory and the Actual Past," 136–37, 142–43; and Brumble, *American Indian Autobiography,* 174). Daniel and Jonathan Boyarin, however, strongly criticize Michaels's perspective. They rightly recognize it as a "radically indi-

6. *Saint Christopher, from a twelfth-century martyrology.* Christopher Columbus's and Kit Carson's namesake, the giant dog-faced "Chananean." Hist fol 415, fol. 50r. Landsbibliothek Stuttgart, Germany. (Foto Marburg/Art Resource, N.Y.)

7. *"One woman,...not able to make good her escape, determined that the dogs should not tear her to pieces...and taking a rope and tying her one-year-old child to her leg, hanged herself from a beam. Yet she was not in time to prevent the dogs from ripping the infant to pieces, even though a friar did arrive and baptize the infant before it died"* (Las Casas, *A Short Account of the Destruction of the Indies,* 73-74). The sixteenth-century Dominican priest Bartolomé de Las Casas was truly a watchdog of God (*Domini canes*) and a tireless defender of Native American rights (see Gutiérrez, *Las Casas,* 8-12). Engraving by Theodore de Bry, plate in *Brevisima relación* (Rare Book and Special Collections Division, Library of Congress)

8. *Vasco Núñez de Balboa sets his European dogs on Indians accused of practicing sodomy.* Engraving by Theodore de Bry, plate 22 in *Americae* Part IV. Frankfurt, 1595 (Rare Book and Special Collections Division, Library of Congress)

Several years ago, while tracing my family history, I found that four Gibson brothers (my father's great grandmother's uncles), volunteered for service in the Mexican-American War and were stationed at Santa Fe in 1848.[26] As part of Company G, First Illinois Volunteers, three of them traveled with Kit Carson west from Missouri along the Santa Fe Trail, and near my first home in Ramona, Kansas. At least one of them, Theodore C. Gibson,[27] probably participated in raids against the Navajo, riding up into the Chuska Mountains in northeastern New Mexico within sight of where I was raised.[28]

A generation later, the Swede Rolf Johnson (my father's mother's uncle) was settling into a sod house with his parents and siblings on the Nebraska prairie, voraciously devouring every *Police Gazette* and American frontier dime novel he could find. He kept a careful journal of his own adventures, mimicking the grand writing style of his favorite pulp authors. On an 1877 hunting expedition in western Nebraska, Rolf managed to kill what must have been one of the last free-roaming buffalo in the state.[29] A year and a half later he was off exploring the Black Hills of Dakota Territory, from Deadwood to Spearfish. Somewhere in those tangled gulches of gold mines, Chinatowns, whorehouses, and saloons he met the notoriously untamed women, Calamity Jane and Bronco Moll.[30]

Rolf's search for the mythic American frontier led him eventually to New Mexico Territory where in 1880 he was laying track for the Santa Fe Railroad

---

vidualist, voluntaristic, and attenuated notion of something that can only with difficulty be called 'identity'" ("Diaspora: Generation and the Ground of Jewish Identity," 702; cf. McKenna, *Violence and Difference,* 139–40).

[26] *Soldiers' and Patriots' Biographical Album,* 172–74.

[27] Why was Theodore C., whose name means "God's gift," the one who remained in Santa Fe under Colonel Edward W. B. Newby's command? Why weren't Theodore's brothers George, William, or John the ones "taking part in the operations against the Indians on the frontier" (Hoffmann, *History of La Salle County, Illinois,* 301)? The name Theodore, like Christopher, is bothersome. I want to erase it.

[28] Myers, "Illinois Volunteers in New Mexico," 10–21; McNitt, "The Navajo Campaigns," 186–91. Carson's military appointment under General Carleton, which led to the Navajo people's exile at Bosque Redondo, would occur twenty years later.

[29] Journal entries for November 6–9, 1877 (Johnson Collection, Phelps County Historical Society Museum Archives, Holdrege, Nebraska, "Journal 1876–1880"). Parts of the first three volumes of Rolf's five-volume journal were printed in the Holdrege newspaper, *The Daily Citizen,* in 1939, and parts of volumes 1–4 were later published as "The Saga of a Wandering Swede" in *The Westerners Brand Book,* 10. However, much of the original journal still remains unpublished.

[30] Journal entries for July 10(?) and August 12, 1879 ("The Saga of a Wandering Swede," 256–60, 262–64).

across the hotly disputed checkerboard strip of the Navajo Reservation.[31] On November 16 of that year, near Mount Taylor (one of the four sacred mountains of the Navajo), he wrote in his diary of meeting the splendidly dressed Navajo leader Cayatanita.[32]

A decade later, in 1891, Rolf suggested the name of his younger brother to William F. Cody's business partners, who were planning to add a new attraction to their Wild West show. As a result, George Johnson joined Buffalo Bill's Congress of Rough Riders late that year,[33] subsequently participating in its many staged Indian battles.[34] For seven years he toured the United States and England with the troupe (see illustrations 9, 10, and 11), beginning with a performance before Queen Victoria in 1892.[35] A few years after he began trav-

---

[31] Hillerman, *Talking God,* 21–22, 72–73. Cf. Kluckhohn and Leighton, *The Navajo,* 11.

[32] Journal entry for November 16, 1880 (Johnson Collection, Phelps County Historical Society Museum Archives, "Journal 1876-1880"). Mount Taylor is called "The Turquoise Mountain" in Navajo mythology (Hillerman, *Coyote Waits,* 231–32). Sadly, the final volume of Rolf's diary, which continued to trace his travels across New Mexico and Arizona, was destroyed by fire around 1920.

[33] Sarah Blackstone describes in detail the origin and development of "The Congress of Rough Riders" (*Buckskins, Bullets, and Business,* 26–27, 54, 65–68, 77–78, 85). The Congress of Rough Riders added the phrase "of the World" to its title just before the Wild West opened alongside the World's Columbian Exposition in Chicago in 1893 (Russell, *The Wild West,* 8, 40; Slotkin, *Gunfighter Nation,* 79–80).

[34] For the role of Native Americans in Buffalo Bill's Wild West, see Blackstone, *Buckskins, Bullets, and Business,* 85–88, 130–31; and Deloria, "The Indians," 45–56. Buffalo Bill argued eloquently: "The bullet is a kind of pioneer of civilization. Although its mission is often deadly, it is useful and necessary. Without the bullet, America would not be a great, free, united and powerful country" (from the official 1906 Italian Program of Buffalo Bill's Wild West, as quoted in Clerici, "Native Americans in Columbus's Home Land: A Show within the Show," 415; cf. Slotkin, "Buffalo Bill's 'Wild West' and the Mythologization of the American Empire," 173–79; and Slotkin, *Gunfighter Nation,* 77).

[35] Passenger List, SS Persian Monarch, New York to London; April 20, 1892 (George Johnson Collection, Phelps County Museum).

We only have one eyewitness account of George's riding capabilities. In a Chicago newspaper article dated May 22, 1893, the reporter writes, "Buffalo Bill's ampitheatre was packed to the eaves. . . . When it came time for the ponies to buck, they bucked so earnestly that the cowboys themselves became interested. Lee Martin was riding Blue Dog when the crazy bronco reared straight up on his hind legs and fell backward. The wiry cowboy managed to squirm out of the way unhurt, although half the people thought he was killed.

"A little later George Johnson mounted Badger. The latter stood on his head a few times and then dashed wildly into the little platform raised in the center of the arena, smashing in one side of it. Johnson leaped just before the horse struck the boards and landed safely on top [of] the platform, a feat not down in the bills. Then the crowd cheered for a full minute. Mr. Johnson was asked if it scared him.

9. *"The Grand Review," Ambrose Park, Brooklyn, New York, 1894.* During the summer of 1894, articles about Buffalo Bill's "Wild West" ran regularly in the *New York Times.* Here and in the following caption are two typical entries. "In addition to the amusing and entertaining qualities of the Wild West, there is much of an educative character which is equally valuable to the old and young.... As an ethnological study, [it shows] the human race from primitive man, as represented by the Indian, Cossack, and Gaucho, to the perfect representative in the person of the educated and trained soldiers of the four great armies of the world [German, French, British, and American]..." (*New York Times,* "Wild West Show Attracts," 27 May 1894, p. 9).

George Johnson is at the extreme left of the photograph, in the third row from the front. He has marked his position with a small *x* above his head. (George Johnson Collection. From the files of Phelps County Museum, Holdrege, Nebraska; reproduction by Wayne Carlson)

10. FACING PAGE,TOP: *American Cowboys Putting on an Act, Ambrose Park, Brooklyn, New York, 1894.* "The scenes enacted by savages, scouts, and cowboys are pictures of what has occurred and will occur just as long as the Indian remains a savage and the great lands on our immense frontier are unsettled. But it should not be forgotten that this period is fast drawing to a close, and these scenes may never again be witnessed" (*New York Times,* "The Wonderful Wild West," 2 September 1894, p. 11).

George Johnson is seated second from the right, beside a horse lying on the ground. He has marked himself with an x on his shirt. (George Johnson Collection. From the files of Phelps County Museum, Holdrege, Nebraska; reproduction by Al Achterberg)

11. *American Cowboys of the "Wild West" at the World's Columbian Exhibition, Chicago, 1893.* The cowboys of the "Congress of Rough Riders of the World" pose for a formal photograph in the arena at 63rd Street. George Johnson, sans moustache, is standing in the back row, second from the right. He has put an *x* over his head.

Although "the World's Columbian Commission did not exactly invite Buffalo Bill to take part in the celebration of the four hundredth anniversary of the discovery of America,...few visitors considered that they had seen the sights until they had also visited Buffalo Bill's Wild West" (Russell, *The Wild West,* 43). (George Johnson Collection. From the files of Phelps County Museum, Holdrege, Nebraska; reproduction by Wayne Carlson)

eling with Buffalo Bill's Wild West, George, with help from Rolf's numerous contacts, was working hard to add Navajo Indians[36] to the show's ever-expand-

---

"'Not on your life,' he replied. 'But if you give Badger six weeks of bunch grass, this place wouldn't [hold] him'" (George Johnson Collection, Phelps County Museum).

[36] W. J. Rouse, New York, N.Y., to George Johnson, location unknown, 20 October 1894(?), and W. J. Rouse, Santa Ana, Calif., to George Johnson, Phelps, Neb., 5 January 1895. The Wild West show with its entourage of American Indians was extremely popular in Europe, particularly in Germany, where Karl May was one of its early attendees. May became one of his generation's most popular authors, drawing inspiration for his American Western novels in part from watching the show (Conrad, "Mutual Fascination: Indians in Dresden and Leipzig," 457–59, 469–70; Feest, "Indians and Europe? Editor's Postscript," 619–20). His most widely sold volumes, *Winnetou* and *Old Shatterhand*, have recently been translated into English (Gillespie, "The Wild West Thrives, but Guess Where? In Germany, That's Where," 13–14).

A brief generation later, Adolf Hitler "is said to have recommended [May's novels] to his generals, all seventy-some volumes in his personal library" (Doerry, "Literary Conquista: The Southwest as a Literary Emblem," 440; see also Rosa and May, *Buffalo Bill and His Wild West,* 146–47; Frayling, *Spaghetti Westerns,* 105; and Mann, "Cowboy Mentor of the Führer," 218, 222). Karl Doerry writes that "on the whole May shows the Indians as doomed to extinction. But not because they are inherently inferior; they are just not given the time to acquire the culture and education that would allow them, for instance, to see through and resist the nefarious schemes of the villains who are smart enough to exploit the Indians' savage energy for their own plans" ("Literary Conquista: The Southwest as a Literary Emblem," 444; cf. Brumble, *American Indian Autobiography,* 149–51; Fiorentino, "'Those Red-Brick Faces': European Press Reactions to the Indians of Buffalo Bill's Wild West Show," 403–11; and Clerici, "Native Americans in Columbus's Home Land: A Show within the Show," 415–23). Not surprisingly, Doerry's assessment of May's books fits remarkably well with Churchill's critique of the Navajo victims portrayed in Hillerman's detective novels (*Fantasies of the Master Race,* 269–71).

Richard Rubenstein also picks up this tangled thread of Romantic Racialism in America and Europe, arguing: "The link between genocidal settler societies of the eighteenth and nineteenth centuries and twentieth century genocide can be discerned in Adolf Hitler's Lebensraum program. As a young man, Hitler saw the settlement of the New World and the concomitant elimination of North America's Indian population by white European settlers as a model to be followed by Germany on the European continent" ("Modernization and the Politics of Extermination," 8; see also Churchill, *Fantasies of the Master Race,* 120, 141–43, 177; Thornton, *American Indian Holocaust and Survival,* 3–90; and v. Feilitzsch, "Karl May: The 'Wild West' as seen in Germany," 173–74).

Thus, it cannot be mere coincidence that the Nazi historian Edgar von Schmidt-Pauli, writing "history in such a way as to demonstrate the inevitability of the rise of the German race and Adolf Hitler in particular," should elicit and edit the 1929 autobiography of Big Chief White Horse Eagle, an Osage of dubious character, and title it *We Indians: The Passing of a Great Race* (Brumble, *American Indian Autobiography,* 152; cf. Conrad, "Mutual Fascination: Indians in Dresden and Leipzig," 459). Nor should one be surprised at Lisa Bartel-Winkler's

ing program. So far as I know, the Johnson brothers were not successful in this venture.[37]

Although we soon learned not to make family pets out of the stray dogs roaming the mission compound, it continued to be inundated by the troublesome pests. Invariably, the problem would be compounded early each spring when the females were in heat. Navajos would come to the mission for water, mail, or medicine, and after they left we would invariably find another four or five puppies foraging for food in the dump. Much to the annoyance of other mission staff, my mother had a habit of naming each stray and feeding them by tossing unwanted leftovers outside our yard, just beyond the mission fence. It wasn't long before she was stretching the boundaries of propriety even further by inviting Navajo women into her home for cookies, coffee, and conversation—a foolish and scandalous activity by most missionary standards.

Sometimes, in the white heat of a summer Sunday,[38] the door of the two-room school where we had Morning Meeting would be propped open to circulate the cool Colorado Plateau breeze. Occasionally a stray dog would

conclusion regarding May's books. Also known by the pen name Barwin, she wrote pulp novels during the Nazi period "in which the heroism of Indian leaders was explained by their assumed Viking ancestry," and had argued as early as 1918 that through his Indian hero Winnetou, "Karl May delineates . . . the German drama. Winnetou is the noble man of his race—he knows about the purity of the blood, the longing, and the hope of his brothers, but they have to founder because they are worn down by discord. . . . This is Indian, this is also German. Who has grasped the meaning of the Indian drama has also grasped the meaning of the German drama" (Feest, "Indians and Europe? Editor's Postscript," 612). So if Rubenstein and others are correct in elaborating this genealogy of genocide, then the American West as popularized by Buffalo Bill's Wild West show and May's novels may be said to have laid the groundwork for much of Hitler's racial policy. And if Ward Churchill is to be believed, Hillerman's wildly successful detective novels continue to disseminate a similar ideology to the American public—albeit in a more sophisticated manner (*Fantasies of the Master Race,* 258–59, 276–79).

[37] George left Buffalo Bill's Wild West at the end of the 1898 season, just a few months before "'Custer's Last Fight' was replaced by 'The Battle of San Juan Hill'" in the show (Slotkin, *Gunfighter Nation,* 82–83). Shortly after leaving the show, George and his younger brother Robert rode north from Nebraska to work as cowboys at Square Butte, Montana, a ranch owned by Milton E. Milner, one of Cody's major business partners. During the fall roundup, on November 12, 1899, George Johnson's horse stepped in a prairie dog hole and fell on top of him. George was killed instantly. After his brother's death, Robert Johnson, my father's namesake, continued to work on Milner's ranch for eleven more years.

[38] White notes the association of dogs with the summer and winter solstices, arguing that "in Homer, Sirius was the dog of Orion who, during the dog days [of summer] 'redoubled the fiery heat of the sun, bringing, in the afternoon, suffering to all living creatures'" (*Myths of the Dog-Man,* 38; cf. 14, 40).

wander in and slowly approach the communion table—perhaps drawn there by the smell of fresh baked bread and store-bought grape juice. But the alert eyes and quick hands of a senior missionary were always able to maintain the sanctity and order of the hour. Much to the disappointment of us giggling children, no dog ever stayed around long.[39]

But after the service, if the dog had been patient and could follow its nose, it would find scraps of food under the outdoor picnic tables set up in the shade of tamarisk trees, where the Navajo faithful were fed hot dogs, beans, and Kool-Aid. In my more reflective moments, which sometimes jolt me with a sudden sharp pain, I have thought that perhaps the real communion on those Sundays took place outside, under the damask veil of the tamarisk trees.[40]

When the stray dogs became too plentiful and threatened to run in wild packs, my father and other mission staff would gather the young ones together, along with the old and weak, stuff them into dusty potato sacks, and tie them to the exhaust pipe of our idling car. Before too long they would stop squirming and yelping. Then they would be buried in shallow pits at the far end of the mission garden. Afterward my brothers, sisters, and I could again run freely and play without fear in front of our home.[41]

---

[39] Mark's Gospel puts it this way, "He said to her, 'Let the children be fed first, for it is not fair to take the children's food and throw it to the dogs'" (Mark 7:27). According to the Mishnah (*Baba Kamma* 7:7), "[a] man may not rear a dog [within the land of Israel] unless it is kept bound by a chain" (cf. Stager, "Why Were Hundreds of Dogs Buried at Ashkelon?" 30–42; Smith and Stager, "Ashkelon—Views and Reviews," 13–18; Wapnish and Hesse, "Pampered Pooches or Plain Pariahs? The Ashkelon Dog Burials," 72).

[40] David White writes: "The pious fiction of the simple heathen glimpsing, through an act of divine grace, the superiority of the Christian path is one that has served missionary colonialism down to the present day. Only the names of the heathens . . . have changed. The medieval propagandists had much of the raw material of their gospel ready to hand in the accounts of the monstrous races bequeathed to them by the ancients. These were the peoples, in the medieval myths, who were first missionized by the apostles (Bartholomew, Andrew, Thomas, Matthew, etc.), following the Pauline evangelization of the Mediterranean world.

"The legend of the cynocephalic Abominable is a prime instance of this new medieval genre. The monster remains the same—only the hand holding the mighty sword has changed: instead of Alexander and his army, it is God himself who, through the works of his military saints, causes the wild savage to surrender himself" (*Myths of the Dog-Man*, 197).

[41] Jane Tompkins, in reflecting upon her visit to the Buffalo Bill Museum in Cody, Wyoming, writes: "Major historical events like genocide and major acts of destruction are not simply produced by impersonal historical processes or economic imperatives or ecological blunders; human intentionality is involved and human knowledge of the self. Therefore, if you're really interested in not having any more genocide or killing of animals, no matter what else you might do—condemning imperialism or shaking your finger at history—if you don't

Funerals at our mission were common occurrences, especially in summer-time. And although I was never allowed to be in the room while my mother washed and dressed the Navajo corpses, I used to watch as my father helped build the pine coffins. I discovered that coffins could be built in many different sizes, and quite often I would help dig the holes to put them in. The smallest holes were the easiest to dig. But since there were usually also more of them, things had a way of balancing out by summer's end. Burials in winter, on the other hand, were nearly always difficult, regardless of the coffin size. Sometimes we would have to build a bonfire over the grave site to thaw the frozen ground before we could begin to dig.

When my mother died of a heart attack on the eve of Passover in 1984, we decided to bury her body on the reservation in the mission cemetery. As we had done so often in the past, we built a coffin of pine. Then, during a mid-April snowstorm, we dug her grave.

> so lovely the grave
> feather-dusting of white lies
> on muddy red skein

When her funeral was over we slowly trudged home. The family dog, like the beloved disciple, remained behind, keeping vigil beside the fresh mound of half-frozen sod.

---

first, or also, come to recognize the violence in yourself and your own anger and your own destructiveness, whatever else you do won't work. It isn't that genocide doesn't matter. Genocide matters and it starts at home" (*West of Everything,* 202–3; cf. White, *Myths of the Dog-Man,* 209; McKenna, *Violence and Difference,* 132, 139–40).

Or as the character Henry Highhawk puts it in one of Hillerman's novels, "Here [in the Smithsonian Museum of Natural History] you see the gods of conquered people displayed like exotic animals in the public zoo. . . . Above your head, lining the halls and corridors of this very building, are thousands of cases and bins and boxes. In them you will find the bones of more than eighteen thousand of your fellow humans. You will find the skeletons of children, of mothers, of grandfathers. They have been dug out of the burials where their mourning relatives placed them, reuniting them with their Great Mother Earth" (*Talking God,* 290–91; cf. 292–94; Vizenor, *The Trickster of Liberty,* 123–25; Williams, *The Alchemy of Race and Rights,* 160; see also Churchill, *Fantasies of the Master Race,* 234–35, 274; Bruner, "Ethnography as Narrative," 140, 152; and cf. Greenblatt's analysis of Prague's "State Jewish Museum" founded by the Nazis, in *Learning to Curse,* 173–76).

It is not without a certain degree of irony that the new National Holocaust Museum in Washington, D.C., stands a block off the Mall just out of sight of the Smithsonian Museum of Natural History (Boyarin, "Europe's Indian, America's Jew: Modiano and Vizenor," 207).

DIFFERENCE[42]

Today, as my mother's bones slowly erode and mix with the red Arizona soil, I cannot help but remember that we were aliens in that foreign land. Outside our childhood home, white-skinned people were dirty, smelly, and stupid. To most of the Navajo children we played with, our heads were strangely shaped, protruding out from the backsides of our necks like grossly overgrown tumors;[43] likewise our genitals were curiosity pieces, a topic of frequent speculative conversations.[44] We transmitted ghost-sicknesses,[45] and a strange, cow-like odor followed us wherever we went.[46]

One event in particular has imprinted itself in my memory as typifying my brothers' and my radical differentness. On a hot summer day when I was ten years old, Greg and I decided to build a raft and float it in the small irrigation reservoir a mile east of the mission. After about an hour of leisurely swimming and lolling in the sunshine we were startled by a sudden shower of baseball-sized stones splashing all around us. Looking up, we saw three Navajo men standing on the shore near our clothes and shoes, gesturing wildly and yelling. We quickly swam out into deeper water and clung to the side of the raft, trying to use it as a shield against the volleys. I was not a strong swimmer at the time and was quickly losing my strength to dodge the stones. I began to panic. I

---

[42] Derrida writes: "To hear oneself is the most normal and the most impossible experience. One might conclude from this, first, that the source is always other, and that whatever hears itself, not itself hearing itself, always comes from elsewhere, from outside and afar" ("Qual Quelle: Valéry's Sources," in *Margins of Philosophy*, 297; cf. "Différance," in *Margins of Philosophy*, 14–16).

[43] Up until the 1960s, most Navajo children spent the first few months of life bound to cradleboards. The backs of their soft-boned skulls naturally became flattened by their heads' constant pressure against the cradleboard frames. By contrast, our heads were shaped like footballs.

[44] Since Navajo boys were not circumcised, a white boy's exposed penis in the dormitory bathroom always drew a crowd of laughing, pointing, curious bystanders. Needless to say, we quickly learned that it was best to go home when we needed to relieve ourselves.

Daniel Boyarin and Jonathan Boyarin observe how "bodies are marked as different and often as negatively different to the dominant cultural system, thus producing a dissonance or gap between one's practices and affects" ("Diaspora: Generation and Ground of Jewish Identity," 704).

[45] We were carriers of ghost-sicknesses probably because we liked to play around abandoned hogans. We learned later that these hogans were inhabited by the *ch'iindii* (ghosts) of the people who had died there, and that was why they had been abandoned (cf. Hillerman, *The Ghostway*, 13, 40–43).

[46] The rank smell came from eating beef and drinking cow's milk.

told Greg that we had to head to the shore. Breathlessly treading water, we worked out a desperate plan. Greg would swim toward the men and try to get our clothes and shoes while I would use the raft to carry me to the shore opposite them. Greg would explain to them what we were doing, apologize for being on their land—if that was the problem—and bring my clothes to me.

I quickly landed the raft and watched Greg swim toward the men. But as he neared the shore, my blood ran cold. While I had been rafting to land, a fourth Navajo, brandishing a shotgun, had joined the other three awaiting Greg's arrival. As soon as he stepped out of the water they grabbed him, shoved him to the ground, and stuck the gun in his face. Terrified, clad only in a swimming suit, I set out for home as fast as my bare feet could carry me. The desert sand blistered my feet and the hot afternoon air seared my lungs. I arrived home shaking with fear and exhaustion, blurted out the story to my parents, and collapsed on the living room couch. My father ran to the car and raced up the road to investigate the incident.

Fifteen minutes later he was back with my brother sitting beside him in the front seat, very much alive. Greg held up my abandoned clothes and grinned from ear to ear. As it turned out, the Navajos were afraid that our pallid skin would somehow wash off in the coffee-colored water, spreading deadly diseases to their sheep that drank from the reservoir. Needless to say, Greg and I never swam there again.[47] And thankfully—as far as I know anyway—no sheep died as a result of our trespass and impurity.

A few years later I joined my older brothers in Atascadero, California, for my freshman year of high school, where the three of us boarded with our uncle's family. For the first time since we had moved to the Navajo reservation in 1959 I was completely surrounded by people who were white-skinned like myself. Initially I thought nothing of that, until one day at lunch time. I happened to be eating with a group of my friends when the high school's four or five Hispanic students walked by. Without any exchange of words or looks I instantly felt my friends' temperatures rising. Suddenly I could taste their sticky-sweet whiteness. It oozed from their pores and ran in little rivulets down the steps that we were sitting on, toward the Mexican kids who were hurrying past us. In that revelatory moment which I will treasure for a lifetime, I discovered that white epidermis could indeed infect and destroy other living things.

Because Navajo is a tonal language, many linguists consider it to be one of

---

[47] However, we discovered a few years later that the gardens adjacent to the reservoir were great places to look for ancient Indian pottery that often would be exposed after the soil had been plowed.

the most difficult human dialects to master.[48] During the Second World War, for example, Ralph Begay and other Navajo men in our valley served in the Pacific theater and were asked to use their native language as a code for sending top secret military messages. The Japanese never did break that "code," nor did we. None of us white children at the mission was ever capable of speaking Navajo as well as a native three-year-old.[49]

At the ages of eight, nine, and ten, my two brothers and I were also as ignorant of our sexuality as a toddler might be. Good Christian families didn't talk about certain bodily functions, body places, or touch themselves "there." So I knew the proper Navajo words for male and female sex organs long before I heard their corresponding English terms, and I learned about sexual intercourse by watching the ever present, shameless dogs humping awkwardly across the mission compound. But it was the Navajo children who connected that bewildering animal behavior with humans. They would grin and poke me in the ribs, saying, "Your mudder an' fodder go like dis ever' night." Of course I vehemently contested their jocular asides, much to their more worldly-wise amusement. I was learning by fits and starts that brown skin denoted intelligence, along with beauty, cleanliness, and everything that was good in the world.[50]

Not coincidentally, when I grew up I fell in love with a darker-skinned woman. On Barbara's first visit to the mission, her waist-length, raven-black hair immediately hypnotized the young Navajo girls. They followed her wherever she walked, crowded around her, and ran their fingers through her hair, whispering, "*Nizhóní, nizhóní*" ("beautiful, beautiful").[51] I noted their spontaneous reactions with deep interest and knew that I had found the woman I would marry.[52]

But like the *Diné* whom my Western European ancestors named Navajo and Indian, my wife's Asian-American surname Wong is not her family's original last name. That name was Lee. The name Wong came from the American

---

[48] Hillerman, *Dance Hall of the Dead*, 139.

[49] Not only could I not speak Navajo; I only barely could speak recognizable English, having developed a severe overbite and, with it, a lisp. Strangely, I never knew a Navajo child who lisped or stuttered.

[50] This was true, at least insofar as brown skin signified a Navajo worldview. From my perspective at the time, the similarly colored Hopis, Zunis, Utes, and Hispanics had none of the Navajos' more natural beauty or intelligence (cf., for example, Joe Leaphorn's discomfort with Zunis, in Hillerman, *Dance Hall of the Dead*, 7, 9–10).

[51] Like Changing Woman of Navajo mythology, she "walked in beauty" (Hillerman, *The Blessing Way*, 40–42; *Coyote Waits*, 119–20; cf. *Sacred Clowns*, 51).

[52] We were married May 22, 1982.

citizenship records that her paternal grandfather, Mee Yim, illegally bought in 1913 to circumvent the restrictive quotas placed on Asians trying to enter California. Today on the walls of our home, next to the pictures of our children, hang my wife's family photographs. One photograph in particular includes the family's "paper grandmother" prominently seated in the center of the frame. Out of the family's fear of deportation, this unrelated Wong woman was posed in Lee family portraits for years (see illustration 12).[53]

Somewhat similarly, my wife's maternal great grandfather, You Dong, changed his surname to the Spanish sounding Don to enable him to buy property in Tucson, Arizona, in 1906. Thanks to that missing *g*, my mother-in-law was able to slip into nursing school in San Francisco two generations later. Thinking that Marjorie Don was a Caucasian name, the admission committee accepted her, even though they had already met their quota of minorities.

Outfitted with his newly acquired name, You Don[g] built an adobe grocery store and house on Meyers Street near Fourth Street.[54] He bought a pair of six-shooters to protect his worldly goods and then, as insurance, had his children baptized in the First Baptist Church of Tucson. He had prepared carefully for life in America. With a working knowledge of the Papago and Yaqui languages and with the pistols holstered at his waist, he developed a profitable business among the Indians of southern Arizona. When the revolutionary Dr. Sun Yat-Sen came to Tucson in the early 1900s he visited in the Don home; and in 1919, You's eldest son, Hoy Chu, became the first Chinese boy to graduate from Tucson High School.[55]

Hoy Chu went on to college at the University of California in Berkeley and, upon graduating, married my wife's grandmother, May Chun (Maude Laverne) Lai. Since daughters were an economic liability for most Chinese families, May Chun Lai had been abandoned by her parents at the age of four, left on the doorstep of the Methodist Oriental Home in San Francisco. As part of the orphanage choir, she sang before President Theodore Roosevelt at the White House in 1908 and went on to become the first Chinese woman to graduate from an American conservatory of music.[56] Although she was an

---

[53] "Memory heals the scars of time. Photography documents the wounds," writes Michael Ignatieff (*The Russian Album*, 7; cf. Sontag, *On Photography*, 164–65).

[54] The building, still standing in 1990 when I visited it in Tucson, is presently occupied by the Elks Club.

[55] Lee, "The Chinese in Tucson, Arizona," 9.

[56] She graduated from the College of the Pacific in San Jose, California, in 1921 (*San Jose Evening News*, 17 June 1921).

12. *The Lee Family, ca. 1930.* The Wong "paper grandmother" is the older woman seated with her hands clasped on her lap. My wife's father, Walter Gin Wong, is the boy standing at the far right. Mr. Wong Si Wei, the "paper grandmother's" husband, owned a mortuary near Portsmouth Square, in San Francisco's Chinatown.

American citizen, born in the United States, by law she lost her citizenship when she married Hoy Chu, who had been born in China.[57] Her battle to regain her American citizenship was fought in the federal courts of Arizona,[58] and when she finally won her case, she became one of the first Chinese women to cast a vote in a presidental election.

Although I grew up being different and would later marry into difference, being different didn't always separate me from the Navajo people. My two older brothers and I learned to climb mesas and buttes with the help of Tom and Harry Yazzie, our nearest Navajo neighbors to the north. With them beside us we played tag on paper-thin ledges, chiseled hand and toe holds in sandstone cliffs and, like the Titans of Greek mythology, hurled gigantic boulders off breathtaking precipices, teetering on the edge to watch them ricochet like thunder on their way to the distant earth beneath our feet. Then, as some sort of concluding act of cosmic fecundity or canine marking, we would unzip our pants and reverently piss hundred-foot arcs of amber rain down upon the arid, alkaline adobe below.

Amazingly, we had only one serious accident in all our years of climbing, and that came much later, after a new missionary couple and their adopted Navajo son moved to the mission. Sam Minkler and I were in the same grade and quickly became best friends. Late one summer afternoon we decided to take a visitor up to the mesa for a climb. Our family had only one rule about climbing: Never climb in the dark. And so as the sun began to set, I headed home alone, having failed to convince Sam and the visitor to follow me. As the two boys began their descent by moonlight, the visitor fell and was seriously injured. For the next two hours Sam stood on the mesa, a quarter of a mile from the mission, and screamed for help. Finally, after reassuring the visiting boy's parents of their Indian son's instinctual native wisdom, Sam's parents went out looking for the two eighth grade boys. It was another four hours before we knew that the visitor had broken three ribs, punctured a lung, and broken an arm.

But in those early years, with Tom and Harry beside us, we never had such problems. We were the first whites to know what every Navajo knew—that the presence of wild creatures and monsters could be felt less than a quarter-mile from the mission compound. We saw them all and smelled their scorch-

---

[57] The United States Immigration Act of 1924 stated: "Any American who married a Chinese woman lost his citizenship; any Chinese man who married an American woman caused her to lose her citizenship" (Kingston, *China Men,* 154). The last of the Chinese exclusionary laws were repealed in 1965.

[58] From an undated Arizona newspaper clipping in my possession.

ing breath: ferocious looking, emerald colored lizards that would stand on their rear legs and fearlessly charge at humans; seventeen-inch, fossilized dinosaur footprints in an ancient seabed of sandstone; and a cougar, hardly a stone's throw away, crouching for an instant in the eroded crotch of our favorite mesa-hideout. And when we were occasionally confined to the mission compound for some significant breech of parental boundaries, we could always hunt golden-plumed birds in the tamarisk trees, shooting them with our slingshots or bows and selling the sacrificial victims' Croesus-like feathers for a dime apiece to Billy Bluff, understudy of Big Whiskers,[59] a local medicine man.

The Yazzie boys also taught us to ride their horses bareback, clutching tangled manes in white-knuckled fists; in return, we let them ride our battered bicycles. From them we learned to swim in quicksand, wiggling nude across its treacherous, quivering surface like a sidewinder rattlesnake on a rippled sand dune, and the barren sand dunes were magical zones where zero-degree gravity prevailed. From their constantly shifting, wind-shaped crests we could soar twenty feet through thin air before disappearing into clouds of lunar fluff. Finally, after hours of play, we would wander homeward; five exhausted, dust-encrusted adams, to eat lunches of fry bread and mutton stew in the cool shade of Yazzies' *chaha'oh*,[60] while Judge, their stolen greyhound, hungrily watched us. In the evenings, Tom and Harry would come for picnics of tuna fish sandwiches and potato chips outside our two-room basement apartment. Together we would read comic books and play card games until the shimmering swath of the summer night's Milky Way could point them northward to their kerosene-lamp-lit hogan silhouetted against the back of the sleeping mesa.

Looking back I know now that I learned to write naturally:[61] watching the patterns bending tufts of wind-blown grass made in drifting snow; fingering thousand-year-old petroglyphs etched high on isolated canyon walls; tracing the silvery plumes of jet planes as they sped across the turquoise sky on their way to distant lands.

---

[59] This, of course, was his nickname, not his secret war name (see Hillerman, *People of Darkness,* 106–7). My father's Navajo nickname was simply "The Teacher." Our maintenance man, Donald Perrault, was given the nickname "Little Round Man."

[60] The word means "shade." Hillerman calls the summer dwelling either a "pole arbor" (*Listening Woman,* 136), or a "brush shelter" (*The Blessing Way,* 92; see illustration 4).

[61] Or as Christopher Norris writes, "once [language] passes beyond the stage of a primitive cry, [it] is 'always already' inhabited by writing, or by all those signs of an 'articulate' structure. . . ." (*Deconstruction,* 36; cf. Derrida, "The Supplement of Origin," in *Speech and Phenomena,* 103).

I fine tuned my thinking by piecing together the three-dimensional puzzles of shattered Anasazi pottery;[62] by walking barefoot in the light of full-orbed desert moons. Their spidery webs were woven into my inner ear. They taught me balance. Harmony. *Hózhó.* Everything was about harmony: the intertwining of a people with a sinuous, symmetrical cosmos. A Navajo rug of earthen-made dyes, framed against a vermillion sky.

As I write these words in a bleak, northern Indiana December, I feel that I am haunted by the differentness of that place: the smell of cedar smoke wafting from an isolated hogan on Sheepskin Mesa: an old woman—Was it Toothless Man's Widow? I don't know—knee-deep in snow and up to her elbows in the bloody entrails of a half butchered donkey, her dogs excitedly barking and gnawing the still steaming-warm hide.

Nestled in another soft, canyon-like crevice of my brain is the more familiar form of Lee Benally. Crippled by polio and smelling of horses, leather, and sweat, he hangs on, a weathered, twisted trunk of a man, seated cross-legged in his horse-drawn wagon. His willowy, imbecilic nephew stands by to answer his every need. When Lee died, I think that his wagon must have been buried with him. It was the last I ever saw in the valley. Today, I imagine his shriveled legs as gnarly roots, forever anchored to smooth-worn floorboards.

Then there were my classmates in the little two-room mission school: lovely Anna Horse, who limped like Twisted Foot,[63] the stray with the bullet-shattered leg who always knew where to hide when the gun-toting dog killers came around; giggly Virginia Benally, who as a young child lost an eye in a woodcutting accident; William Scott, another partially crippled polio victim and my soulmate for many years; and Gladys Luna, who survived a childhood battle with tuberculosis only to contract scleroderma as a teenager, a mysterious disease that stretched the skin and sinews of her body ever more tightly over her bones until she could do nothing but lie in a Gallup hospital bed, a crumpled mass of open, weeping wounds.

When Anna was in the fifth grade, doctors miraculously rebuilt her hip, and years later Virginia got a natural looking glass eye when she went to work for

---

[62] Hillerman, *A Thief of Time,* 14, 23, 67–68, 150–51. The word "Anasazi" (ancient ones) is the name that the Navajos, as predatory late arrivals to the Southwest, gave to the people who previously inhabited the numerous pueblo culture sites. These sites, from the thirteenth century and earlier, dot the high plateau landscape of the Four Corners region (Bowden, *American Indians and Christian Missions,* 6–7).

[63] I named this dog after the lame, Comanche boy hero of a book my father read to us when I was in the fourth grade. In the story, the boy managed to steal a horse from the Spanish conquistadores, becoming the first Indian to learn to ride the fearsome animals.

the Bureau of Indian Affairs in Washington, D.C. William, through extended therapy and special shoes, eventually developed a nearly normal gait. And Gladys, mercifully, died a year earlier than the doctors expected. They were all Mephibosheths in their own ways, dead-dog offspring of Jonathan, touched by the dappled grace of a different David (cf. 2 Sam 9:1–13).

My father was my teacher for four of my eight years of grammar school. He was an avid reader and had a natural curiosity about the new world to which he had brought his family. Often in the fall or spring, when we had science class, he would take us on hikes around the area with the Navajo children as his guides. We would collect insects, rocks, and plants, take them back to school, then catalogue and display them as if we were explorers from some distant planet. Scientific names would be written beside Navajo names, with a brief explanation of the object's use in Navajo culture.

It was the beginning of my father's Navajo language, history, and culture course, and he was perhaps the first to teach such a class on the reservation. Using books and the Navajo children themselves as resources, he fed back to them what he was taking from them, now filtered through the critical observer's pale blue eyes.[64] The blind were gaining sight, the dumb were speaking, and the lame were beginning to walk.

Whenever I return to the mission—and the times become fewer and farther between as I grow older—I still find myself reverting to pidgin English, the language I unconsciously spoke as a young boy in order to be accepted by the Navajos. Then Navajo words, unused for decades, come rushing back to me in a flash flood. Like a dog searching for a buried bone, I sniff the sage-scented air with its hints of juniper and pungent mountain piñon,[65] and find myself retracing steps to old familiar places: to the Red Hill—to look for that one last shard that would complete my fractured self and my first reconstructed Anasazi pot; or to Fort Rock, where we carved our names with pocket knives in shadowed sandstone, and where passionate young lovers traced the outlines of newly discovered terrain far from the prying eyes of mission staff.

Thousands of miles, a score of years, a family, and a career now crowd out my past, separating me from that world. So now I must put distance as well as differentness into writing. Of course, Jacques Derrida tells us that difference

---

[64] Sheehan discusses in detail the origins of such programs within the education policies of Euro-American missionaries (*Seeds of Extinction,* 119–47; see also Bowden, *American Indians and Christian Missions,* esp. 164–201; and Vizenor, "Ruins of Representation: Shadow Survivance and the Literature of Dominance," 27–28).

[65] Hillerman, *Skinwalkers,* 244–45.

is already "there" in language, both as writing and as speech.[66] But that dif-férance is too much; it is a threat to the well-ordered universes of most bibli-cal scholars. And so my academic discipline demands critical distance; a means to step outside the difference, the différance, to put a stop to the sup-plementarity of language and to try to contain it. Distance is the rhetoric of our professional discourse;[67] distance trains it and feeds upon it, then vomits it up. I know all about distance. I grew up with that too.

### DISTANCE[68]

Unless you've been in the Southwest, you can't imagine the distances people regularly travel to do their business. We drove ninety miles one way to "town," just to shop for groceries. Later on, my brothers and I daily made a hundred-and-ten-mile circle to Shiprock, New Mexico, to go to high school. It was a miracle that we survived all those miles on the road. We encountered horses, cattle, sheep, and dogs all crossing the highway on the open range of the reservation. We hit one horse, drove off an embankment to miss another, and were rear-ended once by an inattentive tourist while stopping to let a

---

[66] "[L]anguage as such is already constituted by the very distances and differences it seeks to overcome," says Barbara Johnson in her introduction to Derrida's *Dissemination* (p. ix; see also Derrida's essay "Différance," in *Speech and Phenomena*, 129–60).

I must confess that I really haven't read much of Derrida, although I probably should since I seem to find traces of his thought echoing in my cross-cultural experience. Christopher Norris (*Derrida; Deconstruction;* and *What's Wrong with Postmodernism*) and other dissemina-tors like him are a lot easier for me to follow. What I read of Derrida, I tend to read in the mar-gins and in the prefaces of his work, relegating myself to the role of a listening ear in others' erudite conversations.

[67] Norris, *Deconstruction,* 22–24. See also Stephen Moore's discussion regarding the rhetor-ical nature of biblical criticism (*Literary Criticism and the Gospels,* 66–67), and Elisabeth Schüssler Fiorenza's perspective ("The Ethics of Interpretation," 10–13). For a more positive view of distance in scholarly discourse, see Mary Gerhart's comments on academic genres in *Genre Choices, Gender Questions* (pp. 12–15, 151–52); Stephen Greenblatt's appropriation of the term for the "New Historicists," in *Learning to Curse* (pp. 168–70); and Sandra Schnei-ders's summary of Paul Ricoeur's concept of distanciation in *The Revelatory Text* (pp. 142–44, 169–72).

[68] "Distance," writes Wallace Stegner, "space, affects people as surely as it has bred keen eye-sight into pronghorn antelope. And what makes that western space and distance? The same condition that enforces mobility on all adapted creatures, and tolerates only small or tempo-rary concentrations of human or other life. Aridity" (*Where the Bluebird Sings to the Lemonade Springs,* 75; cf. Erisman, "Hillerman's Uses of the Southwest," 11–12).

herd of sheep cross in front of us. I have no idea of how many dogs and other small animals we killed in our travels.

We saw many bad accidents in those years, but one in particular stands out in my mind. We were on our way to the trading post to get the mission mail when we saw it. A pickup truck had hit a horse. Pinned underneath the vehicle, the horse was still alive and struggling to get up. The driver's wife was in the cab of the truck, clinging to the door in a shocked stupor while the truck rocked back and forth. The driver took a shotgun out of a rack in the cab and shot the horse in the head. I'll never forget the look in that animal's eyes as it fought to get out from beneath the truck.

Signs everywhere warned drivers about the wandering animals, but "Open Range" meant nothing to tourists from New Jersey or Pennsylvania on summer vacations to the Grand Canyon or Mesa Verde. The state finally had to put up fences along all the major travel routes.

Halfway between Shiprock and Farmington, the town where we did our shopping, stood the Turquoise Bar. It was one hundred feet off the reservation line. Built in a circular shape, a gross parody of a hogan, it beckoned to the Navajos with promises of warmth, safety, and friendship. There, family and home could be bought for a buck.[69] But the few hundred yards of highway on either side of the bar were the most dangerous in all of New Mexico. The state finally had to put up warning signs. "Watch for Pedestrians" they said. But there were no pedestrians—just another kind of open range. Half-sleeping Navajos littered the roadside ditches and highway dividers around the bar, especially on weekends. We hit one once, reeling drunkenly across the road, mesmerized by the headlights of our onrushing vehicle.[70] With a thud he smashed into the side of the car. My father pulled over to the shoulder of the

---

[69] For the role of alcohol in U.S. Indian relations, see Sheehan, *Seeds of Extinction,* 232–42. According to Hillerman, the Navajo word for whiskey, *tódiłhił,* means "water of darkness" (*Coyote Waits,* 122). With a typical Navajo play on the word, it can also be manipulated to mean "sucking in darkness" (ibid). While the Navajo word can mean the former, probably a better translation is "water that makes one dizzy."

[70] Hillerman describes a similar experience in *Coyote Waits.* There, Jim Chee is investigating a murder when "[t]hree miles east of the intersection, the high beams of his headlights reflected from the back of a man walking down the asphalt. Chee braked and stared. The man was walking erratically down the center of the westbound lane. . . . He seemed totally oblivious of Chee's headlights, now just a few yards behind him. Without a backward glance, with no effort to move to the side of the road, he walked steadily onward, swinging something in his right hand, zigzagging a little, but with the steady, unhurried pace of a man who has walked great distances, who will walk great distances more" (pp. 15–16; see also *Talking God,* 186; *Sacred Clowns,* 198–99, 269–70).

road. We jumped out and looked for him for half an hour. But like a frightened dog licking its wounds, he had lurched off into the night. We never found him.

In a land of such vast distances you would think that most aspects of American culture never reached us. As late as 1969 there were still only two or three radio stations that we could pick up in the daytime and, along with one snowy, undependable television signal, these were our only daily contacts with the outside world. But we knew what the Cold War was and who the bad guys of the world were. Since the mission was not far from a major missile test flight site in Utah, we occasionally saw misguided U.S. military wizardry exploding high over the uninhabited Southwest. Meanwhile, down below on the desert floor, government geologists and oil company drillers annually crisscrossed our valley looking for high-grade uranium and natural gas reserves that would break U.S. dependence on Middle Eastern crude and ensure supremacy in the arms race. Their prospecting roads and drilling sites periodically tore the skin from the earth while she was in heat, exposing her pulsating fertility to the leering eyes of sweaty-faced hardhats and white-smocked technicians. When they left after a few months, as they always did, we would rush to explore her scattered entrails and uncovered orifices with our own open-mouthed silence.[71]

---

[71] Churchill notes how Hillerman "has managed to write *nine consecutive novels* providing ostensibly detailed descriptions of the habitat of Navajoland, and the people who reside in it, without ever once mentioning the vast proliferation of uranium tailings piles abandoned by U.S. corporations—with full government complicity—on the reservation since 1952" (*Fantasies of the Master Race,* 272). Churchill goes on to argue that "'politically sensitive' issues [such as this] are strictly off-limits within the framework of the author's literary project" (p. 3). Although the latter critique may be generally true, Churchill fails to note that the plot of at least one of Hillerman's early novels, *People of Darkness,* revolves around oil drilling and uranium mining near Mount Taylor (a sacred mountain to the Navajo), and a deadly talisman carved out of its radioactive stone. Furthermore, his most recent book, *Sacred Clowns,* focuses on a large corporation's concerted efforts to turn an abandoned strip mine on the reservation into a toxic waste dump (pp. 4, 6, 8, 67–78).

Speaking of these two books, it seems to me that Churchill overlooks a much more crucial motif that runs through most of Hillerman's novels: that Indian rituals and symbols, when touched by Euro-American colonizers, are inevitably destructive and allied with death. Moreover, the ideology underlying this motif is never made entirely clear to the reader. Is it that all Indian lifeways—whether ceremonial masks or sandpaintings, skinwalkers, an Anasazi flute player, a sacred clown, or a talisman—are potentially life-threatening to Euro-Americans? Or that all Indian lifeways, when subjected to the meddling hands of Euro-Americans, are turned inside out and become destructive to Indians (cf. Bahr's and Fenger's discussion of the victimist mode of writing Indian history in "Indians and Missions: Homage to and Debate with

In 1969, just a few weeks away from high school graduation, I made my customary stop for mail at Teec Nos Pos Trading Post one bright May afternoon. As I sorted the mission mail I saw a letter from the U.S. Army addressed to my father.

My oldest brother, Rob, had volunteered for military service after high school and a year later had volunteered for duty in Vietnam. He had come back to the States in February, visited the family for a few weeks, married one of my best high school friends,[72] then gone up to Fort Lewis, Washington, for his final year in the army. But three days earlier my English teacher had told me that over the weekend he had seen Rob in Flagstaff, Arizona. I knew that something was not right, since he had recently used up his leave. Now, without opening the letter, I knew what my brother had done. He had deserted.

A week later my other brother, Greg, came swaggering into my high school graduation ceremony with a story to tell. High on drugs and full of braggadocio, he announced to the family that he had just gotten back from driving Rob and Becky to Canada. They were safe and well and living in Toronto.

Our good Christian missionary family was on the verge of falling apart, and my soul was one of the major pieces of debris left to fight over. I, as the third child, had always been overly eager to please; and Rob, Greg, and I had always done everything together. At six years old, when Robbie gave his heart to Jesus, Greg did the same thing a few weeks later. At the tender age of four, I followed suit shortly thereafter. When Robbie decided he wanted to be baptized, Greg and I said we did too. And when Rob and Greg became interested in girls and fell in love for the first time, so did I—always with their girlfriends.[73] Now I was caught between my two older brothers with whom I had shared every life passage, my parents who had lost their hold on their two eldest children and didn't want to lose their third, and my two younger sisters who idolized me.

Over the previous six months, whenever Greg would come to visit from college, he would bring home with him a suitcase full of dirty clothes and hallucinogenic drugs. He was always generous. Anything I wanted, I could try.

---

Rupert Costo and Jeanette Henry," 315–19; and Bruner, "Ethnography as Narrative,"140, 143–44, 152)?

[72] Rob and Becky were married at the San Juan County courthouse in Aztec, New Mexico, with Greg and me as witnesses. Afterwards we celebrated with dinner at the Kentucky Fried Chicken Drive-In in Farmington.

[73] I was ever the voyeur, sneaking around after dark to watch Robbie and Sarah Tsosie standing toe to toe, kissing passionately behind the school. They had learned the value of hiding but had not yet discovered the virtue of lying.

His favorites were mescaline and peyote, the latter being a drug the Native American Church used to induce apocalyptic visions.[74] But I was afraid to use any of them.[75] Instead, being the good missionary kid that I was, I would take them to school and pass them out to my friends after gym class. Two hundred and fifty miles from the closest college campus and twenty-five miles from a post office, our household was hopelessly caught up in the generational war of the late 1960s. There would be casualties and an uneasy twelve-year cease-fire before peace was fully restored to our family.

On our way home from my high school graduation, my father stopped at the trading post and called the Military Police to tell them where his son was. And when we got home, my parents made it clear to Greg that he was no longer welcome in the house where he had grown up. In that one memorable week of May I felt I had lost my two brothers and possibly my parents as well. Our high school graduation song that year was from *The Man of La Mancha:* "To Dream the Impossible Dream." I couldn't sing it. I had never had time to learn the words.

Later that summer, Greg had a dramatic conversion experience. And true to form, his return to the fold reaffirmed my own faltering faith. So with a restored trust in God and a family on the mend, Greg and I went off together for a year of Bible school. The following year I enrolled at Wheaton College in Illinois,[76] far away from my family and the Navajo reservation. My plan to

---

[74] Peyote is the buttonlike top of a small, spineless cactus that grows in the southwestern United States and northern Mexico. It has been used in Native American religious ceremonies for centuries (Hillerman, *Dance Hall of the Dead,* 4, 60; *People of Darkness,* 173). The drug mescaline is derived from it.

[75] From about the age of five to seven I suffered from terrifying nightmares and had to be given sweet-tasting sedatives in order to sleep at night. The memories of those inarticulatable, terror-filled experiences made me hesitant in adolescence to try any drug that might conjure up those nameless demons. Having been born on December 22, only a few hours after the winter solstice, perhaps I was haunted by the Eastern European folk traditions of St. Thomas, who, on that particular night, takes the form of a dog and devours little children (White, *Myths of the Dog-Man,* 40). But whatever their origin, my dreams became less threatening and more revelatory once I left home. Three of these I remember distinctly (1969, 1974, 1984), and each focused on a problem in the interpretation of writing. In the first dream I was writing Greek as though I actually knew the language—a full year before I even considered studying it. In the second dream I was analyzing a poem that I had written in high school, one that I had never quite understood. (This dream turned into a demonic nightmare.) In the third dream I was working on my dissertation, dispassionately exegeting the Greek text of John's Gospel (cf. Berg, "Suppressing the Language of (Wo)man: The Dream as a Common Language," 15–24).

[76] Originally founded by Wesleyan abolitionists in the early 1850s as Illinois Institute, the school was reorganized as Wheaton College in 1860. Today, it is probably best known for

attend Wheaton was the first completely independent decision that I had ever made, and for the first time in my life I found myself totally on my own, with no older brothers to rely on. But even there, in suburban Chicago, the reservation dogged me.

First Michael McKenzie came to Wheaton. Along with his brother Marvin, who followed him the next year, they were the elite of the Navajo tribe and model American Indians. They were "good apples": red on the outside and white on the inside. As sons of the only Navajo physician, their parents had taught them nothing about their native culture. David Dennison came the same year Marvin did. Although he was half Navajo and half Mohawk-Seneca, the son of our most respected lay preacher, he was Navajo through and through. His younger sister was the first girl I ever kissed, in spite of my lies to the contrary.

I had encouraged Michael, Marvin, and David to come to Wheaton, where I was in my senior year. They had been part of a high school Bible study group that I led during summers and Christmas vacations, and I had nurtured them in the Christian faith. I made sure that I was their "big brother" during their freshman orientation, and I introduced them to all my friends. But they were freaks at Wheaton.

"What is it like being an Indian?" and "Can you speak some Navajo for us?" rang in their ears at every turn.

George and Rolf Johnson would have been proud of me. On the eightieth anniversary of Buffalo Bill's appearance at the memorable Columbian Exposition of 1893, their great-great-grandnephew had finally made Navajo Indians part of a Wild West show in a wealthy suburb of Chicago.[77]

One of my most poignant memories from my final semester at Wheaton is of Michael McKenzie walking across the college campus in the dead of winter, a stack of books under his arm. Every title he was carrying had something to do with Navajos, and I knew he wasn't taking any anthropology courses. Michael went to Wheaton College and discovered his cultural roots in the ethnological monographs added to the library collection to help prospective missionaries with their evangelization of foreign peoples.

---

being the alma mater of the world-famous evangelist Billy Graham. But for me, a no less significant fact is that John Wesley Powell, the great ethnologist, natural scientist, and methodical explorer of the vast Colorado Plateau, began his college education at the Institute (Stegner, *Beyond the Hundredth Meridian,* 15). Among his many cartographic credits is the discovery and first accurate charting of the mouth of the San Juan River (ibid., 89–90).

[77] Vizenor, "Manifest Manners: The Long Gaze of Christopher Columbus," 223–24.

But David was different. He had a nose for finding live Navajos. He sniffed them out on the corner of Madison and Monroe, Chicago's skid row, stinking of stale cigarettes, cheap wine, and urine. Soon he was spending his weekends there, walking the streets, and talking to them in their native language.

Did I destroy those friends of mine or did I liberate them? The question troubles me. I don't know its answer. My inherited Protestant sense of guilt keeps telling me that I abandoned them, that I left them to self-destruct in the flatlands of Illinois. I do know that none of them finished college at Wheaton. The last I heard, David was a silversmith in Bluff, Utah, making jewelry the old-fashioned way, in sand cast, squash-blossom patterns. Michael married a traditional Navajo girl, much to his parents' displeasure, and was living in an isolated canyon on the reservation. Marvin, I think, eventually graduated from college somewhere in New Mexico.

Distance. In order to be a good biblical scholar I must put distance between my past and my present;[78] between those nebulous names, nearly impossible to bring into focus, and the closer, more familiar names of my own family and children; between the mission on the reservation and my office at the university.

Our family has always had problems handling distance. Out of the six children, only Rob and I have never returned to the reservation or its environs to live for an extended period of time. And because of problems with the U.S. Army, for many years Rob couldn't have returned even if he had wanted. So I am the one left. The one who throws left-handed but writes right-handed; the one with a ruptured left Achilles tendon. I'm the one with the prenatal hemorrhage on the left occipital horn of his brain which left him with no right-side peripheral vision; the one who left it all behind. I've earned my right to speak authoritatively, with the tools of nuanced objectivity. So now listen to my voice as its tone changes, as the distance becomes greater. Here, I promise you, there will be no passion, no memory, no lying. Neutral tone is what counts.[79] Like a northern Indiana December sky.

---

[78] Andrée Collard writes: "Interfering with memories in any way is dangerous to one's integrity. Doing it with scientific precision has devastating implications for women: without memories there are no dreams, no imagination, no future, and above all, no present" (*Rape of the Wild*, 92).

[79] As Theodore Roszak puts it, the scientist "does not wish to see with the lively, wayward eye [I] of the artist, which allows itself to be seduced by what is charming, dramatic or awesome—and to remain there, entranced. It seeks a neutral eye [I] . . . in effect the eyes of the dead wherein reality is reflected without emotional distortion" (as quoted in Collard, *Rape of the Wild*, 66).

TOOLS[80]

Because of the two different environments in which I was immersed as a child, I grew up with a natural curiosity about contrasting ways of perceiving the world. Existential questions regarding the inherent correctness of those perceptions and their mutual claims of certitude arose which otherwise might never have surfaced. Eventually, this same inquisitiveness led me to challenge the authoritarian, anti-intellectualism of my Plymouth Brethren upbringing, replacing it with a mindful curiosity and a natural pluralism.[81]

Perhaps because of the double-minded bind in which I grew up, this slow-forming New Testament scholar had no interest in studying John's Gospel. The Fourth Gospel's message seemed too obvious, too transparent (John 3:7, 16–18). Everything divided up nicely into two camps: the seeing and the blind (9:39–40), the truth-holding believers and the unbelieving liars (8:44, 54–55). There seemed to be no room for openness, intellectual curiosity, or ambiguity in John's narrative world. Moreover, the Johannine Jesus was the type of character who pounded the truth into people's heads whether or not they wanted to hear his message—most, of course, did not.

But then in graduate school, while I was taking seminars in literary theory, I began to use the text of John to teach beginning Greek. Suddenly I began to read the Gospel with a new set of lenses.[82] I began to see that although the Gospel had a clear message to impart (20:31), *how* the reader was transported to that end could be as important as the text's final words. And the *how* that I was beginning to find in John's Gospel was one that undermined, tricked, and played games with the reader's naïve grasp of the story.[83]

In my more objective moments of reflecting on my critical approach to the Fourth Gospel, I will argue that I have been drawn to reader-response criticism primarily because it has offered me a way to read the Bible closely and cohesively, yet critically and differently. And secondarily (a reflective perspec-

---

[80] Probably my earliest and still most treasured tools are the various sorts of writing instruments that I possess (sticks, pocket knives, pencils, pens, typewriters, and computers), which, as Elaine Scarry notes, are alterations or redesigns of the hand, for they "endow the hand with a voice that has more permanence than the speaking voice, and reliev[e] communication of the requirement that speaker and listener be physically present in the same space" (*The Body in Pain,* 254).

[81] My official break with the Plymouth Brethren occurred in 1978 when I began regularly attending St. John's Presbyterian Church in Culver City, California.

[82] Mieke Bal discusses narratology both as a microscopic lens and as a distorting lens (*Death and Dissymmetry,* 240).

[83] Cf. Wayne Meeks, "The Man from Heaven in Johannine Sectarianism," 168–69.

tive that I do not want to share openly in the academic arena), it has allowed me to do what I most like to do—read imaginatively and dramatically. Assuming that no text (or worldview) has the whole truth, reader-response criticism has given me a set of critical tools with which to ask questions about the Gospel's imaginative, dramatic story and how it intends to affect its audience.[84] Narrative poetics and pragmatics are the operative words here.

As I noted in the introduction to this book, reader-response criticism has always been concerned with analyzing the effects of literature. It is interested in the persuasive goals of texts: how texts work readers and how readers work texts. And in reader-response criticism's more formalist expressions, careful, "close readings" of texts are common practice. But in these two foci I also hear resonances from my past.[85]

I grew up in a home where John Nelson Darby's torturous, literalistic readings of biblical texts (those that gave birth to dispensationalism and theories of a pre-tribulational rapture) were the ideal model of exegesis and translation.[86] But in our house these were coupled with a devotionally focused ethos. "What does this verse mean to you? What is God trying to tell you today?" were the classic questions asked around our dinner table.[87] We may have given lip service to Darbyite, "literal readings" of the Bible, but a self-taught, Spirit-centered devotion was what really mattered.[88]

A number of years ago I discovered that this unconventional, Spirit-centered devotion runs thick in my veins, back to the 1650s when my maternal grandmother's ancestors, the Bowerman and Harper families, were

---

[84] In a particularly insightful discussion, Scarry points out how the weapon and the tool "seem at moments indistinguishable" (*The Body in Pain,* 173). The tool, however, is finally "the concrete record of the connection between the worker and the object of his or her work; it is the path from the object back to its sentient source; it is the path that if eclipsed from attention allows the object to be severed from its source" (ibid., 176; cf. Collard's discussion of "living tools," in *Rape of the Wild,* 58–71; and Slicer's feminist assessment of animal research, in "Your Daughter or Your Dog?" 108–24).

[85] Frein, "Fundamentalism and Narrative Approaches to the Gospels," 13–14.

[86] Gosse, *Father and Son,* 229–31.

[87] Edmund Gosse's nineteenth-century description of Plymouth Brethren hermeneutics still fit when I was a child, a hundred years after he wrote: "[M]y parents read injunctions to the Corinthian converts without any suspicion that what was apposite in dealing with half-breed Achaian colonists of the first century might not exactly apply to respectable English men and women of the nineteenth" (*Father and Son,* 57–58; see also 76–77).

[88] For example, see my grandfather Leonard Sheldrake's books, *Our Lord Jesus Christ "A Plant of Renown"; Tabernacle Types and Shadows;* and my great-grandfather George Gray's *One Mediator: A Fourfold Revelation.*

expelled from Plymouth Colony for joining the Society of Friends.[89] A little over a hundred years later my Bowerman forebears were on the move again, this time for remaining neutral during the American Revolution. They were accused of being Tories and harboring pro-British sympathizers. Their lands in Dutchess County, New York, were confiscated and the family was forced to flee to Ontario, Canada.[90] The Bowermans remained within the Quaker tradition, following the inner guidance of the Spirit, until the 1890s, when they became Plymouth Brethren.

But these are not my only dissident, "Tory" roots. Another line in my mother's ancestry is Dutch Reformed, a line diluted by English blood in 1743 when the scheming John Dies married a wealthy, God-fearing woman named Jane Goelet.[91] John Dies was bound by a different spirit from that of my Quaker ancestors. Like that of Rip Van Winkle, his addiction to the little brown jug was legendary in the Catskill Mountains of the Hudson Valley.[92] But John was also a hard worker. He was an important military supplier of

[89] I am a thrice-born son of Plymouth. I was raised within the Plymouth Brethren denomination; I have ancestral roots in the family of William Brewster and the seventeenth century, New England colony of Plymouth; and I was born on December 22, the same day the Mayflower unloaded its cargo at Plymouth Rock (Krupat, "Native American Autobiography and the Synecdochic Self," 184).

[90] Bowerman, "'Bowerman' Family of Ontario Canada (1633 to 1916 inclusive). Being the Descendants of Ichabod Bowerman and Lydia Mott," 5–6.

[91] Randolph, with additions by Hastings, "Jacob Boelen, Goldsmith of New York and his Family Circle," 283–85.

Another New York Dutch ancestral line of mine is that of the Stryker family, which married into the Canadian Bowerman line in the mid-nineteenth century. The New World immigrant, Jacobus Gerritson Strjcker, married Ytie Hubrechts and settled in New Amsterdam in the 1640s. His portraits, some of which are displayed in the National Gallery in Washington D.C., are reminiscent of Rembrandt's style, and are among the earliest produced in colonial America.

The five most recent generations of my mother's family have each had their artists, my brother Greg and his middle son, Jonathan, being the latest in that line. Perhaps it is only coincidence, but it is worth noting that a woman with the same surname as Jacobus's wife married Rembrandt's son (Stryker, *The Stryker Family in America,* 13). Curiously, dogs play an iconographic role in many of Rembrandt's biblical scenes (Bal, *Reading Rembrandt,* 185–200; see illustration 13).

[92] Due to his drinking bouts, the mansion which John built in Catskill, New York was derisively known as "Dies Folly" and "The Stone Jug" (Mattice, *They Walked These Hills Before Me,* 114). The Dies house was especially known for its ornate ceramic tile fireplaces. Among their many imported, hand-painted biblical scenes, one was particularly memorable. It was of the resurrected Lazarus, striding out of his tomb with an upraised Dutch flag clutched in his hands (Beers, *History of Greene County, New York,* 88).

Like Rip Van Winkle, John Dies also wandered off from home in the 1760s, never to

13. *The Good Samaritan, 1633.* Rembrandt Harmensz van Rijn, Dutch 1606-1669. The inclusion of three additional males in the picture (bringing the total to six), and the presence of the woman in the background drawing water from a well all work to evoke an additional New Testament Samaritan story: the Samaritan woman of John 4:4-42 (cf. esp. 4:7, 18). For the iconographic role of dogs in Rembrandt's biblical scenes, see Bal, *Reading Rembrandt,* 185-200). Etching with burin 257 x 208 mm. (Gift of Mr. and Mrs. Jack F. Feddersen, The Snite Museum of Art, University of Notre Dame).

Crown Point during the French and Indian War, and a surveyor and land speculator who, with the help of his father-in-law, bought up patents from the Seneca and Mohawk Indians. One record has him trying to buy the islands just above Niagara Falls for the British Crown—no doubt after getting the Indians dead drunk on the firewater from his ever-present jug.[93]

On my father's side, however, the more rational and well-ordered Puritan blood ran thicker—at least in the Prudden and Coe families. Like many of the nineteenth-century founders of the Plymouth Brethren, John Prudden, son of Oxford-trained Reverend Peter Prudden, was professionally educated in theology and the Bible. He was a 1668 graduate of Harvard and took his first church in Jamaica, Long Island.[94] The Prudden family soon married into the Coe family, also of hearty Puritan stock, and a large branch of the Coes eventually moved to western Pennsylvania by way of Morristown, New Jersey.[95] Near Fort Pitt, Matthew Lamb, the young husband of Jane Coe, volunteered for military service under George Rodgers Clark. A few weeks later, on August 24, 1781, near the confluence of the Great Miami and Ohio Rivers, he was killed by Joseph Brant (Theyandoga), Simon Girty, and their Mohawk warriors, nearly putting an end to the staunch Puritan foundations of my family.[96] Today, I find myself wondering whether my friend David Dennison, half Mohawk-Seneca and half Navajo, was a descendant of a member of that war party. Perhaps my forefather, the devious drunkard John Dies, was involved in the woozy-eyed parleys over David's ancestral lands.

So it is not coincidental that my family, all genetically engineered Protestants rooted in the competing ideals of a youthful America, should emphasize the persuasive element of Scripture over everything else. And it is only natural that there should be little or no critical reflection on that element, and no sense of the differentness of Scripture. In our Plymouth Brethren home,

---

return. No one knows when or where he died (cf. Fetterley's discussion of Rip Van Winkle, in *The Resisting Reader*, 1–12).

[93] Johnson, *The Papers of Sir William Johnson*, 1:674–75; 3:326–29, 396–98, 642–43; 13:240–41; see also Howland, "Navy Island and the First Successors to the Griffon," 23–24; and Paltsits, *Minutes of the Commissioners for Detecting and Defeating Conspiracies in the State of New York: The Albany Sessions 1778–1781*, 2:522–23.

[94] Sibley, *Biographical Sketches of Graduates of Harvard University in Cambridge Mass. 1659–1677*, 2:258–63. See also Carman, *Thomas C. Carman and Phebe Pruden Carman*, 39–47; and Horton Prudden, *Rev. Peter Prudden and his Descendants in America*.

[95] Bartlett, *Robert Coe, Puritan: His Ancestors and Descendants 1340–1910*, 80–83, 90–92, 104–5.

[96] Funk, *The Revolutionary War Era in Indiana*, 23–31; see also Calloway, "Simon Girty: Interpreter and Intermediary," 48.

scriptural meaning was always simple and crystal clear. Interpretive conflicts did not arise from honest intellectual questions but from willful acts of rebellion.[97] In view of my family history, then, reader-response criticism functions as a chain linking my ancestral past to my present. Like a chromosome chain, it is wound tightly around the persuasive effects of narrative and my own personal history, yet it provides the critical tension (distance and attention) needed to assess those effects.[98]

When I secured my first professional position in 1985 at a small university adjacent to the St. Johns district of Portland, Oregon, one of my goals as a teacher was to defamiliarize the Bible so that it could be reappropriated afresh by individuals and communities of faith. I firmly believed that in order for growth and learning to begin, one had to be able to see Scripture simply as different from one's own experience of the world—without necessarily being better or worse. Furthermore, I thought that difference, distance, and defamiliarization (sharpened and polished through my years of academic research) were crucial to the critical and hermeneutical task of the biblical scholar. Thus, for example, I sought to show my students how sensitivity to the Johannine manipulation of narrative order (a special emphasis in much of more formalist reader-response criticism), sometimes seemed to subvert the narrator's own explicit agenda.[99] Among other things, this type of reading was intended to undermine students' naïve assumptions that they were reading straightforward, historical accounts of events from the life of Jesus. My hope was that, as a consequence, students would more critically evaluate their own unexamined ideological, theological, and historical assumptions regarding canonical texts and the life of faith.[100]

But again, the ability to "see things differently" is not something that came to me purely through reader-response criticism, nor was it necessarily something I "discovered" in the text of John. Contrary to my earlier assumptions, I do not believe that I developed this ability merely through appropriating the critical, distance-creating tools of scientific, objective research and the rhetorical techniques of academic discourse. As I have begun to think more recently in terms of how my own social context, geographic location, and personal

---

[97] For example, see Gosse, *Father and Son,* 233–40.

[98] Myers's description of the "genogram" is helpful here (*Who Will Roll Away the Stone?* 102–8).

[99] For example, see my exegetical work in chapters 1–3.

[100] Cf. Moore, *Literary Criticism and the Gospels,* 171–78; Johnson, "Teaching Deconstructively," 140–48; and Crain, "The Implications of Deconstruction in Teaching Servanthood," 88–95.

experience interpret the biblical text, I have come to believe that difference, distance, and defamiliarization have been part of my psychological makeup from the age of seven, when my family moved to the Navajo Indian Reservation. Indeed, as Jacques Derrida would argue, difference, distance, and defamiliarization characterize language itself.

## PLACE[101]

From the classic western films of John Ford, to the wilderness of John the Baptist and Jesus in *The Greatest Story Ever Told,* and the "Forbidden Zone" out of which an alien human savior comes in *Planet of the Apes,* the otherworldly landscapes of northern Arizona have served Hollywood's budget-conscious directors well.[102] But to the university-trained geologist, the country is a vast stratigraphic laboratory of sedimentary rock, volcanic plugs, and intrusive, igneous dikes. Over eons, erosion has cut deeply into the Southwest's mile-high Colorado, Kaibab, and Paria plateaus allowing the modern-day scientist to read the earth's history like an open book. Similarly to Johannine aporias, the mesas, canyons, buttes, and escarpments of the great plateaus break up the cohesive unity of the Rocky Mountain shield and expose in those erosive processes its own myth of origins.[103] For the naïve explorer, however, this erosion-induced, fantastic world can also be a death-trap, a bewildering wilderness of waterless false leads and deadends.

From the clear, arid air of the Carrizo Mountains or the tabletop of Sheepskin Mesa, the topography of our valley seemed full of easily identifiable signs and naturally plotted trails.[104] But it could quickly confuse and surprise the uninitiated hiker who had to wrestle with its unseen cliffs, hundred-foot-

---

[101] "If you don't know where you are, says Wendell Berry, you don't know *who* you are" (as quoted in Stegner, *Where the Bluebird Sings to the Lemonade Springs,* 199; cf. Krupat's attempt to account for "place" in his explication of an ethnically grounded literary criticism, *Ethnocriticism,* 115–16; Alcoff, "The Problem of Speaking for Others," 25; and Myers, *Who Will Roll Away the Stone?* xix–xx, 47–48, 125, 137–38, 324–29, 369–79, 416–18).

[102] Slotkin, *Gunfighter Nation,* 305, 518.

[103] Alan Culpepper, using geologists' and archaeologists' language, reminds his readers that "Johannine scholars have generally approached the text looking for tension, inconsistencies, or 'aporias' which suggest that separate strains or layers of material are present in the text. The next step is usually to place the 'layers' in some sequence by noting the way they are embedded in the gospel and the probable direction of theological development" (*Anatomy of the Fourth Gospel,* 3).

[104] "Aridity, more than anything else, gives the western landscape its character. It is aridity

deep canyons, and meandering washes. To give only one very mundane example: two miles south of the mission the 350-foot-high butte, *Tsé sá'á* (see illustration 14),[105] squatted half-naked and in full view from our living room window. Visitors from the Midwest who were hoping for a fifteen-minute evening stroll to the butte would often laugh incredulously at our suggestions that they plan for an hour hike, and begin by walking east in order to get on the south side of an invisible, twenty-foot-deep, thirty-foot-wide wash a hundred yards beyond the mission fence. To them, the land between our house and *Tsé sá'á* was an unbroken, half-mile plain of saltbush, greasewood, and cacti. They knew nothing of the wash with its clear-flowing stream, night-chirping frogs, and feathery-green tamarisk trees. It was impossible to see its banks from our living room window, even for those of us who knew its precise location. Only the actual experience of walking across the desert could confirm its problematic existence[106] Unless one knew exactly where to cross the wash, one could wander up and down its edges for a quarter of a mile before finding a suitable fording place. Furthermore, once a person descended into the wash, there was no guarantee that he or she could quickly find a route up the opposite embankment. Inattentive hikers could enter the stream bed a hundred yards southeast of our house and not walk out until it finally broadened into a grassy swale near the sheep dip and branding corral, a mile northwest and completely out of sight of the mission.

I think I read the Gospel of John in the same way I explored those lower reaches of the San Juan Basin: with the natural sense that a hiker's experience of plodding through that tortuous terrain was much different from the stationary perspective of the sentinel seated atop a butte or mesa. Only as a reader begins to move temporally through a specific narrative region is he or she able to feel the lay of the land and negotiate its texture with all its detours,

---

that gives the air its special dry clarity; . . . aridity that erodes the earth in cliffs and badlands. . . ." (Stegner, *Where the Bluebird Sings to the Lemonade Springs,* 46).

[105] The Navajo word translates as "the rock that sits." On the U.S. Geological Survey map below, it is spelled *Tseh Any.*

[106] In words that fit the contemporary literary critic of the Bible as well as the westward-headed traveler, Stegner writes, "[a]s we have gone about modifying the western landscape, it has been at work modifying us. . . . Perceptions trained in another climate and another landscape have had to be modified. That means we have had to learn to quit depending on perceptual habit. Our first and hardest adaptation was to learn all over again how to see. Our second was to learn to like the new forms and colors and light and scale when we had learned to see them. Our third was to develop new techniques, a new palette, to communicate them. And our fourth, unfortunately out of our control, was to train an audience that would respond to what we wrote or painted" (*Where the Bluebird Sings to the Lemonade Springs,* 52).

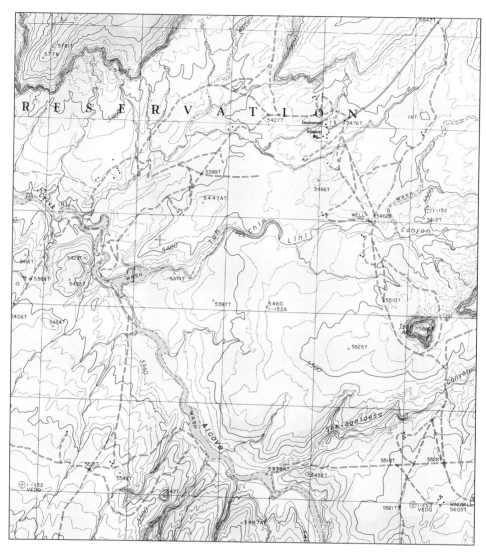

14. *Walker Butte, Arizona Quadrangle.* "When everything else has gone from my brain – the President's name, the state capitals, the neighborhoods where I lived, and then my own name and what it was on earth I sought, and then at length the faces of my friends, and finally the faces of my family – when all this has dissolved, what will be left, I believe, is topography: the dreaming memory of land as it lay this way and that" (Dillard, *An American Childhood,* 3). (Map U.S. Geological Survey)

surprises, traps, and gaps. For me, then, geology gave birth to theology; geography and topography metamorphosed into narratology.[107]

When I was a student at Shiprock High School on the banks of the San Juan River in northern New Mexico, the word *john* was pejorative reservation slang derisively used by Anglos and "town Navajos" for any Navajo who had not made the transition from traditional Indian culture to the dominant Caucasian culture and its values. Like a chapter from my childhood (like the redletter text of John in my missionary parents' home or the two-dimensional topographical map on our schoolroom wall), John seems to me to be a Gospel that outwardly has a simple message, clearly stated and transparent. But underneath that message there is another which—like the john world outside my childhood front door, or the three-dimensional desert floor—often seems to subvert and controvert the previously established norm. As I approach the end of my fifth decade of life, I am beginning to think that I have long been the unsuspecting victim of two johns, two geographies, and two existential ironies.

Having long since left my fundamentalist roots and the Navajo Reservation, I am now discovering that that context with its values still remains with me, affecting the way I read and influencing my own persuasive, scholarly agenda.[108] But whether I am wrestling with geography or theology, Saint John or San Juan, I will always treasure my initial probings into that Gospel. Like the red desert sand of my reservation childhood, the book is my blood. So I am now beginning to believe that the critics of formalist reader-response criticism have an important point to make. Perhaps all our readings of Scripture are autobiographical and circular. Perhaps an objectively obtainable, "textu-

---

[107] "I think of two landscapes—" writes Barry Lopez, "one outside the self, the other within. The external landscape is the one we see—not only the line and color of the land and its shading at different times of the day, but also its plants and animals in season, its weather, its geology, the record of its climate and evolution. . . . The second landscape I think of is an interior one, a kind of projection within a person of a part of the exterior landscape. . . . The interior landscape responds to the character and subtlety of an exterior landscape; the shape of the individual mind is affected by land as it is by genes. . . ." Then, using the Navajo people's "indigenous philosophy" of beauty as a model, Lopez argues: "Each individual, further, undertakes to order his interior landscape [or story] according to the exterior landscape. To succeed in this means to achieve a balanced state of mental health" ("Landscape and Narrative" in *Crossing Open Ground*, 64–68; cf. Engel, "Landscape and Place in Tony Hillerman's Mysteries," 112; and Erisman, "Hillerman's Uses of the Southwest," 10–12).

[108] As the ancient Hebrew proverb puts it, "Like a dog that returns to its vomit is a fool who reverts to his folly" (Prov 26:11). Or to put it more positively, "Train children in the right way, and when old, they will not stray" (Prov 22:6).

ally defined," formalist "encoded reader" is impossible to isolate in the Bible. Perhaps that reader must finally be recognized for what it really is: an invention of modernism, essentialism, and the scientific mind.[109]

But then another possibility stirs my thinking. My curiosity regarding the relationship between autobiography and exegesis was initially aroused by a criticism that Mary Ann Tolbert raised,[110] and that criticism led me to pose her question to myself. "Let's assume that she is right," I said. Suppose that the encoded reader I had previously "discovered" in the Johannine text was merely myself, discreetly hiding behind the objectivistic mask of formalist reader-response criticism. What, then, might I discover if I were consciously to lift that mask and investigate my life in the way that I had previously investigated the Gospel of John? It was that question which spawned the final three chapters of this book.

Of course, what I have found in investigating my life is that I can just as easily find the Gospel of John in my life as I can find my life in the Gospel of

---

[109] Moore, *Literary Criticism and the Gospels,* 173–74.

[110] Echoing Stephen Moore's general observations about biblical reader-response criticism (*Literary Criticism and the Gospels,* 106–7), Mary Ann Tolbert wrote: "What Staley's generalized reader masks . . . is the critic himself: Staley's reader reads the way Staley does" ("A Response from a Literary Perspective," 206; cf. Porter, "Why Hasn't Reader-Response Criticism Caught on in New Testament Studies?" 281–82). Similarly, Danna Fewell and David Gunn say that Meir Sternberg's "poetics of foolproof composition [e.g., *The Poetics of Biblical Narrative*] depends not only on the notion of an omnipotent narrator but also on the notion of an ideal, competent reader, presumably the reader epitomized by Sternberg himself" ("Tipping the Balance: Sternberg's Reader and the Rape of Dinah," 194; cf. Sternberg's rejoinder, "Biblical Poetics and Sexual Politics: From Reading to Counterreading," 466–67; and Carlton, "Rereading *Middlemarch,* Rereading Myself," 240–41).

Interestingly, Jacques Derrida also exposes the problematics of a writer's masks. In discussing Friedrich Nietzsche's peculiar habit of using pseudonyms in his autobiographical *Ecce Homo,* Derrida writes that Nietzsche "advances behind a plurality of masks or names that, like any mask and even any theory of the simulacrum, can propose and produce themselves only by returning a constant yield of protection, a surplus value in which one may still recognize the ruse of life. However, the ruse starts incurring losses as soon as the surplus value does not return again to the living, but to and in the name of names, the community of masks" (*The Ear of the Other,* 7; cf. Bakhtin, *Rabelais and His World,* 39–40; Kazin, "Autobiography as Narrative," 214).

Not surprisingly, masks have an important function in Navajo religion, although outsiders are rarely allowed to view them or the ceremonies in which they are used (Hillerman, *Talking God,* 49–51, 131–33, 189–193, 290). And as Derrida notes, removing them can be life-risking (*The Ear of the Other,* 16-17). One never knows precisely what will be uncovered in that process. In the novel *Talking God,* for example, the only time a mask is taken off in public is when the Navajo detective Chee rips one from a mannequin at the Smithsonian Museum. What lies behind it, attached to it, is a plastic bomb about to detonate (pp. 314–15, 322–23).

John.[111] John's Gospel has been a place for me to abide. It has been my abode; an adobe-framed hiding place. But St. John has also hounded me, dogging my footsteps as I crisscrossed the western United States. Wallace Stegner writes that "if every American is several people, and one of them is or would like to be a placed person, another is the opposite, the displaced person, cousin not of Thoreau but to Daniel Boone, dreamer not of Walden Ponds but of far horizons, traveler not in Concord but in wild unsettled places, explorer not inward but outward."[112] The Gospel of John has been all these things to me, both my sense of place and my displacement; my mask and my unmasking; equally the source of unfulfilled dreams and the unsettling impetus to exploration.

I have uncovered St. John every time that I have peered into my past. In my childhood years on the Navajo reservation it flowed with the muddied waters of the San Juan River of northern New Mexico and southern Utah. It lay deep beneath the snowcapped San Juan Mountains of southern Colorado.[113] San Juan grit nourished me like Navajo fry bread. The air that scraped its peaks was a sweet-tasting, heady wine.

In early adulthood St. John appeared again, this time in the form of a Presbyterian congregation in southern California. It nurtured me when I was making the difficult decision to leave the Plymouth Brethren. When I crossed the divide into married life, St. John was beside me once more. Now it was the Presbyterian church in Berkeley where Barbara and I pledged our love for each other, across the street from where we conceived our first child.[114] Most

[111] Cf. John 17:23. Or as James Olney puts it: "Man creates, in fact, by the very act of seeking, that order that he would have" (*Metaphors of Self*, 4).

[112] Stegner, *Where the Bluebird Sings to the Lemonade Springs*, 199.

[113] Wallace Stegner quotes approvingly George Stewart's incredibly romantic vision, how "once from eastern ocean to western ocean, the land stretched away without names. Nameless headwaters split the surf; nameless lakes reflected nameless mountains; and nameless rivers flowed through nameless valleys into nameless bays" (from *Names on the Land*, as quoted in *Where the Bluebird Sings to the Lemonade Springs*, 166). While Stegner is correct to go on to note that "Catholic invaders planted innumerable Old World saints in the New World" (ibid., 168), the mountains, rivers, lakes, and valleys were by no means nameless prior to the arrival of Europeans. Around our mission, for example, every topographical feature had a name—each butte, mesa, mountain, spring, valley, and canyon. There was Whirling Mountain, Bad Canyon, Dancing Rocks, The Rock that Sits, Sweetwater, No Water Mesa, Cottonwood Trees in a Circle, and hundreds more descriptive, nearly untranslatable Navajo names. Every one of them predated Spanish or English place-names (cf. Cheyfitz, *The Poetics of Imperialism*, 137–38; Kelly and Francis, "Places Important to Navajo People," 151–69).

[114] Our son, Benjamin Walter, was born June 7, 1985, in Berkeley. Our daughter, Allison Jean, was born October 15, 1988, in Portland, Oregon.

recently, St. John has been the troubled neighborhood in north Portland, Oregon, near the university where I was denied tenure.

I know no St. John sans Juan–or, for that matter, sans Jean. For my wife and I both were carried in the wombs and suckled at the breasts of women named Jean.[115]

FULL CIRCLES, STRAIGHT LINES

I have discovered nothing from reading myself as a reader. Nothing except that I can as easily hide and lie about myself as I can about the Gospel of John. And if the critics of reader-response criticism tell me my Johannine "reader" is a fiction, critics of autobiography tell me that the "self" I have read reading the Gospel of John is no less a fiction.[116] The "I" of this chapter is nothing more than print and paper conceived from the unholy trinity of Tony Hillerman's popular, quasi-anthropological detective novels, my own piecemeal memory, and sacred Scripture. But then, the same can be said of Jesus' self-disclosing "I Am" in John's Gospel. It is not his own either. It is merely the text of Exodus 2:14 pinned precariously to his lips by some nameless author. All our reconstructed personae are intertextual and linguistic fictions, whether the referent (or "deferent") is "Jesus," "Jeffrey," or the "Johannine encoded reader."[117]

So I return to the place where I began, beside the westward-headed Santa Fe Trail.[118] But now I find myself doing the same thing with the challenging

---

[115] My mother's name was Mary Elizabeth Jean, and my mother-in-law's name is Marjorie Jean. Both of my sister's middle names are also derivations of the name John: Brenda Joan, and Beth Janette.

[116] To put it a different way, "the problem of autobiography lies in the threat of ideology which dogs all narrative in its compulsion toward wholes" (Gunn, *Autobiography,* 119). Or again: "'Chaos,' Henry Adams said in his *Education,* 'is the law of nature, order is the dream of man.' Both fiction and autobiography attempt to impose order on the only life the writer knows, his own" (Stegner, *Where the Bluebird Sings to the Lemonade Springs,* 219).

[117] As Wallace Stegner writes, "we [writers] are all practiced shape-shifters and ventriloquists; we can assume forms and speak in voices not our own. We have to have in some degree, . . . the capacity to make ourselves at home in other skins" (*Where the Bluebird Sings to the Lemonade Springs,* 217). In Navajo culture, those who have this capacity are the changelings, the coyote-faced skinwalkers (Hillerman, *The Blessing Way,* 38, 67, 121–22; *Skinwalkers,* 46). And in contemporary literary theory, the cynocephalic "boundary crossers," those who insist on "betweenness," and the "shifting processes of 'transculturalization'" are the ethnocritics (Krupat, *Ethnocriticism,* 3–45, esp. 28, 37; cf. Vizenor, "Trickster Discourse: Comic Holotropes and Language Games," 206–7; and Vizenor, *The Trickster of Liberty,* ix–xviii).

[118] The conjunction of circular and linear metaphors here is intentional (cf. Krupat, *Ethno-*

question about "the critic himself" as I had done previously with reader-response criticism's questions about encoded readers. To put matters quite simply, once again I have found what I wanted to find: a plausible way of construing data (now defined as text-plus-memory) so as to render critical insight theoretically possible. As a Johannine scholar I have been cursed with having a vivid imagination. As an autobiographer I have been anathematized by a fragmentary memory. Ironically, both imagination and memory are blessings for the author of fiction—whether author of academic fictions or autobiographical fictions.

Perhaps it is time to don a new mask in biblical exegesis, time to move to a different stage. Perhaps what we need today is an openly expressive, human creation; an artistic invention; some form of discourse that will allow the reflected subjectivity of the person to speak as freely as the critically distanced exegete.[119] With this in mind, the next chapter returns to the Gospel of John under an old dramatic guise (the medieval passion play),[120] but with contemporary content (a fictional conversation juxtaposing the three different perspectives that have guided my interpretive adventures). In utilizing the dramatic genre of the passion play, I intend to move toward the formation of a reader-critic (myself) who is increasingly aware of how autobiographical matters (my reconstructed past, personal values, and present social context), formalist reader criticism, and cultural studies all affect his readings of the Fourth Gospel.

Difference—or à la Jacques Derrida, *différance*—cannot be escaped in any reading strategy. (*Vive la différance!*) But in my final exegetical explorations, the reader will find distance being strangely twisted—the tools of exegetical practice being telescoped into a personal present, and place obtruding incongruously into the biblical text. In this process, the scientific model of binocular, microscopic readings to which I adhered in my exegesis of John 5 and 9, 11, and 18 will give way to a dramatic, subjective colliding of kaleidescopic readings.

---

*criticism,* 38–43). As T. S. Eliot wrote somewhere: "The end of all our exploring / Will be to arrive where we started / And know the place for the first time."

[119] For example, see Patrocinio Schweickart's discussion of the interpreter's subjectivity ("Reading Ourselves: Toward a Feminist Theory of Reading," 528–39, 541; cf. Tompkins, "Me and My Shadow," 36–37; and Freedman, "Border Crossing as a Method and Motif in Contemporary American Writing, or How Freud Helped Me Case the Joint," 14–15).

[120] The model of Mikhail Bakhtin's carnivalesque is apropos here (*Rabelais and His World,* xviii–xxii, 10–15).

# CHAPTER SIX

# Postmortem Passion Play: John 18:28–19:42 and the Erosion of the Reader

[No] one has ever done exegesis of John's writings until the reader has received, as a vital reality, the message of the work and has felt its impact in his own life and existence.

—John Dominic Crossan

I am going to . . . read the Gospel of St. John as an Indian. Secondly, this Indian is not a hypothetical being, . . . whom I have imagined. This Indian is myself.

—M. A. Amaladoss

[R]eading is a species of self-discovery, but it may also be a neurosis or hysteria.

—Elizabeth Freund

Let us . . . cast lots for it to see who will get it.

—John 19:24

## PROLOGUE

As a literary genre, the Christian passion play had its historical origins in medieval Europe and in the liturgy of the church. But as Mikhail Bakhtin points out, its social roots go back much earlier, to the ancient marketplace and the chthonic carnival, "which celebrated temporary liberation from the prevailing truth and from the established order; [and] marked the suspension of all hierarchical rank, privileges, norms and prohibitions."[1]

The earliest reference to passion dramas comes from the tenth-century

---

[1] Bakhtin, *Rabelais and His World,* 10; cf. McKenna, *Violence and Difference,* 35, 172.

English monk Ethelwold, who "described the 'praiseworthy custom' of celebrating the death and resurrection of Christ by a representation, with mime and dialogue, to be performed in church during or after the liturgical rites."[2] In the same century, Hrosvit, a Benedictine nun from Saxony, began writing the first Christian dramas, based largely on the martyrdoms of saints. Hrosvit envisioned the dramatic form as a way of instilling Christian virtues in the laity, and, before long, the form was being adapted to the life of Christ.

The passion play owed much of its popularity to the mixture of folk traditions and cultural stereotypes, especially after the thirteenth century, when it was gradually banished from performances on church property and began to be presented in town squares and in the vernacular.[3] Today, the most famous European passion drama is that performed by the villagers of Oberammergau, in upper Bavaria, Germany. Except for the years 1870 and 1940, it has been performed every ten years since 1634, when, as legend has it, it began as an expression of gratitude for the cessation of a plague.[4]

One of the most popular, long-running passion plays in the United States is the annual summer production at Spearfish, South Dakota. First performed in 1938, with the Black Hills as an expansive backdrop (hills that had been stolen seventy years earlier from the Lakota and Cheyenne Indians for their gold-bearing streams), its geographic setting subtly combines the mythic themes of American Manifest Destiny with Jesus' victory over Satan and death. But I am interested in readers and readings of the passion narrative, not in the history of the dramatic genre. Thus, this chapter's passion play will not be set in Spearfish, South Dakota, or Oberammergau, Germany, but somewhere within the postmodern struggle against totalizing theories of texts and selves.

As with the formless, wordless memories of our professional, pre-autobiographical selves, in John's Gospel the physical pain of the crucified victims has no voice. In sharp contrast to Mark's Gospel, there is no cry of dereliction, nor are there any tortured screams.[5] Although the beaten and crucified Jesus

---

[2] Cross and Livingstone, eds., "Christian Drama," in *The Oxford Dictionary of the Christian Church,* 425. This "praiseworthy custom" probably had its origins in the *Quem quaeritis* trope which was especially well developed in the liturgical worship of the Gallican Rite (ibid).

[3] Mikhail Bakhtin points out the numerous parodic connections between the medieval carnival and the liturgy and mystery plays of the church (*Rabelais and His World,* 5, 15, 27, 78–88, 229–31, 347–48).

[4] According to Richard Pierard, "Hitler admired the play for its alleged anti-Semitic qualities, and it was rewritten for the tricentennial performance in 1934 to make Jesus and the disciples appear as Aryan heroes" ("Oberammergau," 720).

[5] Cf. Mark 15:34 and John 19:26–28; cf. Mark 15:37 and John 19:30.

can speak (he converses with Pilate, with his mother, and with the Beloved Disciple; he says he is thirsty; and he acknowledges the completion of his divinely appointed task [John 19:1–12, 26–30]), he is never portrayed as suffering.[6] The Johannine narrator and the crucified victim remain silent, for to acknowledge the pain is to confess the mastery and power of the one inflicting it, and this neither Jesus nor the narrator can do (19:1–3, 10–11).[7] Like others who have undergone torture, the Johannine Jesus somehow seems to have disciplined himself to transcend the limits of physical pain. From an ideological perspective, perhaps the "food" he has to eat and his commitment to "laying down his life" have made the pain of a tortuous death bearable (4:32; 10:17).[8]

Yet if that physical agony were to find its voice, if Jesus' pain had a pen, I believe that it would begin to tell another story. And, as Elaine Scarry writes, the story that it would tell would be "about the inseparability of . . . three subjects, their imbeddedness in one another."[9] For her, these three subjects are: "first, the difficulty of expressing pain; second, the political and perceptual complications that arise as a result of that difficulty; and third, the nature of both material and verbal expressibility. . . ."[10]

---

[6] As Robert Brawley rightly notes, the narrator's aside explaining Jesus' statement "I thirst" as "a completion of Scripture" (19:28), argues against interpreting it as a sign of agony ("An Absent Complement and Intertextuality in John 19:28–29," 427; see also Moore, *Poststructuralism and the New Testament,* 54–57).

[7] See, for example, Elaine Scarry's discussion of pain and interrogation (*The Body in Pain,* 28–38, esp. 37–38) and her observation that in the Christian symbol of the cross the relationship between power and pain has been eliminated. She notes: "They are no longer manifestations of each other: one person's pain is not the sign of another's power. The greatness of human vulnerability is not the greatness of divine invulnerability. They are unrelated and therefore can occur together: God is both omnipotent and in pain" (ibid., 214).

[8] Perhaps the Roman soldier in Mark's Gospel exclaims, "This man must have been a son of God" (15:39), because he is impressed with Jesus' fortitude. See, for example, Judith Perkins's gruesome examples of self-inflicted pain ("Representation in Greek Saints' Lives," 260–65) and, closer to home, the descriptions of both Euro-American settlers' and Indians' apparent stoicism when tortured (Sheehan, *Seeds of Extinction,* 185–212; and Namias, *White Captives,* 3–4, 54–56). Scarry is aware of the wide variety of cultural responses to pain described by anthropologists, but does not discuss the differences in any detail (see, for example, *The Body in Pain,* 5, 109–10; cf. Collard, *Rape of the Wild,* 60–64; Levi, *Survival in Auschwitz,* 135–36).

[9] Scarry, *The Body in Pain,* 3.

[10] Ibid. Similarly Andrée Collard, in writing about the pain inflicted in animal research, says: "Researchers go to great lengths to avoid naming it, even when they purposely set out to study pain. To look at pain without naming it is to objectify pain, to transmute it into a category of knowledge" (*Rape of the Wild,* 60).

In the following passion play, Scarry's trinity of subjects can be viewed as a plot that is given its peculiar shape by the conversation of the three corpses on their crosses. These three imaginary voices can, in turn, be associated to a certain extent with the hermeneutical voices that Mieke Bal discusses in her theoretical work, although there is actually no one-to-one correspondence between Bal's hermeneutical voices and those of the corpses. Her voices are the text (which is a subject that speaks to us), the interpretation (the plausible interaction with the text), and the witness (who checks what happens in interpretation and "will refuse to go along when the interpreter overwrites the text").[11] I have appropriated these three voices in an effort to raise up my own resistant, painful silences and the resistant, painful silences of the Johannine text.

To paraphrase and interweave Scarry's and Bal's insights, the "difficulty in expressing pain" gives rise to "political and perceptual complications" as the characters in the passion play wrestle with the Johannine text's silences. Next, the characters propose various interpretations, or "plausible interactions with the text," in response to the text's resistance to expressing Jesus' pain.[12] Finally, the characters act as witnesses who check what happens in interpretation and "refuse to go along when [an] interpreter overwrites the text."

I think that Elaine Scarry's threefold theory of pain as an experience out of which worlds are made and unmade, and Mieke Bal's three hermeneutical voices both may be suggestive for contemporary communities dedicated to the liberation of oppressed peoples in a postcolonial world and may help to orient the reader to the discussions of the three corpses which follow. But neither Scarry's nor Bal's theories are meant to act as metanarratives that somehow seek to legitimate or center any one of the interpretive voices over the other. In other words, my exegetical play does not represent a postmortem autopsy on postmodernism's resistance to totalizing theories.[13] It has no obvious savior figure. So with these introductory comments in mind, let the Roman begin the postmortem task.

[11] Bal, *Death and Dissymmetry*, 240–41.

[12] Traditionally, in commentaries and exegetical articles on the Fourth Gospel's passion narrative, christological questions have dominated these "political and perceptual complications."

[13] Is postmodernism's resistance to metanarratives and totalizing theories simply another Western European metanarrative (see, for example, Krupat, *Ethnocriticism*, 9–13; Hutcheon, *The Politics of Postmodernism*, 14–17; Holub, *Crossing Borders*, 194–95, 200–201; Spivak, *The Post-Colonial Critic*, 18–20; cf. Tolbert, "The Politics and Poetics of Location," 309–11; and The Bible and Culture Collective, *The Postmodern Bible*, 145–47)? Perhaps.

ACT I

A Roman soldier begins to cut the leather thongs that hold the three bloodied bodies to their crosses. He rips the valuable iron nails from the still-warm flesh. They will be saved, straightened, and reused another day for another grim demonstration of Pax Romana.[14] As he drops the first corpse on the ground, Death rattles their throats and the tale begins.[15]

The first corpse falls in a heap, face in the dirt, and one of those left hanging addresses the other two. "You know, I must confess to you that I have never written about the Johannine passion narrative before, primarily because it has always struck me as a passionless passion. Ignace de la Potterie has recently said the same thing, only more in terms of character analysis. He says, 'The careful reader will be struck by two details: the complete self-awareness of Jesus, several times indicated, and also the majesty with which he goes forward to his Passion.'[16] But Raymond Brown describes it in a manner which I find to be more disturbing theologically; as a passion narrative where 'there is no victimizing of the Johannine Jesus, [who] is in such control that only when he affirms 'It is finished,' does he bow his head and hand over his Spirit' (19:30).[17] Suddenly, those strategies of subversion and victimization that so intrigued me in my earlier analysis of the Fourth Gospel's story world seem to have disappeared. If they're here at all, I'll have to work hard to find them."[18]

The corpse lying face down in the dirt intones, "And I'm absolutely repulsed by this Johannine Jesus, a person sent from God who is so sure of himself, so hypersensitized and aware of the hour's significance that 'he passes through death without turmoil and with jubilation.'[19] So how can I be anything less than a radically resistant reader to this 'take-two-aspirin-and-call-me-in-the-morning' story? I've got to know this passion narrative in a painful, passionate

---

[14] "Roman crucifixion was state terrorism; . . . its function was to deter resistance or revolt, especially among the lower classes . . ." (Crossan, *Jesus*, 127).

[15] "To degrade an object does not imply hurling it into the void of nonexistence, into absolute destruction, but to hurl it down to the reproductive lower stratum, the zone in which conception and new birth take place. Grotesque realism knows no other lower level; it is the fruitful earth and the womb. It is always conceiving" (Bakhtin, *Rabelais and His World*, 21; cf. Booth, *The Company We Keep*, 394–416; esp. 402, 410).

[16] De la Potterie, *The Hour of Jesus*, 16.

[17] Brown, *The Community of the Beloved Disciple*, 118.

[18] See, for example, chapter 3.

[19] Käsemann, *The Testament of Jesus According to John 17*, 20; cf. Thompson, *The Humanity of Jesus in the Fourth Gospel*, 87–89.

way, in a carnal way. I will find a way to strip it and lay it bare, shuddering and convulsing, before the faithful mother and Beloved Disciple."

The third corpse, still hanging on its cross, enters the conversation: "Frankly, I'm repulsed by both of you. One of you has refused to talk about this text previously because it annoys your sophisticated literary and theological sensitivities, while the other of you dislikes the text's passionless characterization of Jesus, yet has decided to read it anyway—any way you want. You both seem to recognize intuitively that these crosses reflect the radical difference between two social worlds—the ancient Mediterranean and the contemporary Euro-American—yet you can't let the difference stand by itself and try to understand that cultural difference for what it is.[20] So why don't we just let our crosses stand for difference, for the Other? Let's investigate, critically evaluate, question, and interpret the text, but then let's leave our crosses to turn to stone in the sun. Let them be discovered by chance as artifacts of a different time, culture, and place."[21]

The second corpse, oblivious to the previous comments, plunges on in its soliloquy. Its voice deepens and grows more confident as it continues. "Listen to me for a minute, you two wind-filled bags of bones! From my vantage point up here I can see that the passion narratives are the most carefully, proleptically plotted parts of the Synoptic Gospels, and the Fourth Gospel is no exception to this. Straightforward predictions, foreshadowings, allusions, and reliable commentary all work together to announce significant elements of Jesus' final days, and purposely leave little room for passion, surprise, or imagination in the narrative. As many scholars have pointed out, from the opening scenes of the Gospel, incidental characters, the narrator, and Jesus himself all make oblique or explicit references to his death and its significance. John's witness starts things off (1:29); Jesus alludes to it[22] and seems actually to contrive it (6:70–71; 13:11–21; 17:12); the narrator expands on it

---

[20] Part of that difference has to do with the contrasting experience of personhood in the ancient Mediterranean world and the contemporary Euro-American world (see pp. 147–48, nn. 1, 2). Bruce Malina and Jerome Neyrey, following Mary Douglas, would argue that the Jesus of the Johannine passion narrative is a typical "strong group person" ("First Century Personality: Dyadic, not Individual," 72; see also Bal, "The Point of Narratology," 731–32).

[21] Elaine Scarry writes that "in any culture, the simplest artifact, the simplest sign, is the single mark on wood, sand, rock, or any surface that will take the imprint" (*The Body in Pain*, 238). Here, as in the ancient Hebrew tradition, that sign is blood on a human-made surface (cf. 220, 233–41, 325–26).

[22] See, for example, John 2:4, 19; 3:14–16; 10:14–18; 12:7–8, 23–24, 31–32; 15:13; 18:11.

(2:21–22; 11:51–52; 12:33); and eventually even a minor character such as Caiaphas inadvertently prophesies it" (11:49–50).[23]

The other hanging corpse impatiently interrupts to interject a slightly different perspective. "I can play your literary game too, although I reject your anachronistic, ethnocentric notion of story worlds.[24] But, assuming for the sake of argument that I am reading the text as so-called closely as you are, I note that within the passion narrative itself the actions of political powers dominate the sequence of events as nowhere else in the story.

"For example, this is the only section of the narrative where Jesus is passively moved from one place to the other. Only in the passion narrative is Jesus bound (*deō*, 18:12, 24; 19:40),[25] brought (*syllambanō*, 18:12), or led to someone (*agō*, 18:13, 28; 19:4, 13). And it is the actions and intentions of the soldiers and temple police that move your plot along—not Jesus' moment-by-moment decisions.

"As a matter of fact, earlier in the Gospel the chief priests had sent the temple police to arrest Jesus (7:32), but precisely because they were reluctant to do so, the action was not carried out (7:45–52). And at other times Jesus quite easily escaped or withdrew from people whenever he wished.[26] Finally, when Jesus was asked to intervene in situations of need, there was always an immediate sense that Jesus' own prerogatives governed the plot movement—not the second party's interests.[27] So the intentions of both the protagonist and the antagonists do seem capable of affecting plot developments. Clearly, then, the Fourth Gospel's plot is not based on a Greek idea of the Fates.

---

[23] Alan Culpepper correctly discusses many of these references within the context of "plot" (*Anatomy of the Fourth Gospel*, 86–98; see also Senior, *The Passion of Jesus in the Gospel of John*, 31–44).

[24] The term "story world" expresses the biblical narrative critics' notion that stories can have their own natural laws, social codes, and symbolic connections, which might be quite different from any "real world" outside the text. For example, science fiction and fantasy are two contemporary genres that construct story worlds which are often at odds with the world as we know it (cf. Powell, *What Is Narrative Criticism?* 6–8; Moore, *Literary Criticism and the Gospels*, 8–10).

[25] Note Sylva's discussion of the word ("Nicodemus and his Spices," 148–51).

[26] See, for example, John 4:3; 5:13, 18; 6:15; 7:1, 10, 19, 25, 30, 44; 8:20, 37, 40; 9:12; 10:39; 11:8, 54; cf. Stibbe, "The Elusive Christ: A New Reading of the Fourth Gospel," 21–25.

[27] Note especially John 2:3–7; 4:46–49; 7:2–14; 11:1–6. In his study of these texts, Giblin concludes that "there is [no] inconsistency or change of mind on Jesus' part." For Jesus is disassociated "from the predominantly human concerns of those who, by merely human standards, would seem to be rather close to him. . . . He never fails to attend to the situation presented to him, but in doing so he acts radically on his own terms" ("Suggestion, Negative Response and Positive Action in St. John's Portrayal of Jesus," 210).

Rather, Jesus is acting like a good and loyal son in a Mediterranean house-hold. To paraphrase Bruce Malina and Jerome Neyrey, the Jesus of the Fourth Gospel is one who internalizes and makes his own what God, his 'father' says, does, and thinks about him because he believes it is necessary, if he is to be an honorable son, to live out the expectations of God, his 'father.'[28]

"Furthermore, although your encoded reader has been given numerous clues early on that Jesus would willingly be 'lifted up,'[29] in the passion narrative there are only minimal references to Jesus' ultimate power over the events or the plot. These come equally from Jesus (18:5–8, 11; 19:28–29) and the narrator (18:4, 9; 19:30), but only at the beginning and end of the passion narrative. They seem to be clumsily tacked on by your timorous implied author. One would think that in such an important part of the story, your implied author could have given your encoded reader consistently stronger clues regarding Jesus' self-awareness or commitment to God's purposes. But the closest we come to this is a remark by Jesus in his conversation with Pilate (19:11). By comparison, in the raising of Lazarus your encoded reader can find numerous references to Jesus' control and his near manipulation of events (11:4, 11–15, 23–27, 40–42).

"It seems to me, then, you could argue that in this juxtaposing of power and powerlessness there is a subversive and doubly ironic undermining of the passion plotting. Jesus may indeed willfully step forward into his captors' arms at the beginning of the passion narrative (18:4–11),[30] but once he does that, he becomes a mere pawn in the hands of Jewish and Roman authorities. And for a few moments, anyway, you can legitimately say that things move beyond Jesus' personal control. Why? Simply because the sociopolitical order (*kosmos*) hates and persecutes him (15:18–25; 18:36; cf. 11:50).[31] Even Jesus can't control that."

---

[28] Malina and Neyrey, "First Century Personality: Dyadic, not Individual," 73; cf. John 5:19–20, 22.

[29] See, for example, John 3:14–16; 10:17–18; 12:32; cf. Nicholson, *Death as Departure,* 164–65.

[30] Mark Stibbe wonders rhetorically whether Jesus' captors falling on the ground couldn't be understood as a response of amazement. Couldn't it be "[t]hat after so many great escapes Jesus is at last in a place where he will not and does not escape? Where he can be sought *and found*" ("The Elusive Christ: A New Reading of the Fourth Gospel," 23; his emphasis)?

[31] Or to put it another way, "that which resists integration," or "elude[s] the security umbrella of order" (like Jesus does) is the originating "chaos" that makes "cosmos" possible (White, *Myths of the Dog-Man,* 3–4).

With regard to Pilate, who is a representative of the cosmos, David Rensberger astutely observes that "he is callous and relentless, indifferent to Jesus and to truth, and contemptuous

ACT II

"Dogs! Dogs! There are dogs all around me!" The first corpse, face still in the dirt, suddenly screams out in its darkness. "Thin ones, with ribs protruding, ears down, and their tails between their legs. There are dogs in this story, *téchąą'í,* hungrily sniffing and licking my dried sweat, blood, and excrement—just like the dogs of Jezreel that gnawed Jezebel's bones.[32] First come the flies and dogs, then come the beady-eyed rats!"

The second corpse interrupts: "You're out of your mind! Lift your head out of the dirt and look about carefully, you babbling idiot! If you just open your eyes you'll see that there are no dogs in this story world. Sheep, shepherds, and sheepfolds, yes. But nowhere in John will you find a dog mentioned. They're only the mad dreams of your disembodied mind."

"It may be true that there are no dogs in your Johannine story world," the third corpse breaks in, "but every Mediterranean crucifixion scene would have had them: the shameless dogs; watching, silently sitting on their haunches, waiting for the corpses to be dropped so they could finish the work left undone. The scavenging dogs surrounding crucified victims would have been one more element of the public shaming of criminals in that ancient social world."[33]

"So now you believe it too? A corpse with its nose stuck in our filth shrieks 'dogs,' and just like that you're off in the world of cultural-anthropology and honor/shame societies![34] That's precisely what I find so disconcerting about

---

of the hope of Israel that Jesus fulfills and transcends. . . . Pilate is thus a hostile figure second only to 'the Jews' themselves" ("The Politics of John: The Trial of Jesus in the Fourth Gospel," 406).

[32] 2 Kgs 9:30–37.

[33] In his study of honor in the ancient Mediterranean world, Paul Friedrich has shown how dogs are "an illuminating key to the Iliadic idiom of honor. [They] emerge in the fourth line of the epic and reappear at least once in all but five of the remaining twenty-three books, thirty-five times in connection with the eating of corpses, mainly in metaphors, invectives, and similies. Dogs come in pairs, and packs, devouring the myriad corpses on the battelfield [*sic*] or even rushing in to gnaw the testicles of their dead master. . . . Numerous threats and entreaties involve being thrown to the dogs, the worst form of defilement" ("Sanity and the Myth of Honor," 289; cf. Crossan, *Jesus,* 123–27, 153–54; Neyrey, "'Despising the Shame of the Cross': Honor and Shame and the Johannine Passion Narrative," 15; Sloterdijk, *Critique of Cynical Reason,* 167–69).

Recent films on the life of Jesus have also mentioned dogs at the crucifixion scene. Note, for example, the narrator's comments at the crucifixion scene in the film *Jesus of Montreal,* and Judas's remarks to Jesus in the film *The Last Temptation of Christ.*

[34] For a comprehensive analysis of the ancient Mediterranean world as one whose values

your kinds of interpretive moves," the second corpse says exasperatingly. "You have no sensitivity for how implied authors imaginatively create story worlds. You want to bring any and every detail of the ancient Mediterranean social world into the Gospel—all from other first-century *texts,* of course—and then you act as though they are part of this particular story world. But not every aspect of that ancient social world is in here!"

"Oh no, it *is* all here," replies the third corpse. "It's just that the ancient Mediterranean world is a 'high context society' which 'produce[s] sketchy and impressionistic texts, leaving much to the reader's or hearer's imagination. . . . Hence, much can be assumed.'[35] Western Europeans and Euro-Americans, on the other hand, are 'low context societies,' which 'produce detailed texts, spelled out as much as possible, and leave little to the imagination.'[36]

"Everyone here knows what a crucifixion is like. We don't have to spell out all the gory details."

"Your twofold description may work for societies at large, but it won't work for storytelling," interjects the second corpse, trying to stretch out tall on its cross. "It seems to me that narratives always reflect 'high contexts.'[37] No story can hold its hearers' attention if every detail of that narrative world must first be spelled out. Authors who had to do that would never get around to telling their stories! This is part of what is meant by beginning a story *in medias res,* and it is as much a dictum of modern Euro-American prose as it was of Greek literature when Aristotle first observed it. Enormously high-context demands are placed upon readers of all narratives. It's not just a peculiar identifying mark of ancient stories from Mediterranean cultures.

"I will grant you the point that it is important to know how shaming and how shameful crucifixions were in your so-called honor/shame society. But I

center around honor and shame, see Malina and Neyrey, "Honor and Shame in Luke-Acts: Pivotal Values of the Mediterranean World," 25–65.

[35] Malina, "Reading Theory Perspective: Reading Luke-Acts," 20.

[36] Ibid., 19.

[37] Bruce Malina's concept of the sociorhetorical "context" would be called the text's "repertoire" in Wolfgang Iser's theory of aesthetic response, which for him, "consists of all the familiar territory within the text. This may be in the form of references to earlier works, or to social and historical norms, or to the whole culture from which the text has emerged . . ." (*The Act of Reading,* 69). Yet Iser can go on to make the important observation that "[l]iterary communication differs from other forms of communication in that those elements of the sender's repertoire which are familiar to the reader through their application in real-life situations, lose their validity when transplanted into the literary text. And it is precisely this *loss* of validity which leads to the communication of something new" (ibid., 83; his emphasis).

will still maintain, after all is said and done, that it is just as important to recognize how this implied author refuses to dwell on its most shameful details.[38] This implied author's narrowly constructed story world—no less socially constructed than any so-called real world, mind you—wishes to convince its encoded reader of a different ideology: that in spite of outward appearances, the final event of Jesus' life is bringing honor to his 'father.' Thus, many shameful, real-world elements have been purposely omitted from this particular 'fantastic' story world.[39] So don't go bringing into the story those elements which the author may have purposely left out."

"You don't think I understand how stories work? Well, you don't understand how different cultures work!" snaps the third corpse. "Don't you see that you can't understand what was 'left out' of a text without first understanding what was socially implicit 'in' the text? Your ethnocentric dogmatism just appalls me!"[40]

The corpse crumpled on the ground tries to jerk out of its deathly slumber. "What is all the yapping I keep hearing? I've dreamed of those damned dogs, and I can still hear them sniffing and barking around me. Hidden inside every mad dog is a god, damned to suffer for our sins.[41] So I say let's keep them here beside us. They add a realistic note of passion to an otherwise passionless story. And besides, it's two against one. You're the odd corpse out."

"Say, all your talk about dogs reminded me of a joke someone once told me.[42] Have you heard the one about the dyslexic atheist?

---

[38] The author of 4 Maccabees graphically depicts the torture of the Jewish faithful (4 Macc 5:28–6:30; 9:10–11:27; see also Perkins's examples of ancient Mediterranean torture narratives in "Representation in Greek Saints' Lives," 257–65; Hengel, *Crucifixion in the Ancient World,* 22–32, 87; and Crossan, *Who Killed Jesus?* 135).

[39] Ernst Käsemann says: "Judged by the modern concept of reality, our [Fourth] Gospel is more fantastic than any other writing in the New Testament (*The Testament of Jesus According to John 17,* 45; cf. Aichele, "Literary Fantasy and the Composition of the Gospels," 56–59).

[40] See Mieke Bal's criticism of enthnocentrism in biblical literary criticism and ethnographers' need for narrative theory ("The Point of Narratology," 730–37).

[41] David White writes, "There is much of man in his dogs, much of the dog in us, and behind this, much of the wolf in both the dog and man. And, there is some of the Dog-Man in god" (*Myths of the Dog-Man,* 15). Or, I might add, there is some of the Dog-Man in Christ (cf. Sloterdijk and Crossan, who both describe much of Jesus' behavior as dog-like, or cynic-inspired [*Critique of Cynical Reason,* 161–62; *The Historical Jesus,* 72–88, 421–22; see also Kitchell, *God's Dog,* 19–23]).

[42] "Whatever is sacred *must* become, somehow or other, a joke, if we want to free ourselves from mental tyranny (Ostriker, *Feminist Revision and the Bible,* 29; her emphasis). For "laughter is always transgressive. The moment of laughter ruptures the principles of authority, whatever they may be" (ibid., 125; cf. Bakhtin, *Rabelais and His World,* 13–15, 73).

"No, I haven't. And I hope it's not funny. It hurts like hell when I laugh."

"He didn't believe there was a dog."

"Ha, Ha. Thank Dog, my ribs didn't move."

"Oh, stop encouraging the fool!" the second corpse retorts. "Your joke stank, and you're beginning to sound just as absurd as the corpse below us.

"And as for you"—the corpse continued, trying to look down—"you've got to stop bringing your personal, autobiographical *'téchąą'í* into this story world just because you've seen them in your dreams! Everything is so arbitrary, so cynical with you! You have no sense of argumentation or logic.

"Where's the scholarly discourse; any semblance of plausible interaction with the text? At least the corpse hanging beside me has a reason for bringing in its scavenger dogs. Historical, social-world reconstructions of first-century crucifixions would demand their presence. But you shamelessly add elements to the story based simply on your own idiosyncratic desire to have them here."

"Oh, so you want a reason for the dogs' presence, do you? Some 'plausible interaction with the text?' If you require that for legitimizing interpretations, I can give it to you.[43] Everyone knows there are intertextual allusions to Psalm 22:14–18 in John 19:24 and 28. The narrator even adds, 'This was to fulfill what the scripture says.' So what do you think is the referent of the third person plural verb 'they divided' and the antecedent of the reflexive pronoun 'themselves' in the phrase 'They divided my clothes among themselves' (19:24)? It's the 'dogs' of Psalm 22:16 and 20 (Psalm 21:17/21 [LXX])![44] So you see, the dogs are too here. Some may watch us silently from their haunches, waiting to gnaw our bones. Others merely playfully tug and rip apart our discarded clothing" (see illustrations 15, 16, and 17).

But the second corpse continues to speak from its cross, dismissing its companions' voices with an attempted twitch of its head. "You can't have those dogs either. In Psalm 22:16 and 20 'dogs' is a pejorative epithet for 'evildoers.' Even there the dogs aren't real. They're just a metaphor. And besides, it's neither the third person plural verb nor the reflexive pronoun that is significant here in John, but rather the action of dividing the clothes. That's what fulfills Scripture."

"You bitches! You just don't get it, do you? What I want is the metaphor:

---

[43] To paraphrase Mieke Bal, "the argument I am trying to make is to prove the presence of the absent, and it is up to the reader to evaluate to what extent they are there or not" (*Death and Dissymmetry,* 239–40).

[44] Brawley recognizes this ("An Absent Complement and Intertextuality in John 19:28-29," 438).

15. *The Last Supper.* Sebastiano Ricci, 1713/1714. A dog lies near Judas Iscariot's feet as Judas leaves the Last Supper with the money bag, on his way out to betray Jesus (John 13:21-30). (Samuel H. Kress Collection, © 1994 Board of Trustees, National Gallery of Art, Washington)

16. *Road to Calvary*. Albrecht Dürer, 1527. In the lower right-hand corner a dog excitedly runs alongside Jesus as Jesus carries his own cross to Golgotha (John 19:17). Following on the heels of the dog are Veronica, with a cloth in her hands; the curly-headed apostle John; Mary, the mother of Jesus; and John's mother, Salome. (Alinari/Art Resource, N.Y.)

17. *Crucifixion at Calvary.* Albrecht Dürer, ca. 1500. Although many of Dürer's woodcuts of Christ's passion include a dog in the foreground, only one of his renditions of the crucifixion depicts a dog near the cross. In this Johannine-inspired scene, a slinking dog is strategically positioned between Jesus' grieving mother, the curly-headed apostle John, and John's mother Salome on the left (John 19:25-27); and the Roman soldiers on the right, who are casting lots for Jesus' clothing (John 19:23-25; cf. Ps 22:16-18). (Foto Marburg/Art Resource, N.Y.)

people as dogs, or dogs as people—either way, it doesn't make any difference to me.[45] You say your implied author has historicized the Psalmist's metaphor, turning it into a prophetic reference to events at Jesus' crucifixion.[46] Well, I just want to keep the Psalm's original metaphoricity.[47] What's wrong with that? Can't you hear my pain and my groaning? 'I have given a name to my pain and call it 'dog.' It is just as faithful, just as obtrusive and shameless, just as entertaining, just as clever as any other dog—and I can scold it and vent my bad mood on it as others do with their dogs. . . .'[48] So you can keep the sheepherders, the sheep, and the rock-enclosed corrals. I just want the dogs. And you can't take them away from me! They're here, they're mine, and they're eating me up inside!"

## ACT III

Attempting to get the scholarly debate back on course, the second corpse decides to ignore the last outrageous outburst. "Frankly, I think we've all been barking up the wrong tree for some time. Hadn't one of you just brought up the issue of irony before we were led off track? Now there's an important topic in the Fourth Gospel and a Johannine strategy that we can all agree on. Everyone says the Johannine passion narrative is highly ironic.[49] And, I believe, we

---

[45] Andrée Collard argues that in Pavlov's "scientific experiments" on dogs, he faulted his animals for exhibiting antisocial behavior in much the same way that women's resistance to oppressive male power is often used to label them as "men-haters" (*Rape of the Wild*, 62). David White notes the reciprocal relationship between the "domestication" of the dog and the "'humanization' of the human species" (*Myths of the Dog-Man*, 12–13; cf. McKenna, *Violence and Difference*, 132).

[46] According to Ernst Haenchen,"[t]he scene itself, the division of the clothes and the casting of lots for 'the tunic without seams,' is derived from Ps 22:18(19)" (*The Gospel of John*, 2:193). Raymond Brown, however, thinks that "the interpretation of the psalm is stretched to cover an incident that the evangelist found in his tradition rather than vice versa," since one would expect to find the psalmist's expression *ebalon klēron* for casting lots rather than the verb *lachōmen* (John 19:24) if the evangelist were simply inventing the scene (*The Gospel according to John*, 2:920, cf. 2:903).

[47] Eric Cheyfitz writes: "Figurative language, of which metaphor, or translation, is the model, is the driving force of interpretation, that is, of language itself. For this language within language that is the force of language opens up a space between signified and signifier, a rupture of identity, where the conflictive play of dialogue takes place that constitutes the speakers (writers/readers) for and significantly through each other" (*The Poetics of Imperialism*, 38).

[48] Nietzsche, *The Gay Science*, 249–50. Or as John Crossan writes, "if you seek the heart of darkness, follow the dogs" (*Jesus*, 127).

[49] For example, see Culpepper, *Anatomy of the Fourth Gospel*, 173–74; Duke, *Irony in the*

were just talking about the contrasting views of power in the text, weren't we? Who is really in control? God or the earthly, ruling authorities? Surely, as you said, the contrast between Jesus willfully stepping forward at his arrest and being led here and there is ironic.[50] And of course, Jesus' conversations with the 'powers that be' are ironic (18:19–24, 28–19:16).

"As everyone notes, those so-called powerful characters in the text think they are in control, but, in fact, the encoded reader knows all along that they are not. Clearly, all Jesus' and the narrator's talk about 'the hour' (*hōra/kairos*) has been supplying the encoded reader with that ironic, binocular perspective from the first scenes of the Gospel.[51] So I don't see your focus on the contrasts in power and powerlessness as subversively undermining the theological theme of God's salvific power (10:17–18). As with the portrayal of the Jewish leaders' concern for pollution (18:28; 19:14, 31), these multifaceted ironies simply bind the implied author's and encoded reader's ideological/theological points of view more closely together over against those of the ruling authorities: in spite of earthly appearances, God and Jesus are in control. Or to put it in your terms, the faithful, honorable son is acting out his socially prescribed role according to his father's wishes."

Another leather thong is cut and the third corpse drops to the ground beside the first. "I suppose it's time for me to jump back into your interpretive game. So answer me this. Wouldn't you say that one of the most dramatic ironies is when Pilate asks the offhanded question 'What is truth?' (18:38) of the very one who had earlier told his disciples, 'I am the way, and the truth, and the life. . . .' (14:6)?[52] Yet curiously, neither Jesus, the narrator, nor Pilate responds to the question. In John 19:9–10 Jesus will again fail to answer Pilate, and there both the narrator and Pilate note Jesus' silence. But here, strangely, there is no narrative mark of the silence. Why not? Jesus responded to the high priest's earlier question, and he has responded to every other question of Pilate up to this point. Why is there no response, no uptake, not even a narrator's remark 'And he said nothing?'"

The second corpse quickly answers. "Well, obviously the implied author

---

*Fourth Gospel,* 129–37; Senior, *The Passion of Jesus in the Gospel of John,* 68, 152; and Giblin, "John's Narration of the Hearing before Pilate (John 18,28–19,16)," 238; et al.

[50] Stibbe, "The Elusive Christ: A New Reading of the Fourth Gospel," 20–25, 29.

[51] See John 2:4; 4:21–23; 5:25–29; 7:6–8, 30; 8:20; 12:27; 13:1; 17:1. Paul Duke, following many before him, speaks of the "double-layered" quality of irony in the Fourth Gospel (*Irony in the Fourth Gospel,* 14).

[52] Foucault, *Power/Knowledge,* 66.

expects the encoded reader to fill in the correct answer: 'Jesus is the Truth.'[53] And Pilate's question—Is it asked in jest, pensiveness, or sarcasm?—proves only that he is an outsider.[54] So at Pilate's expense, Jesus, the implied author, and encoded reader are all joined together. Ideologically they are one."

"But I'm not so sure," the third corpse interjects. "Did you know that this is the last time the noun 'truth' is used in the book? Pilate and your implied author both know that the answer to the question 'What is truth?' does not lie in some abstract quality of historical accuracy or confessional correctness (cf. 1:49–51; 7:27, 52; 11:27, 40). Irrespective of 'the truth,' Jesus only becomes a threat in this Gospel when people rightly or wrongly 'believe in him' and 'follow him' (6:15; 7:3–9, 12, 45–49; 11:45–53; 12:12–19). So whether Jesus really is or is not a king is beside the point. Pilate's inscription on Jesus' cross and the chief priests' objections to it will be the ultimate joke here (19:19–22).[55] Contrary to your opinion, here I think Pilate and Jesus are both aligned with your implied author."

"Yes! I think you've found the correct answer to this text's question 'What is truth?' I would only want to add that whether Jesus fed five thousand people with five loaves and two fish is also beside the point for your implied author (6:15, 21–65). Maybe even whether he is or is not a son of God is beside the point (5:18; 10:31–39). Neither who Jesus historically is nor what people confess him to be—nor even who Jesus confesses himself to be—is the crucial question for your implied author or Pilate at this juncture. As the next dialogue between Jesus and Pilate will show (19:8–11), the important question underlying all others is whether Jesus is a threat to power (11:45–53; 12:12–19). The question of truth cannot be separated from the body that stretches out the hand" (18:22; 19:3; 20:27).[56]

"So as I was about to say, in handing over Jesus (18:30), the chief priests

---

[53] Paul Duke writes, "It is just as possible that the unanswered question concludes the scene because the Johannine ironist invites us to reflect upon what—and who—the Answer is" (*Irony in the Fourth Gospel*, 131; cf. Edwards, "The World Could not Contain the Books," 192; Neyrey, "'Despising the Shame of the Cross': Honor and Shame in the Johannine Passion Narrative," 12).

[54] Following Rudolf Schnackenburg (*The Gospel according to St. John*, 3:251) and Raymond Brown (*The Gospel according to John*, 2:869), David Rensberger says that "Pilate's final 'What is truth?' (18:38) [is not] the question of a serious seeker; if it were, he would stay for an answer" ("The Politics of John: The Trial of Jesus in the Fourth Gospel," 403; cf. Stibbe, *John as Storyteller*, 107).

[55] Duke, *Irony in the Fourth Gospel*, 136–37; Senior, *The Passion of Jesus in the Gospel of John*, 153–54.

[56] In the ancient Mediterranean world, the hands of the human body represented power

have safeguarded their positions of power against the threat of their Roman overlords (11:48–50). In handing over Jesus (19:16), Pilate is safeguarding his position of power (*exousia*, 19:10–11) against the possible threat of Caesar (19:12). And in handing over his spirit (19:30), Jesus will safeguard his place of power (*exousia*, 17:1–5) before God (10:17–18). We all know that '[p]ower is cautious. It covers itself.'"[57]

"Thus, the power of the dialogue between Jesus and Pilate resides precisely in Jesus' possible threat to Roman power—not in the truth or falsity of his claim to kingship.[58] So Jesus doesn't answer Pilate's question and there is no uptake. Why? Because in the presence of power, the question of some independent truth source is ultimately irrelevant. Jesus, your implied author, and Pilate know that."[59] I guess what I'm trying to say is that '[t]ruth is a thing of this world [*kosmos*]: it is produced only by virtue of multiple forms of constraint.' It 'is linked in a circular relation with systems of power which produce and sustain it.'"[60]

"That's the most absurd, convoluted argument I've ever heard!" The second corpse shouts, its voice shaking with anger. "Why do you have to jump into this discussion too? First you tried to force your ridiculous Navajo dogs into the story, and now you're trying to turn one simple, offhandedly ironic question of Pilate into some radically deconstructive metaphor that shapes the entire narrative and empties its claim to truth. I wish you would just keep your mouth shut and your head buried down there in the dirt!

"From my vantage point up here, it is perfectly clear that right at the very start of the narrative the prologue revealed an implied author who would be vitally concerned with truth—who it is, where it comes from, what it does, and where it goes (1:14, 17).[61] I mean, 'truth' and its cognates occur forty-

---

(Malina, *The New Testament World*, 73–75; cf. Scarry, *The Body in Pain*, 173, 252–53). And in the words of Page DuBois, "the desire to create an other and the desire to extract truth are inseparable" (*Torture and Truth*, 152).

[57] Scarry, *The Body in Pain*, 59; cf. McKenna's discussion of "state agents" in *Violence and Difference*, 160–72.

[58] Charles Giblin instinctively recognizes this when he says, in regard to John 18:38b–40, that "[t]o Pilate's mind *thus far in the hearing* [my emphasis], the King of the Jews is no threat to Roman rule or to Pilate's own position" ("John's Narration of the Hearing Before Pilate [John 18,28–19,16]," 227). Once he perceives Jesus to be a threat to his position, however, he immediately moves to get rid of him (19:12).

[59] Cf. Foucault, *Politics, Philosophy, Culture*, 106–9, 118–19; and Kitchell, *God's Dog*, 93–95.

[60] Foucault, *Power/Knowledge*, 131, 133. See also Mailloux, *Rhetorical Power*, 141–44.

[61] Warner, "The Fourth Gospel's Art of Rational Persuasion," 176–77.

eight times in the book! So let me tell you, your deconstructive agenda simply won't work here. I won't let it happen!

"But I do think the former observation, that there is no narrative uptake to Pilate's question, is an interesting one. Yet I can't see how it is significant—other than as a joke between the implied author and encoded reader, both of whom, I will still maintain over your objections, are laughing at Pilate and his earthbound sensibilities.

"And if you really want to talk about power in the passion narrative, then talk about it in the resurrection account, where God's power is ultimately triumphant over human power.

"Now, let's move on to talk about something more basic; something more objective, empirical, and countable. Let's look at the implied author's use of repetition in the story. This is an important topic, and the passion narrative is full of repetitions."

"Now wait just a minute! Who's talking about poststructuralist literary theory and a Johannine metaphor that deconstructs itself? I wasn't! I was thinking that perhaps what is operative in the Fourth Gospel is a commonly overlooked, ancient Mediterranean social-world code of patronage 'based on a strong element of inequality and difference in power.'[62] It does seem to fit. I mean, think of it this way: Jesus is the truth because he is the broker who has been 'sent' from the patron 'above,' the place of ultimate honor and power.[63] That's the language of patronage.

"Now, listen to what you were just saying. You were agreeing with me that in this narrative, power (illustrated by your reference to the resurrection) is ultimately more important than some anachronistic, abstract quality of truth. The one with the power at the end, who has the right connections, is therefore the one who is 'the truth.' Power—either honorably acquired or ascribed—is truth, and in the Fourth Gospel truth does not exist apart from authority and power. That, my friend, is a description of the patronage system in an honor/shame society."

"All your talk of patronage sounds objective and scientific, but how far can you really press it in the Fourth Gospel? After all, Jesus never calls God his 'patron' in this story.[64] Instead, he always uses the relational language of father and son. Isn't that difference in metaphors significant? Isn't fictive kinship finally more important than patronage?[65]

[62] Moxnes, "Patron-Client Relations and the New Community in Luke-Acts," 242.
[63] Cf. John 3:31–36; 5:31–44; 7:16–18; 8:12–18; 10:36–39; 12:44–50; 17:25–26.
[64] Cf. *1 Clement* 36:1; 61:3; 64.
[65] Cf. John 19:7, 26–27; 20:31.

"You know me, I'd hate to have to give up any Johannine metaphor for some broader, ancient social-world scenario—regardless of its apparent usefulness—if it meant destroying the peculiar ideology and narrative world of the Fourth Gospel in the process."

"Well, don't forget that 'father/son' language is often used interchangeably with patron/client language in the Mediterranean world.[66] Fictive kinship and patronage are much more closely linked than you might think."[67]

"God! I'm confused. Am I awake or dreaming? Now that the two of you are on the ground, your voices are beginning to erode, intermingle, and coalesce. Perhaps if I could just lift my head from my chest to look at you. . . . But I can't. And I can't seem to connect voices with bodies anymore. Ancient Mediterranean social code of patronage or deconstructive metaphor—name it what you will, the effect still seems to be the same.

"For example, just look around us! No one is really listening to our conversation. Everyone who cared about us has left, convinced that we're dead. The only one still here is the cursing Roman, trying to cut me down from my cross before sunset. Needless to say, I'm worried that both of your strategies, no matter how necessary or novel for the modern world, will cut us off from the very communities we're seeking to nourish. This exercise is really beginning to bring me down."

"Oh come off it! You're the only corpse left up there with its head in the clouds, and you talk about us being cut off from community? As far as I'm concerned, the sooner you join us down here, the better off you'll be."

ACT IV

After a few moments of painful silence, the corpse remaining on its cross decides to ignore its own misgivings and the grunts and groans of the two on the ground below. Once more it picks up its commentary.

---

[66] For example, see Matt 5:43–6:15.

[67] Halvor Moxnes writes: "In Roman models of society the relations between public, professional life and personal, family life were different from those of most modern societies. We make a clear distinction between the role of individuals as parents, spouses, or friends on the one hand and their role as public officials on the other. Within one set of relations we might expect them to show preferential treatment (parents, friends), but in others we expect strict impartiality (public officials). In Roman ideology, however, there were no such distinctions. . . . Even the emperor played a patronal[/paternal] role. He was looked upon more as a powerful father figure than as an imperial administrator" ("Patron-Client Relations and the New Community in Luke-Acts," 245).

"Look,[68] let's try this conversation one last time. As I noted earlier, the passion narrative is the most carefully plotted section of the story. Throughout it, repetitions of key words and phrases fill out and confirm the implied author's theological point of view. For example, the basic plot line is fourfold: (1) arrest (18:1–18); (2) legal charges (18:19–19:16); (3) crucifixion (19:17–37); and (4) burial (19:38–42). But plot developments in each of the first three narrative sequences are slowed down by the numerous repetitions, repetitions that primarily assess blame for the final events of Jesus' life. From the implied author's perspective, Jesus' arrest, trial, and death are the result of collusion within the *kosmos* of Jewish and Roman power.[69]

"The three most dominant repetitions are those which deal with 'the handing over' of Jesus to someone, the attempt to release Jesus, and his ultimate punishment by crucifixion. In the first case, the Greek verb *paradidōmi* is used twice as the narrator's epithet for Judas (18:2, 5). It is also used four times in reference to the Jewish leaders (by the Jewish leaders themselves, 18:30; by Pilate, 18:35; and by Jesus, 18:36, 19:11). Finally, the narrator uses it once in reference to Jesus' spirit (19:30). Interestingly, the six references of 'handing over' earlier in the Gospel are all related to Judas. Moreover, the narrator never implicates 'the Jews' in Jesus' *paradidonai*. This is something 'the Jews' themselves do, almost with a sense of pride (18:30), and it is echoed by Jesus and Pilate.

"The most common repetitions in the passion narrative are those that mention the crucifixion. There are fifteen references to it: 19:6 (twice), 10, 15 (twice), 16, 17, 18, 19, 20, 23, 25, 31, 32, and 41. The narrator uses the verb 'crucify' or noun 'crucifixion' ten times, while 'the Jews' (chief priests and servants) only use the verb in the imperative mood (two times). Pilate, on the other hand, always uses the verb in questions (three times). Similarly, references of the kingship charge leveled against Jesus are repeated five times (18:33, 37, 39; 19:14, 15), four of which are couched in questions Pilate asks. The remaining reference is the chief priests' climactic response to Pilate, 'We have no king but Caesar' (19:15). Finally, there are eight different references to Pilate's acquittal and intended release of Jesus (*aitian* in 18:38; 19:4, 6; *apolyō* in 18:39 [twice]; 19:10 and 12 [twice]). Six come from Pilate, one

---

[68] "Looking may be called enchanted when the act of attention draws a circle around itself from which everything but the object is excluded, when intensity of regard blocks out all circumambient images, stills all murmuring voices" (Greenblatt, *Learning to Curse*, 176).

[69] John 15:18–19; 17:14–16; 18:36. David Rensberger correctly points out that "Pilate too becomes an agent of the 'world'" in the Johannine trial scene ("The Politics of John: The Trial of Jesus in the Fourth Gospel," 402; see further, 403–6).

comes from the narrator, and one comes from 'the Jews.' Clearly, all these repetitions strongly reinforce the implied author's ideological point of view, one that cannot be misinterpreted by the encoded reader."

The third corpse grins up at the second one still hanging above it. "Whenever I interrupt one of your dramatic soliloquies, you're forced to shut up for a while. So let me thrust another splinter in your tender, bloated side. Someone once said 'Sometimes the challenge posed by a text is not excessive obscurity but, rather, some form of excessive clarity.'[70]

"You talk of repetitions in the passion narrative, and how they seem to slow down the plot and emphasize your implied author's ideological point of view. But curiously, it is not until one gets to the crucifixion itself, which you argued earlier was the most emphasized element in the narrative's plot, that the action begins to speed up significantly. While it takes from 18:12–19:16 (five pages of Greek text) just to get a death verdict against Jesus, it only takes from 19:16b–42 (two and a half pages of text) to get Jesus crucified, killed, and buried. Thus, in the first half of the passion account, narrative time and story time more closely parallel each other. But in the second half, narrative time is greatly constricted, while story time remains roughly the same.[71]

"Furthermore, there are fewer repetitions in John 19:16b–37, more scene changes, and more characters on stage than in the first half of the passion narrative. Only the four unusual references to Scripture being fulfilled (19:24, 28, 36, 37), the five references to Jesus' mother (19:25 [twice], 26 [twice], 27),[72] and the narrator's five necessary references to crucifixion (19:18, 20, 23, 31, 32) reflect those earlier, emphatic repetitions. Finally, and most importantly, at the crucial moment when Jesus is 'lifted up,' your encoded reader's eyes are immediately averted from that central glorious event. Paradoxically, at this point, your encoded reader is made to look anywhere but at Jesus" (19:19–25).

"If you ask me, you've still listed quite a number of repetitions for that section of text," snaps the hanging corpse. "And I must say that you've failed to mention one of the most fascinating redundancies in the entire passion narra-

---

[70] Johnson, "Teaching Deconstructively," 145.

[71] Alan Culpepper describes this narrative duration nicely, but in a general manner, without trying to point out the variations in duration on the last day of Jesus' life. He says: "The 'speed' of the narrative reduces steadily [throughout the Gospel], . . . until it virtually grinds to a halt at the climactic day" (*Anatomy of the Fourth Gospel*, 72).

[72] Robert Brawley notes the fivefold repetition, calling it a "sentimental scene" ("An Absent Complement and Intertextuality in John 19:28–29," 435), but surely this misses the rhetorical implications of the repetitions (see below).

tive: the six additional references to writing which introduce the crucifixion scene (19:19 [twice], 20, 21) and conclude with Pilate's final words, 'What I have written I have written' (19:22). It can hardly be inconsequential that Pilate's own writing, in a gross parody of Jewish Scripture, will not be modified (cf. 7:23; 10:35), and is an object of debate among 'the Jews' who read it (cf. 1:45–46; 7:51–52).[73] Nor can it be insignificant that it directly precedes the last three explicit citations of Jewish Scripture in the Gospel."

"Yes, Pilate seems to be saying, 'I am one thing, [but] my writings are another matter,'"[74] the first corpse mumbles drowsily.

"What's that?"

"Oh nothing. It's just something else about intertextuality. An echo of another text, I suppose," responds the third corpse, trying to look at its companion.

"Well, I'm not interested in those sorts of intertextual echoes," the hanging corpse says. "That corpse beside you exasperates the hell out of me. Can't you get it to shut up? It has absolutely nothing to add to our conversation.

"Anyway, irrespective of your failure to note the important repetition I just pointed out, you would still need to account for the change in narrative point of view at the crucifixion scene. The focalization in 19:26–28 is from the perspective of Jesus. Jesus is the focalizer. This, I think, is really significant, for it means that the encoded reader is indeed with Jesus at the moment of his glorification, gazing down at those around his cross.[75] There are, therefore, other ways of emphasizing the implied author's ideological perspective besides repetition. And in this case, the encoded reader is uniquely made to share Jesus' view of both 'his mother and the disciple whom he loved standing beside her' (the latter being a person whom the narrator had left out of his earlier scenic description [19:25]), and Jesus' knowledge 'that all was now finished' (19:28). So even if there isn't as much repetition here, the encoded reader is clearly in a most privileged position."

The first corpse is aroused out of its restless dreams by this new turn. "Are

---

[73] Rudolf Bultmann correctly observes that Pilate's "inscription . . . is undoubtedly to be understood as a prophecy" (*The Gospel of John*, 669), and Thomas Brodie calls it the "implication of a new scripture" (*The Gospel According to John*, 546). But Robert Brawley, strangely, fails to discuss any possible metaphorical or ironic connection between these references to writing and the subsequent fulfillment of Scripture ("An Absent Complement and Intertextuality in John 19:28-29," 431–32).

[74] Nietzsche, *Ecce Homo*, 259, as quoted in Derrida, *The Ear of the Other*, 20.

[75] For, as Bultmann can say, in the crucifixion "everything has happened that had to happen; the work of Jesus is completed; he has carried out that which his Father had commanded him" (*The Gospel of John*, 674–75, cf. 632).

the dogs gone yet? I'm sick of hearing them panting and sniffing around my head. Where the hell did they go?

"It's true that your encoded reader is where Jesus is, seeing what Jesus sees, and knowing what Jesus knows, but I wouldn't say your encoded reader is in a privileged position because of that. Your encoded reader is actually offered only the most literal, rudimentary interpretation of Jesus' words. Jesus' statements to his mother and the Beloved Disciple (19:26) are interpreted by the narrator simply as Jesus' interest in her welfare ('the disciple took her into his own home' [19:27]), something that is a rather mundane concern for oldest sons in ancient Mediterranean kinship structure.[76] And Jesus' next statement initially seems to be a straightforward fulfillment Scripture (19:28). Yet almost everyone sees Jesus' 'mother/son' language as reflecting more than a mundane concern for his mother, and Jesus' thirst as more than a request for a drink. People say these must be symbolic, related somehow to the foundation of the new community and Jesus' mission.[77] But why do people say that? Where are the explicit textual clues?

"Damn it! The dogs are back. Now I think they're beginning to dig a hole to bury my bones.

"You know, I once heard how in ancient Mesopotamia (which is not too far to the east of here, I need hardly add) dogs were often severed in two, split longitudinally, so that the offerer could then 'pass between . . . [the] two parts which, like a magnet, attracted . . . impurit[ies].'[78] Rituals such as this are good illustrations of how 'the body tends to be brought forward in its most extreme form only on behalf of a cultural artifact or symbolic fragment or made thing (a sentence) that is without any other basis in material reality: that is, it is only brought forward when there is a crisis of substantiation.'[79] Well, as far as I'm concerned, our own little 'crisis of substantiation' here makes this the perfect time to cut up those cowering canines. Now, if I could just find something sharp. . . ."

"Well you can forget about chopping up your phantasmic dogs. There are actually substantive, intratextual clues that Jesus' mother, the Beloved Disciple,

---

[76] Neyrey, "Despising the Shame of the Cross': Honor and Shame in the Johannine Passion Narrative," 15. Cf. Stibbe, *John as Storyteller,* 161–66.

[77] Brown, *The Gospel According to John,* 2:922–27, 929–30; Senior, *The Passion of Jesus in the Gospel of John,* 113–20; Foster, "John Come Lately: The Belated Evangelist," 127–28; Brawley, "An Absent Complement and Intertextuality in John 19:28–29," 427–28, 442–43, et al.

[78] Wapnish and Hesse, "Pampered Pooches or Plain Pariahs? The Askelon Dog Burials," 72; cf. Stager, "Why Were Hundreds of Dogs Buried at Ashkelon?" 30–42.

[79] Scarry, *The Body in Pain,* 127, cf. 14; Gen 15:7–11.

and thirst have symbolic significance here. Just look up John 2:1–11; 4:1–30; 6:52–56; 7:37–39; and 13:21–25."

"Yes, you're probably right," adds the third corpse. "Those probably are intratextual cues. But I think what really interests my companion is how real readers get sidetracked, entangled, and mesmerized by the narrator's seemingly mundane observations, wanting to turn them all into deeply symbolic codes. I mean, here, at what appears to be the moment of greatest clarity, when the 'hour' comes, when all things converge at the cross—that place of Jesus' 'lifting up'—your encoded reader is suddenly overwhelmed by the narrator's excruciatingly attentive descriptions of seemingly peripheral and extraneous details."[80]

"For example," chimes in the first corpse, "why should anyone care that Jesus' robe is 'seamless, woven in one piece from the top' (19:23–25)? Simply because your encoded reader knows Psalm 22:18? Or is it because your encoded reader also knows the high priest's vestments were seamless (Exod 39:27–31)?[81] Perhaps your encoded reader is expected to recall Mark 15:38 and the ripping of the temple veil. Who knows?"

"And just to continue that line of questioning," the third corpse adds, staring up into the sky, "how much ink has been spilled over the symbolic significance of the hour of crucifixion (19:14); the mother and the Beloved Disciple near the cross (19:25–27); the jar and the hyssop stalk which cannot support a sponge dripping with wine (19:29); the thirst that completes Scripture; the lance thrust, the unbroken bones, and the wound that pours forth water and blood (19:34–35)?[82] As the extensive repetitions we talked about earlier diminish, readers have a need to find more and more intertextual and intratextual allusions in order to give themselves some interpretive direction and a sense of control over the text.[83] But instead, overt opacity and a strange, metaphoric murkiness abound."[84]

---

[80] Robert Brawley writes, "Petty detail repeatedly takes on notable importance," and "[t]he insignificance of details can be the other side of their importance as symbols" ("An Absent Complement and Intertextuality in John 19:28–29," 434; cf. Moore, *Poststructuralism and the New Testament*, 54–59).

[81] Cf. Senior, *The Passion of Jesus in the Gospel of John*, 105–7; de la Potterie, *The Hour of Jesus*, 98–104.

[82] For the relationship between the human body and the belief system of the Judeo-Christian tradition, see Scarry, *The Body in Pain*, 214–21.

[83] Michael Riffaterre tries to determine the sorts of indices which would "direct readers towards the specific and relevant intertexts" of a given narrative, but without much success ("Compulsory Reader Response: The Intertextual Drive," 58, 76–77, note esp., 60–62; see also his "The Mind's Eye: Memory and Textuality," 7–8, 20–21; and Stibbe, *John as Storyteller*, 117–19).

[84] Marianne Thompson has a nice summary of the text's various symbolic possiblities and

"So it's not the referentiality of all the scenic minutiae that I find so intriguing," says the first corpse, trying one last time to lift its face out of the dirt. "Rather, it's the fact that the inconsequential details are so concentrated here and tied so tenuously to the fulfillment/completion of Scripture—or to anything else, for that matter. What clues is your encoded reader given in order to understand these concrete statements as allusions and metaphors? Why don't these kinds of illusive allusions appear earlier or elsewhere in the passion narrative?

"Most think that a seismic *sēmeion* is on the verge of erupting. If so, it would appear to be one that calls into question the apparent clarity and translucence of those carefully constructed *sēmeia* preceding this climax.[85] Ironically, when Jesus whispers 'It is finished,' or 'It is completed' (*tetelestai*), your encoded reader's task is just beginning."

"Well, at least we've established from the preceding narrative that the encoded reader knows this is the key scene in the Gospel," sniffs the hanging corpse. "And if that is the case, the encoded reader has been primed in every way to overread the death scene."

"Yes, I can agree with that. Like Jesus, we have been led to cry 'I am thirsty!'[86] We want to wring the text dry; to squeeze from it every last bit of wet, slippery symbolism that we can, in order to satisfy our craving for unity and meaning."

## ACT V

"Wait, you can't do this to me!" screams the last hanging corpse as it is finally cut loose from its cross and dropped down on the ground next to the other two. "I'm not finished! I still want to talk about the use of emphatic pronouns in the passion narrative.

*Egō! Sy! Hymeis!* They're all over the place, and no one has ever made a detailed study of their usage here. I think I can squeeze them in, if you'll let me—but you're not going to! Now I can't even find them! Someone help me! Tie me back up where I belong!

---

intertextual connections (*The Humanity of Jesus in the Fourth Gospel,* 109–10; cf. Senior, *The Passion of Jesus in the Gospel of John,* 99). For a deconstructive analysis of the Johannine cruxifiction and its signs, see Moore, *Poststructuralism and the New Testament,* 54–59.

[85] For example, at this point in his interpretation of the crucifixion scene, Stephen Moore says that he is "as interested in what might be out of the control of the Johannine writers . . . as in anything that has traditionally been said to be within their control" (*Literary Criticism and the Gospels,* 162).

[86] Bakhtin, *Rabelais and His World,* 86.

"Oh no, it's dogs! My God! It's the dogs! I can hear them sniffing around my face. They're here and the bitches are gnawing[87] my eyes! My eyes! They've eaten my eyes!"

"Don't get so upset," laughs one of the dogs, its mouth full of dirt, sinew, and bone. "Just think of it as part of erosion."[88]

"Yes, that's it," whispers the second corpse. "It must be erosion, and it's going to destroy the text in the same way that it's eating away every trace of us.

"Once upon a time there was an encoded reader, who, with penetrating force, was erected upon this hallowed, hollow hill. But now there is only an eroded reader.[89] Our titular should have read, 'Here hung the eroded reader. Broken and pierced, stripped bare of its outer and inner tunics, it was finally devoured by the dream dogs of a croaking corpse.' Put that in Latin, Hebrew, and Greek, hang it over our heads, and see what real readers do with it."

"At least the image of erosion fits you," chuckles the third corpse. "And when rosy-fingered Eos appears you'll be completely gone. But perhaps the dog was inventing some narratological neologism, and yelped 'errorscission.' Maybe the cut of that Roman blade is beginning to bring you to your senses."

"No, no, you two still haven't gotten it!" hisses the first corpse. "The dog said 'erosion.' 'Eros-eon.' It's all about eros, can't you see? 'The cravings for

---

[87] The Greek verb here would be *trōgō* (John 6:56; cf. Bakhtin, *Rabelais and His World,* 296; Scobie, "Slums, Sanitation and Mortality in the Roman World," 86). For as David Jasper argues, "the text itself . . . becomes the sacred space of eucharistic celebration," a physical sign of "dismemberment" and "fragmentation" (*Rhetoric, Power, and Community,* 161).

[88] In this play I have tried to avoid the danger of the "Lone Ranger" mentality (Hillerman, *Talking God,* 39–40), or the "would-be practitioner of ethnocriticism," that is, "to speak *for* the 'Indian' [dogs], 'interpreting' . . . [them] in a manner that would submit . . . [them] to a dominative discourse" (Krupat, *Ethnocriticism,* 30; his emphasis). However, as with Arnold Krupat, "the danger *I* run . . . is the danger of leaving the Indian [dogs] silent entirely in my discourse. I don't know of any way securely to avoid this danger, for all that I hope it may somewhat be mitigated by a certain self-conscious awareness" (Krupat, *Ethnocriticism,* 30; his emphasis; cf. Parsons, "Anatomy of a Reader," 24; Alcoff, "The Problem of Speaking for Others," 24–29; Cheyfitz, *The Poetics of Imperialism,* 139–40; McKenna, *Violence and Difference,* 172).

For two recent examples of writing that intermingle Native American and biblical stories, see Warrior, "A Native American Perspective: Canaanites, Cowboys and Indians," 287–95; and Jahner, "Transitional Narratives and Cultural Continuity," 176–79; cf. The Bible and Culture Collective, *The Postmodern Bible,* 284–86.

[89] "Listen to this. 'The top of the hill is round and smooth, worn down by centuries of eroticism.' Is she pulling my leg . . . ?"

"I suppose she means 'erosion.'"

"I suppose she does. But yearning speaks between the lines" (Stegner, *Crossing to Safety,* 49).

unity, for essence, for the total picture, for the real and the true, are primitive,'[90] and eros will live on in readers for eons, regardless of what happens to us or the text. No wine-sopped hyssop can quench the tanha-like thirst for completion, nor will a tightly wrapped linen cloth ever silence its voice."

EPILOGUE

"Socialization is training in allegorical interpretation," Barbara Johnson says,[91] and the strong temptation for me at the end of this drama is simply to defer any conclusion, allowing my readers, in good postmodern fashion, to infer their own allegorical preferences from their own particular ideological perspectives and social locations. However, if confessions and original intentions count for anything in allegory (and I suppose that they do not), I should also add that I did not intend to write this chapter as a drama. I did not begin with a plan to fictionalize scholarly discourse.

The chapter began like any other academic project: with sniffing out a text, developing a bare-boned thesis, digging into the secondary literature, and carefully covering the various perspectives.[92] But as I began to reflect on some of the objections raised against reader-response criticism and how I might "own my own views,"[93] I realized that I could not simply write autobiographically as I did in the last chapter and then let that stand apart from any critical discourse on the Johannine text. To do that would be to perpetuate uncritically the very fiction that I have been attempting to problematize in the last two chapters. That fiction, composed as it is of a number of rhetorical conceits within the discourse of modern, scientific exegesis, allows us scholars to talk to each other and "separate" our nonprofessional selves from our professional readings of texts.[94] Thus, in spite of a growing sense that "auto-

---

[90] Szabados, "Autobiography after Wittgenstein," 10. Cf. Ostriker, *Feminist Revision and the Bible,* 122.

[91] Johnson, "Teaching Deconstructively," 148. Cf. Frye, *Anatomy of Criticism,* 89; and Bloomfield, "Allegory as Interpretation," 301–2.

[92] "[T]he writer's emblem is the badger, Old High German *dahs,* an animal who builds; thus the critic's symbol would be that animal specially bred for ferreting out badgers, the *dachshund,* like so many of my colleagues, long of nose and low of belly" (Holland, "Unity Identity Text Self," 118; cf. Vizenor, *The Trickster of Liberty,* xi–xii).

[93] Tolbert, "A Response from a Literary Perspective," 206. Cf. Moore, *Literary Criticism and the Gospels,* 105–6; and Porter, "Why Hasn't Reader-Response Criticism Caught on in New Testament Studies?" 283–90.

[94] The rhetorical tropes of scientific discourse have become common knowledge since Hayden White's seminal work on historiography and Clifford Geertz's work in anthropology

biographical intention begins in contradiction, ends in falsification, and is characterized throughout by the writer's alienation from the very self the writer seeks to remember and present,"[95] I decided that I would somehow have to find a way to integrate that "autobiographical self" into my professional reading in such a way that whatever came out would express both the polyvalence and intersubjectivity of the autobiographical self, and the polyvalence and intersubjectivity of the Johannine text.

As Stephen Moore states, "you must be several in order to write, and you must write with several hands."[96] So, at the risk of error or self-deception, the double-edged polyvalency of text and reader has been represented by a triad of voices in my exegetical play. No doubt there are more voices in me,[97] but three is a fine number—especially since I was the completion of my parents' trinity of sons, all born within a three-year span.[98] Of course, the number three has also held a position of honor in the Christian tradition and sounds surprisingly contemporary when placed alongside postmodernism's rejection

---

(not to mention Jacques Derrida's work in philosophy). For example, see Mieke Bal's references to the problems of "third person narrative" and "the . . . notion of subjectivity," in narratology and ethnography ("The Point of Narratology," 732, cf. 750).

To skirt and hide the shame of subject in biblical criticism, we use the passive voice or the first person plural as circumlocutions for "I," then tacitly agree to name these grammatical choices "objectivity" (cf. Tompkins, "Me and My Shadow," 31–33; Carlton, "Rereading *Middlemarch*, Rereading Myself," 241–42; and Ostriker, *Feminist Revision and the Bible*, 113, 122). "[E]ven ordinary pronouns become a political problem" (Rich, *Blood, Bread, and Stone*, 224).

[95] Kaplan, "The Rhetoric of Circumstance in Autobiography," 71–72; cf. Sloterdijk, *Critique of Cynical Reason*, 537–47.

[96] Paraphrasing Derrida in *Truth in Painting*, 152 (*Mark and Luke in Poststructuralist Perspectives*, 154–55; cf. 3). In biblical criticism, I might add, we have more often had to pretend we were writing with severed hands than with "several hands" (see Scarry, *The Body in Pain*, 176; Tompkins, "Me and My Shadow," 31–36).

[97] To paraphrase Bela Szabados, "I have a feeling that many people speak through my mouth. Yet my aim has been to create myself out of this chaos of voices" ("Autobiography after Wittgenstein," 5). Or as Mikail Bakhtin puts it: "Language . . . lies on the borderline between oneself and the other. The word in language is half someone else's. . . . [T]he word does not exist in a neutral and impersonal language . . . but rather it exists in other people's mouths, in other people's contexts, serving other people's intentions: it is from there that one must take the word and make it one's own" (*Discourse on the Novel*, as quoted in Gates, "Editor's Introduction: Writing, 'Race' and the Difference it Makes," 1; cf. Booth, *The Company We Keep*, 238–39).

[98] Our birth years were 1949, 1950, and 1951, respectively. The last two digits of each of those years add up to the number 150, a deeply theological number made up of threes and sevens: $3 \times (7 \times 7) + 3$.

of the modernist fascination with binary oppositions. Besides all that, the three subjects were right there in the text from the very beginning.[99]

But, "Whatever happened to narratology?" asks Christine Brooke-Rose plaintively.[100] Is there still a place in biblical exegesis for the more formalist type of reader-response criticism with which you began this book?

I stammer for an answer. After all, my professional career began with narratology—with Gérard Genette, Mieke Bal, Christine Brooke-Rose, Seymour Chatman, and others as my guides. Indeed, what *has* happened to narratology? But Christine replies before I can collect my thoughts.

"It got swallowed up into story seems to be the obvious answer," she responds to her own question. "It slid off the slippery methods of a million structures and became the story of its own functioning. . . ."[101]

And then comes her final challenging query. "[So] was it a good story?"[102]

Again I'm silent. I don't know, and I'm not sure I care. Let others be the judge of that, if it is important. But, like a pup happily chasing its own tail, I can't resist telling one more story; the true tale of how the dogs made their way onto the paper, or how they were housebroken.[103]

The dogs were not a part of the first draft of this chapter or the preceding chapter, which were originally part of one paper read at the Pacific Northwest Regional Meeting of the Society of Biblical Literature, in May 1992. The dogs made their way into the project, first into the preceding chapter, in order to illustrate dramatically the difference between Navajo values and the dominant values of my Euro-American home. Only after some thought did I decide to add the dogs to the developing exegetical drama of the passion nar-

---

[99] Cf. Bal's three hermeneutical voices as discussed at the beginning of this chapter, p. 203 (*Death and Dissymmetry,* 240–41).

[100] Brooke-Rose, "Whatever Happened to Narratology?" 283.

[101] Ibid. Perhaps Christine Brooke-Rose has exaggerated slightly in saying, "It slid off the slippery methods of a *million* structures . . ." (my emphasis). In my story, for example, only three methods have slid off their slippery structures.

[102] Ibid.

[103] Leif Vaage describes "Cynic 'transgression'" as "less a 'criminal' crossing over of an imagined or inscribed line of containment, and more like the movement of children 'criss-crossing' every attempted ordering of things, like excited puppies, never housebroken, wreaking havoc in the living room" ("Like Dogs Barking: Cynic parresia and Shameless Asceticism," 37–38). Vaage's description of "Cynic transgression" can be assimilated nicely within Bakhtin's literary theory of the carnivalesque (*Rabelais and His World,* 5–17)—or with Vizenor's postmodern literary criticism, which has its roots in the "comic sign" and "social antagonism" of the trickster figure (often a coyote) of Native American mythologies ("Trickster Discourse: Comic Holotropes and Language Games," 192, 207; cf. McKenna's discussion of the court fool, in *Violence and Difference,* 179–81).

rative. In this latter part of the project, they were simply intended to stand as a metaphor for how we read our own interests and proclivities into canonical texts—or, better yet, they would become a sinister allegory for the intermingling of text and reader—the erosion of the one into the other. The more I thought about the dogs, the more they seemed the perfect metaphor for this intermingling phenomenon. First, dogs were despicable creatures in some ancient Mediterranean cultures, and thus could symbolize the "social-world" perspective of many New Testament scholars. Second, dogs were despised animals in Navajo culture and thus reflected my own cross-cultural childhood experiences and memories (only much later, and purely by chance, did I discover the mythic significance of dogs).[104] Third, and most importantly, I knew that there were no dogs in the Gospel of John, and so any imposition of them on the Johannine text would appear incongruous and artificial.

But now I had a real problem: How could I make dogs "appear" in a text where they were so obviously absent? The narratologist in me wanted some quirky evidence of their presence in the Fourth Gospel—and the more fantastic the argument for their presence, the better. An illusory sighting of dogs in John would point out the arbitrariness and subjectivity of some types of reader-responses, and the masked illogic of some of our guild's interpretive moves. Knowing that the Greek word for dog (*kyōn*) did not appear in the Fourth Gospel, I began by looking for a backwards *kyōn*. The genitive form of night (*nyktos*) seemed to offer possibilities, as did several Greek participial constructions. But nothing fit "perfectly." I couldn't find a dog in John to save my soul, no matter how cynically I toyed with the text. It made no difference whether I was reading the text forward or backward, up or down.[105]

Then, totally by chance, and to my complete surprise, the dogs reared up in the passion narrative itself, in the quotation from Psalm 22. I just hadn't seen them there before—or had I? If I had seen them before, they had long

---

[104] I found David White's book *Myths of the Dog-Man* by browsing through the University of Chicago book display at the national AAR/SBL meeting in San Francisco, November, 1992. Coincidentally, an hour later I met the author when he overheard me telling a friend about his strange book which I had just discovered. David then came over and introduced himself to me.

[105] I guess I'm not the first to read the Fourth Gospel in peculiar ways. For example, Ernst Käsemann once wrote: "Eighteen hundred years of [Johannine] exegesis have investigated each line and each syllable from all possible perspectives, reading it backwards and forwards, turning it upside down. . . . It is [therefore] easy for outsiders to ridicule us, that we think we can hear the grass grow and the bedbugs cough" (*The Testament of Jesus,* 75 n. 1). For the relationship of the apostle John to bedbugs, see *The Acts of John,* 60–61.

since been reburied, like an old bone, deep in the dirt of my subconscious.[106] But they were obvious to me now. Why hadn't I seen them there before? Suddenly, arguments about the arbitrariness of signifiers and signifieds took on new meaning. For what had begun as a conscious attempt to read something purely arbitrary into a text had ended up cohering nicely, intertextually stuck in the muck of a Johannine narrative world.

I found myself wanting to go back and reread that neglected, subjectivist reader-response critic, Norman Holland. For example, according to Holland's theory of reader-response, the phenomenon of "nice coherence" in my interpretation would be evidence of a psychological "identity theme," where "*interpretation is a function of identity,*"[107] "a fantasy pushing for gratification, pressing upward toward coherence and significance."[108] Even the subsequent historical evidence that John Crossan has lent me, supporting my argument that there were dogs at Jesus' crucifixion,[109] can be seen as another part of my own "press upward toward coherence and significance."

As I sit typing these lines, I recall a phone conversation I had with my family just last night. It began with my seven-year-old son getting on the line and barking like a Chinese dog. Once, twice.[110] Then a long, pregnant pause.

---

[106] I realize now that the dogs first made their appearance in a poem I wrote for Easter, 1984; the day after my mother's funeral. The poem, written in the structure of four linked haiku, is entitled "The Stone."

> Like friends at midnight,
> we pleaded for bread, O Lord.
> But you gave us stone.
> We took it, shaped it;
> then grim-faced, rolled it upright
> on a fresh filled grave.
> Dawn came; it was gone,
> crushed and mixed with blood-flecked sweat,
> a finely ground flour.
> Now gaunt bellies roam,
> stop and sniff the altered stone—
> cryptic, hand-held crumbs.

No, that can't be right. The dogs must go back much earlier, to the countless times Donald Perrault, the senior missionary at Immanuel Mission, stood up during Morning Meeting and with tears rolling down his cheeks, read Psalm 22.

[107] Holland, "Unity Identity Text Self," 123; his emphasis. For an important, postmodern critique of Holland's view of the self, see The Bible and Culture Collective, *The Postmodern Bible,* 28–29, 123–58.

[108] Ibid., 127. Cf. Michaels, "The Interpreter's Self: Peirce on the Cartesian 'Subject,'" 199.

[109] See Crossan's chapter entitled "The Dogs Beneath the Cross," in *Jesus,* 123–58.

[110] There is an ancient Zen koan that goes something like this: "When asked by a monk, 'Is

"Daddy, two big dogs chased Allie tonight and knocked her down."
My wife picks up the phone in the bedroom. "Yes, that's right. And she has
cuts and bruises all over her face to prove it. Your baby was flat on her back, in
the middle of the street, screaming, and these two dogs were pawing her and
drooling in her face. She was petrified, but the dogs just thought it was a
game. One of the neighbors kept yelling at the dogs' owner, 'God damn it,
that's why cities have leash laws! To keep dogs like yours under control!'"[111]
"Keep your dogs under control!" I can hear my fellow biblical scholars
echoing that response. "You can't do critical, responsible exegesis with a
bunch of half-wild dogs cavorting about your neighborhood, living room, or
study, continually disrupting your work and pissing all over it."[112]
If, indeed, my readers (both the formalist ones inside the text and the autobiographical ones outside the text) have proved to be fictions, fossilized rem-
nants on the verge of eroding away into nothing, then who—or what—is left
to control the free-roaming, boundary-breaking, barking dogs that remain
behind?[113] For as surely as the sun rises, there will be caninical constraints and
controls. I suppose the answer to that question, dishearteningly, is to be
found among the same whos and whats that have always been in control:
those cosmos-creating, sociopolitical structures that stand together as a
human wall against the ever-present chaos outside. Paradoxically, however,
those structures are nourished by the "life-giving power" of the monstrous
chaos they seek to exclude.[114]
But sometimes I like to imagine a different scenario. I pretend that some

---

there a Buddha-nature in a dog?' Chao-chu barked, 'Wu.'" (Wu is the negative symbol in
Chinese, meaning "No thing" or "No.")

[111] Cf. Williams, *The Alchemy of Race and Rights,* 12–13.

[112] Using words that, today, still describe many New Testament scholars' dogged resistance
to new developments in biblical studies and hermeneutics, Robert Roberts admiringly wrote
fifteen years ago of Rudolf Bultmann: He "has not ambled through his career sniffing every
pole and fire hydrant of modernity [or postmodernity, we might now add] for an object upon
which to bestow his theological blessings" (*Rudolf Bultmann's Theology,* 9; Vaage, "Like Dogs
Barking: Cynic parresia and Shameless Asceticism," 38).

[113] Or, as Jane Tompkins writes: "The questions that propose themselves within this critical
framework therefore concern, broadly, the relations of discourse and power. What makes one
set of perceptual strategies or literary conventions win out over another? If the world is the
product of interpretation, then who or what determines which interpretive system will pre-
vail?" ("The Reader in History: The Changing Shape of Literary Response," 226).

[114] Jonathan Z. Smith, *Map Is Not Territory: Studies in the Histories of Religions,* 98, as
quoted in White, *Myths of the Dog-Man,* 4; cf. Haraway, "A Manifesto for Cyborgs: Science,
Technology, and Socialist Feminism in the 1980s," 99.

form of postmodern ethnocriticism is really possible. I bring the nightmare out of the closet and dance with it in the privacy of my room.[115] The dancing monster will combine the Native American trickster, medieval carnivalesque, and the cynocephalic and lycanthropic creatures of Eurasian mythologies in such a way as to traverse the borderlands of theories, epistemologies, and genres with humor and abandon.[116] At the same time, however, the monster will try not to lose sight of the crucial fiction—or any cursive fiction[117]—that is connected and committed to those inhabitants on both sides of the border, the burghers and the peasants, who are forever seeking to define, categorize, and constrain it.[118]

I am a man of the American West. I wonder if I could construct a postmodern, ethnically and gender sensitive biblical criticism based on that indigenous western carnival: the rodeo.[119]

[115] Cf. Berg, "Suppressing the Language of (Wo)man: The Dream as a Common Language," 15–24.

[116] For the significance of borders in literary theory, see Diane Freedman's discussion "Border Crossing as Method and Motif in Contemporary Feminist Writing" in *An Alchemy of Genres,* 31–65; esp. 47–50; cf. Bach, "Slipping Across Borders: The Bible and Popular Culture," 1–7.

[117] For me, of course, at the heart (*coeur*) of the crucifixion are the curs, who represent both curse and cure.

[118] Articulating a theory of ethnocriticism that exhibits a concern for community, Arnold Krupat says, "there will always be something paradoxical about a criticism that insists on its betweenness [which is a particularly canine characteristic, I might add]—while seeking a certain privilege or centrality; a criticism that insists upon a commitment to dialogue and the shifting processes of 'transculturalization'—in the name of such apparently monologous and fixed categories as accuracy, knowledge, and truth. But this is only to recognize that ethnocriticism is not only at but of the frontier, its situation and its epistemological status the same" (*Ethnocriticism,* 28; see further 25–26, 36–37; cf. Clifton, "Alternate Identities and Cultural Frontiers," 24, 29–30; and Freedman, "Bordercrossing as Method and Motif in Contemporary American Writing, or, How Freud Helped Me Case the Joint," 14–15).

[119] The metaphorical foundation for this project has already been laid by the Idahoan, Robert Kysar, who wrote a book on the Gospel of John and entitled it *John: The Maverick Gospel* (the term "maverick" refers to an unbranded calf).

The Spanish word *rodeo* translates as "roundup," and both words originally described the *vaquero* or the cowboy's task of gathering cattle together and driving them to pasture or market (Russell, *The Wild West,* 1–10). While many Indians compete on the rodeo circuit today, the rodeo-carnival is indigenous only to the American West of the *conquistadores.* It was not a part of any ancient Native American tribal tradition (cf. Lawrence, *Rodeo,* 44–47, 157–60, 270).

# Things Not Written
# in This Book

Our belief in language's capacity for reference is part of our contract with the world; the contract may be playfully suspended or broken altogether, but no abrogation is without consequences, and there are circumstances where the abrogation is unacceptable. The existence or absence of a real world, real body, real pain, makes a difference. The traditional paradigms for the uses of history and the interpretation of texts have all eroded—this is a time in which it will not do to invoke the same pathetically narrow repertoire of dogmatic explanations—but any history and any textual interpretation worth doing will have to speak to this difference.

—Stephen J. Greenblatt

There are many things that I have not read in the writing of this book. Take Paul Ricoeur's newly translated book *Oneself as Another,* for example. Now there's a catchy title and a topic that seems appropriate to my interests. Next week I think I'm going to sit down and read it from cover to cover.

I probably should also read a lot more of those French feminists and post-structuralists. It would have been nice if I had disciplined myself to read more of Michel Foucault; cast at least a sidelong glance at Jacques Lacan, for goodness sake; and taken Julia Kristeva, Luce Irigaray, and Hélène Cixous more seriously. Astoundingly, most of those scholars are hardly mentioned in the book. Talk about blindness and reading gaps!

And another thing. Why should I spend so much time with feminist theory when men are beginning to discover a more holistic, inclusive sense of personhood? Male woundedness and all that.[1] None of that material is in this book either. Finally, there are all those Continental biblical scholars whom I scarcely mention. Don't they have anything to add to my analysis of the Fourth Gospel? My bibliography looks pretty sparse there, too.

But you can't fault me on my footnotes. I've worked hard on them and they look pretty impressive. And almost all of the sources I quote actually exist. I must confess, however, that the idea of putting footnotes in chapter 5, the autobiographical chapter, started out simply as a joke. Who but a biblical scholar would think of footnoting an autobiography? But the joke quickly got out of hand and became a significant part of that chapter. I plan someday to write a scholarly article consisting of a single sentence and a twenty-page footnote.

On a more serious note, what reading I have done has convinced me that recent literary theories of autobiography may help us biblical reader-response critics reinvent ourselves for a postcolonial, postmodern age. But I also see a couple of looming dangers in my autobiographical move. First, I would feel that I was being sadly misunderstood if someone were to read the final two chapters of this book as an attempt to reconfigure biblical readers in radically individualistic terms. Second, I would be doubly upset if someone were to find a way to read those chapters as advocating a return to naïve, unreflective readings of the Bible.[2] At the risk of sounding elitist, I am not attempting to empower a particular species of pre-Enlightenment devotionalism, or an overly simplistic this-is-what-God-is-saying-to-me-today mentality. And in retrospect, I probably should have added a section to my autobiographical chapter on community and the influence that community has had on the way I read.[3] That addition might have helped clear up any misreadings along individualistic lines. Here again, a sense of community and its value in interpretation have been nourished by my childhood experience.

Wait a minute. I feel a credo rising to a crescendo inside me.

---

[1] Parsons, "Anatomy of a Reader," 25–26; Patte and Phillips, "A Fundamental Condition for Ethical Accountability in the Teaching of the Bible by White Male Exegetes," 20. See also Myers, *Who Will Roll Away the Stone?* 84–90.

[2] This teary-eyed language of "feeling misunderstood" seems way out of line with postmodern turns in criticism. Are the specters of essentialism, communication models, and the unified self somehow still haunting me? Why should I care if I am misunderstood? And who is the *I* that cares about that anyway? Cf. Miller's reflections on Tompkins's essay "Me and My Shadow," in *Getting Personal,* 3–25.

[3] See, for example, Cochrane, "The Grave, the Song and a *Gestalt* Theology as Pregnant with Context: Contextual Impregnation as the Substance of Theology (Local Theologies and the Integrity of Faith)," 127–29.

I believe that critically reflective, readerly fictions that give voice to the voiceless, which give a place at table to the dogs, the *łéchąą'í* of the world,[4] are those that ultimately are theologically and socially constructive and useful.

And a large table is crucial. In our home there always seemed to be lots of "company" at table. Sometimes the company would be people we knew— relatives, farmer friends from Kansas bringing us a side of beef, or former Navajo students, now grown. But just as often our guests were people who had introduced themselves to us just moments before sitting down to a meal. In summers, and after the state highway system brought us within fourteen miles of smooth, black pavement, Immanuel Mission became an informal bed and breakfast inn. Curious explorers of the mythical American "out- back," devout Christian pilgrims in search of sixteenth-century Spanish mis- sions, lost oil drillers, occasional spacey-faced hippies, along with plodding government geologists and looters of ancient Anasazi ruins, all found their way to our door. And in the mornings my mother would be collecting addresses instead of cash, handing out recipes instead of receipts. She col- lected people and stories the way other women collect china teacups and sil- ver spoons.

In my thinking, then, chapter 4, the theoretical chapter (which, coinciden- tally, lies chiastically near the center of the book), is crucial to my postmod- ern, autobiographical reader-response agenda. For in summarizing the ways that Euro-Americans tend to read themselves, postmodern, autobiographical literary criticism opens a door to communal values and a shared story which, in spite of ethnic, regional, and religious pluralisms, and in spite of our uniquely individual stories, invigorate and/or infect our collective conscious- ness. Thus, insofar as people living in the United States have internalized the

---

[4] As I noted in the preceding chapter, Arnold Krupat observes with sympathetic insight, that "the danger the would-be practitioner of ethnocriticism must try to avoid is . . . to speak *for* the 'Indian,' 'interpreting' him or her . . . in a manner that would submit her or him to a dominative discourse" (*Ethnocriticism,* 30, his emphasis; cf. Bal, *Reading Rembrandt,* 200–201; and Tolbert, "The Politics and Poetics of Location," 314–17). Similarly, my silence in the last chapter regarding the interpretive implications of the Johannine passion narrative for Navajo Indians ought to be read as resisting this same dangerous temptation—a tempta- tion, to which, I might add, Euro-American liberation theology has often succumbed.

"The question is not so much, to borrow a formulation from Gayatri Spivak, whether the subaltern can speak but whether and to what effect she can be heard" (Krupat, *Ethnocriticism,* 19). Or, to put the issue another way, it is not a question of *giving* them voices, but of recog- nizing their space and then listening for their voices. As Euro-Americans, all too often we begin by taking away the subalterns' space and then wonder why we can't hear their voices (see Patte, "Acknowledging the Contextual Character of Male, European-American Critical Exegeses: An Androcritical Perspective," 40, 42–47).

Euro-American story, they will share common reading strategies of the Bible that can be critically examined against theories of American autobiography and other national or cultural stories. But insofar as an individual's personal history is reflected in a reading, in a form different from the Euro-American norm, that reading will be evaluated against the background of a different hermeneutic.[5] That hermeneutic, I believe, can be found in the type of ethno-criticism advocated by Arnold Krupat and others.

Now with regard to my fear that my autobiographical turn in reader-response criticism might be viewed as a return of the naïve reader, I should add this rejoinder. First, I don't wish automatically to denigrate "naïve" readings of the Bible.[6] They do, in fact, often function to undercut systems of oppression, and they can sometimes be liberating. Still, a devotional type of reading that is insensitive to either the social location of the reader or the ideology of the text is precisely the type of reading that most of us in the teaching profession today try to wean our students of. But much of the reading that goes on in our gelded guild of biblical scholarship is just as often an instrument of oppression as is naïve reading. The only difference is that with naïve readings, the voice of God is a stand-in for the authoritative and authoritarian

---

[5] As Nancy Miller writes: "Though the reign of the Master Narratives, we are told, has passed, micro-narratives abound, and with them a massive reconsideration of the conditions grounding authorization itself" (*Getting Personal,* 20; cf. Jahner, "Transitional Narratives and Cultural Continuity," 176–79; MacIntyre, *After Virtue,* 191–209; Kerby, *Narrative and the Self,* 32–59; McAdams, *The Stories we Live By,* 19–38; and Patte and Phillips, "A Fundamental Condition for Ethical Accountability in the Teaching of the Bible by White Male Exegetes," 18–19). In reaction to this loss of "master Narratives," Brian Swimme and Thomas Berry have been trying to develop a sort of meta-Master Narrative of the universe—but without any sensitivity to the "conditions grounding [its own] authorization" (ibid., Swimme and Berry, *The Universe Story,* 3, 264–68; cf. Silko, *Ceremony,* 245–46). But for Miller, as well as for much of my thinking, that "reconsideration of the conditions grounding authorization" is bound up *in part* with the "personalization of cultural analysis" found in the "personal criticism" of recent feminist criticism (Miller, *Getting Personal,* 21, cf. 1–2; see also Myers, *Who will Roll Away the Stone?* 132–39, 369–79; and Patte, "Acknowledging the Contextual Character of Male, European-American Critical Exegeses: An Androcritical Perspective," 38–40).

[6] The naïve readings I have in mind would be close to what Paul Ricoeur calls "the first naïveté," or the "spontaneous immediacy of reader to subject matter" (Schneiders, *The Revelatory Text,* 169; cf. Schüssler Fiorenza, "Biblical Interpretation and Critical Commitment," 11). For a theoretical appraisal of "ordinary readers," see West, "The Relationship Between Different Modes of Reading (the Bible) and the Ordinary Reader," 87–110; Patte and Phillips, "A Fundamental Condition for Ethical Accountability in the Teaching of the Bible by White Male Exegetes," 25–26; and The Bible and Culture Collective, *The Postmodern Bible,* 64–67.

voice of the scholar. Clearly, I do not wish to be viewed as attempting or advocating such an unreflected, enslaving turn in reader criticism. Reading should
be done with passion, but not without reservations.[7]

Second, and more important, my emphasis on the autobiographical
impulse in reader-response criticism is rooted in a particularly feminist and
postcolonial insight. This perspective grounds the crucial noetic moment in
particular experiences of oppression and seeks to utilize that experiential
insight in critical conversation with androcentrist and colonialist acceptance
of "the way things are." Furthermore, I would argue that any personal experience that is critically reflected upon in the context of competing metanarratives, ideologies, and cultural theories should become an essential part of
biblical interpretation.[8]

And on that heavily laden note, I think I'll stop. I'm beginning to overdose
on metamatter. Those AIDS symptoms are recurring. Strange voices in
unusual forms are beginning to inhabit my deteriorating body.

I feel as though "I have arrived at a point where everything I have ever
learned is running around and around in my head; and little bits of [theory]
and pieces of everyday life fly out of my mouth in weird combinations,"[9] says
a Patricia Williams inside me.

Yes, but that's because "[y]ou have to do a lot of unlearning before you get
to the position when you start growing a tongue of your own," responds a
Nicole Jouve from another corner of my body.[10]

Besides, with the "demise of New Criticism, and the rise of reader-response
theory, poet-critics are in ascendance,"[11] chimes in a Diane Freedman from
somewhere near my ear.

Okay, Okay, that settles it, says Nancy Miller. "I would rather end personally,
but I'm afraid to go too far, though it may be worse not to go far enough. . . .

---

[7] Or as Schuyler Brown puts it: "the crucial value judgment is the reader's consciousness of
the interests which are actually motivating him" ("Reader Response: Demythologizing the
Text," 235; see also his "John and the Resistant Reader: The Fourth Gospel after Nicea and
the Holocaust," 254; cf. Patte, "Textual Constraints, Ordinary Readings, and Critical Exegeses: An Androcritical Perspective," 68–69).

[8] Cf. Schüssler Fiorenza, "Biblical Interpretation and Critical Commitment," 9–12;
Wuellner, "Where is Rhetorical Criticism Taking Us?" 460–63; Patte and Phillips, "A Fundamental Condition for Ethical Accountability in the Teaching of the Bible by White Male
Exegetes," 17–18, 23; and West, "No Integrity without Contextuality: The Presence of Particularity in Biblical Hermeneutics and Pedagogy," 134–36.

[9] Williams, *The Alchemy of Race and Rights,* 14.

[10] Jouve, *White Woman Speaks with Forked Tongue,* 5.

[11] Freedman, *An Alchemy of Genres,* 44.

"What remains, I think, is to give the last word. . . ."[12]

So here it is. A last word.

My mother's father, orphaned at age eleven, left England for Canada when he was twenty years old. But he imprinted the memories of his childhood homeland in my mother's mind by reading her A. A. Milne's children's books. As an adult, Milne was second only to the book of Proverbs in her list of appropriated wisdom. Not surprisingly, I, too, grew up loving the stories about Winnie the Pooh. Yet my most vivid childhood nightmare was one in which I heard a terrified Piglet scream, "Pooh! Wake up! Pooh! Wake up!"

That shrill voice of Piglet originated in a 45 rpm record that my parents had bought for me one afternoon when I was about six years old. Since I had been sick and unable to accompany them to the grocery store, I had received the record as a reward for being a good boy while they were gone.

I'm thinking now that perhaps the dream I mentioned at the end of the last chapter, in which I envisioned myself dancing with a monster, should also have Piglet in it. After all these years, I still sometimes hear Piglet's squeaky, frightened voice ringing in my head. And that voice still has the power to send cold chills tingling down my middle-aged spine.

I will allow A. A. Milne to introduce Piglet:

> The Piglet lived in a very grand house in the middle of a beech-tree, and the beech-tree was in the middle of the forest, and the Piglet lived in the middle of the house. Next to his house was a piece of broken board which had: "TRES-PASSERS W" on it. When Christopher Robin asked the Piglet what it meant, he said it was his grandfather's name, and had been in the family for a long time. Christopher Robin said you couldn't be called Trespassers W, and Piglet said yes, you could, because his grandfather was, and it was short for Trespassers Will, which was short for Trespassers William. And his grandfather had had two names in case he lost one—Trespassers after an uncle, and William after Trespassers.
>
> "I've got two names," said Christopher Robin carelessly.
>
> "Well, there you are, that proves it," said Piglet.[13]

Piglet's sign arouses in me a latent Lacanian and Foucauldian curiosity. I wonder what that broken, eroded signpost outside Piglet's front door originally said: "Trespassers will be prosecuted"? "Trespassers will be fined fifty shillings"? "Trespassers will be shot on sight"? Who can say, for sure? Is it a signpost of postmodernism? Postcolonialism? All I know is that Piglet under-

[12] Miller, *Getting Personal,* 138.
[13] Milne, *Winnie the Pooh,* 32–33.

stood the sign quite differently from the way most readers would understand it today.

I like the timid Piglet. He took what could have been a life-threatening prohibition against bordercrossing and created from it a family history, a place to belong.

But then I hesitate for a moment. Perhaps Piglet is too androcentric, too colonialist and too European to be used as an illustration for the species of postmodernism that I have in mind. After all, Piglet is male and living in the British Isles, and the ancestors he evokes are all males. Nevertheless, as a pig-child, he must be relatively powerless. And traditionally, pigs have been marginalized members of barnyard society. Moreover, the Piglet and I do have a good deal in common. We both grew up on someone else's land—through no choice of our own—and we both have lived our lives trying to find ways to incorporate that otherness into our own living space and identity.

I shall indeed write Piglet into my new nightmare. Piglet, my out-of-the-closet cynocephalic monster, and I, afflicted with literary AIDS, will have a pretend rodeo in my room. Then we'll go downstairs and outside, onto an Arizona mesa top[14] where we'll teach the world a bawdy, postmodern, giddy-up dance step or two.

I have always dreamed of living in two stories:

A house fenced with white pickets
and shuttered in pale blue.
It would have bright rooms upstairs
sheltered under broad eaves,
and bay windows on the ground floor
fluttering in snowflake-lace.
Tall maples would shield me from neighbors
and smaller trees would speckle the back lawn
with late autumn fruit.

I always thought love would come
easily, like the spring blossoms falling
from my dreamyard pear. It would be golden,
the comforter mother

[14] Hillerman, *Talking God,* 34–54.

fitted so snugly
to the double bed in her room;
the same one a quavering-voiced boy of four
had once pulled over his head
while forming his first prayers
to a god-fearing forty-five.
(Fully loaded, revolving in an oak cabinet,
that hot cylinder used to fire heavenly bulletins
and send gospel choruses zinging
toward his brain every afternoon at nap time.)

And children—they, too, would come in time—
bouncing tousle-headed onto my lap; girl first,
then boy. They would be blue-eyed and fair-skinned,
and I would tickle and hug them,
then finally tuck them into comfortable beds
far above the glowering cold
that crept across wooden floors
during fierce prairie winters.

Perhaps I have always lived in two stories:

A doll house set up
in my parents' bedroom
during quiet afternoons; pulled out
of a Sears and Roebuck catalog in late November,
with pleading eyes.
(It had appeared like magic
under a Kansas Christmas tree in 1956,
while my two older brothers looked on,
grinning wickedly.)

And a blackened disk
still spinning, shot through the center
with a hole so large
that I can push three fingers into it:
perfectly round,
a marksman's bull's-eye.

# Works Cited

Abel, Elizabeth. "Black Writing, White Reading: Race and the Politics of Feminist Interpretation." *Critical Inquiry* 19 (1991): 470–98.

Adams, Timothy. *Telling Lies in Modern American Autobiography.* Chapel Hill: University of North Carolina Press, 1990.

Aichele, George, Jr. "Literary Fantasy and the Composition of the Gospels." *Forum* 5 (1989): 42–59.

Alcoff, Linda. "The Problem of Speaking for Others." *Cultural Critique* 20 (1991): 5–32.

Alter, Robert. *The Art of Biblical Narrative.* New York: Basic Books, 1981.

———. *The Pleasure of Reading in an Ideological Age.* New York: Simon & Schuster, 1989.

Amaladoss, M. A. "An Indian Reads St. John's Gospel." In *India's Search for Reality and the Relevance of the Gospel of John,* edited by Christopher Duraisingh and Cecil Hargreaves, 7–24. Delhi: SPCK, 1975.

Anderson, Janice C. "Mapping Feminist Biblical Criticism: The American Scene, 1983–1990." *Critical Review of Books in Religion* (1991): 21–44.

———. "Matthew: Gender and Reading." *Semeia* 28 (1983): 3–28.

———, and Stephen D. Moore, eds. *Mark and Method: New Approaches in Biblical Studies.* Minneapolis: Fortress, 1992.

Anderson, Paul N. *The Christology of the Fourth Gospel: Its Unity and Disunity in Light of John 6.* WUNT 2. Tübingen: Mohr, 1995.

Anzaldúa, Gloria. *Borderlands/La Frontera: The New Mestiza.* San Francisco: Aunt Lute, 1987.

Appiah, Kwame Anthony. "Is the Post- in Postmodernism the Post- in Postcolonialism?" *Critical Inquiry* 17 (1991): 336–57.

Arens, W. *The Man-Eating Myth: Anthropology and Anthropophagy.* New York: Oxford University Press, 1979.

Auerbach, Erich. *Mimesis: The Representation of Reality in Western Literature.* Princeton, N.J.: Princeton University Press, 1953.

Bach, Alice. "Slipping Across Borders: The Bible and Popular Culture." *Biblical Interpretation* 2 (1994): 1–7.

Bahr, Donald, and Susan Fenger. "Indians and Missions: Homage to and Debate with Rupert Costo and Jeannette Henry." *Journal of the Southwest* 31 (1989): 300–329.

Bakerman, Jane. "Cutting Both Ways: Race, Prejudice, and Motive in Tony Hillerman's Detective Fiction." *MELUS* 11 (1984): 17–25.

Bakhtin, Mikail. *Rabelais and His World.* Translated by Hélène Iswolsky. Bloomington: Indiana University Press, 1984.

Bal, Mieke. *Death and Dissymmetry: The Politics of Coherence in the Book of Judges.* Chicago: University of Chicago Press, 1988.

———. "The Point of Narratology." *Poetics Today* 11 (1990): 727–54.

———. *Reading "Rembrandt": Beyond the Word-Image Opposition.* New York: Cambridge University Press, 1991.

Bar-Efrat, Shimon. *Narrative Art in the Bible.* Bible and Literature Series 17. Sheffield: Almond, 1989.

Bartlett, J. Gardner. *Robert Coe, Puritan: His Ancestors and Descendants 1340–1910.* Boston: J. Gardner Bartlett, 1911.

Bassler, Jouette. "Mixed Signals: Nicodemus in the Fourth Gospel." *Journal of Biblical Literature* 108 (1989): 635–46.

Bauer, Walter, W. Arndt, F. Gingrich, and F. Danker. *A Greek-English Lexicon of the New Testament and other Early Christian Literature.* Chicago: University of Chicago Press, 1979.

Bauman, Zygmunt. *Modernity and the Holocaust.* Ithaca, N.Y.: Cornell University Press, 1989.

Beasley-Murray, George R. *John.* Word Commentary 36. Waco, Tex.: Word, 1987.

Beck, David R. "The Narrative Function of Anonymity in Fourth Gospel Characterization." *Semeia* 63 (1993): 143–58.

Beers, F. *History of Greene County, New York, with Biographical Sketches of Its Prominent Men.* New York: J. B. Beers, 1884.

Benstock, Shari. "Authorizing the Autobiographical." In *The Private Self: Theory and Practice of Women's Autobiographical Writings,* edited by Shari Benstock, 10–33. Chapel Hill: University of North Carolina Press, 1988.

———, ed. *The Private Self: Theory and Practice of Women's Autobiographical Writings.* Chapel Hill: University of North Carolina Press, 1988.

Berg, Temma. "Reading in/to Mark." *Semeia* 48 (1989): 187–206.

———. "Suppressing the Language of (Wo)man: The Dream as a Common Language." In *Engendering the Word: Feminist Essays in Psychosexual Poetics,* edited by Temma F. Berg, 3–28. Urbana: University of Illinois Press, 1989.

Berlin, Adele. *Poetics and Interpretation of Biblical Narrative.* Bible and Literature Series 9. Sheffield: Almond, 1983.

Bernard, J. H. *A Critical and Exegetical Commentary on the Gospel According to St. John.* Edinburgh: T. & T. Clark, 1928.

Beutler, Johannes. "Response from a European Perspective." *Semeia* 53 (1991): 191–202.

Bible and Culture Collective. *The Postmodern Bible.* Edited by Elizabeth A. Castelli, Stephen D. Moore, Gary A. Phillips, and Regina M. Schwartz. New Haven: Yale University Press, 1995.

Blackstone, Sarah. *Buckskins, Bullets, and Business: A History of Buffalo Bill's Wild West.* Contributions to the Study of Popular Culture 14. New York: Greenwood, 1986.

Blass, F., and A. Debrunner. *A Greek Grammar of the New Testament and Other Early Christian Literature.* Translated and revised by Robert W. Funk. Chicago: University of Chicago Press, 1961.

Bloom, Harold. *The Anxiety of Influence: A Theory of Poetry.* New York: Oxford University Press, 1973.

Bloomfield, Morton W. "Allegory as Interpretation." *New Literary History* 3 (1972): 301–17.

Boers, H. "Narrative Criticism, Historical Criticism, and the Gospel of John." *Journal for the Study of the New Testament* 47 (1992): 35–48.

Booth, Wayne C. *The Company We Keep: An Ethics of Fiction.* Berkeley: University of California Press, 1988.

———. *The Rhetoric of Fiction.* Second Edition. Chicago: University of Chicago Press, 1983.

———. *A Rhetoric of Irony.* Chicago: University of Chicago Press, 1974.

Borg, Marcus J. *Jesus: A New Vision: Spirit, Culture, and the Life of Discipleship.* San Francisco: Harper & Row, 1987.

———. *Meeting Jesus Again for the First Time: The Historical Jesus and the Heart of Contemporary Faith.* San Francisco: HarperSanFrancisco, 1994.

———. "Portraits of Jesus in Contemporary North American Scholarship." *Harvard Theological Review* 84 (1991): 1–22.

Botha, J. Eugene. *Jesus and the Samaritan Woman: A Speech Act Reading of John 4:1-42.* Supplements to Novum Testamentum 65. New York: E. J. Brill, 1991.

———. "Reader 'Entrapment' as Literary Device in John 4:1-42." *Neotestamentica* 24 (1990): 37–47.

Bowden, Henry Warner. *American Indians and Christian Missions: Studies in Cultural Conflict.* Chicago: University of Chicago, 1981.

Bowerman, A. C. "'Bowerman' Family of Ontario Canada (1633 to 1916 Inclusive). Being the Descendants of Ichabod Bowerman and Lydia Mott." 1916 (?) [photocopy].

Boyarin, Daniel. "The Politics of Biblical Narratology: Reading the Bible Like/As a Woman." *Diacritics* 20 (1990): 31–42.

———, and Jonathan Boyarin. "Diaspora: Generation and the Ground of Jewish Identity." *Critical Inquiry* 19 (1993): 693–725.

Boyarin, Jonathan. "Europe's Indian, America's Jew: Modiano and Vizenor." *Boundary 2* 19 (1992): 197–222.

Braun, Willi. "Resisting John: Ambivalent Redactor and Defensive Reader of the Fourth Gospel." *Studies in Religion/Sciences religieuses* 19 (1990): 59–71.

Brawley, Robert L. "An Absent Complement and Intertextuality in John 19:28-29." *Journal of Biblical Literature* 112 (1993): 427–43.

Breen, Jon L. "Interview with Tony Hillerman." In *The Tony Hillerman Companion: A Comprehensive Guide to his Life and Work,* edited by Martin Greenberg, 51–70. New York: HarperCollins, 1994.

Breytenbach, Breyten. *Buffalo Bill.* Johannesburg: Taurus, 1984.

Brodie, Thomas L. *The Gospel According to John.* New York: Oxford, 1993.

Brooke-Rose, Christine. *A Rhetoric of the Unreal: Studies in Narrative and Structure, Especially of the Fantastic.* New York: Cambridge University Press, 1981.

———. "Whatever Happened to Narratology?" *Poetics Today* 11 (1990): 293–94.

Brown, Raymond E. *The Community of the Beloved Disciple.* New York: Paulist, 1979.

———. *The Gospel According to John.* Anchor Bible 12, 12A. 2 vols. Garden City, N.Y.: Doubleday, 1966, 1970.

Brown, Schuyler. "John and the Resistant Reader: The Fourth Gospel after Nicea and the Holocaust." *Journal of Literary Studies* 5 (1989): 252–61.

———. "Reader-Response: Demythologizing the Text." *New Testament Studies* 34 (1988): 232–37.

Brumble, H. David III. *American Indian Autobiography.* Berkeley: University of California Press, 1988.

Bruner, Edward M. "Ethnography as Narrative." In *The Anthropology of Experience,* edited by Victor W. Turner and Edward M. Bruner, 139–55. Urbana: University of Illinois Press, 1986.

Bultmann, Rudolf. *The Gospel of John: A Commentary.* Translated by G. R. Beasley-Murray et al. Philadelphia: Westminster, 1971.

———. *History of the Synoptic Tradition.* Translated by John Marsh. New York: Harper & Row, 1963.

Bunyan, John. *The Pilgrim's Progress.* Harvard Classics 15. New York: Collier, 1961.

Burnett, Fred W. "Reflections on Keeping the Implied Author an 'It': Why I Love Wolfgang Iser." Paper presented to the Matthew Group, Society of Biblical Literature Annual Meeting, Chicago, 1988 [photocopy].

Byrne, Brendan. *Lazarus: A Contemporary Reading of John 11:1-46.* Collegeville, Minn.: Liturgical Press, 1991.

Calinescu, Matei. *Rereading.* New Haven: Yale University Press, 1993.

Calloway, Colin C. "Simon Girty: Interpreter and Intermediary." In *Being and Becoming Indian,* edited by James A. Clifton, 38–58. Chicago: Dorsey, 1989.

Carlton, Peter. "Rereading *Middlemarch,* Rereading Myself." In *The Intimate Critique: Autobiographical Literary Criticism,* edited by Diane P. Freedman, Olivia Frey, and Frances Murphy Zauhar, 237–44. Durham, N.C.: Duke University Press, 1993.

Carman, Albert Pruden. *Thomas C. Carman and Phebe Pruden Carman.* Urbana-Champaign, Ill.: By the author, 1935.

Carter, Harvey L. *'Dear Old Kit': The Historical Christopher Carson.* Norman: University of Oklahoma Press, 1968.

Charbonneau, André. "L'interrogatoire de Jésus, d'après la facture interne de Jn 18,12-27." *Science et Esprit* 35 (1983): 191–210.

Chatman, Seymour. *Story and Discourse: Narrative Structure in Fiction and Film.* Ithaca, N.Y.: Cornell University Press, 1978.

Chevallier, Max-Alain. "La comparution de Jésus devant Hanne et devant Caïphe (Jean 18/12-14 et 19-24)." In *Neues Testament und Geschichte: Historisches Geschehen und Deutung im Neuen Testament,* edited by Heinrich Baltensweiler and Bo Reicke, 179–85. Zurich: Theologischer Verlag, 1972.

Cheyfitz, Eric. *The Poetics of Imperialism: Translation and Colonization from "The Tempest" to "Tarzan."* New York: Oxford University Press, 1991.

Chrysostom, John. *Commentary on Saint John the Apostle and Evangelist: Homilies 1-47.* Translated by Sister Thomas Aquinas Goggin. New York: Fathers of the Church, 1957.

Churchill, Ward. *Fantasies of the Master Race: Literature, Cinema and the Colonization of American Indians.* Edited by M. Annette Jaimes. Monroe, Me.: Common Courage, 1992.

Clerici, Naila. "Native Americans in Columbus's Home Land: A Show within the Show." In *Indians and Europe: An Interdisciplinary Collection of Essays,* edited by Christian F. Feest, 415–26. Aachen: Rader, 1987.

Clifton, James. "Alternate Identities and Cultural Frontiers." In *Being and Becoming Indian,* edited by James A. Clifton, 1–37. Chicago: Dorsey, 1989.

Cochrane, James. "The Grave, the Song and a *Gestalt* Theology as Pregnant with Context: Contextual Impregnation as the Substance of Theology (Local Theologies and the Integrity of Faith)." *Scriptura* S11 (1993): 116–30.

Collard, Andrée, with Joyce Contrucci. *Rape of the Wild: Man's Violence Against Animals and the Earth.* Bloomington: Indiana University Press, 1989.

Collins, Raymond F. "The Representative Figures in the Fourth Gospel." *Downside Review* 94 (1976): 26–46; 95 (1976): 118–32.

———. *These Things Have Been Written: Studies on the Fourth Gospel.* Louvain Theological & Pastoral Monographs 2. Grand Rapids: Eerdmans, 1990.

Conrad, Rudolf. "Mutual Fascination: Indians in Dresden and Leipzig." In *Indians and Europe: An Interdisciplinary Collection of Essays,* edited by Christian F. Feest, 455–473. Aachen: Rader, 1987.

Costello, Jeanne. "Taking the 'Woman' out of Women's Autobiography: The Perils and Potentials of Theorizing Female Subjectivities." *Diacritics* 21 (1991): 123–34.

Countryman, L. William. *The Mystical Way in the Fourth Gospel: Crossing Over into God.* Philadelphia: Fortress, 1987.

Crain, Maxine E. "The Implications of Deconstruction in Teaching Servanthood." *Literature and Belief* 9 (1990): 88–95.

Cross, F. L., and E. A. Livingstone, eds. *The Oxford Dictionary of the Christian Church.* Second Edition. New York: Oxford University, 1974.

Crossan, John Dominic. *The Gospel of Eternal Life: Reflections on the Theology of St. John.* Milwaukee: Bruce, 1967.

———. *The Historical Jesus: The Life of a Mediterranean Peasant.* San Francisco: HarperSanFrancisco, 1991.

———. *Jesus: A Revolutionary Biography.* San Francisco: HarperSanFrancisco, 1994.

———. *Who Killed Jesus? Exposing the Roots of Anti-Semitism in the Gospel Story of the Death of Jesus.* San Francisco: HarperSanFrancisco, 1995.

Culbertson, Diana. *The Poetics of Revelation: Recognition and the Narrative Tradition.* Studies in American Biblical Hermeneutics 4. Macon, Ga.: Mercer University Press, 1989.

Culler, Jonathan. *On Deconstruction: Theory and Criticism after Structuralism.* Ithaca, N.Y.: Cornell University Press, 1982.

Cullmann, Oscar. *The Johannine Circle.* Translated by John Bowden. Philadelphia: Westminster, 1976.

Culpepper, R. Alan. *Anatomy of the Fourth Gospel: A Study in Literary Design.* Philadelphia: Fortress, 1983.

———. "Un exemple de commentaire fondé sur la critique narrative: Jean 5,1-18." In *La Communauté Johannique et son Histoire,* edited by Jean Michel Poffet and Jean Zumstein, 136–52. Geneva: Labor et Fides, 1990.

———. *The Johannine School: An Evaluation of the Johannine-School Hypothesis Based upon an Investigation of the Nature of Ancient Schools.* Society of Biblical Literature Dissertation Series 26. Missoula, Mont.: Scholars, 1975.

Danby, Herbert. *The Mishnah: Translated from the Hebrew with Introduction and Brief Explanatory Notes.* London: Oxford University Press, 1933.

Darr, John A. "Narrator As Character: Mapping A Reader-Oriented Approach to Narration in Luke-Acts." *Semeia* 63 (1993): 43–60.

———. *On Character Building: The Reader and the Rhetoric of Characterization in Luke-Acts.* Louisville: Westminster/John Knox, 1991.

Davies, Margaret. *Rhetoric and Reference in the Fourth Gospel.* Journal for the Study of the New Testament Supplement 69. Sheffield: JSOT Press, 1992.

Davies, Stevan L. *Jesus the Healer: Possession, Trance, and the Origins of Christianity.* New York: Continuum, 1995.

Davis, Michael. "The Moral Status of Dogs, Forests, and Other Persons." *Social Theory and Practice* 12 (1986): 27–59.

Dawsey, James. *The Lukan Voice: Confusion and Irony in the Gospel of Luke.* Macon, Ga.: Mercer University Press, 1986.

Deeks, David. "The Structure of the Fourth Gospel." *New Testament Studies* 27 (1968–69): 107–28.

de la Potterie, Ignace. *The Hour of Jesus: The Passion and the Resurrection of Jesus According to John.* New York: Alba, 1989.

Deloria, Vine, Jr. "The Indians." In *Buffalo Bill and the Wild West,* by The Brooklyn Museum; Museum of Art, Carnegie Institute; Buffalo Bill Historical Center, 45–56. New York: The Brooklyn Museum, 1981.

de Man, Paul. *Allegories of Reading: Figural Language in Rousseau, Nietzsche, Rilke, and Proust.* New Haven: Yale University Press, 1979.

———. "Autobiography as De-facement." *Modern Language Notes* 94 (1979): 919–30.

Derrida, Jacques. *Dissemination.* Translated, with an introduction and additional notes, by Barbara Johnson. Chicago: University of Chicago Press, 1981.

———. *The Ear of the Other: Otobiography, Transference, Translation.* Edited by Christie McDonald. Translated by Peggy Kamuf. Lincoln: University of Nebraska Press, 1988.

———. *Speech and Phenomena and Other Essays on Husserl's Theory of Signs.* Translated by David B. Allison. Evanston, Ill.: Northwestern University Press, 1973.

Des Pres, Terrence. "Excremental Assault." In *Holocaust: Religious and Philosophical Implications,* edited by John K. Roth and Michael Berenbaum, 203–20. New York: Paragon House, 1989.

Detweiler, Robert, and Vernon K. Robbins. "From New Criticism to Poststructuralism: Twentieth Century Hermeneutics." In *Reading the Text: Biblical Criticism and Literary Theory,* edited by Stephen Prickett, 225–80. Cambridge: Basil Blackwell, 1991.

Dillard, Annie. *An American Childhood.* New York: Harper & Row, 1987.

Dinnerstein, Dorothy. *The Mermaid and the Minotaur: Sexual Arrangements and Human Malaise.* New York: Harper & Row, 1977.

Dirlik, Arif. "The Postcolonial Aura: Third World Criticism in the Age of Global Capitalism." *Critical Inquiry* 20 (1994): 328–56.

Dodd, C. H. *The Interpretation of the Fourth Gospel.* Cambridge: Cambridge University Press, 1953.

Doerry, Karl. "Literary Conquista: The Southwest as a Literary Emblem." *Journal of the Southwest* 32 (1990): 438–50.

DuBois, Page. *Torture and Truth: The New Ancient World.* New York: Routledge, 1990.

Duke, Paul D. *Irony in the Fourth Gospel.* Atlanta: John Knox, 1985.

Du Rand, J. "The Characterization of Jesus as Depicted in the Narrative of the Fourth Gospel." *Neotestamentica* 19 (1985): 18–36.

Durber, Susan. "The Female Reader of the Parables of the Lost." *Journal for the Study of the New Testament* 45 (1992): 59–78.

Eakin, Paul John *Fictions in Autobiography: Studies in the Art of Self-Invention.* Princeton: Princeton University Press, 1985.

———, ed. *American Autobiography: Retrospect and Prospect.* Madison: University of Wisconsin Press, 1991.

Eco, Umberto. *The Role of the Reader: Explorations in the Semiotics of Texts.* Bloomington: Indiana University Press, 1979.

Edwards, Michael. "The World Could not Contain the Books." In *The Bible as Rhetoric: Studies in Biblical Persuasion and Credibility,* edited by Martin Warner, 178–94. New York: Routledge, 1990.

Ellis, Peter. *The Genius of John: A Composition-Critical Commentary on the Fourth Gospel.* Collegeville, Minn.: Liturgical Press, 1984.

Engel, Leonard. "Landscape and Place in Tony Hillerman's Mysteries." *Western American Literature* 28 (1993): 111–22.

Erisman, Fred. "Hillerman's Uses of the Southwest." *Roundup Quarterly* 1 (1989): 9–18.

Eslinger, Lyle. "The Wooing of the Woman at the Well: The Reader and Reader-Response Criticism." *Journal of Literature and Theology* 1 (1987): 167–83.

Estés, Clarissa Pinkola. *Women Who Run with the Wolves: Myths and Stories of the Wild Woman Archetype.* New York: Ballantine, 1992.

Feest, Christian. "Indians and Europe? Editor's Postscript." In *Indians and Europe: An Interdisciplinary Collection of Essays,* edited by Christian F. Feest, 609–28. Aachen: Rader, 1987.

Fetterley, Judith. *The Resisting Reader: A Feminist Approach to American Fiction.* Bloomington: Indiana University Press, 1978.

Fewell, Danna Nolan, and David M. Gunn. "Tipping the Balance: Sternberg's Reader and the Rape of Dinah." *Journal of Biblical Literature* 110 (1991): 193–211.

Fiorentino, Daniele. "'Those Red-Brick Faces': European Press Reactions to the Indians of Buffalo Bill's Wild West Show." In *Indians and Europe: An Interdisciplinary Collection of Essays,* edited by Christian F. Feest, 403–14. Aachen: Rader, 1987.

Fischer, Michael M. J. "Ethnicity and the Post-Modern Arts of Memory." In *Writing Culture: The Poetics and Politics of Ethnography,* edited by James Clifford and George E. Marcus, 194–233. Berkeley: University of California Press, 1986.

Fish, Stanley. *Is There a Text in This Class?* Cambridge, Mass.: Harvard University Press, 1980.

Fisher, David H. "Self in Text, Text in Self." *Semeia* 51 (1990): 137–54.

Flax, Jane. "Postmodernism and Gender Relations in Feminist Theory." *Signs: Journal of Women in Culture and Society* 12 (1987): 621–43.

Foldenyi, Laszlo F. "Novel and Individuality." *Neophilologus* 73 (1989): 1–13.

Folkenflik, Robert. "The Self as Other." In *The Culture of Autobiography: Constructions of Self-Representation,* edited by Robert Folkenflik, 215–34. Stanford: Stanford University Press, 1993.

———, ed. *The Culture of Autobiography: Constructions of Self-Representation.* Stanford: Stanford University Press, 1993.

Forster, E. M. *Aspects of the Novel.* New York: Harcourt, Brace & World, 1927.

Fortna, Robert T. *The Fourth Gospel and Its Predecessor: From Narrative Source to Present Gospel.* Philadelphia: Fortress, 1988.

Foster, Dennis. *Confession and Complicity in Narrative.* New York: Cambridge University Press, 1987.

Foster, Donald. "John Come Lately: The Belated Evangelist." In *The Bible and the Narrative*

*Tradition,* edited by Frank McConnell, 113–31. New York: Oxford University Press, 1986.

Foucault, Michel. *Politics, Philosophy, Culture: Interviews and Other Writings, 1977-84.* Edited with introduction by Lawrence D. Kritzman. Translated by Alan Sheridan and others. New York: Routledge, 1988.

———. *Power/Knowledge: Selected Interviews and Other Writings 1972–77.* Edited by Colin Gordon. Translated by Colin Gordon, Leo Marshall, John Mepham, and Katie Soper. New York: Pantheon, 1980.

Fowler, James W. *Stages of Faith: The Psychology of Human Development and the Quest for Meaning.* San Francisco: Harper & Row, 1981.

Fowler, Robert M. *Let the Reader Understand: Reader-Response Criticism and the Gospel of Mark.* Minneapolis: Fortress, 1991.

———. *Loaves and Fishes: The Function of the Feeding Stories in the Gospel of Mark.* Society of Biblical Literature Dissertation Series 54. Chico, Calif.: Scholars Press, 1981.

———. "Postmodern Biblical Criticism." *Forum* 5 (1989): 3–30.

Frayling, Christopher. *Spaghetti Westerns: Cowboys and Europeans from Karl May to Sergio Leone.* Boston: Routledge & Kegan Paul, 1981.

Freedman, Diane P. *An Alchemy of Genres: Cross-Genre Writing by American Feminist Poet-Critics.* Charlottesville: University Press of Virginia, 1992.

———. "Border Crossing as Method and Motif in Contemporary American Writing, or How Freud Helped Me Case the Joint." In *The Intimate Critique: Autobiographical Literary Criticism,* edited by Diane P. Freedman, Olivia Frey, and Frances Murphy Zauhar, 13–22. Durham, N.C.: Duke University Press, 1993.

———, Olivia Frey, and Frances Murphy Zauhar, eds. *The Intimate Critique: Autobiographical Literary Criticism.* Durham, N.C.: Duke University Press, 1993.

Frein, Brigid Curtin. "Fundamentalism and Narrative Approaches to the Gospels." *Biblical Theology Bulletin* 22 (1992): 12–18.

Freund, Elizabeth. *The Return of the Reader: Reader-Response Criticism.* New York: Methuen, 1987.

Friedman, Susan Stanford. "Creativity and the Childbirth Metaphor: Gender Difference in Literary Discourse." In *Feminisms: An Anthology of Literary Theory and Criticism,* edited by Robyn R. Warhol and Diane Price Herndl, 371–96. New Brunswick, N.J.: Rutgers University Press, 1991.

Friedrich, Paul. "Sanity and the Myth of Honor." *The Journal of Psychological Anthropology* 5 (1977): 281–305.

Frye, Northrop. *Anatomy of Criticism.* Princeton: Princeton University Press, 1957.

Funk, Arville L. *The Revolutionary War Era in Indiana.* Corydon, Ind.: Alfco, 1975.

Funk, Robert. *The Poetics of Biblical Narrative.* Sonoma, Calif.: Polebridge, 1988.

Gates, Henry Louis, Jr. "Editor's Introduction: Writing, 'Race' and the Difference it Makes." *Critical Inquiry* 12 (1985): 1–20.

Genette, Gérard. *Narrative Discourse: An Essay in Method.* Translated by Jane E. Lewin. Foreword by Jonathan Culler. Ithaca, N.Y.: Cornell University Press, 1980.

Gerhart, Mary. *Genre Choices, Gender Questions.* Oklahoma Project for Discourse and Theory 9. Norman: University of Oklahoma Press, 1992.

Giblin, Charles H. "Confrontations in John 18,1–27." *Biblica* 65 (1984): 210–32.

———. "John's Narration of the Hearing Before Pilate (John 18,28–19,16)." *Biblica* 67 (1986): 221–39.

———. "Suggestion, Negative Response and Positive Action in St. John's Portrayal of Jesus (John 2.1–11.; 4.46–54.; 7.2–14.; 11.1–44.)." *New Testament Studies* 26 (1979–80): 191–211.

Gillespie, Phyllis. "The Wild West Thrives, but Guess Where? In Germany, That's Where." *Arizona Highways* 70 (October 1994): 13–17.

Gilmore, Leigh. *Autobiographics: A Feminist Theory of Women's Self-Representation.* Ithaca, N.Y.: Cornell University Press, 1994.

Gloege, Martin E. "The American Origins of the Postmodern Self." In *Constructions of the Self,* edited by George Levine, 59–80. New Brunswick, N.J.: Rutgers University Press, 1992.

Goleman, Daniel. *Vital Lies, Simple Truths: The Psychology of Self-Deception.* New York: Simon & Schuster, 1985.

Gosse, Edmund. *Father and Son: A Study of Two Temperaments.* New York: W. W. Norton, 1963.

Gottlieb, Alma. "Dog: Ally or Traitor?" *American Ethnologist* 13 (1986): 477–88.

Gottwald, Norman K. "Social Class as an Analytic and Hermeneutical Category in Biblical Studies." *Journal of Biblical Literature* 112 (1993): 3–22.

Gray, George. *One Mediator: A Fourfold Revelation.* New York: Loizeaux Brothers, 1951.

Grayston, Kenneth. "Who Misunderstands the Johannine Misunderstandings?" *Scripture Bulletin* 20 (1989): 9–15.

Green, Rayna. "Poor Lo and Dusky Ramona: Scenes from an Album of Indian America." In *Folk Roots, New Roots: Folklore in American Life,* edited by Jane S. Becker and Barbara Franco, 77–101. Lexington, Ky. Museum of our National Heritage, 1988.

Greenblatt, Stephen J. *Learning to Curse: Essays in Early Modern Culture.* New York: Routledge, 1990.

Guild, Thelma S., and Harvey L. Carter. *Kit Carson: A Pattern for Heroes.* Lincoln: University of Nebraska Press, 1984.

Gunn, David M. "New Directions in the Study of Biblical Hebrew Narrative." *Journal for the Study of the Old Testament* 39 (1987): 65–77.

———. "Reading Right: Reliable and Omniscient Narrator, Omniscient God, and Foolproof Composition in the Hebrew Bible." In *The Bible in Three Dimensions: Essays in Celebration of Forty Years of Biblical Studies in the University of Sheffield,* Journal for the Study of the Old Testament Supplement 87, edited by D. J. A. Clines, 53–64. Sheffield: JSOT Press, 1990.

Gunn, Janet Varner. *Autobiography: Toward a Poetics of Experience.* Philadelphia: University of Pennsylvania Press, 1982.

Gutiérrez, Gustavo. *Las Casas: In Search of the Poor of Jesus Christ.* Translated by Robert R. Barr. Maryknoll, N.Y.: Orbis, 1993.

Haenchen, Ernst. *The Gospel of John.* 2 vols. Edited by Robert W. Funk with Ulrich Busse. Translated by Robert W. Funk. Philadelphia: Fortress, 1984.

Hägg, Tomas. *Narrative Technique in Ancient Greek Romances: Studies of Chariton, Xenophon Ephesius and Achilles Tatius.* Stockholm: Swedish Institute in Athens, 1971.

Haraway, Donna. "A Manifesto for Cyborgs: Science, Technology, and Socialist Feminism in the 1980s." *Socialist Review* 80 (April 1985): 65–107.

———. *Simians, Cyborgs, and Women: The Reinvention of Nature.* New York: Routledge, 1991.

Hasitschka, Martin. *Befreiung von Sünde nach dem Johannesevangelium: Eine bibeltheologische Untersuchung.* Innsbrucker theologische Studien 27. Innsbruck: Tyrolia-Verlag, 1989.

Hedrick, Charles H. "Authorial Presence and Narrator in John: Commentary and Story." In *Gospel Origins & Christian Beginnings: In Honor of James M. Robinson,* edited by James E. Goehring, Charles W. Hedrick, Jack T. Sanders, with Hans Dieter Betz, 74–93. Sonoma, Calif.: Polebridge, 1990.

Henaut, Barry W. "John 4:43-54 and the Ambivalent Narrator: A Response to Culpepper's *Anatomy of the Fourth Gospel.*" *Studies in Religion/Sciences religieuses* 19 (1990): 287–304.

Hengel, Martin. *Crucifixion in the Ancient World and the Folly of the Message of the Cross.* Translated by John Bowden. Philadelphia: Fortress, 1977.

Henking, Susan E. "The Personal is the Theological: Autobiographical Acts in Contemporary Feminist Theology." *Journal of the American Academy of Religion* 49 (1991): 511–25.

Hillerman, Tony. *The Blessing Way.* New York: HarperPaperbacks, 1970.

———. *Coyote Waits.* New York: HarperPaperbacks, 1990.

———. *Dance Hall of the Dead.* New York: HarperPaperbacks, 1973.

———. *The Dark Wind.* New York: HarperPaperbacks, 1982.

———. *The Fly on the Wall.* New York: HarperPaperbacks, 1971.

———. *The Ghostway.* New York: Avon Books, 1984.

———. *Listening Woman.* New York: HarperPaperbacks, 1978.

———. *People of Darkness.* New York: HarperPaperbacks, 1980.

———. *Sacred Clowns.* New York: HarperCollins, 1993.

———. *Skinwalkers.* New York: HarperPaperbacks, 1986.

———. *Talking God.* New York: HarperPaperbacks, 1989.

———. *A Thief of Time.* New York: HarperPaperbacks, 1988.

Hitchcock, F. R. M. "Is the Fourth Gospel a Drama?" In *The Gospel of John as Literature: An Anthology of Twentieth-Century Perspectives,* edited by Mark W. G. Stibbe, 15–24. New York: E. J. Brill, 1993.

Hochman, Baruch. *Character in Literature.* Ithaca, N.Y.: Cornell University Press, 1985.

Hoffmann, U. J. *History of La Salle County, Illinois.* Chicago: S. J. Clarke, 1906.

Holland, Norman N. "Unity Identity Text Self." In *Reader-Response Criticism: From Formalism to Post-Structuralism,* edited by Jane P. Tompkins, 118–33. Baltimore: Johns Hopkins University Press, 1980.

Holub, Robert C. *Crossing Borders: Reception Theory, Poststructuralism, Deconstruction.* Madison: University of Wisconsin Press, 1992.

———. *Reception Theory: A Critical Introduction.* New York: Methuen, 1984.

Hoskyns, Edwyn. *The Fourth Gospel.* London: Faber & Faber, 1947.

Howard-Brook, Wes. *Becoming Children of God: John's Gospel and Radical Discipleship.* Maryknoll, N.Y.: Orbis, 1994.

Howell, David B. *Matthew's Inclusive Story: A Study in the Narrative Rhetoric of the First Gospel.* Journal for the Study of the New Testament Supplement 42. Sheffield: JSOT Press, 1990.

Howland, Henry R. "Navy Island and the First Successors to the Griffon." *Publications of the Buffalo Historical Society* 6 (1903): 17–26.

Hutcheon, Linda. *The Politics of Postmodernism.* New York: Routledge, 1989.

Ignatieff, Michael. *The Russian Album.* New York: Viking, 1987.

Iser, Wolfgang. *The Act of Reading: A Theory of Aesthetic Response.* Baltimore: Johns Hopkins University Press, 1978.

———. *The Implied Reader: Patterns of Communication in Prose Fiction from Bunyan to Beckett.* Baltimore: Johns Hopkins University Press, 1974.

Jahner, Elaine A. "Transitional Narratives and Cultural Continuity." *Boundary 2* 19 (1992): 149–79.

Jasper, David. *Rhetoric, Power and Community: An Exercise in Reserve.* London: Macmillan, 1993.

Jaspert, Bernd, ed. *Karl Barth/Rudolf Bultmann Letters 1922-1966.* Translated and edited by Geoffrey W. Bromiley. Grand Rapids: Eerdmans, 1981.

Jauss, Hans Robert. *Toward an Aesthetic of Reception.* Theory and History of Literature 2. Translated by Timothy Bahti. Minneapolis: University of Minnesota Press, 1982.

Johnson, Barbara. "My Monster/My Self." *Diacritics* 12 (1982): 2–10.

———. "Teaching Deconstructively." In *Writing and Reading Differently: Deconstruction and the Teaching of Composition and Literature,* edited by Douglas C. Atkins and Michael L. Johnson, 140–48. Lawrence: University of Kansas Press, 1985.

Johnson, Marshall D. "Power Politics and New Testament Scholarship in the National Socialist Period." *Journal of Ecumenical Studies* 23 (1986): 1–24.

Johnson, Rolf. "Journal, 1876-1880." Transcript in the hand of Rolf Johnson. Johnson Collection, Phelps County Historical Society Museum Archives. Holdrege, Nebraska.

———. "The Saga of a Wandering Swede." Edited by Don Bloch. *The Westerners Brand Book* 10 (1954): 239–93.

Johnson, William. *The Papers of Sir William Johnson.* Vols. 1, 3. Edited by James Sullivan. Albany: State University of New York Press, 1921.

———. *The Papers of Sir William Johnson.* Vol. 13. Edited by Milton W. Hamilton. Albany: State University of New York Press, 1962.

Jones, Ann Rosalind. "Writing the Body: Toward an Understanding of *l'écriture féminine.*" In *Feminisms: An Anthology of Literary Theory and Criticism,* edited by Robyn R. Warhol and Diane Price Herndl, 357–70. New Brunswick, N.J.: Rutgers University Press, 1991.

Jouve, Nicole Ward. *White Woman Speaks with Forked Tongue: Criticism as Autobiography.* New York: Routledge, 1991.

Kaplan, Andrew. "The Rhetoric of Circumstance in Autobiography." *Rhetorica* 10 (1992): 71–98.

Karris, Robert J. *Jesus and the Marginalized in John's Gospel.* Collegeville, Minn.: Liturgical Press, 1990.

Käsemann, Ernst. *The Testament of Jesus According to John 17.* Translated by Gerhard Krodel. Philadelphia: Fortress, 1968.

Kazin, Alfred. "Autobiography as Narrative." *Michigan Quarterly Review* 3 (1964): 210–16.

———. "The Self as History: Reflections on Autobiography." In *Telling Lives: The Biographer's Art,* edited by Marc Pachter, 74–89. Philadelphia: University of Pennsylvania Press, 1981.

Kelly, Klara, and Harris Francis. "Places Important to Navajo People." *American Indian Quarterly* 17 (1993): 151–69.

Kerby, Anthony Paul. *Narrative and the Self.* Studies in Continental Thought. Bloomington: Indiana University Press, 1991.

Kingsbury, Jack D. *Matthew as Story.* Second edition. Philadelphia: Fortress, 1988.

Kingston, Maxine Hong. *China Men.* New York: Ballantine, 1977.

Kitchell, Webster. *God's Dog: Conversations with Coyote.* Boston: Skinner House Books, 1991.

Kitzberger, Ingrid Rosa. "Love and Footwashing: John 13:1–20 and Luke 7:36–50 Read Intertextually." *Biblical Interpretation* 2 (1994) 190–206.

———. "Mary of Bethany and Mary of Magdala—Two Female Characters in the Johannine

Passion Narrative: A Feminist, Narrative-Critical Reader-Response." *New Testament Studies* (forthcoming).

Kluckhohn, Clyde, and Dorthea Leighton. *The Navaho.* Cambridge, Mass.: Harvard University Press, 1946.

Knapp, Steven. "Collective Memory and the Actual Past." *Representations* 26 (1989): 123–49.

Koester, Craig. "Hearing, Seeing, and Believing in the Gospel of John." *Biblica* 70 (1989): 327–48.

Kolodny, Annette. "Dancing through the Minefield: Some Observations on the Theory, Practice, and Politics of a Feminist Criticism." *Feminist Studies* 6 (1980): 1–25.

Krupat, Arnold. *Ethnocriticism: Ethnography, History, Literature.* Berkeley: University of California Press, 1992.

———. *For Those Who Come After: A Study of Native American Autobiography.* Berkeley: University of California Press, 1985.

———. "Native American Autobiography and the Synecdochic Self." In *American Autobiography: Retrospect and Prospect,* edited by Paul John Eakin, 171–94. Madison: University of Wisconsin Press, 1991.

Kysar, Robert. "Johannine Metaphor—Meaning and Function: A Literary Case Study of John 10:1-8." *Semeia* 53 (1991): 81–111.

———. *John: The Maverick Gospel.* Atlanta: John Knox, 1976.

———. *John's Story of Jesus.* Philadelphia: Fortress, 1984.

Las Casas, Bartolomé de. *A Short Account of the Destruction of the Indies.* Edited and translated by Nigel Griffin, with an introduction by Anthony Pagden. New York: Penguin, 1992.

Lawrence, Elizabeth Atwood. *Rodeo: An Anthropologist Looks at the Wild and the Tame.* Knoxville: University of Tennessee Press, 1982.

Lee, Lim P. "The Chinese in Tucson, Arizona." *Chinese Digest* 3 (1938): 8–9, 19.

Lejeune, Philippe. *On Autobiography.* Theory and History of Literature 52. Edited by Paul John Eakin. Translated by Katherine Leary. Minneapolis: University of Minnesota Press, 1989.

Levi, Primo. *Survival in Auschwitz.* Translated by Stuart Woolf. New York: Macmillan, 1961.

Lewis, C. S. *The Lion, the Witch and the Wardrobe.* Middlesex: Puffin Books, 1959.

Liebert, Elizabeth. "That You May Believe: The Fourth Gospel and Structural Development Theory." *Biblical Theology Bulletin* 14 (1984): 67–73.

Lieu, Judith. "Blindness in the Johannine Tradition." *New Testament Studies* 34 (1988): 83–95.

Lindars, Barnabas. *The Gospel of John.* The New Century Bible Commentary. Grand Rapids: Eerdmans, 1982.

———. "Rebuking the Spirit: A New Analysis of the Lazarus Story of John 11." *New Testament Studies* 38 (1992): 89–104.

Lionnet, Françoise. *Autobiographical Voices: Race, Gender, Self-Portraiture.* Ithaca, N.Y.: Cornell University Press, 1989.

Lombard, H. A., and W. H. Oliver. "A Working Supper in Jerusalem: John 13:1-38 Introduces Jesus' Farewell Discourses." *Neotestamentica* 25 (1991): 357–78.

Lopez, Barry. *Crossing Open Ground.* New York: Charles Scribner's Sons, 1988.

Machor, James L. "Introduction: Readers/Texts/Contexts." In *Readers in History: Nineteenth-Century American Literature and the Contexts of Response,* edited by James L. Machor, vii–xxix. Baltimore: Johns Hopkins University Press, 1993.

MacIntyre, Alasdair. *After Virtue: A Study in Moral Theory.* Notre Dame: University of Notre Dame Press, 1981.

Mahoney, Aidan. "A New Look at an Old Problem (John 18,12-14, 19-24)." *Catholic Biblical Quarterly* 27 (1965): 137–44.

Mailloux, Steven. *Interpretive Conventions: The Reader in the Study of American Fiction.* Ithaca, N.Y.: Cornell University Press, 1982.

———. "Misreading as a Historical Act: Cultural Rhetoric, Bible Politics, and Fuller's 1845 Review of Douglass's Narrative." In *Readers in History: Nineteenth-Century American Literature and the Contexts of Response,* edited by James L. Machor, 3–31. Baltimore: Johns Hopkins University Press, 1993.

———. *Rhetorical Power.* Ithaca, N.Y.: Cornell University Press, 1989.

Maldonado, Robert D. "'¿La Conquista?' Latin American (Mestizaje) Reflections on the Biblical Conquest." *Journal of Hispanic/Latino Theology* (forthcoming).

Malina, Bruce J. *The New Testament World: Insights from Cultural Anthropology.* Second edition. Louisville: Westminster/John Knox, 1993.

———. "Reading Theory Perspective: Reading Luke-Acts." In *The Social World of Luke-Acts: Models for Interpretation,* edited by Jerome H. Neyrey, 3–24. Peabody, Mass.: Hendrickson, 1991.

———, and Jerome H. Neyrey. "First-Century Personality: Dyadic, not Individual." In *The Social World of Luke-Acts: Models for Interpretation,* edited by Jerome H. Neyrey, 68–96. Peabody, Mass.: Hendrickson, 1991.

———, and Jerome H. Neyrey. "Honor and Shame in Luke-Acts: Pivotal Values of the Mediterranean World." In *The Social World of Luke-Acts: Models for Interpretation,* edited by Jerome H. Neyrey, 25–65. Peabody, Mass.: Hendrickson, 1991.

Mann, Karl. "Cowboy Mentor of the Führer." *Living Age* 352 (November 1940): 217–22.

Marchadour, Alain. *Lazare: Histoire d'un récit. Récits d'une histoire.* Paris: Cerf, 1988.

Martyn, J. Louis. *History and Theology in the Fourth Gospel.* Revised edition. Nashville: Abingdon, 1979.

Matera, Frank J. "Jesus Before Annas: John 18, 13-14, 19-24." *Ephemerides Theologicae Lovanienses* 66 (1990): 38–55.

Mattice, Beatrice H. *They Walked These Hills Before Me: An Early History of the Town of Conesville.* Cornwallville, N.Y.: Hope Farm, 1980.

May, Antoinette. *The Annotated Ramona.* San Carlos, Calif.: Wide World/Tetra, 1989.

McAdams, Dan P. *The Stories We Live By: Personal Myths and the Making of the Self.* New York: William Morrow, 1993.

McCane, Byron. "'Where No One Had Yet Been Laid': The Shame of Jesus' Burial." *Society of Biblical Literature Seminar Papers* 32 (1993): 473–84.

McGann, Jerome J. *A Critique of Modern Textual Criticism.* Chicago: University of Chicago Press, 1983.

McKee, John. *Literary Irony and the Literary Audience: Studies in the Victimization of the Reader in Augustan Fiction.* Amsterdam: Ropodi, 1974.

McKenna, Andrew. *Violence and Difference: Girard, Derrida, and Deconstruction.* Chicago: University of Illinois Press, 1992.

McKnight, Edgar V. *Post-Modern Use of the Bible: The Emergence of Reader-Oriented Criticism.* Nashville: Abingdon, 1988.

McNitt, Frank. "The Navajo Campaigns and the Occupation of New Mexico 1847-1848." *New Mexico Historical Review* 43 (1968): 173–94.

Meeks, Wayne. "The Man From Heaven in Johannine Sectarianism." *Journal of Biblical Literature* 91 (1972): 159–69.

Metzger, Bruce M. *A Textual Commentary on the Greek New Testament.* New York: American Bible Society, 1971.

Meyer, Ben F. "The Challenges of Text and Reader to the Historical-Critical Method." In *The Bible and its Readers,* edited by Wim Beuken, Sean Freyne, and Anton Weiler, 3–12. Philadelphia: Trinity, 1991.

Michaels, J. Ramsey. "John 12:1-11." *Interpretation* 43 (1989): 287–91.

Michaels, Walter Benn. "The Interpreter's Self: Peirce on the Cartesian 'Subject.'" In *Reader-Response Criticism: From Formalism to Post-Structuralism,* edited by Jane P. Tompkins, 185–200. Baltimore: Johns Hopkins University Press, 1980.

———. "Race into Culture: A Critical Genealogy of Cultural Identity." *Critical Inquiry* 18 (1992): 655–85.

Miller, Nancy K. *Getting Personal: Feminist Occasions and Other Autobiographical Acts.* New York: Routledge, 1991.

Milne, A. A. *Winnie the Pooh.* New York, E. P. Dutton, 1926.

Mlakuzhyil, George. *The Christocentric Literary Structure of the Fourth Gospel.* Analecta Biblica 117. Rome: Pontifical Biblical Institute, 1987.

Moloney, Francis J. *Belief in the Word: Reading John 1-4.* Minneapolis: Fortress, 1993.

———. Review of *The Print's First Kiss: A Rhetorical Investigation of the Implied Reader in the Fourth Gospel,* by Jeffrey L. Staley. *Revue Biblique* 97 (1990): 617–18.

Moore, Stephen. "How Jesus' Risen Body Became a Cadaver." In *The New Literary Criticism and the New Testament,* edited by Edgar V. McKnight and Elizabeth Struthers Malbon, 269–82. Valley Forge, Penn.: Trinity Press International, 1994.

———. *Literary Criticism and the Gospels: The Theoretical Challenge.* New Haven: Yale University Press, 1989.

———. *Mark and Luke in Poststructuralist Perspectives: Jesus Begins to Write.* New Haven: Yale University Press, 1992.

———. "'Mirror, Mirror . . .': Lacanian Reflections on Malbon's Mark." *Semeia* 62 (1993): 165–71.

———. *Poststructuralism and the New Testament: Derrida and Foucault at the Foot of the Cross.* Minneapolis: Fortress, 1994.

Mosala, Itumeleng. *Biblical Hermeneutics and Black Theology in South Africa.* Grand Rapids: Eerdmans, 1989.

Moxnes, Halvor. "Patron-Client Relations and the New Community in Luke-Acts." In *The Social World of Luke-Acts: Models for Interpretation,* edited by Jerome H. Neyrey, 241–68. Peabody, Mass.: Hendrickson, 1991.

Myers, Ched. *Who Will Roll Away the Stone? Discipleship Queries for First World Christians.* Maryknoll, N.Y.: Orbis, 1994.

Myers, Lee. "Illinois Volunteers in New Mexico." *New Mexico Historical Review* 47 (1972): 5–31.

Namias, June. *White Captives: Gender and Ethnicity on the American Frontier.* Chapel Hill: University of North Carolina Press, 1993.

Newton, Judith. "Historicisms New and Old: 'Charles Dickens' Meets Marxism, Feminism, and West Coast Foucault." *Feminist Studies* 16 (1990): 449–70.

Neyrey, Jerome H. "'Despising the Shame of the Cross': Honor and Shame in the Johannine Passion Narrative." *Semeia* (forthcoming).

———. "The Footwashing in John 13:6-11—Transformation Ritual or Ceremony?" In *The*

*First Christians and Their Social World,* edited by L. Michael White and Larry Yarborough, 200–215. Minneapolis: Fortress, 1995.

Nicholson, Godfrey. *Death as Departure: The Johannine Descent-Ascent Schema.* Society of Biblical Literature Dissertation Series 63. Chico, Calif.: Scholars, 1983.

Nietzsche, Friedrich. *Beyond Good and Evil: Prelude to a Philosophy of the Future.* Translated with commentary by Walter Kaufmann. New York: Vintage, 1966.

———. *The Gay Science: with a Prelude in Rhymes and an Appendix of Songs.* Translated with commentary by Walter Kaufmann. New York: Vintage, 1974.

Norris, Christopher. *Deconstruction: Theory and Practice.* Revised edition. New York: Routledge, 1986.

———. *Derrida.* Cambridge, Mass.: Harvard University Press, 1987.

———. *What's Wrong with Postmodernism: Critical Theory and the Ends of Philosophy.* Baltimore: Johns Hopkins University Press, 1990.

Nortjé, S. J. "The Role of Women in the Fourth Gospel." *Neotestamentica* 20 (1986): 21–28.

O'Day, Gail. *The Word Disclosed: John's Story and Narrative Preaching.* St. Louis: CPB, 1987.

Olney, James. "Autobiography and the Cultural Moment: A Thematic, Historical, and Bibliographic Introduction." In *Autobiography: Essays Theoretical and Critical,* edited by James Olney, 3–27. Princeton: Princeton University Press, 1980.

———. *Metaphors of the Self: The Meaning of Autobiography.* Princeton: Princeton University Press, 1972.

——— , ed. *Autobiography: Essays Theoretical and Critical.* Princeton: Princeton University Press, 1980.

O'Neill, John. "The Experience of Error: Ironic Entrapment in Augustan Narrative Satire." *Papers on Language and Literature* 18 (1982): 278–90.

Osiek, Carolyn. "The 'Liberation Theology' of the Gospel of John." *Bible Today* 27 (1989): 210–17.

———. "The Social Sciences and the Second Testament: Problems and Challenges." *Biblical Theology Bulletin* 22 (1992): 88–95.

Østenstad, Gunnar. "The Structure of the Fourth Gospel: Can it be Defined Objectively?" *Studia Theologica* 45 (1991): 33–55.

Ostriker, Alicia Suskin. *Feminist Revision and the Bible.* Cambridge: Blackwell, 1993.

Painter, John. "John 9 and the Interpretation of the Fourth Gospel." *Journal for the Study of the New Testament* 32 (1986): 596–608.

———. "Quest and Rejection Stories in John." *Journal for the Study of the New Testament* 36 (1989): 17–46.

Paltsits, Victor Hugo. *Minutes of the Commissioners for Detecting and Defeating Conspiracies in the State of New York: Albany County Sessions, 1778-1781.* Vol. 2. Albany: State University of New York Press, 1909.

Pamment, Margaret. "Focus in the Fourth Gospel." *Expository Times* 97 (1985): 71–75.

Pancaro, Severino. *The Law in the Fourth Gospel: The Torah and the Gospel of Moses and Jesus, Judaism and Christianity According to John.* Supplements to Novum Testamentum 42. Leiden: E.J. Brill, 1975.

Parsons, Mikeal C. "Anatomy of a Reader." *Biblical Interpretation* (forthcoming).

———. "What's 'Literary' about Literary Aspects of the Gospels and Acts?" *Society of Biblical Literature Seminar Papers* 31 (1992): 14–39.

Pascal, Roy. *Design and Truth in Autobiography.* Cambridge, Mass.: Harvard University Press, 1960.

Patte, Daniel. "Acknowledging the Contextual Character of Male, European-American Critical Exegeses: An Androcritical Perspective." In *Reading From This Place.* Volume 1: *Social Location and Biblical Interpretation in the United States,* edited by Fernando F. Segovia and Mary Ann Tolbert, 35–55. Minneapolis: Fortress, 1995.

———. "Textual Constraints, Ordinary Readings, and Critical Exegesis: An Androcritical Perspective." *Semeia* 62 (1993): 59–79.

———, and Gary Phillips. "A Fundamental Condition for Ethical Accountability in the Teaching of the Bible by White Male Exegetes." *Scriptura* S9 (1991): 7–28.

Payne, James Robert, ed. *Multicultural Autobiography: American Lives.* Knoxville: University of Tennessee Press, 1992.

Pease Donald E. "National Identities, Postmodern Artifacts, and Postnational Narratives." *Boundary 2* 19 (1992): 1–13.

Perkins, Judith. "Representation in Greek Saints' Lives." In *Greek Fiction: The Greek Novel in Context,* edited by J. R. Morgan and Richard Stoneman, 255–71. New York: Routledge, 1994.

Petersen, Norman R. *Literary Criticism for New Testament Critics.* Philadelphia: Fortress, 1978.

Phillips, Gary. "'What is Written? How are You Reading?' Gospel, Intertextuality and Doing Lukewise: A Writerly Reading of Lk 10:25–37 (and 38–42)." *Society of Biblical Literature Seminar Papers* 31 (1992): 266–301.

Pierard, Richard V. "Oberammergau." In *The New International Dictionary of the Christian Church,* edited by J. Douglas, Earle E. Cairns, and James E. Ruark, 721. Grand Rapids: Zondervan, 1974.

Pierson, James C. "Mystery Literature and Ethnography: Fictional Detectives as Anthropologists." In *Literature and Anthropology,* edited by Philip Dennis and Wendell Aycock, 15–30. Lubbock: Texas Tech University Press, 1989.

Pilch, John. "Sickness and Healing in Luke-Acts." In *The Social World of Luke-Acts: Models for Interpretation,* edited by Jerome H. Neyrey, 181–209. Peabody, Mass.: Hendrickson, 1991.

Porter, Stanley. "Reader-Response Criticism and New Testament Study: A Response to A. C. Thiselton's *New Horizons in Hermeneutics.*" *Literature and Theology* 8 (1994): 94–102.

———. "Why Hasn't Reader-Response Criticism Caught on in New Testament Studies?" *Journal of Literature and Theology* 4 (1990): 278–92.

Powell, Mark Allan. *What Is Narrative Criticism?* Minneapolis: Fortress, 1990.

Pratt, Mary Louise. "Interpretive Strategies/Strategic Interpretations: On Anglo-American Reader-Response Criticism." In *Postmodernism and Politics,* edited by Jonathan Arac, 26–54. Minneapolis: University of Minnesota Press, 1986.

Prudden, Horton R. *Rev. Peter Prudden and his Descendants in America.* Palm Beach: By the author, 1983.

Randolph, Howard S. F., with additions by Mrs. Russel Hastings. "Jacob Boelen, Goldsmith of New York and his Family Circle." *New York Genealogical and Biographical Record* 72 (1941): 265–94.

Reinhartz, Adele. "Great Expectations: A Reader-Oriented Approach to Johannine Christology and Eschatology." *Journal of Literature and Theology* 3 (1989): 61–76.

———. *The Word in the World: The Cosmological Tale in the Fourth Gospel.* Atlanta: Scholars Press, 1992.

Rensberger, David. *Johannine Faith and Liberating Community.* Philadelphia: Westminster, 1988.

———. "The Politics of John: The Trial of Jesus in the Fourth Gospel." *Journal of Biblical Literature* 103 (1984): 395–411.

Resseguie, James L. "John 9: A Literary-Critical Analysis." In *Literary Interpretations of Biblical Narratives,* Vol. 2, edited by Kenneth R. R. Gros Louis, 295–303. Nashville, Abingdon, 1982.

Rhoads, David, and Donald Michie. *Mark as Story: An Introduction to the Narrative of a Gospel.* Philadelphia: Fortress, 1981.

Rich, Adrienne. *Blood, Bread, and Poetry: Selected Prose 1979-1985.* New York: W. W. Norton, 1986.

Richter, David. "The Reader as Ironic Victim." *Novel* 14 (1981): 135–51.

Riffaterre, Michael. "Compulsory Reader Response: The Intertextual Drive." In *Intertextuality: Theories and Practices,* edited by Michael Worton and Judith Still, 56–78. New York: Manchester University Press, 1990.

———. "The Mind's Eye: Memory and Textuality." *Romanic Review* 79 (1988): 7–21.

Rissi, Mathias. "Der Aufbau des Vierten Evangeliums." *New Testament Studies* 29 (1983): 48–54.

Roberts, Robert C. *Rudolf Bultmann's Theology: A Critical Interpretation.* Grand Rapids: Eerdmans, 1976.

Rorty, Amelie Oskenberg. "A Literary Postscript: Characters, Persons, Selves, Individuals." In *The Identity of Persons,* edited by Amelie O. Rorty, 301–23. Berkeley: University of California Press, 1976.

Rosa, Joseph G., and Robin May. *Buffalo Bill and his Wild West: A Pictoral Biography.* Lawrence: University of Kansas Press, 1989.

Rouse, W. J. From New York, N.Y., to George Johnson, location unknown, 20 October 1894(?). Typewritten transcript. George Johnson Collection, Phelps County Historical Society Museum Archives, Holdrege, Nebraska.

———. From Santa Ana, Calif., to George Johnson, Phelps, Neb., 5 January 1895. Typewritten transcript. George Johnson Collection, Phelps County Historical Society Museum Archives, Holdrege, Nebraska.

Rubenstein, Richard L. "Modernization and the Politics of Extermination." In *A Mosaic of Victims: Non-Jews Persecuted and Murdered by the Nazis,* edited by Michael Berenbaum, 3–19. New York, New York University Press, 1990.

———, and John K. Roth. *Approaches to Auschwitz: The Holocaust and Its Legacy.* Philadelphia: John Knox, 1987.

Russell, Don. *The Wild West: A History of the Wild West Shows.* Fort Worth: Amon Carter Museum of Western Art, 1970.

Sabbe, M. "John 10 and Its Relationship to the Synoptic Gospels." In *The Shepherd Discourse on John 10 and its Context,* edited by Johannes Beutler and Robert Fortna, 75–93. SNTS Monograph Series 67. Cambridge: Cambridge University Press, 1991.

Sayre, Robert F. "Autobiography and the Making of America." In *Autobiography: Essays Theoretical and Critical,* edited by James Olney, 146–68. Princeton: Princeton University Press, 1980.

Scarry, Elaine. *The Body in Pain: The Making and Unmaking of the World.* New York: Oxford University Press, 1985.

Scheick, William J. *The Half-Blood: A Cultural Symbol in 19th Century American Fiction.* Lexington: University of Kentucky Press, 1979.

Schnackenburg, Rudolf. *The Gospel According to St. John.* 3 Vols. Vol. 1 translated by Kevin Smyth; vol. 2 translated by Cicily Hastings, Francis McDonagh, David Smith, and Richard Foley, S.J.; vol. 3 translated by David Smith and G. A. Kon. New York: Seabury, 1980.

Schneiders, Sandra M. "Death in the Community of Eternal Life: History, Theology, and Spirituality in John 11." *Interpretation* 41 (1987): 44–56.

———. *The Revelatory Text: Interpreting the New Testament as Sacred Scripture.* San Francisco: HarperCollins, 1991.

Scholes, Robert, and Robert Kellogg. *The Nature of Narrative.* New York: Oxford University Press, 1966.

Schüssler Fiorenza, Elisabeth. "Biblical Interpretation and Critical Commitment." *Studia Theologica* 43 (1989): 5–18.

———. *Bread not Stone: The Challenge of Feminist Biblical Interpretation.* Boston: Beacon, 1984.

———. "The Ethics of Biblical Interpretation: Decentering Biblical Scholarship." *Journal of Biblical Literature* 107 (1988): 3–17.

———. *In Memory of Her: A Feminist Theological Reconstruction of Christian Origins.* New York: Crossroad, 1983.

Schweickart, Patrocinio. "Reading Ourselves: Toward a Feminist Theory of Reading." In *Gender and Reading: Essays on Readers, Texts, and Contexts,* edited by Elizabeth A. Flynn and Patrocinio Schweickart, 31–62. Baltimore: Johns Hopkins University Press, 1986.

Scobie, Alex. "Slums, Sanitation and Mortality in the Roman World." *Klio* 68 (1986): 399–433.

Segovia, Fernando. "'And They Began to Speak in Other Tongues': Competing Modes of Discourse in Contemporary Biblical Criticism." In *Reading from This Place.* Volume 1: *Social Location and Biblical Interpretation in the United States,* edited by Fernando F. Segovia and Mary Ann Tolbert, 1–32. Minneapolis: Fortress, 1995.

———. *The Farewell of the Word: The Johannine Call to Abide.* Minneapolis: Fortress, 1991.

———. "The Final Farewell of Jesus: A Reading of John 20:30-21:25." *Semeia* 53 (1991): 167–90.

———. "The Journey(s) of the Word of God: A Reading of the Plot of the Fourth Gospel." *Semeia* 53 (1991): 23–54.

———. "Toward a Hermeneutics of the Diaspora: A Hermeneutics of Otherness and Engagement." In *Reading from This Place.* Volume 1: *Social Location and Biblical Interpretation in the United States,* edited by Fernando F. Segovia and Mary Ann Tolbert, 57–73. Minneapolis: Fortress, 1995.

———. "Towards a New Direction in Johannine Scholarship: The Fourth Gospel from a Literary Perspective." *Semeia* 53 (1991): 1–22.

Seim, Turid Karlsen. "Roles of Women in the Gospel of John." In *Aspects on the Johannine Literature: Papers Presented at a Conference of Scandinavian New Testament Exegetes at Uppsala, June 16-19, 1986,* edited by Lars Hartman and Birger Olsson, 56–73. Coniectanea Biblica New Testament Series 18. Uppsala: Almqvist & Wiksell International, 1987.

Senior, Donald. *The Passion of Jesus in the Gospel of John.* Collegeville, Minn.: Liturgical Press, 1991.

Shea, Daniel B. "The Prehistory of American Autobiography." In *American Autobiography:*

*Retrospect and Prospect,* edited by Paul John Eakin, 25–46. Madison: University of Wisconsin Press, 1991.

Sheehan, Bernard W. *Seeds of Extinction: Jeffersonian Philanthropy and the American Indian.* New York: W. W. Norton, 1973.

Sheldrake, Leonard. *Our Lord Jesus Christ "A Plant of Renown."* Grand Rapids: Gospel Folio, 1950.

———. *Tabernacle Types and Shadows.* Grand Rapids: Gospel Folio, n.d.

Sibley, John Langdon. *Biographical Sketches of Graduates of Harvard University in Cambridge Mass. 1659-1677.* Cambridge: Charles William Sever, 1881.

Silko, Leslie Marmon. *Ceremony.* New York: Penguin, 1977.

Slicer, Deborah. "Your Daughter or Your Dog? A Feminist Assessment of the Animal Research Issue." *Hypatia* 6 (1991): 108–24.

Sloterdijk, Peter. *Critique of Cynical Reason.* Theory and History of Literature 40. Translated by Michael Eldred. Foreword by Andrew Huyssen. Minneapolis: University of Minnesota Press, 1987.

Slotkin, Richard. "Buffalo Bill's 'Wild West' and the Mythologization of the American Empire." In *Cultures of United States Imperialism,* edited by Amy Kaplan and Donald E. Pease, 164–81. Durham, N.C.: Duke University Press, 1993.

———. *Gunfighter Nation: The Myth of the Frontier in Twentieth-Century America.* New York: Atheneum, 1992.

Smith, D. Moody. *John.* Proclamation Commentaries. Second edition. Philadelphia: Fortress, 1986.

Smith, Morton, Lawrence E. Stager, Thomas E. Levy, T. Vago. "Askelon–Views and Reviews." *Biblical Archaeology* 17:6 (1991): 13–18.

Smith, Sidonie. *A Poetics of Women's Autobiography: Marginality and the Fictions of Self-Representation.* Bloomington: Indiana University Press, 1987.

*Soldiers' and Patriots' Biographical Album Containing Biographies and Portraits of Soldiers and Loyal Citizens in the American Conflict, Together With the Great Commanders of the Union Army also A History of the Organizations Growing out of the War: The Grand Army of the Republic, The Loyal Legion, The Sons of Veterans, and the Woman's Relief Corps.* Chicago: Union Veteran Publishing, 1892.

Sontag, Susan. *AIDS and Its Metaphors.* New York: Farrar, Straus & Giroux, 1989.

———. *On Photography.* New York: Farrar, Straus & Giroux, 1973.

Spengemann, William C. *The Forms of Autobiography: Episodes in the History of a Literary Genre.* New Haven: Yale University Press, 1980.

Spivak, Gayatri Chakrovorty. *The Post-Colonial Critic: Interviews, Strategies, Dialogues.* Edited by Sarah Harasym. New York: Routledge, 1990.

Sprinker, Michael. "Fictions of the Self: The End of Autobiography." In *Autobiography: Essays Theoretical and Critical,* edited by James Olney, 321–42. Princeton: Princeton University Press, 1980.

Stager, Lawrence E. "Why Were Hundreds of Dogs Buried at Ashkelon?" *Biblical Archaeology* 17:3 (1991): 27–42.

Staley, Jeffrey L. *The Print's First Kiss: A Rhetorical Investigation of the Implied Reader in the Fourth Gospel.* Society of Biblical Literature Dissertation Series 82. Atlanta: Scholars Press, 1988.

———. "The Structure of John's Prologue: Its Implications for the Gospel's Narrative Structure." *Catholic Biblical Quarterly* 48 (1986): 241–64.

Steckmesser, Kent. *The Western Hero in History and Legend.* Norman: University of Oklahoma Press, 1965.

Stegner, Wallace. *Beyond the Hundredth Meridian: John Wesley Powell and the Second Opening of the West.* New York: Penguin Books, 1992.

———. *Crossing to Safety.* New York: Penguin Books, 1987.

———. *Where the Bluebird Sings to the Lemonade Springs: Living and Writing in the West.* New York: Penguin Books, 1992.

Stein, Gertrude. *Everybody's Autobiography.* New York: Random House, 1937.

Sternberg, Meir. "Biblical Poetics and Sexual Politics: From Reading to Counterreading." *Journal of Biblical Literature* 111 (1992): 463–88.

———. *The Poetics of Biblical Narrative: Ideological Literature and the Drama of Reading.* Bloomington: Indiana University Press, 1985.

Stibbe, M. W. G. "The Elusive Christ: A New Reading of the Fourth Gospel." *Journal for the Study of the New Testament* 44 (1991): 19–38.

———. *John as Storyteller: Narrative Criticism and the Fourth Gospel.* SNTS Monograph Series 73. New York: Cambridge University Press, 1992.

———. *John's Gospel.* New Testament Readings. New York: Routledge, 1994.

———. "A Tomb with a View: John 11.1-44 in Narrative-Critical Perspective." *New Testament Studies* 40 (1994): 38–54.

Stokes, Michael C. *Plato's Socratic Conversations: Drama and Dialectic in Three Dialogues.* Baltimore: Johns Hopkins University Press, 1986.

Stone, Albert E. *Autobiographical Occasions and Original Acts: Versions of American Identity from Henry Adams to Nate Shaw.* Philadelphia: University of Pennsylvania Press, 1982.

Stryker, William Norman. *The Stryker Family in America.* Rome, N.Y.: Canterbury, 1979.

Suleiman, Susan R., and Inge Crosman, eds. *The Reader in the Text: Essays on Audience and Interpretation.* Princeton: Princeton University Press, 1980.

Swearingen, Jan. *Rhetoric and Irony: Western Literacy and Western Lies.* New York: Oxford University Press, 1991.

Swimme, Brian, and Thomas Berry. *The Universe Story: From the Primordial Flaring Forth to the Ecozoic Era—A Celebration of the Unfolding of the Cosmos.* San Francisco: HarperSanFrancisco, 1992.

Sylva, D. "Nicodemus and his Spices." *New Testament Studies* 34 (1988): 148–51.

Synnott, Anthony. *The Body Social: Symbolism, Self and Society.* New York: Routledge, 1993.

Szabados, Bela. "Autobiography after Wittgenstein." *Journal of Aesthetics and Art Criticism* 50 (1992): 1–11.

Tannehill, Robert C. *The Narrative Unity of Luke-Acts: A Literary Interpretation.* Vol. 1. Philadelphia: Fortress, 1986.

Tatius, Achilles. *Leucippe and Clitophon.* Translated by John J. Winkler. In *Collected Ancient Greek Novels,* edited by B. P. Reardon, 170–284. Berkeley: University of California Press, 1989.

Teloh, Henry. *Socratic Education in Plato's Dialogues.* Notre Dame: University of Notre Dame Press, 1986.

Thompson, Marianne Meye. *The Humanity of Jesus in the Fourth Gospel.* Philadelphia: Fortress, 1988.

Thornton, Russell. *American Indian Holocaust and Survival: A Population History since 1492.* Norman: University of Oklahoma Press, 1987.

Thyen, Hartwig. "Die Erzählung von den Bethanischen Geschwestern (Joh 11,1-12,19) als 'Palimpsest' über Synoptischen Texten." In *The Four Gospels 1992: Festschrift Frans*

*Neirynck,* Vol. 3, Bibliotheca Ephemeridum Theologicarum Lovaniensium 100, edited by F. Van Segbroeck, C. M. Tuckett, G. Van Gelle, and J. Verheyden, 2021–50. Louvain: Louvain University Press, 1992.

Tolbert, Mary Ann. "The Politics and Poetics of Location." In *Reading from This Place.* Volume 1: *Social Location and Biblical Interpretation in the United States,* edited by Fernando F. Segovia and Mary Ann Tolbert, 305–17. Minneapolis: Fortress, 1995.

———. "A Response from a Literary Perspective." *Semeia* 53 (1991): 203–12.

Tompkins, Jane P. "Me and My Shadow." In *The Intimate Critique: Autobiographical Literary Criticism,* edited by Diane P. Freedman, Olivia Frey, and Frances Murphy Zauhar, 23–40. Durham, N.C.: Duke University Press, 1993.

———. "The Reader in History: The Changing Shape of Literary Response." In *Reader-Response Criticism: From Formalism to Post-Structuralism,* edited by Jane P. Tompkins, 201–32. Baltimore: Johns Hopkins University Press, 1980.

———. *West of Everything: The Inner Life of Westerns.* New York: Oxford University Press, 1992.

———, ed. *Reader-Response Criticism: From Formalism to Post-Structuralism.* Baltimore: Johns Hopkins University Press, 1980.

Torsney, Cheryl B. "'Everyday Use': My Sojourn at Parchman Farm." In *The Intimate Critique: Autobiographical Literary Criticism,* edited by Diane P. Freedman, Olivia Frey, and Frances Murphy Zauhar, 67–74. Durham, N.C.: Duke University Press, 1993.

Trafzer, Clifford E. *The Kit Carson Campaign: The Last Great Navajo War.* Norman: University of Oklahoma Press, 1982.

v. Feilitzsch, Frhr. "Karl May: The 'Wild West' as Seen in Germany." *Journal of Popular Culture* 27 (1993): 173–189.

Vaage, Leif E. "Like Dogs Barking: Cynic parresia and Shameless Asceticism." *Semeia* 57 (1992): 25–39.

van den Heever, Gerhard. "Being and Nothingness." *Theologia Evangelica* 26 (1993): 39–47.

van Tilborg, Sjef. *Imaginative Love in John.* Biblical Interpretation Series 2. New York: E. J. Brill, 1993.

Varner, John G., and Jeannette J. Varner. *Dogs of the Conquest.* Norman: University of Oklahoma Press, 1983.

Vermes, Geza. *Jesus the Jew: A Historian's Reading of the Gospels.* Philadelphia: Fortress, 1981.

Vizenor, Gerald. *Interior Landscapes: Autobiographical Myths and Metaphors.* Minneapolis: University of Minnesota Press, 1990.

———. "Manifest Manners: The Long Gaze of Christopher Columbus." *Boundary 2* 19 (1992): 223–35.

———. "Ruins of Representation: Shadow Survivance and the Literature of Dominance." *American Indian Quarterly* 17 (1993): 7–30.

———. "Trickster Discourse: Comic Holotropes and Language Games." In *Narrative Chance: Postmodern Essays on Native American Indian Literature,* edited by Gerald Vizenor, 187–212. Albuquerque: University of New Mexico Press, 1989.

———. *The Trickster of Liberty: Tribal Heirs to a Wild Baronage.* Minneapolis: University of Minnesota Press, 1988.

Vlastos, Gregory. *Socrates, Ironist and Moral Philosopher.* Ithaca, N.Y.: Cornell University Press, 1991.

von Staden, Heinrich. "Women and Dirt." *Helios* 19 (1992): 7–30.

Waetjen, Herman C. "Social Location and the Hermeneutical Mode of Integration." In *Read-*

*ing from This Place.* Volume 1: *Social Location and Biblical Interpretation in the United States,* edited by Fernando F. Segovia and Mary Ann Tolbert, 75–93. Minneapolis: Fortress, 1995.

Wapnish, Paula, and Brian Hesse. "Pampered Pooches or Plain Pariahs? The Ashkelon Dog Burials." *Biblical Archaeologist* 56:2 (1993): 55–80.

Warner, Martin. "The Fourth Gospel's Art of Rational Persuasion." In *The Bible as Rhetoric: Studies in Biblical Persuasion and Credibility,* edited by Martin Warner, 153–77. New York: Routledge, 1990.

Warrior, Robert. "A Native American Perspective: Canaanites, Cowboys, and Indians." In *Voices from the Margin: Interpreting the Bible in the Third World,* edited by R. S. Sugirtharajah, 287–95. New York: Orbis, 1991.

Weintraub, Karl Joachim. *The Value of the Individual: Self and Circumstance in Autobiography.* Chicago: University of Chicago Press, 1978.

West, Gerald. "No Integrity without Contextuality: The Presence of Particularity in Biblical Hermeneutics and Pedagogy." *Scriptura* S11 (1993): 131–46.

———. "The Relationship between Different Modes of Reading (the Bible) and the Ordinary Reader." *Scriptura* S9 (1991): 87–110.

White, David G. *Myths of the Dog-Man.* Chicago: University of Chicago Press, 1991.

White, Leland. "Historical and Literary Criticism: A Theological Response." *Biblical Theology Bulletin* 13 (1983): 32–34.

"Wild West Show Attracts." *New York Times.* 27 May 1894, p. 9.

Williams, Patricia J. *The Alchemy of Race and Rights: Diary of a Law Professor.* Cambridge, Mass.: Harvard University Press, 1990.

Williams, Walter L. *The Spirit and the Flesh: Sexual Diversity in American Indian Culture.* Boston: Beacon, 1986.

Wilson, Rob. "Producing American Selves: The Form of American Biography." *Boundary 2* 18 (1991): 104–29.

Windisch, Hans. "John's Narrative Style." In *The Gospel of John as Literature: An Anthology of Twentieth-Century Perspectives,* edited by Mark W. G. Stibbe, 25–64. New York: E. J. Brill, 1993.

Wire, Antoinette. "The Structure of the Gospel Miracle Stories and Their Tellers." *Semeia* 11 (1978): 83–113

"The Wonderful Wild West." *New York Times.* 2 September 1894, p. 11.

Wong, Hertha Dawn. *Sending My Heart Back Across the Years: Tradition and Innovation in Native American Autobiography.* New York: Oxford University Press, 1992.

Worton, Michael, and Judith Still. "Introduction." In *Intertextuality: Theories and Practices,* edited by Michael Worton and Judith Still, 1–44. Manchester: Manchester University Press, 1990.

Wuellner, Wilhelm. "Is There an Encoded Reader Fallacy?" *Semeia* 48 (1989): 40–54.

———. "Putting Life Back into the Lazarus Story and Its Reading: The Narrative Rhetoric of John 11 as the Narration of Faith." *Semeia* 53 (1991): 113–32.

———. "Where is Rhetorical Criticism Taking Us?" *Catholic Biblical Quarterly* 49 (1987): 448–63.

Yee, Gale. *Jewish Feasts and the Gospel of John.* Wilmington: Michael Glazier, 1989.

Young-Bruehl, Elisabeth. "Pride and Prejudice: Feminist Scholars Reclaim the First Person." *Lingua Franca* 1:3 (1991): 15–18.

# Author Index

Elisabeth Schüssler Fiorenza
*Jesus: Miriam's Child, Sophia's Prophet*
*Critical Issues in Feminist Christology*

"No Christology today will be adequate that does not take seriously her unsettling challenge to assess critically how social and political forces have shaped Christian doctrine and how those doctrines impact the lives of women and others." — *Commonweal*

"An important contribution to the quest for 'rhetorics' of scholarly and popular Jesus traditions. It is also important for its serious confrontation with Christian anti-Judaism." — *Booklist*

"Provocative. . . . The book provides a good survey of current theological thinking across a broad spectrum. . . ." — *Kirkus Reviews*

"Radical . . . at the heart of cutting-edge critical, political and theological debate. Recommended for feminist and liberation theology collections." — *Library Journal*

Stevan L. Davies
*Jesus the Healer*
*Possession, Trance, and the Origins of Christianity*

"Stevan Davies offers a fascinating reading of the Gospels that takes serious account of their description of Jesus as a spirit-filled exorcist and healer. This is a provocative work which I certainly intend to assign for my course in the New Testament." — *Elaine Pagels*

"The Jesus-quest has spawned a number of seminal studies, but none more brilliant, surprising, and engaging than this one. Davies is able to reclaim as authentic large swaths of Jesus tradition previously regarded by scholars as late additions. The work is a *tour de force* that opens a whole new vista on Jesus and his followers." — *Walter Wink*

Hans Küng
*Christianity*
*Essence, History, and Future*

"A mammoth and important rendering of the Christian faith by one of the most important Roman Catholic theologians. Küng surveys Christianity from its origins to the present in a highly readable account that illuminates without being didactic. . . . Küng does not skirt thorny issues, including papal infallibility, the changing role of women, and the encounter with other faiths."— *Kirkus Reviews*

"This is a big book on a big subject by the biggest name in contemporary theology, and it does not deserve a small welcome. . . . [A]ny reader who is capable of tackling such a work and who is deeply interested in Christianity would find Hans Küng's latest masterpiece a permanent enrichment of the mind."— *Church Times*

Hans Küng
*Judaism*
*Between Yesterday and Tomorrow*

"A stunning achievement. What erudition this man has! The section on the Bible alone would be worthy of an Old Testament specialist." — *The Expository Times*

"Küng's work contains a mine of information about Judaism, and its discussions of issues facing Judaism and the Jewish people today are clear, sympathetic, and insightful." — *The Journal of Religion*

"This is . . . without doubt one of the most serious and learned encounters with Judaism by a non-Jewish scholar and thinker in our time." — *Shofar*

David L. Miller, Editor
*Jung and the Interpretation of the Bible*

Provides in compact form an introduction to the uses of Jung in reading the Bible. Here are accessible studies of some central and exemplary texts relating to the Hebrew Bible, the New Testament, and intratestamental feminist imagery. Contributors: Schuyler Brown, D. Andrew Kille, Michael Willett Newheart, Wayne G. Rollins, and Trevor Watt.

Ita Sheres and Anna Kohn Blau
*The Truth about the Virgin*
*Sex and Ritual in the Dead Sea Scrolls*
Foreword by David Noel Freedman

"[T]here are occasional suggestions in the extant literature—particularly in the more recently published documents of the [Qumran] community—about arcane lore and esoteric practices. The authors of the present new book on the Scrolls have made a special study of these less well known and much more obscure materials. They have probed more deeply than most into sectarian works of a highly speculative kind. . . . [T]hese texts offer glimpses and clues, tantalizing hints about secret doctrines and restricted rites of a very startling nature. . . . This pioneering work is not for the fainthearted but will light the way for intrepid searchers for the truth, no matter how startling or shocking it may prove to be." —David Noel Freedman

*Available at your bookstore or from the publisher:*
The Continuum Publishing Company
370 Lexington Avenue
New York, NY 10017
1-800-937-5557